Microsoft Identity Manager 2016 Handbook

A complete handbook on Microsoft Identity Manager 2016 – from design considerations to operational best practices

David Steadman

Jeff Ingalls

[PACKT] PUBLISHING

enterprise

professional expertise distilled

BIRMINGHAM - MUMBAI

Microsoft Identity Manager 2016 Handbook

First published: July 2016

Production reference: 1150716

Published by Packt Publishing Ltd.
Livery Place
35 Livery Street
Birmingham B3 2PB, UK.

ISBN 978-1-78528-392-5

www.packtpub.com

Credits

Authors
David Steadman
Jeff Ingalls

Reviewers
Jochen Nickel
Tomica Kaniski
Peter Geelen
Brandon James
Jeff Stokes
Arik Noyman

Commissioning Editor
Nadeem Bagban

Acquisition Editor
Meeta Rajani

Content Development Editors
Pooja Mhapsekar
Amey Varangaonkar

Technical Editor
Taabish Khan

Copy Editors
Shruti Iyer
Sonia Mathur

Project Coordinator
Suzanne Coutinho

Proofreader
Safis Editing

Indexer
Rekha Nair

Graphics
Kirk D'Penha

Production Coordinator
Shantanu N. Zagade

Cover Work
Shantanu N. Zagade

About the Authors

David Steadman has been an IT industry influencer and dedicated husband for more than 17 years. He has held prestigious positions at some of the world's most innovative technology companies, including his service as a senior escalation engineer within the identity platform at, possibly, the most famous tech company on the planet, Microsoft. He is an entrepreneur, active learner, and a man constantly looking to develop and expand new skills in order to leverage the technology of the future. When not at his job, David enjoys family time and coaching soccer.

I would like to express my gratitude to the many people who saw me through this book, to all those who provided support; talked things over; read; wrote; offered comments; allowed me to quote their remarks; and assisted in the editing, proofreading, and design of this book.

Above all, I want to thank my wife, Amy, and the rest of my family, who supported and encouraged me despite all the time it took me away from them. It was a long and difficult journey for them. I want to thank the Microsoft Identity Support team, the Engineer team, specifically Steve Light, Ziv Yankelovich, Mark Wahl, Brandon James, Juan Olivencia, and Steve Klem, and my manager, Franz Foster, for all the discussions on this book and off-the-wall questions.

Last but not least, I want to thank my Dad and Grandfather for showing me that hard work and dedication can go a long way!

Jeff Ingalls is a husband, father, and cancer-surviving dyslexic who works out of his Ohio home office in identity and access management. Jeff has been working with Microsoft technologies for over 20 years and with the Microsoft identity software since its conception in 2003. He has provided solutions to various private and public sectors including automotive, DoD, education, health and services, small businesses, and state and local government. He enjoys learning, teaching, and learning some more. Jeff has a graduate degree in information technology and an undergraduate degree in mathematics. In his free time, he enjoys spending time with his family, cooking, and reading non-fiction. You can reach him at jeff@ingallsdesigns.com.

I would like to thank Packt Publishing for the opportunity, David Steadman for running the long writing race with me, the MIM product group team for their speedy replies and assistance, the technical reviewers, and especially my wife and kids for their sacrifices during the writing of this book. I would also like to make a special thanks to industry leaders I have met throughout my career who provided me with a rich personal and professional growing soil: Chuck Mirabitur, Vern Rottmann, Barb Moro, Mark Edwards, and Mikel Hancock.

About the Reviewers

Jochen Nickel is a cloud, identity, and access management solution architect with a focus on and deep technical knowledge about identity and access management. He is currently working for inovit GmbH in Switzerland and spends the majority of each workday planning, designing, and implementing identity and access management solutions, including the Microsoft Identity Manager, Azure Active Directory Premium, and the Microsoft Azure Rights Management Services.

Jochen has been part of many projects, proof of concepts, reviews, reference architectures, and workshops in this field of technology. Furthermore, he is a Microsoft VTSP Security, Identity, and Access Management from Microsoft Switzerland, and he uses his experience for the directly-managed business accounts in Switzerland. He has also been an established speaker at many technology conferences.

Committed to continuous learning, Jochen holds Microsoft certifications such as MCSD Azure Solutions Architect, MCITP, MCSE/A Office 365/Private Cloud, MCTS, and many other security titles, such as the Certified Information Systems Auditor (CISA). He enjoys spending as much time as possible with his family to get the energy to handle such interesting technologies.

As an active writer and reviewer, Jochen has authored the book *Learning Microsoft Windows Server 2012 Dynamic Access Control* and the upcoming book *Mastering Identity and Access Management with Microsoft Azure*, both by Packt Publishing.

He also reviewed the books *Windows Server 2012 Unified Remote Access Planning and Deployment* by Erez Ben-Ari and Bala Natarajan and the book *Windows Server 2012 R2 Administrator Cookbook* by Jordan Krause, both by Packt Publishing.

I would like to thank David and Jeff for the chance and opportunity to be a small helper in this project by serving as a technical reviewer.

Tomica Kaniski has been active in the IT field for years. He started out as a web designer and web developer, did some Windows development during college days, and then finally found out his true passion—systems administration on the Microsoft platform. Systems administration, virtualization, deployment, management, consulting, support, and so on; you name it, he has been doing it since 2008 and teaching about it since 2011, when he got his Microsoft Certified Trainer title.

In 2009, Tomica passed his first MCP exam and became a Microsoft Certified Professional. Certification is something that he continued doing throughout the years, and he now has certificates, titles, and knowledge about almost the entire Microsoft product portfolio. In 2010, Tomica was awarded his first Microsoft MVP title (Management Infrastructure), then got switched to Virtualization (Hyper-V), and lately Cloud and Datacenter Management. He is strongly engaged with communities and is one of the community leads in Croatia.

Nowadays, you can find Tomica presenting at various local and regional conferences, user group meetings, and other events. You can say that he is fully engaged with Microsoft products and technologies (with a strong focus on Windows Server, Hyper-V, System Center, and Azure) and is mostly interested in products that are yet to be released.

In his spare time, he plays bass guitar and also likes to read and travel. He currently works in the telecommunications industry, for VIPnet d.o.o. in Croatia (a Telekom Austria Group/América Móvil company).

Other books on which Tomica has worked include *Microsoft System Center Virtual Machine Manager 2012 R2 Cookbook, Edvaldo Alessandro Cardoso, Packt Publishing*; *Introducing Windows Server 2012, Mitch Tulloch, Microsoft Press*; and *Windows Server 2012 MOAC courseware* from Wiley.

I would like to thank my family for their patience and constant support.

Peter Geelen is the owner of and a managing consultant at Quest For Security. Over the years, he has gathered strong experience in enterprise security and identity and access management, including information protection, cybersecurity, corporate security policies, security hardening, and cloud security.

Committed to continuous learning, Peter holds renowned security certificates such as CCSK, CISSP, CISSP-ISSAP, and CISA. He is also an MCT (Microsoft Certified Trainer), MCSA, MCTS, MCSE:Security, and MCSA:Security. Also, he is ITIL and PRINCE2 foundation certified.

Since 2005, Peter's technical focus is Microsoft identity and access solutions: MIIS, ILM, FIM 2010, MIM 2016, and related platforms such as PKI, UAG, ADFS, single sign-on, and security solutions. You can find a more detailed overview of Peter's career on his LinkedIn profile at `http://be.linkedin.com/in/pgeelen`.

Peter strives to spend time helping the Microsoft community both online as offline through the following:

- Taking care of governance and the administration of TechNet Wiki (`http://aka.ms/wiki`)
- TechNet Wiki Blog (`http://aka.ms/wikiblog`)
- Publishing articles and white papers at TN Wiki ant TN Gallery (`http://aka.ms/pgpage`)
- Being the community lead of the Belgian Microsoft Security User group, which he founded (`http://www.winsec.be`)

You can find his personal blog at `http://blog.identityunderground.be`.

Peter has also reviewed all published FIM books and videos:

- *FIM Best Practices Volume 1: Introduction, Architecture And Installation Of Forefront Identity Manager 2010, David Lundell* (`http://aka.ms/fim2010r2bestpracticesbook`)
- *Microsoft Forefront Identity Manager 2010 R2 Handbook, Kent Nordström, Packt Publishing* (`http://aka.ms/fim2010r2handbook`)
- *Enterprise Identity Management with Microsoft Forefront Identity Management [Video], Kent Nordström, Packt Publishing* (`http://aka.ms/fimvideolearning`)

Brandon James is a support escalation engineer who works with troubleshooting, debugging, and implementing identity management solutions using Forefront Identity Manager and Microsoft Identity Manager. Working with many enterprise customers, he has worked on various on-premise and cloud solutions. He holds a bachelor's degree in computer engineering and a master's degree in computer science.

Jeff Stokes is an old-hand IT pro based in the Southeast United States. He has worked as a reviewer on books such as *MCSA 2012 R2 Study Guide, William Panek, Wiley*, and *Optimizing and Troubleshooting Hyper-V Networking, Mitch Tulloch, Microsoft Press*. He also coauthored *Mastering the Microsoft Deployment Toolkit*, with Manuel Singer, published by Packt Publishing. He is currently a content developer for Microsoft, covering Azure big data solutions.

> I'd like to thank my family for the love and routine care and feeding that allows me to focus on technology while still staying sane.

Arik Noyman grew up in Tel Aviv, Israel, and completed with honors his bachelor's degree in computer science at The Academic College of Tel Aviv. Later, he went on to obtain an MBA from Tel Aviv University.

In parallel, Arik imparted his knowledge as a lecturer in Tel Aviv University and in The Academic College of Tel Aviv, while also working in SAP as a senior team leader in charge of the SAP solutions of e-commerce for SME. He was honored thrice for his tremendous achievements at SAP.

Later on, Arik moved to Microsoft, where he currently works as a senior lead. In Microsoft, he leads the R&D of the new Microsoft Identity Manager 2016. Currently, he leads the cyber security effort to protect Azure resources.

www.PacktPub.com

eBooks, discount offers, and more

Did you know that Packt offers eBook versions of every book published, with PDF and ePub files available? You can upgrade to the eBook version at www.PacktPub. com and as a print book customer, you are entitled to a discount on the eBook copy. Get in touch with us at customercare@packtpub.com for more details.

At www.PacktPub.com, you can also read a collection of free technical articles, sign up for a range of free newsletters and receive exclusive discounts and offers on Packt books and eBooks.

https://www2.packtpub.com/books/subscription/packtlib

Do you need instant solutions to your IT questions? PacktLib is Packt's online digital book library. Here, you can search, access, and read Packt's entire library of books.

Why subscribe?

- Fully searchable across every book published by Packt
- Copy and paste, print, and bookmark content
- On demand and accessible via a web browser

Instant updates on new Packt books

Get notified! Find out when new books are published by following @ PacktEnterprise on Twitter or the *Packt Enterprise* Facebook page.

Table of Contents

Preface

Microsoft Identity Manager 2016 (MIM 2016) is a tool that helps you manage identities and automate identity-related business processes that reduce operational cost and, done right, improve security.

Microsoft Identity Manager 2016 Handbook is an in-depth guide to identity management. You will learn how to manage users and groups and implement self-service parts, troubleshooting, and best practices. You will see how to implement identity management and set up a smart card logon for strong administrative accounts within Active Directory. This book also covers certificate management, reporting, and role-based access control using BHOLD. We will also discuss in detail MIM reports to audit the identity management life cycle.

With *Microsoft Identity Manager 2016 Handbook*, you will be able to implement and manage MIM 2016 almost effortlessly.

The story in this book

Identity management can be thought of as a marriage between business requirements and technology; therefore, implementing and operating MIM 2016 requires technical skill and business acumen. Throughout this book, we will follow a fictional case study, and you will learn to implement all the features of MIM 2016 according to business requirements. You will see how to install a complete MIM 2016 infrastructure, including both test and production environments.

This book aims to guide you through technical aspects and provide some business requirement help too in the form of questions, tips, and common errors. In order to explain MIM 2016 concepts, we have chosen to write this book using a fictitious company as an example.

What this book covers

Chapter 1, Overview of Microsoft Identity Manager 2016, gives an overview of the MIM 2016 product, a history of how the product has evolved, and an overview of each MIM major component: the MIM Synchronization service, MIM Service, the MIM portal, MIM Reporting, certification management, role-based access management, and privileged access management. Important terminology will also be discussed.

Chapter 2, Installation, covers the prerequisites for installing different components of MIM 2016, how to actually install the components, and a few post-installation steps to get it working.

Chapter 3, MIM Sync Configuration, focuses on the MIM Synchronization service; specifically, topics such as configuring Management Agents, schema management, initial load versus scheduled runs, and moving configurations from the development to the production environment. If you have an environment already set up, this chapter can act as a guide for you to verify that you have not missed any important steps that will cause your MIM environment to not work properly.

Chapter 4, MIM Service Configuration, presents the MIM service capabilities, configuring and customizing the web portal, and developing custom activities.

Chapter 5, User Management, covers how to use the MIM portal to provision accounts without any code, how to manage users, policies, and sets. User management is the primary goal for most MIM deployments.

Chapter 6, Group Management, presents the different group scopes and types in AD and MIM, creating criteria-based groups, and working with client add-ins. Once you have user management in place, it is usually time to start looking at group management, which will be covered in this chapter.

Chapter 7, Role-Based Access Control with BHOLD, will show how you can apply role-based access control and attestation to help an organization implement integration with the identity solution. The BHOLD suite provides organizations the ability to define roles and control access based upon those roles.

Chapter 8, Reducing Threats with PAM, demonstrates how to mitigate access escalation and lateral movement risks using privileged access management and its components. MIM helps reduce internal and external threats by working with Active Directory Domain Services to provide a privileged access management interface.

Chapter 9, Password Management, will explore the self-service password reset (SSPR) feature that allows users to reset their own passwords if they have forgotten them. You will learn how password synchronization works and its configuration.

Chapter 10, Overview of Certificate Management, takes you through certificate management and the main components of the CM. We will also uncover the agents accounts and the permission model.

Chapter 11, Installation and the Client Side of Certificate Management, shows how to install and configure the core components of the certificate management solution in continuation to the previous chapter. We will look into what is needed to get the baseline installed and configured. We will also look into deploying the Modern App.

Chapter 12, Certificate Management Scenarios, looks at the organizational scenarios while creating the certificate template and linking to the profile template, which is the final step once the certificate management solution is in place. We will look at implementing cross forest and ADFS scenarios and glance at some other certificate models.

Chapter 13, Reporting, covers the MIM 2016 out-of-box reporting features, how reporting works, the mechanics under the hood, and customizing and deploying reports. MIM 2016 provides built-in reporting functionality to show how user and group memberships change over time.

Chapter 14, Troubleshooting, demonstrates how to troubleshoot core MIM components by enabling logging, reviewing logs, and using tools.

Chapter 15, Operations and Best Practices, covers how to operate MIM 2016 on a daily basis. You will learn suggested monitoring areas, how to back up and restore the MIM configuration, and coding best practices.

What you need for this book

In this book, we install and configure a complete MIM 2016 environment. In this book, all the installations and servers use the following operating system:

- Microsoft Windows Server 2012 R2 Standard Edition
- .NET Framework 3.5.1

The required software are as follows:

- Microsoft Identity Manager 2016
- Microsoft SQL Server 2014
- Microsoft Visual Studio 2013
- Microsoft SharePoint Foundation 2013
- Microsoft System Center Service Manager 2010

Apart from the software required to get MIM 2016 up and running, Microsoft Exchange 2013 is also used or referred to in the book.

Who this book is for

This book is for architects, developers, and operational staff who want to deploy, manage, and operate Microsoft Identity Manager 2016 and for technical decision makers who want to improve their Microsoft Identity Manager 2016 knowledge. Readers should have a basic understanding of Microsoft-based infrastructure using Active Directory. Identity management beginners and experts will be able to apply the examples and scenarios to solve real-world business problems.

Conventions

In this book, you will find a number of text styles that distinguish between different kinds of information. Here are some examples of these styles and an explanation of their meaning.

Code words in text, database table names, folder names, filenames, file extensions, pathnames, dummy URLs, user input, and Twitter handles are shown as follows: "This is done by modifying the web.config file."

A block of code is set as follows:

```
<%@ Page Language="C#" %>
<script runat="server">
protected override void OnLoad(EventArgs e)
{
  base.OnLoad(e);
  Response.Redirect("~/IdentityManagement/default.aspx");
}
</script>
```

Any command-line input or output is written as follows:

```
SETSPN -S http/MIMService svc-mimservice
```

New terms and **important words** are shown in bold. Words that you see on the screen, for example, in menus or dialog boxes, appear in the text like this: "We should make it a habit to right-click and select **Run as administrator**."

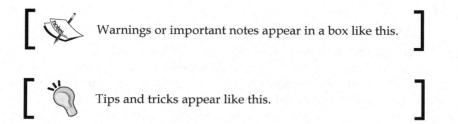

Warnings or important notes appear in a box like this.

Tips and tricks appear like this.

Reader feedback

Feedback from our readers is always welcome. Let us know what you think about this book—what you liked or disliked. Reader feedback is important for us as it helps us develop titles that you will really get the most out of.

To send us general feedback, simply e-mail feedback@packtpub.com, and mention the book's title in the subject of your message.

If there is a topic that you have expertise in and you are interested in either writing or contributing to a book, see our author guide at www.packtpub.com/authors.

Customer support

Now that you are the proud owner of a Packt book, we have a number of things to help you to get the most from your purchase.

Downloading the color images of this book

We also provide you with a PDF file that has color images of the screenshots/diagrams used in this book. The color images will help you better understand the changes in the output. You can download this file from https://www.packtpub.com/sites/default/files/downloads/MicrosoftIdentityManager2016Handbook_ColorImages.pdf.

Errata

Although we have taken every care to ensure the accuracy of our content, mistakes do happen. If you find a mistake in one of our books—maybe a mistake in the text or the code—we would be grateful if you could report this to us. By doing so, you can save other readers from frustration and help us improve subsequent versions of this book. If you find any errata, please report them by visiting http://www.packtpub.com/submit-errata, selecting your book, clicking on the **Errata Submission Form** link, and entering the details of your errata. Once your errata are verified, your submission will be accepted and the errata will be uploaded to our website or added to any list of existing errata under the Errata section of that title.

To view the previously submitted errata, go to https://www.packtpub.com/books/content/support and enter the name of the book in the search field. The required information will appear under the **Errata** section.

Piracy

Piracy of copyrighted material on the Internet is an ongoing problem across all media. At Packt, we take the protection of our copyright and licenses very seriously. If you come across any illegal copies of our works in any form on the Internet, please provide us with the location address or website name immediately so that we can pursue a remedy.

Please contact us at copyright@packtpub.com with a link to the suspected pirated material.

We appreciate your help in protecting our authors and our ability to bring you valuable content.

Questions

If you have a problem with any aspect of this book, you can contact us at questions@packtpub.com, and we will do our best to address the problem.

1
Overview of Microsoft Identity Manager 2016

Microsoft Identity Manager 2016 (MIM 2016) is not one product but a family of products working together to mitigate challenges regarding identity management. In this chapter, we will discuss the MIM family and provide a brief overview of the major components available. The following diagram shows a high-level overview of the MIM family and the components relevant to an MIM 2016 implementation:

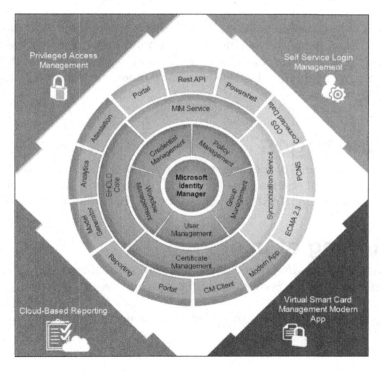

Within the MIM family, there are some parts that can live by themselves and others that depend on other parts. To fully utilize the power of MIM 2016, you should have all the parts in place, if possible. At the center, we have MIM Service and **MIM Synchronization Service (MIM Sync)**. The key to a successful implementation of MIM 2016 is to understand how these two components work — by themselves as well as together.

The Financial Company

The name of our fictitious company is *The Financial Company*. The Financial Company is neither small nor big. We will not give you any indication of the size of this company because we do not want you to take our example setup as being optimized for a company of a particular size, although we will provide some rough sizing guidelines later.

As with many other companies, The Financial Company tries to keep up with modern techniques within their IT infrastructure and is greatly concerned with unauthorized security issues. They are a big fan of Microsoft and live by the following principle:

> *If Microsoft has a product that can do it, let's try that one first.*

The concept of cloud computing is still somewhat fuzzy to them, and they do not yet know how or when they will be using it. They do understand that in the near future, this technology will be an important factor for them, so they have decided that for every new system or function that needs to be implemented, they will take cloud computing into account.

The challenges

During a recent inventory of the systems and functions that their IT department supported, a number of challenges were found. We will now have a look at some of the **identity management (IdM)**-related challenges that were uncovered.

Provisioning of users

The Financial Company discovered a new employee or contractor may wait up to a week before accounts are provisioned to the various required systems, and the correct access is granted to each person to do his/her job. The Financial Company would like account provisioning and proper access granted within a few hours.

The identity life cycle procedures

A number of identity life cycle management issues were found.

Changes in roles took way too long. Access based on old roles continued even after people were moved to a new function or after they changed their job. The termination and disabling of identities was also sometimes missed. A security review found active accounts of users who had left the company more than six months ago.

The security review found one HR consultant who had left The Financial Company months ago that still had VPN access and an active administrative HR account. The access should have been disabled when the project was completed and the consultant's contract had ended.

The Financial Company would like a way of defining identity management policies and a tool that detects anomalies and enforces their business policies. The Financial Company would like business policy enforcement to take no more than a few hours.

Highly privileged accounts (HPA)

The Financial Company has been successful in reducing the number of powerful administrative accounts over the last few years; however, a few still exist. There are also other highly privileged accounts and a few highly privileged digital identities, such as code signing certificates. The concern is that the security of these accounts is not as strong as it should be.

Public key infrastructure (PKI) within The Financial Company is a one-layer PKI, using an Enterprise Root CA without **hardware security module (HSM)**. The CSO is concerned that it is not sufficient to start using smart cards because he feels the assurance level of the PKI is not high enough.

Password management

The helpdesk at The Financial Company spends a lot of time helping users who have forgotten their password. Password resets are done for internal users as well as partners with access to shared systems.

Traceability

The Financial Company found that they had no processes or tools in place to trace the status of identities and roles historically. They wanted to be able to answer questions such as:

- *Who was a member of the Domain Admins group in April?*
- *When was John's account disabled, and who approved it?*

The environment

The following diagram gives you an overview of the relevant parts of the current infrastructure within The Financial Company:

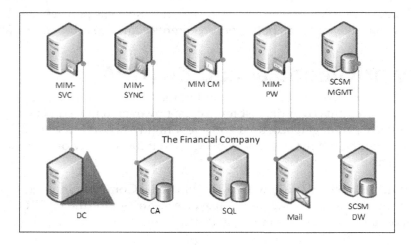

The diagram does not represent any scaling scenarios but rather shows the different functions we will be using in this book.

In the following table, you will find a short summary of the systems involved:

System	Usage	Products installed/to be installed
DC	This is the domain controller for the Active Directory domain `thefinancialcompany.net`.	The AD DS and DNS roles need to be installed.
CA	This is the Enterprise Root CA. The Financial Company uses only a one-layer PKI without any HSM.	AD CS, including the Web Enrollment role, needs to be installed.

System	Usage	Products installed/to be installed
SQL	The central Microsoft SQL server is used by many systems. Among these systems are the HR and Phone systems.	SQL Server 2014, including Integration Services, needs to be installed.
TFCEX01/02	This is the e-mail system.	Exchange 2013 needs to be installed.
TFCMIM02	This is the test and development server for MIM.	SQL Server 2014 and Visual Studio 2013, along with MIM Sync, Service, and Portal, need to be installed.
TFCSYNC01/0	This is the MIM Synchronization server.	MIM Synchronization service.
TFCMIM01	This is the MIM Web Service and Portal server.	MIM Service and MIM Portal need to be installed.
TFCCM01	This is the MIM Certificate Management server.	MIM CM Service and Portal need to be installed.
TFCSSPR01	This is the MIM Password Registration and Reset server.	MIM Password Registration and Reset need to be installed.
TFCSCSM-MGMT01	This is the SCSM Management server used by MIM Reporting.	SQL Server 2014 and System Center Service Manager need to be installed.
TFCSCSM-DW01	SCSM Data Warehouse server used by MIM Reporting.	SQL Server 2014 and System Center Service Manager need to be installed.

All systems have Microsoft Windows Server 2012 R2 as the operating system.

The products installed or to be installed show the status of the systems when we start our journey in this book. Details about the features and products already installed will be explained in *Chapter 2, Installation*.

The Active Directory domain within The Financial Company is thefinancialcompany.net, which uses TFC as the NetBIOS name. The public domain used by The Financial Company is thefinancialcompany.net; this is also the primary e-mail domain used.

Moving forward

The CIO, CSO, and CTO of The Financial Company found that the solutions explained to them by the identity management company would indeed help mitigate the challenges they were facing. They decided to implement MIM 2016.

In this book, we will follow The Financial Company as it implements MIM 2016. We will take a look at how the different features and functions of MIM 2016 will, in the end, solve all the issues that the company detects.

The use of digital identities through smart cards is very new to them, so they decided that this should initially be implemented as a proof of concept.

The history of Microsoft Identity 2016

In 1999, Microsoft bought a company called Zoomit, which had a product called VIA, a directory synchronization product. Microsoft incorporated Zoomit VIA into the product known as **Microsoft Metadirectory Services** (**MMS**). MMS was only available as a Microsoft Consulting Services solution.

Microsoft released **Microsoft Identity Integration Server** (**MIIS**) in 2003, which was the first publicly available version of the synchronization engine we know today as MIM 2016 Synchronization Service.

In 2005, Microsoft bought a company called Alacris. Alacris had a product called IdNexus that managed certificates and smart cards, which Microsoft renamed **Certificate Lifecycle Manager** (**CLM**).

Microsoft took MIIS (now with Service Pack 2) and CLM and consolidated them into a new product in 2007 called **Identity Lifecycle Manager 2007** (**ILM 2007**). ILM 2007 was a directory synchronization tool with the optional certificate management feature.

In 2010, Microsoft released **Forefront Identity Manager 2010** (**FIM 2010**). FIM 2010 added the FIM Service component, which provides workflow capabilities, self-service capabilities, and a codeless provisioning option to the synchronization engine. Many identity management operations that used to require a lot of coding were suddenly available without a single line of code.

Microsoft announced the acquisition of some of the BHOLD suite in 2011, which is a product that provides identity and access governance functionality. A year later, in 2012, FIM 2010 R2 was released, reporting was added, BHOLD and additional browser support for Password Reset Portal were incorporated, performance was improved, and better troubleshooting capabilities were introduced. Support for Active Directory 2012, SQL Server 2012, and Exchange 2013 was added with FIM 2010 R2 Service Pack 1, which was released in 2013.

Components at a glance

Let's take a look at the major components of MIM in the following table:

Component	Description	Details
MIM Synchronization Service, Sync Engine, or MIM Sync	This is the Windows service that handles identity and password synchronization between systems.	The MIM component is required. It uses the SQL database to store its configuration and configured identity information.
MIM Portal	This is the IIS website that can be used for administrative management and user self-service.	It uses SQL database to store its schema, policies, and identity information. This is required for codeless provisioning.
MIM Service	This is the Windows service that provides MIM Portal with web APIs.	It is an optional MIM component. This is required if you want to deploy MIM Portal or the self-service password reset.
BHOLD	This is the suite of services and tools that integrates with MIM and enhances its offerings by adding RBAC, attestation, analytics, and role reporting.	This is an optional MIM component. It uses the SQL database and IIS and is a required component if you want RBAC.
Reporting	Adds new tables and the SQL agent job to allow SCSM to interact with MIM Service to produce historical reports.	This is an optional MIM component. It uses SQL Server Reporting Service, SCSM, and Data Warehouse.

MIM Synchronization Service

MIM Synchronization Service is the *oldest* member of Microsoft's identity family. Anyone who has worked with MIIS 2003, ILM 2007, FIM 2010, or MIM 2016 will find the MIM synchronization engine very similar. Visually, the management tools look the same. MIM Synchronization Service can work by itself without any other MIM component installed, although not all product features are possible using only MIM Synchronization Service.

MIM Synchronization Service is like a heart that pumps identity data between systems. Identity data could be a new user account, an update to someone's department, an updated member of a group, the modification of a contact, and so on. Synchronization is sometimes referred to as data flowing from one system to another, and this is a good way to think of it.

We will explore the MIM Synchronization Service features and dive deeper into why the MIM Synchronization Service is such a powerful tool when leveraged with the rest of the identity management stack.

MIM Portal and Service

MIM Portal is usually the starting point for administrators who configure the MIM Service because of its SharePoint recognizable web components. MIM Service has its own database, in which it stores information about the identities it manages. MIM Portal is the way to make changes to these identities, which can trigger changes in other connected systems.

MIM Service plays many roles in MIM, and during the design phase, the capabilities of MIM Service are often in focus. MIM Service allows you to enforce the Identity Management policy within your organization and also makes sure you are compliant at all times.

MIM Portal can be used for self-service scenarios, allowing users to manage some aspect of the Identity Management process. For example, the self-service password reset is only possible after you deploy MIM service.

MIM Portal is actually an ASP.NET application using Microsoft SharePoint as a foundation, and can be modified in many ways. MIM Service adds custom activities around the MIM and cloud integration story.

The configuration of MIM Service is usually done using MIM Portal, but it may also be configured using PowerShell or even your own custom interface.

MIM Certificate Management

Certificate Management is an optional MIM component. MIM CM can be, and often is, used by itself without any other parts of MIM being present. It is also the component with the poorest integration with other components.

You will find that it hasn't changed much since its predecessor, **Certificate Lifecycle Manager (CLM)**, was released.

MIM CM is mainly focused on managing smart cards, but it can also be used to manage and trace any type of certificate requests. This also includes machine certificates, but there is a slight limitation when we move to machine certs. FIM CM was developed around the user context.

The basic concept of MIM CM is that a smart card is requested using the MIM CM portal. Information regarding all requests is stored in the MIM CM database.

The certification authority, which handles the issuing of the certificates, is configured to report the status back to the MIM CM database.

The MIM CM portal also contains a workflow engine so that the MIM CM admin can configure features such as e-mail notifications as a part of the policies.

In MIM, we add new features, which include the modern app for Windows. Also, a new REST API will be introduced, which we will explore and configure in conjunction with the modern app with MIM CM.

During the configuration, we'll explore the authentication and authorization settings in more detail. This will enable you to fully understand the permission model around MIM CM that is required.

Role-Based Access Control (RBAC) with BHOLD

BHOLD is one of the newest members of MIM and was introduced in Forefront Identity Manager 2010. The acquisition helped customers implement and overcome compliance issues, IT security issues, operational fantasy, and business agility. One of the benefits of BHOLD is that we can easily define and manage access-based user roles that also regularly ensure that access rates are maintained. Also, the integration between BHOLD and FIM enables users with a self-service access request and approval process.

The BHOLD suite encompasses its own reporting analytics, which is the model generator to define working with roles. We will dive into the attestation engine's core role within BHOLD and deployment scenarios. In all these components, the BHOLD core is required. In the coming chapters, we will discuss and touch upon what all of these available suites do and the capability they bring to your organization.

MIM Reporting

Reporting was brand new to FIM and added the capability to audit users and groups via completed MIM Portal requests. This MIM component provides integrated reporting with System Center Service Manager as the main engine.

The purpose of Reporting is to give you a chance to view historical data. There are some reports already built into MIM 2016, and organizations also have the option to develop their own reports that comply with their Identity Management policies.

In *Chapter 13, Reporting*, we will discuss how Reporting works, the main components involved, and how you can create custom reports.

Privilege Access Management

Privilege Access Management (PAM) provides the ability to defend against particular vulnerabilities, such as "pass-the-hash", spear-phishing, and other hacking techniques that attempt to gain high privileges across the enterprise. PAM integrates with Active Directory to apply an expiration to group membership. That is to say, the membership of a highly privileged (and organizationally chosen) group is automatically removed by Active Directory after a specified duration. MIM adds self-service request capabilities, allowing users who are granted the permission to request the membership of a group to receive membership for a specified time. The end result is that people no longer need the permanent membership of highly privileged groups.

Licensing

We will put this part in here, not to tell you how MIM 2016 is licensed but rather to tell you that it can be complex. Depending on which parts you are using — and, in some cases, how you are using them — you need to buy different licenses. MIM 2016 will continue to use both Server licenses and **Client Access Licenses (CALs)**.

In almost every MIM project, the licensing cost has been negligible compared to the benefit of implementing it (for example, adding up the operational cost of provisioning a single user or resetting a password while considering typos, the accounts not done on time, or those left active that should have been disabled). There are strong reasons for having identity management in every business, and if you are reading this book, we would expect you to have already come to the conclusion that identity management will save you money. But even so, make sure you contact your Microsoft licensing partner or your Microsoft contact to clear any questions you might have about licensing.

Also, note that at the time of writing this book, Microsoft has stated that you can install and use Microsoft System Center Service Manager for MIM Reporting without having to buy SCSM licenses.

Read more about MIM Licensing at `http://aka.ms/MIMLicense`.

Summary

The Financial Company will reduce the new employee account provision time by implementing MIM 2016. MIM 2016 will be used to terminate and disable accounts, manage roles, groups, and secure HPA. Empowering end users to perform self-service password resets will reduce helpdesk calls. You now know a little about the company we will be using in this book to explain concepts. We have outlined the bit of the history of how the product evolved and an overview of each component.

As you can see, Microsoft Identity Manager 2016 is not just one product but a family of products. We gave you a short overview of the different components, new and old, and together, we will go through the challenges of The Financial Company and implement some solutions.

For those who have worked with the previous versions of Microsoft Identity Manager 2016, you will see that the platform has not changed much other than a few additional features and platform-supported items. Still, we will explore the components that have been around for years and provide information you may have missed.

In the next chapter, we will look at how to install and configure some of the MIM components. We will then dig into the component details. In some areas, we will go deeper than others because we feel there is a lack of good material on the topic. There is a lot of material to cover, and at one point, we needed to make a judgment call on what would help the largest amount of people while keeping the book at a reasonable size.

2
Installation

As we have already discussed, Microsoft Forefront Identity Manager 2016 (MIM 2016) is not one product but a family of products.

This also means that there are many different ways of installing the product, depending on what parts you want and how you would like to separate them on different systems.

We can choose to separate the different components based on the load or just because we like it clean.

As an example, we will look at the setup used by The Financial Company. They are doing a split installation for the configuration to include sync and service on separate physical nodes.

In this chapter, we will look at the following topics:

- Prerequisites for installing different components of MIM 2016
- How to actually install the components
- A few post-installation steps to get it working

Capacity planning

At the Microsoft download center, you can download the Forefront Identity Manager *Capacity Planning Guide* (`http://bit.ly/MIMCapacityPlanning`). We will not dig deep into capacity planning in this book, but make sure your setup is done in a way that allows you to easily make your MIM environment expand to cope with future needs.

If you look at the following table, you'll see that capacity planning is not easy because there is no straight answer to the problem. When we have 10,000 users, how should we plan our MIM environment? There are many parameters to look at:

Design factor	Considerations
Topology	This is the distribution of MIM services among computers on the network.
Hardware	This is the physical hardware and any virtualized hardware specifications that you are running for each MIM component. It includes CPU, memory, network adapter, and hard drive configurations.
MIM policy configuration objects	This is the number and type of MIM policy configuration objects, which includes sets, **Management Policy Rules** (**MPRs**), and workflows — for example, how many workflows are triggered for operations, how many set definitions exist, and what the relative complexity of each is.
Scale	This is the number of users, groups, calculated groups, and custom object types, such as computers, to be managed by MIM. Also, consider the complexity of dynamic groups, and be sure to factor in group nesting.
Load	This is the frequency of the anticipated use — for example, the number of times you expect new groups or users to be created, the passwords to be reset, or the portal to be visited in a given time period. Note that the load may vary during the course of an hour, day, week, or year. Depending on the component, you may have to design for peak or average load.

The fact that MIM 2015 release includes a number of performance improvements also makes it harder to find relevant facts as so far, most performance testing has been around earlier releases.

We would like to point out one fact, though. In the earlier versions of MIM, FIM, MIIS, and ILM, there were huge performance gains by colocating the synchronization service database with the synchronization service itself. In modern 10-Gigabit networks, and with the changes in the design of MIM, this is no longer the case. Also, as centralized database servers tend to have better CPU and disk performance, you could even gain performance today by having the database and the service separated.

[When looking at the overall performance in MIM, databases are the components to focus on!]

Separating roles

If we look at all the MIM features we are about to install, we need to understand that in theory, we might be able to put them all in one box; however, this is not practical, and in some cases, it is not even supported by Microsoft.

The example setup we will use in this book for The Financial Company can be used as a starting point.

Databases

As you will see, you need quite a few databases. Depending on the load and other factors, you can choose to install the databases locally on each box hosting a MIM feature, or choose to have them all on a central Microsoft SQL server. Alternatively, you can even mix the two approaches.

If you find that your initial approach was not optimal, don't be alarmed. Moving the databases is fully supported. In this book, we will use so-called SQL aliases when referencing the databases. One reason for this is that it makes moving the databases simpler.

System Center Service Manager Data Warehouse, required by the MIM Reporting feature, usually uses a separate SQL server or instance.

MIM features

As with the databases, the MIM features can also be colocated or separated. The only issue here is that MIM Certificate Management should not be colocated with other parts of MIM. The main reason for this is that the MIM CM setup and configuration tool thinks it owns its local web server (IIS). If you have other MIM features using IIS in the same box, you will get a conflict.

Also, System Center Service Manager used for Reporting requires separate servers. Read more about this at http://aka.ms/SCSM2010Deployment.

If we were to give you all the possible scenarios for the ways you could separate the MIM features in order to get fault tolerance, performance, and so on, we would have to add some 50 pages just to cover this topic. We suggest you take a good look at the Microsoft TechNet site (http://bit.ly/MIMplanning) to find out how your company should separate or colocate different parts.

In this book, The Financial Company will use a design that can easily be expanded if the need arises. If you find that your company requires much better performance or that you need to only use a part of the product or colocate more services, this book will still be valid when it comes to the requirements and setup procedures.

Hardware

Whether to virtualize or not is the question for many companies today. All components of MIM 2015 can be virtualized. If you have chosen to virtualize your SQL servers, a starting point for the discussion on virtualization is available at `http://aka.ms/VirtualizationBestPractices`.

Installation order

The MIM CM components can be installed regardless of other MIM pieces.

If you have an existing SCSM environment, the SCSM servers might already be in place, but may still need some updates to support MIM 2016R2 Reporting.

The following SCSM servers need to be installed before we install the MIM Reporting feature, as the MIM service uses the client to communicate with the SCSM server:

- SCSM Management (if the MIM Reporting feature is to be used)
- SCSM Data Warehouse (if the MIM Reporting feature is to be used)

MIM components also have some dependencies that make it logical to install them in a certain order. They should be installed in the following order:

1. MIM Synchronization Service
2. MIM Service
3. MIM Portals
4. MIM Reporting

If you have a configuration similar to that of The Financial Company, the order of installation could be to start off with the test/development environment. We will use the *domain : server name : feature to install* syntax in the following installation lists. For complete server names, refer to the server names used in *Chapter 1, Overview of Microsoft Identity Manager 2016*.

We will then move on to installing the production environment in the following order:

1. TFCSCSM-MGMT01: SCSM Management
2. TFCSCSM-DW01: SCSM Data Warehouse
3. TFCSYNC01: MIM Synchronization Service
4. TFCMIM01 & 02: MIM Service, MIM Portal, and MIM Reporting
5. TFCSSPR01: MIM Password Registration and Reset Portals

MIM CM can be installed at any point, but it also has two components that we usually install in the following order as there are dependencies within MIM CM, as well:

1. TFCCM01 & 02: MIM Certificate Management
2. TFCMIMCA: MIM CM CA Files

Prerequisites

Before we can start installing any components, there are a number of prerequisites that we need to make sure we have in place.

The main reason for errors in MIM is mistakes made during this phase of the installation. Sometimes, it is hard to backtrack the errors, especially if you get Kerberos authentication errors.

Databases

The Company will have several servers running Microsoft SQL Server. The server names in the following list refer to the server names used in *Chapter 1, Overview of Microsoft Identity Manager 2016*:

- TFCSQL01: This is the central SQL server holding all production databases. This will be used by the MIM Sync, MIM Service, and MIM CM servers. This is also where SQL-based CDSes such as the HR system will be found.
- TFCSCSM-MGMT01: This SQL server will be used by SCSM for management. The Financial Company does not have existing SCSM infrastructure and is implementing this for MIM reporting purposes only.
- TFCSCSM-DW01: This SQL server will be used by SCSM for data warehousing and reporting. The Financial Company does not have existing SCSM infrastructure and is implementing this for MIM reporting purposes only.

All instances of SQL Server run the SQL Server 2014 release, except System Center as it requires SQL 2012. This can be upgraded to 2014 once System Center is installed as this is the only supported way at the time of writing this book. A list of supported platforms and useful information can be found at http://bit.ly/MIMSupportedplat. If you're looking for Forefront Identity Manager to see the differences, then this can be found at http://bit.ly/FIMSupportedplat.

The technical requirements for the SQL servers are that they must have at least SQL Server 2008 R2 (64-bit version) installed.

There are many resources on how to install SQL Server, but we have added our own guide here because we would like to point out some things related to MIM 2015.

Collation and languages

In this book, we will not go into the different SQL Server collation settings to support different languages in MIM 2016 or in System Center Service Manager 2012 or later. Read more about the MIM 2016 language packs at http://aka.ms/FIMLanguagePacks.

For more information on SQL Server collations, take a look at http://aka.ms/SQLCollations. SCSM has its own collation problems, which are described at http://aka.ms/SCSMCollations.

We will go over some of these items during the reporting and integration chapters later in the book.

If you need support for other languages, read the information in the previous links. On the TechNet site (http://bit.ly/MIMbefore), the following information can be found, which can also act as guidance:

"Work with your SQL Server database administrator (DBA) to determine the correct collation setting to use for your MIM Service database. The collation setting determines the sorting order and how indexing works.

The default collation set during installation is SQL_LATIN1_General_CP1_CI_AS.

If the server running Windows is using a character set that is different from the Latin alphabet, then you might consider a different collation.

Ensure that the selected collation is case insensitive (indicated by _CI_*).*

If you change the collation setting, ensure that the collation setting is the same on the MIM Service database and on the system databases master *and* tempdb.

If you install the MIM Service and later decide to change the collation setting, you must manually change the collation setting on every table in the MIM Service database."

We have so far only worked with customers using the Latin alphabet and therefore use the collation SQL_LATIN1_General_CP1_CI_AS to begin with.

As not all components of MIM 2015 have the same list of supported languages, you need to figure out at which user interfaces other languages are required within your organization and whether they are supported by the features of MIM you intend to use.

SQL aliases

It is highly recommended that you use SQL aliases for the database connections used by different MIM pieces. The reason for this is that it simplifies the moving of databases to other SQL servers and also makes failover to a mirror SQL easier.

If you want to use aliases for service databases, you need to configure them before starting the installation.

The utility you use on the SQL client is cliconfg and then add an alias server name.

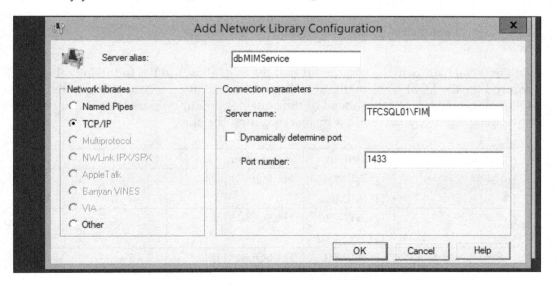

Be careful and specify the port if local. The Windows firewall on your SQL server only allows you to connect to TCP 1433 or whatever port your instance is using; in our case, we will use 1433.

The Financial Company will use this approach for all production servers and SQL **Management Agents (MAs)**. Using SQL aliases on SQL Management Agents makes it easier to move a configuration from test to production, allowing the same SQL alias to point to different SQL instances and making the TFCMIM02 server use the test instances of the databases, while the production TFCSYNC01 Sync server uses production instances.

Depending on the software using the alias, you might need to install the SQL Client Connectivity component. It is required, for example, when using SharePoint Foundation.

If you use SQL aliases in your SharePoint Foundation farm to connect to SQL Server, you must install the SQL client connectivity components on your farm servers in order to use the SPF-VSS writer for backup/restoration. The components include an SQL provider for configuration management, which the SPF-VSS writer needs to resolve SQL aliases to the correct SQL Server. It is not necessary to install any management tool, such as SQL Management Studio. You must use the same installation source (for example, data ISO) that you would use to install the full SQL Server product. Choose to make a custom installation and select only the client components to install.

[Do not use the separate, standalone version of the client components. This version does not include the SQL WMWe provider.]

The Financial Company has identified that the SQL aliases in the following table are required for the MIM implementation. As you can see, we are connecting to the same SQL instance, but doing this ahead of time enables you to prepare later if you need to move the database; you can do it by just updating the alias:

SQL alias	SQL client	SQL Server	IP
dbSharePoint	TFCMIM01 TFCMIM02	TFCSQL01\FIM	.126
dbMIMSync	TFCSYNC01 TFCSYNC02	TFCSQL01\FIM	.127
dbMIMService	TFCMIM01 TFCMIM02	TFCSQL01\FIM	.128
dbMIMCM	TFCCM01 TFCCM02	TFCSQL01\FIM	.129

In DNS, we will add the following records to point to the SQL 2014 named instance:

dbSharePoint	Host (A)	192.168.2.126
dbMIMSync	Host (A)	192.168.2.127
dbMIMService	Host (A)	192.168.2.128
dbMIMCM	Host (A)	192.168.2.129

In the next step, we will add the IP bindings to the SQL server network adapter so that we can bind the alias name to the IP in the SQL configuration.

As you might have noticed, we will not be using aliases for the SCSM databases. This is because the SCSM setup suggests the local SQL server to host the databases used by the SCSM Management and SCSM Data Warehouse features. Take a look at the SCSM 2010 TechNet site (http://bit.ly/SCSMTech).

SQL

The installation of a central SQL server or the adding of instances to an existing SQL server or SQL server cluster is usually not part of the MIM installation, but rather something you order from your database administrators.

The SQL feature requirements for each service database are as follows:

- **MIM Synchronization Service**: Database engine service
- **MIM Service**: Database engine service and full-text search
- **MIM CM**: Database engine service

In many solutions where MIM is used, **SQL Server Integration Services (SSIS)** is also used. This is not a requirement, but with SSIS, we will be able to add some data transformation to our solution if needed.

 Remember to make sure the local Windows firewall is allowing inbound connections to SQL services (TCP 1433) in order for it to be used by the different MIM services hosting their databases on it.

In order for the servers to use a remote SQL server, you need to install SQL Server Native Client on these servers. This can be downloaded separately, or you can install it from the SQL Server media (Client Tools Connectivity). As we have already discussed in this chapter, we prefer to always use Client Tools Connectivity from the SQL Server media.

For troubleshooting purposes, you may also want the SQL Management tools installed on the MIM servers.

SCSM

The Financial Company will have separate servers hosting SCSM and the databases required by SCSM. This is because they are, at the moment, not sure about how to use the Reporting feature, and the MIM Reporting implementation is considered a kind of MIM Reporting test. If this feature is required at full scale in a large organization, you need to take a very close look at how to design the SCSM infrastructure to cope with the possibly very large amount of data the data warehouse might be required to handle.

SCSM requires that:

- System Center Service Manager Management Server be deployed to a standalone machine; a separate SQL server instance is recommended
- System Center Service Manager Data Warehouse and associated database be deployed to a standalone machine; a separate SQL server instance is recommended

So basically, the SCSM installation will use two SQL servers: one on the TFCSCSM-MGMT server and one on the SCSM-DW server.

The Financial Company will use the two-server deployment scenario of SCSM, as described at Microsoft TechNet (http://aka.ms/SCSM2010Deployment).

At The Financial Company, TFCSCSM-MGMT01 is the SCSM-MGMT server and TFCSCSM-DW01 is the SCSM-DW server.

In the SCSM documentation (http://bit.ly/SCSMDeploy), there is a mention of the requirement for an Authorization Manager hotfix (http://support.microsoft.com/kb/975332). This hotfix, however, is included in Windows Server 2008 R2 SP1 or later.

The SQL feature requirements for SCSM-MGMT are as follows:

- **Database engine services**: Full-text search

The SQL feature requirements for SCSM-DW are as follows:

- **Database engine services**: Full-text search
- **Reporting services**: On the **Reporting Services Configuration** page, you should select the **Install the native mode default configuration** option

Web servers

There is a number of web servers involved when installing MIM 2016. Depending on the load and/or **Service Level Agreement** (**SLA**), you may require some kind of load balancing deployment. The goal of the setup at The Financial Company is to make the MIM 2016 deployment as easy as possible to scale out, in case it is needed later on.

One way of making scaling out easier is to use aliases for the websites and run all application pools as domain user accounts. This way, it will be easy for The Financial Company to extend the websites into farms, if required in the future.

MIM Portal

MIM Portal is the interface to administer the MIM service and also for users' self-service.

MIM Portal will be installed on two different servers at The Financial Company, as follows:

- **TFCMIM02**: Primary
- **TFCMIM01**: Secondary

MIM Portal is based on SharePoint and requires that Windows SharePoint Services 3.0 (WSS) be installed.

By default, WSS and SharePoint Foundation use a local Windows internal database, and if you would like to use a central database instead, you need to modify the default setup.

The Financial Company uses Microsoft SharePoint Foundation 2013. The setup of SharePoint Foundation on the setup on the MIM Service server will use the central SQL server for SharePoint databases.

As with SQL servers, web servers may also move from one server to another or need to be scaled out into a farm. In such cases, it is useful to implement some alias for the websites. It is simple to add a new DNS record so that users can type something else in their browser and still end up on the web server you would like them to.

However, as we are dealing with SharePoint and also use Kerberos and SSL, it's a little more complex. For every alias, you need to:

- Add an Alternate Access Mapping in SharePoint
- Add a **Subject Alternative Name** (**SAN**) in a certificate
- Register a new **SPN** (**Service Principle Name**)

MIM password reset

The MIM Password Registration and Reset portals at The Financial Company will be installed on a separate server, MIM-PW.

The requirement of the web server is that it should support ASP.NET and the authentication method (usually Windows Authentication) that you are planning to use in the Password Registration portal.

Add the web server (IIS) role and add the following components to the default ones:

- ASP.NET (will add some additional components automatically)
- Windows Authentication
- IIS 6 management compatibility (including all subcomponents)

It is best practice to use SSL when users access the Password Registration and Reset portals. If you, as The Financial Company, are hosting both portals on the same server, you might also need to consider adding DNS aliases, as well as additional IP addresses if you would like to use the default port TCP 443 for SSL.

The Financial Company uses two different alias URLs for the two portals, register.thefinancialcopmany.net and Reset.thefinancialcompany.net.

Add extra IP addresses to host the different sites. Within IIS, The Financial Company adds two extra IP addresses to be used by the MIM password portals, as you can see in the following screenshot from the DNS manager:

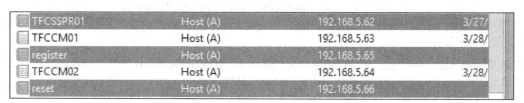

Create the DNS records required for clients to find the two portals.

After installing the MIM password portals, IIS will be configured to bind these portals to the new IP addresses, using SSL on standard port 443.

MIM Certificate Management

The MIM CM server is basically a web application. The setup will not install the required web server roles. The requirements on the MIM CM server before installing MIM CM are as follows:

- Add the web server (IIS) role and add the following components to the default ones:
    ○ HTTP redirection
    ○ ASP.NET (will add some additional components automatically)
    ○ Windows Authentication
    ○ Dynamic content compression
    ○ IIS 6 management compatibility (including all subcomponents)
- MIM CM also requires the .NET Framework 3.5.1 feature to be installed.

> Make sure you only add the .NET Framework 3.5.1 subcomponent. If you happen to select the .NET Framework 3.5.1 Features parent component, you will also get the WCF Activation component, which we do not want in this case.

The MIM CM portal requires you to use SSL, so the web server needs to have an SSL certificate containing the hostnames used to access the website. The Financial Company will use the alias of `cm.thefinancialcompany.net` to access the MIM CM portal. To also enable the use of the actual server name, the certificate used will be requested using the following name information:

- Subject name:
    ○ `CN=cm.thefinacialcompany.net`
- Alternative name:
    ○ `DNS=cm.ad.company.com`
    ○ `DNS=cm`
    ○ `DNS=MIM-cm.ad.company.com`
    ○ `DNS=MIM-cm`

MIM Service accounts and groups

Before we start the installation, we need to create a few service accounts used when installing the MIM environment. The Financial Company uses a separate set of service accounts to be used by the development environment running on MIM Dev.

It is crucial that you know your service accounts and use a good naming standard so that it is easy to understand where and how they is used.

The only service account that is a bit *special* is the service account used by MIM Service. In order for MIM Service to actively take part in (both sending and receiving) e-mail-based workflows, it needs to be an account that has Microsoft Exchange Mailbox. If you do not have Exchange as your e-mail system, MIM Service can only send e-mails but not receive them.

The accounts created by The Financial Company will be listed in the following table:

Username/name	Type	Description
svc-sql	User	SQL service account
svc-scsmwf	User	SM mail-enabled workflow account
svc-scsmrep	User	SM reporting and analysis account
svc-scsm	User	SM server service account
svc-mimsync	User	MIM Sync service
svc-mimservice	User	MIM Service account
SVC-MIMSSPR	User	MIM password registrations
SVC-MIMSPS	User	MIM SharePoint configuration account
svc-mimspsPOOL	User	MIM SharePoint pool account
svc-mimma	User	MIM Service account connector
svc-miminstall	User	MIM master account install
SCSM-Admins	Security group – global	SM administrators security group
MIMCMWebAgent	User	CM web pool agent
MIMCMManagerAgent	User	CM CA manager agent
MIMCMKRAgent	User	CM key recovery agent
MIMCMEnrollAgent	User	CM enrollment agent
MIMCMAuthAgent	User	CM authorization agent
MIMCMAgent	User	MIM CM agent

As you can see, there is quite a number of service accounts required for a complete MIM deployment. Before you go ahead and create all of them, make sure you are actually planning to use the feature requiring the specific service account.

The Kerberos configuration

Everything in MIM is based on Kerberos authentication! MIM Service only accepts Kerberos authentication. Furthermore, there are many occasions when MIM service accounts need to act on behalf of the user using what is called **Kerberos Delegation**. Sometimes, Kerberos Delegation is limited to only specific services, and we usually call this **Kerberos Constrained Delegation (KCD)**.

The primary reason for not getting your MIM deployment working is some mistakes in the Kerberos configuration. Once in place, it will just work, but changes in the environment, such as the use of new aliases, will make it necessary to make adjustments over time.

Let me give you one example to clarify this a little more.

A user accesses MIM Portal, `http://MIMportal`; MIM Portal acts on behalf of the user to access MIM Service on the MIM Service server so that MIM Service thinks it is the original user that is making the request.

To make this a little more complex, Kerberos introduces what is called a Service Principal Name. The SPN is used by the client to retrieve the so-called service ticket used to perform Kerberos authentication against a service. The SPN is a way to tell Active Directory which account is responsible for this service.

In order for an account to act on behalf of others, it needs to be configured in Active Directory to be trusted for delegation.

Let's say that the HTTP service for the name `MIMportal` is owned by the account `svc-MIMSPPool`, and that the `MIMService` service is owned by the account `svc-MIMService`.

We will, then, first tell AD who owns which service using the `setspn` command. In the example, it would be `setspn -S http/MIMportal svc-MIMSPPool` and `setspn -S MIMService/MIM-Service svc-MIMService`. We would then need to configure the `svc-MIMSPPool` account to be trusted for delegation to the `MIMService` service owned by the `svc-MIMService` account.

However, this was just an overview. Let's look at the exact commands used by The Financial Company to configure the Kerberos settings in their environment.

First of all, we need to make sure that IIS is using the application pool account and not the local system account when performing Kerberos authentication. In IIS 7, a new performance enhancement was added that gave IIS the possibility to use what is called Kernel Mode authentication. This, however, means that IIS 7 defaults to using its system account even if you configure the use of a different application pool account.

In MIM, we will use a lot of application pool accounts and will, therefore, need to modify the behavior in IIS on all portal servers.

There are multiple ways of doing this; we usually configure IIS to continue to use the enhanced performance in Kernel Mode authentication and also use the application pool identity whenever possible.

However, SharePoint—at the time of writing—does not support Kernel Mode authentication. On the SharePoint-based MIM Portal servers, the solution is to turn off Kernel Mode authentication. Chun Liu has written a blog post describing why we should do this (`http://blogs.msdn.com/b/chunliu/archive/2010/03/24/why-SharePoint-2010-not-use-kernel-mode-authentication-in-iis7.aspx`). Supported or not, we have used Kernel Mode authentication in almost all our MIM Portal deployments without any errors. If you do, be prepared to turn it off in case you run into any errors that might be related to it.

To configure IIS so as to use both Kernel Mode and the application pool identity, we need to do a little configuration file editing, as follows:

1. On the web server, open an elevated (run as administrator) command prompt and navigate to `C:\Windows\System32\inetsrv\config`.

2. Type `Notepad applicationHost.config`; this will open up the configuration file we need to modify. If you have some kind of XML editor, you can use this instead of Notepad. It would also be best practice to make a backup copy of the `applicationHost.config` file before starting to edit it.

3. In the `applicationHost.config` file, navigate to the `<system.webServer>` section (in one of my example files, it is on line 280, but depending on what you installed, it might be somewhere else).

4. In the `<system.webServer>` section, find the `<security>` section.

5. In the `<security>` section, locate the `<windowsAuthentication>` section.

6. Modify the line `<windowsAuthentication enabled="false">` so that it reads `<windowsAuthentication enabled="false" useAppPoolCredentials="true">`.

7. Save the file and run `iisreset` to have IIS accept the new settings.

In the latest versions of IIS, Internet Information Services Manager can be used to modify this value using the Configuration Editor tool found in the Management section in IIS Manager. If you start Configuration Editor, you can navigate to **system. webServer | Security | Authentication | Windows Authentication** and set the **useAppPoolCredentials** value to **True**.

SETSPN

The SETSPN utility is what you use to configure and verify all the SPNs used by MIM.

If you type SETSPN /?, you will get a list of parameters to use. These vary a little from one version of Windows to another. In my examples, we are using Windows Server 2012 R2.

The most common switches for SETSPN are as follows:

- SETSPN -S: This adds SPN after verifying that no duplicates exist (-A is available in older versions of Windows only; it adds SPN but does not check for duplicates)
- SETSPN -Q: This queries for existence of SPN
- SETSPN -L: This lists the SPNs registered to an account

There are multiple registrations made by The Financial Company.

For the MIM production environment, there are a few more accounts involved as this also involves MIM Certificate Management, MIM Password, and MIM Reporting environments.

For the MIM service and MIM portal in the production environment to work, the following are registered:

```
SETSPN -S http/MIMService svc-mimservice

SETSPN -S http/MIMService.thefinancialcompany.net svc-mimservice

SETSPN -S FIMService/MIMService.thefinancialcompany.net svc-mimservice

SETSPN -S FIMService/MIMService svc-mimservice

SETSPN -S http/MIMPortal svc-mimspspool

SETSPN -S http/MIMPortal.thefinancialcompany.net svc-mimspspool
```

For the MIM Password Registration portal, you do not need any SPN if the URL used is the actual server name, but since The Financial Company uses svc-mimsspr as an alias, the following is registered:

```
SETSPN -S http/register svc-mimsspr

SETSPN -S http/register.thefinancialcompany.net svc-mimsspr
```

The MIM CM server will use an application pool identity. MIMCMWebAgent is the account name used by The Financial Company. This account will be used by the HTTP service of the MIM CM server. The MIM CM configuration wizard will do the registration for some of these SPNs for us, but if we plan to use some alias, like The Financial Company uses cm.thefinancialcompany.net, we need to add it manually. So, The Financial Company needs to add the following registrations:

```
SETSPN -S http/cm.thefinancialcompany.net MIMCMWebAgent
SETSPN -S http/cm MIMCMWebAgent
```

Delegation

A delegation is configured when one account needs to act on behalf of another account.

There are many occasions when this occurs within an MIM deployment. The most common one is when a user accesses MIM Portal, and Web Application Pool Identity needs to perform Kerberos delegation on the MIM service.

Delegation configuration is performed in Active Directory using the **Delegation** tab of the account that needs to perform delegation.

The delegations configured within The Financial Company for different scenarios are as follows:

Account name	Delegation to...	Scenario
SVC-MIMSPSPOOL	FIMService/SVC-MIMService	The MIM Portal on the MIM Service server needs to access the MIM service on the MIM Service server (take a look at the following screenshot)
SVC-MIMSERVICE	FIMService/SVC-MIMService	Used in case a workflow running in the MIM service needs to access the MIM service (take a look at the following screenshot)
SVC-MIMSSPR	FIMService/SVC-MIMService	The Password Registration and Reset portals need to access the MIM service on the MIM Service server
MIMCMWEBAGENT	HOST/TFCMIMCA.thefinancialcompany.net	The MIM CM application pool account needs to access the CA server

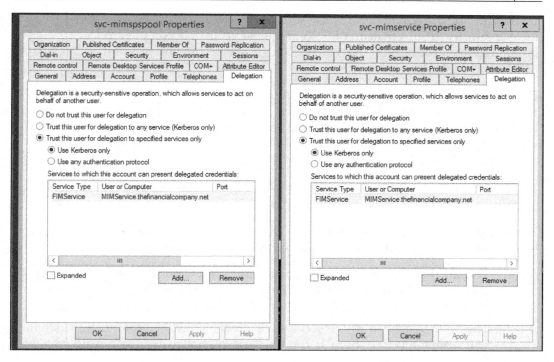

Installation

The installation of different components is quite straightforward once the prerequisites are in place.

The MIM Synchronization service

The Financial Company will have two separate instances of the MIM Synchronization service: one on the MIM Dev server and one on the MIM Sync server.

The MIM Synchronization service setup creates five security groups. The first three groups correspond with the MIM Synchronization service user roles—**Administrator**, **Operator**, and **Joiner**. The other two groups are used to grant access to the **Windows Management Instrumentation (WMI)** interfaces: **Connector Browse** and **Password Set**.

By default, the MIM Synchronization service creates five security groups as local computer groups instead of domain global groups. If you plan to use domain global groups, you must create the groups before you install the MIM Synchronization service.

From a recovery standpoint, it is highly recommended to use domain groups all the time as this will give you the flexibility to manage this group in AD. Also, these groups are stored in the database by SID and when a recovery is needed—that is, when you build a new server—you would have to install and run change mode versus using the domain groups.

The account doing the installation needs to be a local administrator on the server and also needs to have enough permission on the SQL server to create the database.

The setup itself is quite straightforward. The following guide does not cover every step of the wizard, just the ones where you need to pay attention:

1. To start the setup for the MIM Synchronization service, open up the MIM 2016 ISO and run `Setup.exe` in the `Synchronization Service` folder. We should make it a habit to right-click and select **Run as administrator**.

2. The MIM Synchronization service will create a few data folders in which it will store temporary data. If you have a strict policy against storing data in `c:`, you might consider installing it on some other drive:

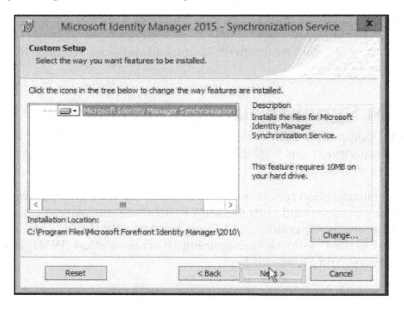

3. As we are using a local SQL alias named `dbMIMSync`, we will configure the
    SQL Server on the install screen, as follows:

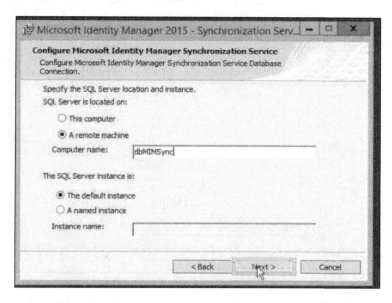

4. By default, the setup will create local groups for different roles in the MIM
    Synchronization service. If you created domain groups instead, specify these
    as `domain\groupname`:

The screen would look like this after the changes:

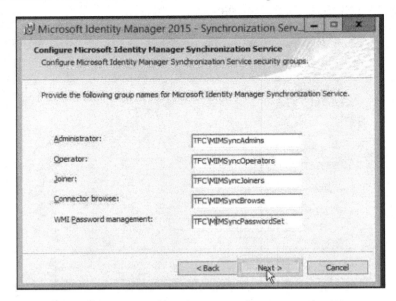

5. You should allow setup to open up the local Windows firewall to allow MIM Service to do, say, password resets. If the local firewall is managed using group policies, make sure to add the appropriate rules to the policy configuration:

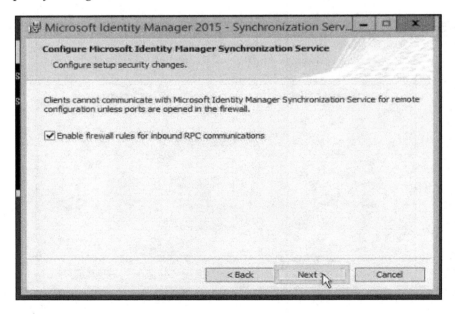

6. If you have not secured the service account as suggested, you will get a warning. To secure this account, it is recommended that you add it to the following User Rights Assignments, either using a group policy or the local security policy:

  ○ Deny log on as a batch job

  ○ Deny log on locally

  ○ Deny access to this computer from the network

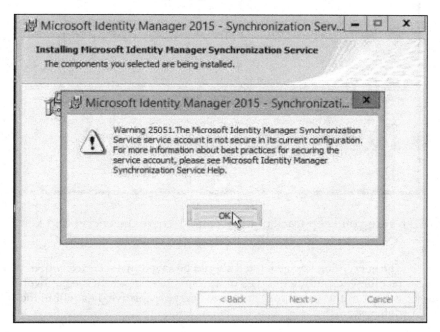

7. At the end of the installation, you will get a prompt about backing up the encryption keys:

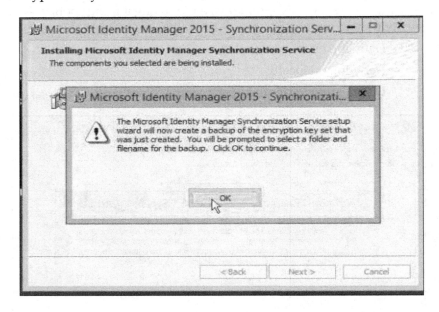

8. Make sure you keep track of the location where the encryption key is saved.

 The encryption key generated should be saved in a secure location. We recommend putting it in TFS or a secure vault in which the password is kept, as this key is for the user to encrypt sensitive data within the database.

9. After finishing the setup, you are prompted to log off and log on again. The account used during installation is automatically added to the MIMSyncAdmins group. The logoff/logon is to make sure that group membership takes effect.

The System Center Service Manager console

If you are going to use the Reporting feature of MIM 2016, you need to install the System Center Service Manager Console on the server(s) running the feature; we will enable this feature later on TFCMIM01.

Installing the SCSM 2012 R2 console is, at the moment, a three-step installation. You will need to install the following components, in order:

1. The SCSM 2012 R2 Service Manager console:

Microsoft SQL Server 2008 Analysis Management Objects	Microsoft Corporation
Microsoft SQL Server 2012 Analysis Management Objects	Microsoft Corporation

2. 2012 AS MO (http://www.microsoft.com/en-us/download/details. aspx?id=42295)

3. 2008 AS AMO (http://www.microsoft.com/en-us/download/details. aspx?id=6375)

On the splash screen of SCSM 2012 R2, select **Install a Service Manager console**.

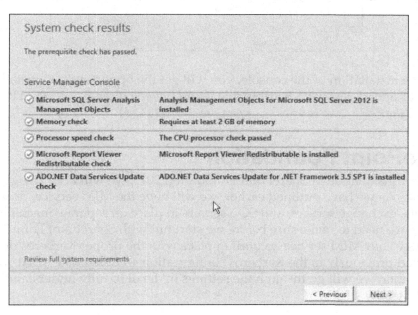

With this, the SCSM 2012 R2 installation is complete, as shown by the following screenshot:

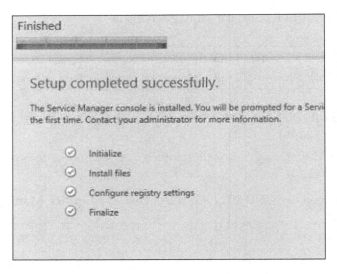

During the installation of the console, you will get the opportunity to install Microsoft Report Viewer Redistributable if you haven't already – KB971119 (https://support.microsoft.com/en-us/kb/971119).

SharePoint Foundation

During our installation of SharePoint Foundation 2013, we will keep things as simple as possible. As we have outlined earlier, we will have the MIM service, domain controllers, exchange servers, and SQL servers in place on separate machines. The first thing we need to make sure before we start out with SharePoint Foundation is that we have our MIM service account in place with the proper Kerberos delegation. As outlined previously in the Kerberos configuration section, this is what we need. As a reminder, we will go through the settings in detail to fully understand what is required, step by step.

For the first step, we need to install the software prerequisites of SharePoint Foundation 2013; this can be done by opening the installer and clicking on **Install software prerequisites**:

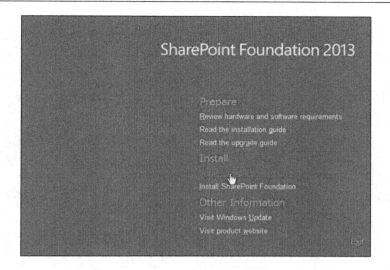

As you can see in the following screenshot, the Preparation Tool installs all the required components, including the roles required for the SharePoint service to be installed on the machine:

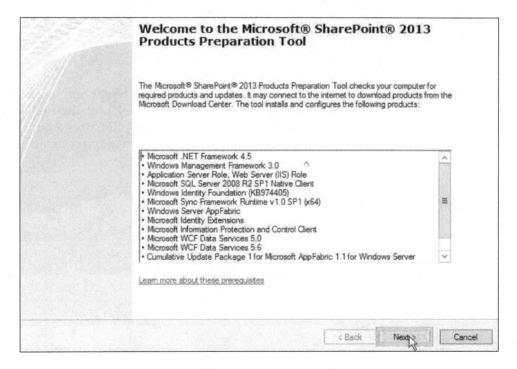

During the installation of the prerequisites, you may have to run the prerequisites installer a couple times. This will make sure you have all the components installed as they may have been skipped due to the previous components needing a restart of the system.

Now, we will begin the installation of the SharePoint Foundation core component; let's run the setup:

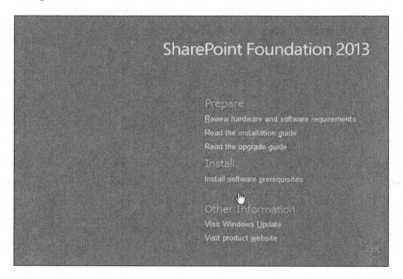

Now, during the setup, we have two options of the installation type: complete and standalone. The complete setup allows us to choose a remote SQL and also allows for the expansion of multiple servers in the farm. The standalone option uses a built-in database, SQL Express. This type is best for lab and development environments:

Server Type

Select the type of installation you want to install on the server.

○ Complete – Use for production environments.
  • Installs all components to a farm that you can expand with more servers.
  • Requires SQL Server 2008 R2 SP1 (minimum requirement).

○ Stand-alone – Use for trial or development environments.
  • Installs all components on a single server.
  • This installation cannot add servers to create a SharePoint farm.
  • Includes SQL Server 2008 R2 Express Edition with SP1 in English.

There has been much debate with previous versions of MIM/FIM as to what the configuration type should be. As we support both variations, we have seen many cases of issues around patching and installation when a SharePoint Foundation server is part of a farm. Now, you do get some gains around configuration along with the replication of this configuration and a farm scenario. In The Financial Company, we will install two individual farms on a remote SQL Server instance. This means that we will select the complete install followed by an NLB that will manage the MIM Service and Portal traffic.

Also, I want to make it clear as we are discussing SharePoint that there is no evidence of any improvement going from SharePoint 2010 to SharePoint 2013. As we know, this importer requires the use of the classic authentication mode, which we know is deprecated in SharePoint 2013. The only reason The Financial Company is going with SharePoint 2013 is to keep it at the cutting edge of technology.

During our install, as previously indicated, we will point our SharePoint install to a SQL alias. A SQL alias provides flexibility around the configuration and management ability to move the backend SQL, if needed, without affecting the application tier.

Once the installation is complete, we will unselect the **Run the SharePoint Products Configuration Wizard now** option and click on **Close**:

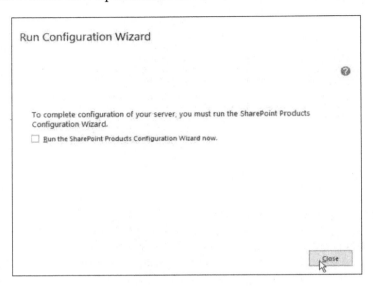

Next, we will run through the SharePoint configuration wizard using elevated credentials; that is, we will run as administrator. Perform the following steps:

1. Run the SharePoint Products Configuration Wizard to configure SharePoint:

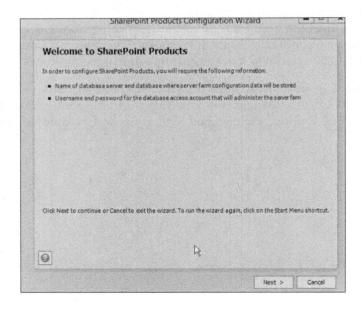

1. Create a new server farm:

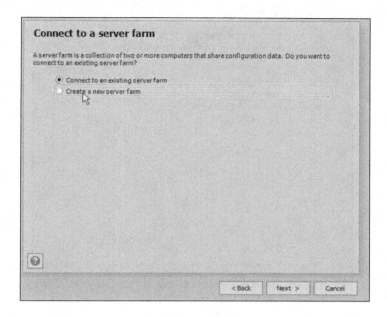

2. Specify **dbSharePoint** as the database server for the configuration database and **TFC\SVC-MIMSPS** as the database access account for SharePoint to use:

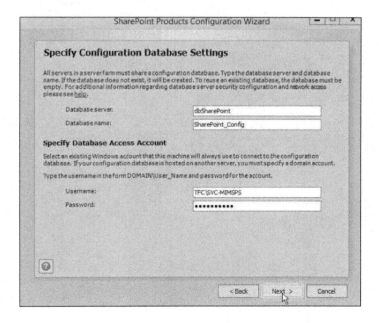

3. For this environment, accept the rest of the SharePoint configuration wizard default settings:

4. When the configuration is complete, at step 10 of 10, a web browser will open. Authenticate as `TFC\svc-miminstall` (or the equivalent domain administrator account) to proceed:

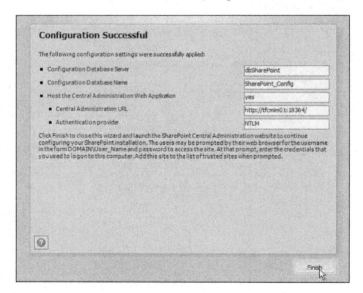

2. After the wizard completes, use PowerShell to create a SharePoint
   Foundation 2013 web application to host MIM Portal.

   Launch SharePoint 2013 Management Shell and run the following
   PowerShell script:

   ```
   $adminCredentials = get-credential TFC\svc-mimspspool

   $dbManagedAccount = New-SPManagedAccount -Credential
   $adminCredentials

   New-SpWebApplication -Name "MIM Portal" -ApplicationPool
   "MIMAppPool" -ApplicationPoolAccount $dbManagedAccount
   -AuthenticationMethod "Kerberos" -Port 80 -URL http://mimportal.
   thefinancialcompany.net
   ```

Note that a warning message will appear that the Windows Classic authentication
method is being used, and it may take several minutes for the final command
to return:

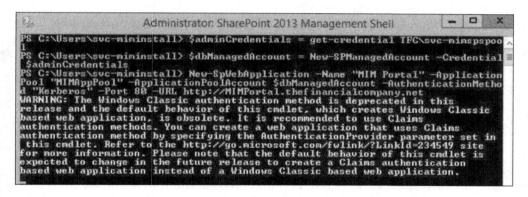

When completed, the output will indicate the URL of the new portal. (Keep
the SharePoint 2013 Management Shell window open as it will be needed in a
subsequent task):

1. Next, create a SharePoint Site collection associated with this web application
   to host MIM Portal.

   ○ If you do not have a web browser window still open for SharePoint
     Central Administration, launch the SharePoint 2013 Central
     Administration program and authenticate via the web browser
     as svc-miminstall.

       °   Alternatively, we can use PowerShell to complete the rest of the task needed for the site collection and Kerberos, as follows:

```
$t = Get-SPWebTemplate -compatibilityLevel 14 -Identity
"STS#1"

$w = Get-SPWebApplication "MIM Portal"

New-SPSite -Url $w.Url -Template $t -OwnerAlias TFC\
svc-mimspspool -CompatibilityLevel 14 -Name "MIM Portal"
-SecondaryOwnerAlias TFC\svc-miminstall

$s = SpSite($w.Url)

$s.AllowSelfServiceUpgrade = $false

$s.CompatibilityLevel

$contentService = [Microsoft.SharePoint.Administration.
SPWebService]::ContentService;

$contentService.ViewStateOnServer = $false;

$contentService.Update();

$fimPortalUrl = "http://mimportal.thefinancialcompany.net"

Set-SPWebApplication -Identity $fimPortalUrl
-AuthenticationMethod Kerberos -Zone Default

cd c:\windows\system32\inetsrv

.\config\applicationHost.config .\config\applicationHost.
config.bak

.\appcmd.exe set config "MIM Portal" /
section:windowsauthentication /useKernelMode:false /
useAppPoolCredentials
```

2.   The final step of SharePoint Foundation configuration is that we need to make sure MIM Portal is using Kerberos and the application pool credentials for Kerberos Delegated Authentication. To do this, we can simply run the following command and then execute `iisreset`:

```
Set-SPWebApplication -Identity $fimPortalUrl -AuthenticationMethod
Kerberos -Zone Default

cd c:\windows\system32\inetsrv

.\config\applicationHost.config .\config\applicationHost.config.
bak

.\appcmd.exe set config "MIM Portal" /
section:windowsauthentication /useKernelMode:false /
useAppPoolCredentials
```

The MIM service and the MIM portal

As with the Synchronization service, The Financial Company will have two separate instances of the MIM service and the MIM portal.

The Financial Company is initially colocating the MIM service and MIM portal on the same boxes. Depending on the load and other parameters, they may in the future decide to separate the two and also scale out into a farm of servers.

To install MIM service and MIM portal, the user running the installation needs to:

- Be a local administrator
- Be an administrator of the SharePoint site that will host the MIM portal
- Have permission to create the database on the database server

The account performing the installation will be given the administrator role within the MIM service. This account is the only account initially able to do anything within MIM portal and MIM service. In this book, we will use the TFC\SVC-MIMInstall account; we need to point out that it is considered best practice to create a separate account to perform the installation and become the MIM service administrator.

To start the setup of the MIM service and the MIM portal, open up MIM 2016 ISO and run Setup.exe in the Service and Portal folder. We should make it a habit to right-click and select **Run as administrator**. Another option I use in this very installation is to run from an elevated command prompt and then execute "Service and Portal.msi" /L*V Install.log. This enables you to have an installer log; that way, if something goes wrong, you can then have a log to investigate the installation of MIM service and MIM portal (which is done by performing the following steps):

```
(c) 2013 Microsoft Corporation. All rights reserved.

C:\Windows\system32>cd C:\Install\CTP3_MIM_Installers\Service and Portal

C:\Install\CTP3_MIM_Installers\Service and Portal>"Service and Portal.msi" /L*v
install.log
```

1. The MIM service and MIM portal setup is used to install many features. Be careful to select the features you want on the current server. If you are not sure, you can leave them out and go back later and add them. On the MIM Service server, we will not install the MIM Reporting feature. In order for MIM Reporting to be installed, the SCSM infrastructure needs to be in place. The Reporting feature will also require the SCSM console to be installed, as discussed in the *Prerequisites* section of this chapter:

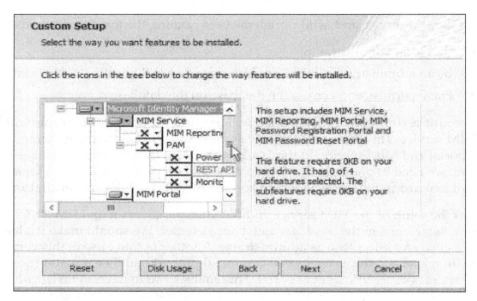

2. We will also skip the installation of the password reset features, as this will be installed on its own dedicated server, and the new **PAM (privilege access management)** features will be installed and configured in *Chapter 8, Reducing Threats with PAM,* as this requires a separate environment than the TFC domain. We will uncover its benefits in that chapter and the challenges it solves.

   As we are using SQL aliases, the database server is dbMIMService for both the MIM Service setups:

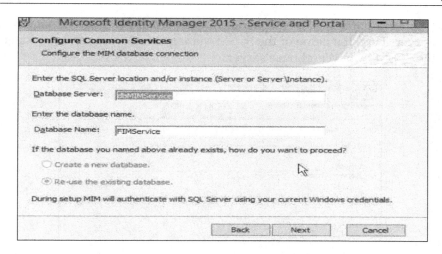

3. If you are running Exchange 2007 or later and the MIM Service service account is assigned a mailbox, you can check all the boxes on the **Configure mail server connection** page. If you do not run Exchange, the MIM service will not be able to receive mails, but it will be able to send mails. Just enter the SMTP server address as **Mail Server** and unselect all the checkboxes:

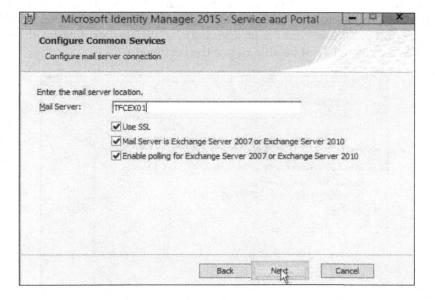

4. If MIM Reporting is to be installed, a question appears on **Management Server**. Type the name of the SCSM Management server and not the name of the SCSM Data Warehouse server:

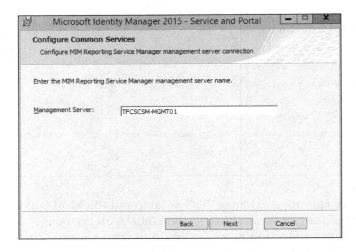

5. We recommend that you allow the MIM setup to generate the certificate used by the MIM service. Note that this is not the SSL certificate used by IIS. If you would like to generate your own certificate to be used, you need to make sure that `CN=ForefrontIdentityManager` is in the certificate; otherwise, the MIM service will not be able to use the certificate:

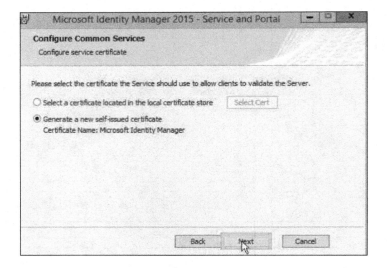

6. Make sure you configure the correct MIM Service service account and the correct e-mail address of the account:

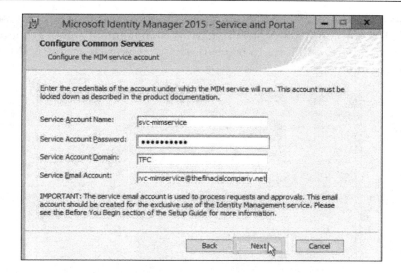

7. If you did not follow the instructions on how to secure the service account, you will get a warning message. To secure this account, it is recommended that you add it to the following User Rights Assignments, either using group policy or using the local security policy:

   ° Deny log on as a batch job

   ° Deny log on locally

   ° Deny access to this computer from the network

8. Make sure the correct MIM Synchronization server and the corresponding MIM MA account are configured. MIM Management Agent account, specified here, will have to be used when we later create the MIM Service Management agent:

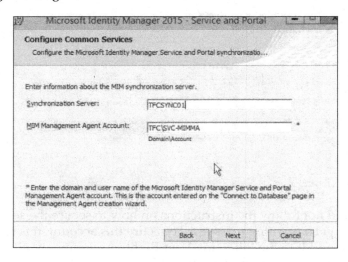

9. If you are not using the server name as MIM Service server address, make sure you have the correct SPN as well as the correct DNS records registered. In a scaled-out solution with clustered MIM Service servers, this would point to the cluster name:

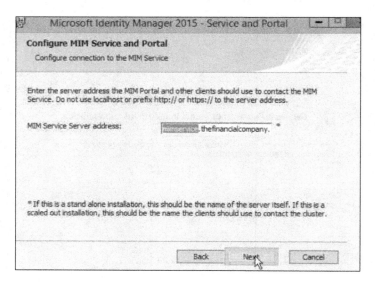

10. If you have configured the SharePoint site to use SSL and an alias as the default name, this alias should be used. At The Financial Company, the URLs used to access the SharePoint sites are environment and `https://MIMportal` for the MIM production environment:

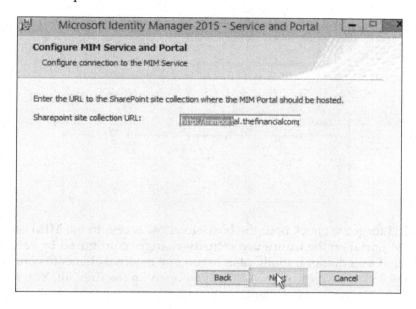

11. The MIM portal will have a link pointing to the Password Registration portal:

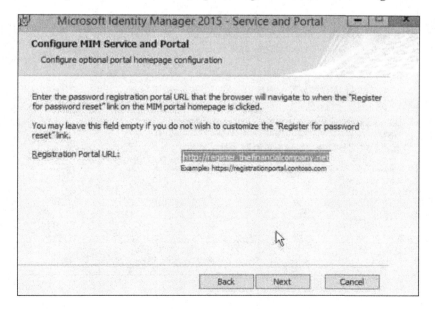

12. The MIM SSPR will be on another server, but we need to define the account being used as there is a special mapping that occurs under the hood that we will speak about in *Chapter 9, Password Management*:

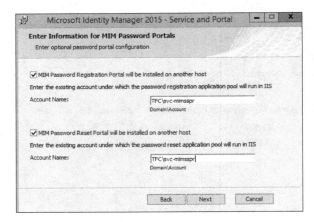

13. Don't forget to check both the boxes to allow access to the MIM service and MIM portal on the **Configure security changes configured by setup** page. Even if you do not initially plan to use any external clients to connect to the MIM service, we recommend that you open up the firewall. You are likely going to have external clients sooner than you imagined:

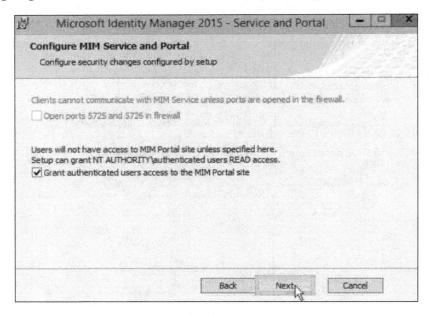

14. The final configuration step is that we need to configure the SharePoint connection to the same service to require Kerberos. In this, we will open up the IIS manager from TFCMIM01, select **MIM Portal**, right-click, and click on **Explore**:

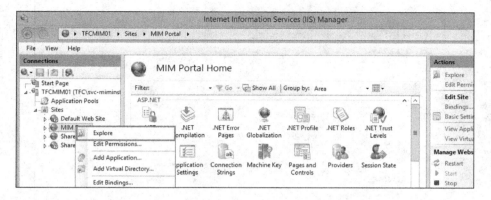

15. Once the directory opens, typically, (C:\inetpub\wwwroot\wss\ VirtualDirectories\80) we would have a web.config file that we would need to modify. We usually make a backup copy of web.config by simply selecting, right-clicking, copying, and then pasting. Let's go ahead and open up web.config:

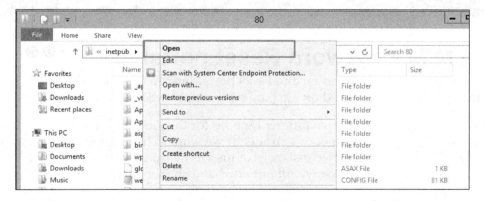

16. Once we have this open, we will scroll all the way down to the bottom of the file. You will notice that we have an entry for the resource management client, and the server space addressed will leave everything default and simply add the following entry (requireKerberos="true"):

```
<resourceManagementClient requireKerberos="true" resourceManagementServiceBaseAddress
```

17. We will save and close this file and then perform an IIS reset. Once this is done, we will open up the MIM portal. Using a Klist, you will be able to see that we have a Kerberos ticket when going to the MIM portal:

```
Cached Tickets: (3)

#0>     Client: svc-miminstall @ THEFINANCIALCOMPANY.NET
        Server: krbtgt/THEFINANCIALCOMPANY.NET @ THEFINANCIALCOMPANY.NET
        KerbTicket Encryption Type: AES-256-CTS-HMAC-SHA1-96
        Ticket Flags 0x40e10000 -> forwardable renewable initial pre_authent name_canonicalize
        Start Time: 6/2/2016 19:53:59 (local)
        End Time:   6/3/2016 5:53:59 (local)
        Renew Time: 6/9/2016 19:53:59 (local)
        Session Key Type: AES-256-CTS-HMAC-SHA1-96
        Cache Flags: 0x1 -> PRIMARY
        Kdc Called: TFCDC02.THEFINANCIALCOMPANY.NET

#1>     Client: svc-miminstall @ THEFINANCIALCOMPANY.NET
        Server: FIMService/mimservice.thefinancialcompany.net @ THEFINANCIALCOMPANY.NET
        KerbTicket Encryption Type: RSADSI RC4-HMAC(NT)
        Ticket Flags 0x40a10000 -> forwardable renewable pre_authent name_canonicalize
        Start Time: 6/2/2016 19:54:12 (local)
        End Time:   6/3/2016 5:53:59 (local)
        Renew Time: 6/9/2016 19:53:59 (local)
        Session Key Type: RSADSI RC4-HMAC(NT)
        Cache Flags: 0
        Kdc Called: TFCDC02.THEFINANCIALCOMPANY.NET

#2>     Client: svc-miminstall @ THEFINANCIALCOMPANY.NET
        Server: HTTP/mimportal.thefinancialcompany.net @ THEFINANCIALCOMPANY.NET
        KerbTicket Encryption Type: RSADSI RC4-HMAC(NT)
        Ticket Flags 0x40a10000 -> forwardable renewable pre_authent name_canonicalize
        Start Time: 6/2/2016 19:53:59 (local)
        End Time:   6/3/2016 5:53:59 (local)
        Renew Time: 6/9/2016 19:53:59 (local)
        Session Key Type: RSADSI RC4-HMAC(NT)
        Cache Flags: 0
        Kdc Called: TFCDC02.THEFINANCIALCOMPANY.NET
```

The MIM Password Reset portal

The MIM Password Registration and Reset portals are, in the example of The Financial Company, installed on a separate server: the MIM-PW server.

In MIM 2016, we can have two different scopes for the Password Reset and Registration portals—**Intranet** or **Extranet**. If we want to have some differentiation between the two, we need two instances of the Password Reset and Registration portals. The Financial Company will initially have one scope: Intranet.

The MIM Password Registration portal and the Password Reset portal will be installed as two separate websites in IIS. If the web server hosting these portals also contains other websites, you need to consider which ports and/or hostnames are available for use by the MIM Password Reset portal.

To start the setup of the MIM Registration and Reset portals, open up MIM 2016 ISO and run Setup.exe in the Service and Portal folder. We should make it a habit to right-click and select **Run as administrator**. Install the MIM Registration and Reset portals by performing the following steps:

1. The MIM Password Registration and MIM Password Reset portals can be installed on separate machines or on the same machine. These portals do not use SharePoint, as you can see in the *Prerequisites* section in this chapter:

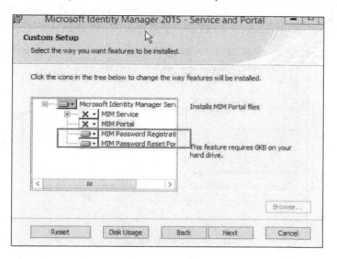

2. The Financial Company will use the same account to run the application pool for both the password portals. The hostname and port need to be unique on the IIS used. During setup, you cannot configure SSL, so we recommend that you use a unique hostname and port 80 and then change the binding in IIS to use SSL afterward:

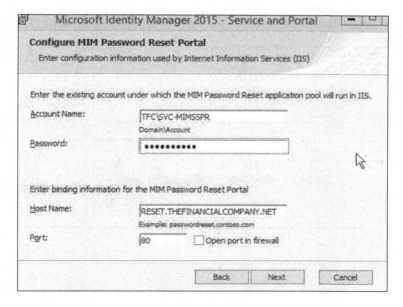

3. Enter the name of the MIM service that the Password Registration and Reset portals should use. At The Financial Company, they only have one set of password portals, so they configure it for Intranet usage. The implications of choosing Extranet and/or Intranet will be explained in *Chapter 9, Password Management*, in which self-service password reset is described in more detail:

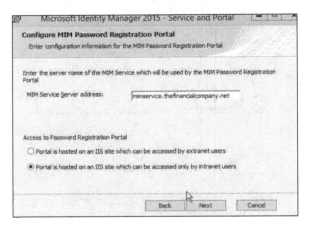

Setup does not configure MIM Password Registration site to use the application pool credentials. Authentication using Kerberos would, therefore, fail as we registered the SPN for the `TFC\SVC-MIMSSPR` account.

You have to manually modify the `useAppPoolCredentials` value to `True` in the `system.webServer.security.authentication.windowsAuthentication` section in Configuration Editor:

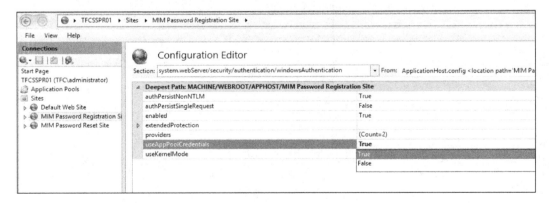

Once the installation is complete, it will look similar to the following screenshot:

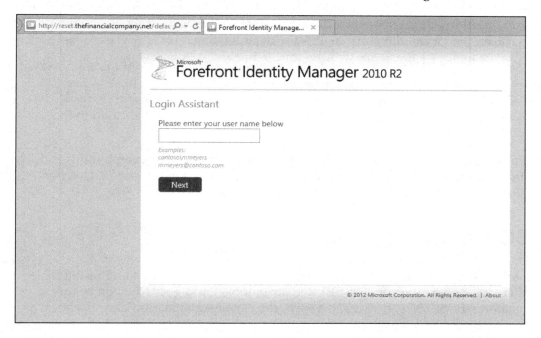

MIM certificate management

The installation of the MIM CM service is actually a group of a few different installations.

One is the installation of the web application, and the other is the installation of the so-called modules on the Certificate Authority server.

The web application is in itself a two-step process in which you first install and then run the MIM CM Configuration wizard to actually tell MIM CM how to operate.

After making sure the web server prerequisites are in place, you can start the MIM CM installation.

To start the setup of the MIM CM service and portal, open up MIM 2016 ISO and run `Setup.exe` in the `Certificate Management\x64` folder. We should make it a habit to right-click and select **Run as administrator**.

On the MIM CM server, you usually do not have the Certification Authority server as well, so only MIM CM portal and MIM CM Update Service should be installed. The only question you will be asked during the installation is what name you would like to use on the virtual directory in IIS—the default being `CertificateManagement`.

The next step will then be to run the Certificate Management Configuration wizard to tell MIM CM how to operate. This will be covered in *Chapter 10, Overview of Certificate Management*; *Chapter 11, Installation and the Client Side of Certificate Management*; and *Chapter 12, Certificate Management Scenarios*, dedicated to the MIM CM service.

We will also need to install the MIM CM CA files on the CA server, but this is done after configuring the CM server and will also be covered in *Chapter 10, Overview of Certificate Management*.

SCSM management

The SCSM setup contains a version of the Microsoft Report Viewer 2008 Redistributable Package, but we recommend that you download and install the Microsoft Report Viewer 2008 SP1 Redistributable Package before you begin installing the SCSM software. This way, you can ensure that you have the latest version of Report Viewer.

On the System Service Manager 2012 R2 media, navigate to the `amd64` folder and run `Setup`. On the splash screen, select **Install a Service Manager management server**. Perform the following steps during setup:

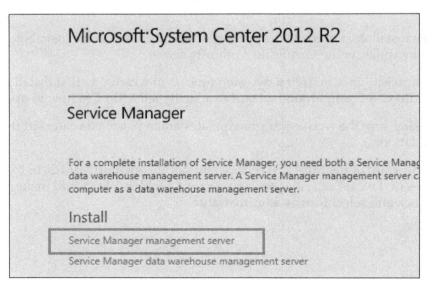

1. A warning message appears if you are using the default collation (`SQL_Latin1_General_CP11_CI_AS`). Support for multiple languages in Service Manager is not possible when you are using the default collation. If you later decide to support multiple languages using a different collation, you have to reinstall SQL Server. For more information on this, go to `http://bit.ly/MIMSCSMCollations` and `http://bit.ly/MIMSQLCollations`.

2. If the setup detects a local SQL instance, it will suggest using this one and creating a new database in the default instance:

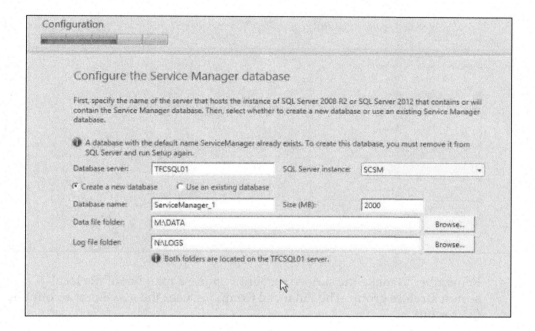

3. Management group names must be unique. Do not use the same management group name when you deploy a Service Manager management server and a Service Manager data warehouse management server. Furthermore, do not use the management group name that is used for Operations Manager:

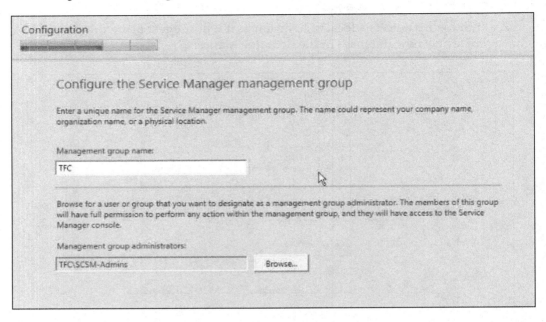

4. Remember to make the service account you use a member of the local administrators group. The Financial Company uses the `svc-SCSM` account in their setup:

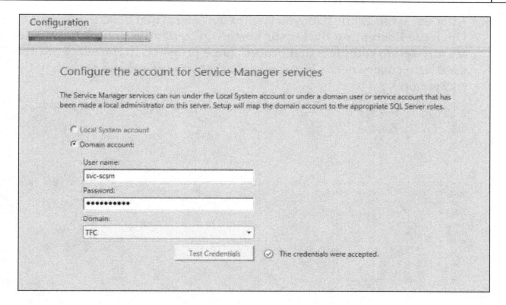

5. The Financial Company uses the `svc-SCSMWF` account as the workflow account:

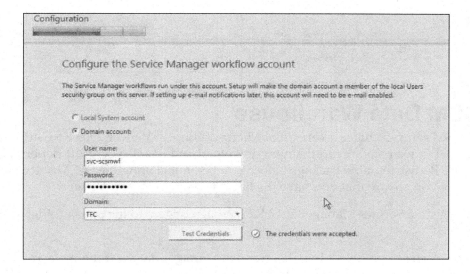

6. After the setup is finished, you should make sure that the checkbox for **Open the Encryption Backup or Restore Wizard after Setup closes. You are advised to complete that process to be prepared in the event of future disaster recovery needs.** is selected, so that you can make a backup of the encryption keys used by SCSM:

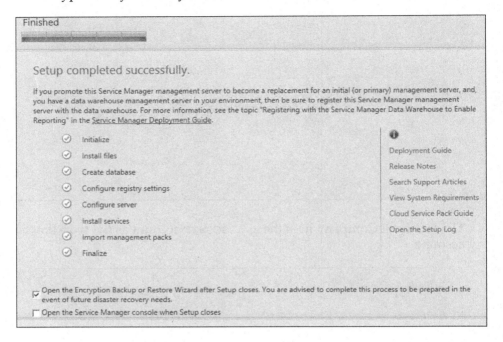

SCSM Data Warehouse

The SCSM setup contains a version of Microsoft Report Viewer 2008 Redistributable Package, but we recommend that you download and install Microsoft Report Viewer 2008 SP1 Redistributable Package before you begin installing the SCSM software. This way you ensure that you have the latest version of Report Viewer.

On the System Service Manager 2012 R2 media, navigate to the amd64 folder and run Setup.

On the splash screen, select **Install a Service Manager data warehouse management server**. Perform the following steps during setup:

1. During setup, a check is made to verify that prerequisites are met. You will also see a warning about not having enough memory, the other items being missing, and the action needed, such as whether the server has less than 8 GB of RAM:

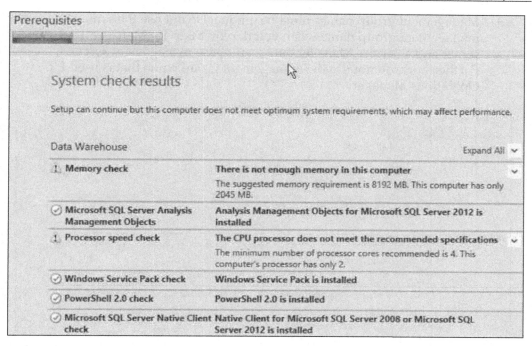

2. If setup detects a local SQL instance, it will suggest using this one and creating a new database in the default instance:

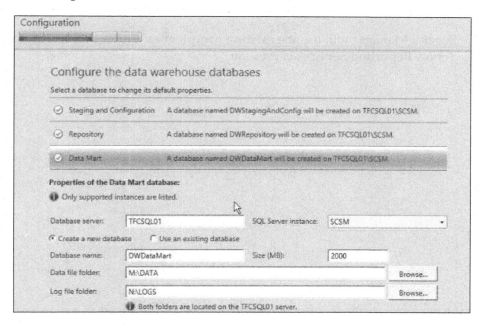

3. Management group names must be unique. Do not use the same management group name when you deploy a Service Manager management server and a Service Manager data warehouse management server. Furthermore, do not use the management group name that is used for Operations Manager:

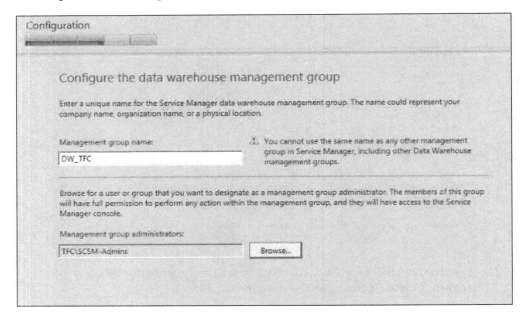

4. Service Manager will use the existing computer as a reporting server if SQL Server Reporting Services is present:

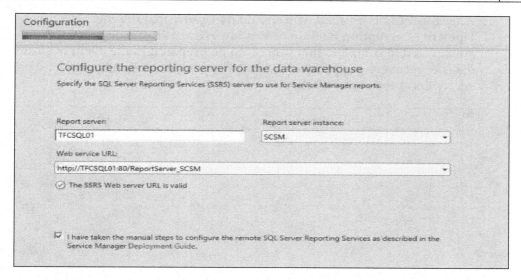

5. Remember to make the service account you use a member of the local administrators group. The Financial Company will use the same service account, svc-SCSM, for both the TFCSCSM-MGMT01 and TFCSCSM-DW01 servers in their SCSM setup.

6. The Financial Company will use svc-scsmrep as the reporting account:

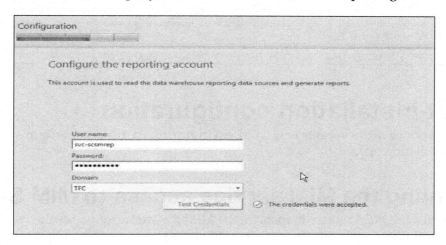

7. After the setup is finished, you should make sure that the checkbox for **Open the Encryption Backup or Restore Wizard after Setup closes. You are advised to complete that process to be prepared in the event of future disaster recovery needs.** is selected so that you can make a backup of the encryption keys used by SCSM:

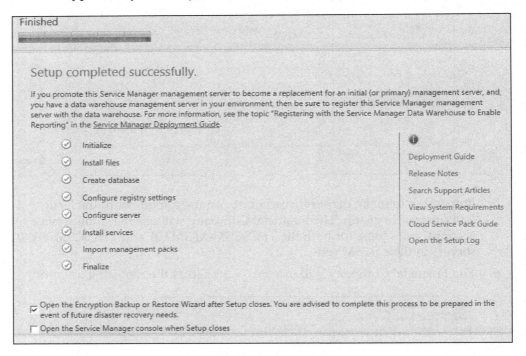

Post-installation configuration

Before we can start to use our new MIM environment, we need to perform some post-installation tasks.

Granting the MIM service access to MIM Sync

In order for the MIM service to manage the MIM Synchronization service, we need to add the MIM Service service account to the MIMSyncAdmins group. If you are implementing Password Reset, you also need to add the MIM Service service account to the MIMSyncPasswordSet group.

After adding the MIM Service service account to the new groups, you need to restart the MIM Service service in order for the new group membership to take effect.

Securing the MIM Service mailbox

This is not required, but it is best practice to take a look at the mailbox used by the MIM service (if you're running Exchange). A few things you might consider are as follows:

- Secure the mailbox, making sure only internal users can send a mail to it.
- Configure the mailbox quota to make sure the MIM Service mailbox does not get blocked by default quota settings.
- Configure maximum mail sizes to make sure no one can send large e-mails to the MIM Service. Usually, you can limit this to 1 MB.

Disabling indexing in SharePoint

If SharePoint is used only for the MIM portal, you will gain performance if you disable the indexing within SharePoint because you will not use the search capabilities of SharePoint. This is done a little differently in WSS 3.0 and SharePoint Foundation 2010, so take a look at the documentation to see how to turn this off.

For SharePoint 2013, you can run the following command:

```
Get-SPTimerJob hourly-all-sptimerservice-health-analysis-job | disable-SPTimerJob
```

Redirecting to IdentityManagement

If you want to redirect the MIM Portal URL, say to let the user type `http://servername` and be redirected to `http://servername/identitymanagement`, this can be useful to users; as the default behavior, they would see an empty screen of a SharePoint site. Perform the following steps:

1. Navigate to the SharePoint website directory. By default, this path is `c:\inetpub\wwwroot\wss\VirtualDirectories\80`.
2. Make sure the filesystem is showing file extensions.
3. Create a new text file named `default.aspx`.

4. Edit `default.aspx` as follows:

```
<%@ Page Language="C#" %>
<script runat="server">
protected override void OnLoad(EventArgs e)
{
  base.OnLoad(e);
  Response.Redirect("~/IdentityManagement/default.aspx");
}
</script>
```

5. Save the file and run `iisreset`.

Enforcing Kerberos

If you have set all the prerequisites correctly, your clients should be able to authenticate to your MIM portal using Kerberos. However, they might try, say, to connect using a client/browser that does not support Kerberos and end up with NTLM instead.

We can configure the MIM portal to require Kerberos, as we did in the previous steps.

This is done by modifying the `web.config` file used by the SharePoint website. Perform the following steps to modify the `web.config` file:

1. The `web.config` file is located at `C:\inetpub\wwwroot\wss\VirtualDirectories\80`.

   Before modifying the file, make sure you make a backup copy.

2. In order to be able to save the file, you need to run your editor (Notepad, maybe) in an elevated mode (that is, run as administrator).

3. Open the file and locate the `<resourceManagementClient . . . />` section.

4. Add `requireKerberos="true"`, so that it reads
   `<resourceManagementClient requireKerberos="true" . . . />`.

5. After saving the file, run `iisreset`.

Editing binding in IIS for MIM Password sites

After installing the MIM Password Registration and Reset portals, you might need to change the binding of the websites created by the MIM Password Portal setup.

If you, as in the example used in this book, used a separate host header name during installation, you would need to add the binding of `https`, using the correct certificate and the correct IP. You may then also configure IIS to force the use of SSL for the MIM Password websites if you like.

Registering the SCSM manager in data warehouse

After you have deployed the Service manager and data warehouse management servers, you must run the Data Warehouse Registration wizard. This wizard registers the Service manager management group with the data warehouse management group and deploys management packs from the Service manager management server to the data warehouse management server. The management pack deployment process can take several hours to complete. It is best practice not to turn off any Service manager computers or stop any Service manager services during this time. During this registration process, you can continue to use the Service manager console to perform any Service manager functions that you want.

To ensure that the reporting data will be available, use the following procedure to register the data warehouse and deploy the management packs:

1. Using an account that is a member of the Service manager and data warehouse management administrators group, log on to the computer that hosts Service Manager Console. In our example, this is the TFCSCSM-MGMT01 server.

2. In Service Manager Console, select **Administration**.

3. In the **Administration** pane, expand **Administration**.

4. In the **Administration** view in the **Register with Service Manager's Data Warehouse** area, click on **Register with Service Manager Data Warehouse**.

5. In the **Data Warehouse Registration** wizard on the **Before You Begin** page, click on **Next**.

6. On the **Data Warehouse** page, in the **Server name** box, type the name of the computer hosting the data warehouse management server and then click on **Test Connection**. If the test is successful, click on **Next**. In our example, the server name is TFCSCSM-DW01.

7. On the **Credentials** page, you can accept the default entry in the **Run as account** list and click on **Next**, or you can enter credentials from a user or group of your own choosing.

8. On the **Summary** page, click on **Create**.

9. On the **Completion** page, when the data warehouse registration succeeded is displayed, click on **Close**.

10. A dialog box states that the report deployment process has not finished. This is to be expected. In the **System Center Service Manager** dialog box, click on **OK**.

11. In a few minutes, after closing the **Data Warehouse Registration** wizard, the **Data Warehouse** button will be added to the Service Manager console.

You could get an error message that the Service Manager Data Warehouse SQL Reporting Services server is currently unavailable.

This might be due to the fact that the local firewall on the Reporting Services (SCSM-DW, in our example) server does not allow inbound connections to the ports used by Reporting Services. This is also true for SQL ports such as TCP 1433. In order for connections to work, you need to open up the ports in the firewall or disable the firewall.

To open port 80 on the TFCSCSM-DW01 server for Reporting services to work, perform the following steps:

1. From the **Start** menu, click on **Control Panel**, then on **System and Security**, and finally on **Windows Firewall**. If **Control Panel** is not configured for **Category** view, you only need to select **Windows Firewall**.

2. Click on **Advanced Settings**.

3. Click on **Inbound Rules**.

4. Click on **New Rule** in the **Actions** window.

5. Select **Port** on the **Rule Type** page.

6. Click on **Next**.

7. On the **Protocol and Ports** page, click on **TCP**.

8. Select **Specific Local Ports** and type a value of 80.

9. Click on **Next**.

10. On the **Action** page, click on **Allow the connection**.

11. Click on **Next**.

12. On the **Profile** page, click on the appropriate options for your environment.
13. Click on **Next**.
14. On the **Name** page, enter the name `ReportServer` (TCP on port `80`).
15. Click on **Finish**.
16. Restart the computer.

Repeat the previous steps for TCP `1433`, if you need to remotely manage or connect to the database engine.

In order for Reporting to work, we also need to allow the SCSM Data Warehouse server where SQL reporting is running to access the SQL server used by SCSM management. In our example, that means we also need to open up the firewall on the SCSM-MGMT server to allow inbound connections to TCP `1433`.

For a complete list of ports required by SCSM 2010, take a look at `http://aka.ms/SCSM2010Ports`.

MIM post-install scripts for data warehouse

If you are installing and planning to use Reporting, you will have to run some scripts on the SCSM Data Warehouse server that will (among other things) grant the MIM service account permissions to the SCSM databases.

The scripts can be found on the MIM 2016 ISO, in the `Data Warehouse Support Scripts` folder. Copy the folder containing the scripts to your SCSM 2010 data warehouse server and execute the PowerShell script, `MIMPostInstallScriptsForDataWarehouse.ps1`.

Summary

Installing the prerequisites is, as you can see, the toughest part, while installing the products involved in the MIM family is quite straightforward.

In this chapter, we showed you what it would look like if you installed all MIM 2016 components using the setup that my example company, The Financial Company, uses.

The *key* to a successful MIM 2016 installation is to really understand the prerequisites, making sure you understand all your service accounts, aliases, and Kerberos settings.

Remember that if you are not planning to use parts of the product, you might be able to reduce the number of machines involved. If you, for example, are not interested in MIM Reporting, the whole setup of the SCSM infrastructure is not required.

Now that we have our installation in place, it is time to start using our MIM 2016 infrastructure. In the next chapter, we will start off by looking at the initial configuration of the MIM Synchronization, MIM Service, and MIM Portal components.

3
MIM Sync Configuration

If you have followed the previous chapters closely, you will now have a newly installed MIM environment. In this chapter, we will discuss some of the basic configurations we need to look at, no matter how our environment looks, or how we plan to use MIM.

We will focus on the initial configuration of the MIM Synchronization Service. Specifically, we will cover the following topics:

- MIM Synchronization interface
- Creating Management Agents
- Schema management
- Initial load versus scheduled runs
- Moving the configuration from development to production

MIM Synchronization interface

Let's start by examining the MIM Synchronization graphical interface, and describing some of the tools and options available. Launching the Synchronization Service program will show an interface divided into five primary tools: **Operations**, **Management Agents**, **Metaverse Designer**, **Metaverse Search**, and **Joiner**. The basic features of these tools are as follows:

- The **Operations** tool provides the connection status, details of new objects, object deletions, changes, errors, and internal MIM actions such as projections, provisions, and joins.

- The **Management Agents** tool allows you to create, configure, control, and view management agents or the way we connect the synchronization engine to the various systems and pull and push data between those systems.

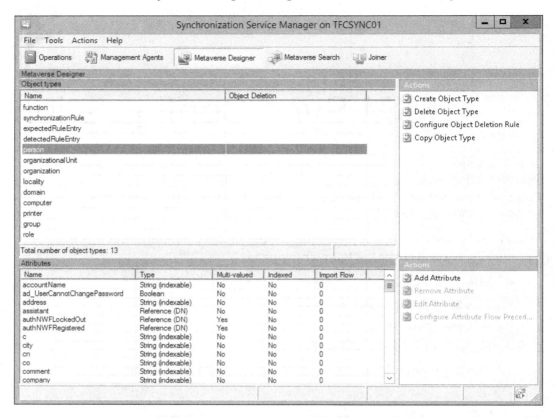

- The **Metaverse Designer** controls the Metaverse schema, the objects, the attributes associated with these objects, object deletion rule, as well as controlling which system is authoritative for each attribute. Recall that the Metaverse is where MIM combines multiple connector space object attributes that are related to the same identity into a unique, single object.

- The **Metaverse Search** allows you to look at Metaverse objects and their details. Clauses can be specified that allow you to narrow down the search to a specific object or a group of objects.

- Finally, the **Joiner** tool enables you to manually create and destroy connections between connector space objects and their respective Metaverse objects.

Creating Management Agents

Before we start to use our MIM implementation to manage identities, we need to decide where the information about the identities will come from, and where that information will go. It is best that we start off with the essential connections, and add more as we verify that the basics are working.

A very typical scenario is the one we have—The Financial Company has an **HR (human resource)** system that will, for the most part, work as the source of identity information. Then it has Active Directory, which is the primary system to receive the identity information.

The basic flow will be: *HR -> MIM -> AD*.

But that is only the basic flow. As you will see later in this book, there will be other sources of information and additional targets.

Active Directory

Most MIM implementations have at least one Management Agent connected to Active Directory.

There are a few things to consider before creating this Management Agent. First, you should have already sat down with business partners and technology teams, and determined which systems you will be connecting to, which objects, which attributes, and how an attribute should flow through MIM to other systems. These identity discovery and processing mapping discussions are extremely useful, because you will effectively be configuring MIM to coincide with those business processes. Secondly, keep things as simple as possible, and don't try to do everything at once.

 Do not try to implement everything at once!

If, for example, your plan is to have MIM manage both users and groups in AD, start off by implementing the management of users, and then add groups when the user part is working.

Are we interested in the whole AD or only its parts?

Some businesses specifically exclude parts of Active Directory from MIM. There's nothing wrong with excluding parts, but keep in mind that this decision may impact other requirements. For example, if a collection of users is excluded from MIM, those people will then also be excluded in MIM group management. If Active Directory has group nesting, excluding a collection of groups could have serious repercussions.

Do I need a test environment?

Yes! You should always develop and verify your MIM configuration in a testing environment before applying the configuration to your production environment. What is the worst that can happen? A lot! Depending on what you've configured in MIM and the permissions your service accounts have, you could overwrite or clear data, mistakenly create new accounts, or inadvertently delete accounts. The authors have worked in support long enough to tell you that this is one lesson you do not want to learn the hard way.

Least-privileged approach

The **Management Agent (MA)** will use a service account to talk to Active Directory. The Financial Company is using the approach to have as few MA accounts as possible rather than having one account for each connected system.

In the case of The Financial Company, the SVC-ADMA account will be the account that we will use to connect to Active Directory. What we need to do is to give this account the permissions needed to manage relevant objects in AD.

You should always apply a *least-privileged* approach to all your accounts, especially service accounts such as the ones we will be using with our MIM Management Agents.

To keep things simple, our environment has user accounts in an OU named **TFC Users**. We then need to give MIM the required permissions to manage the objects. Right-click on the OU, and run the delegate control wizard. Give the AD MA account, SVC-ADMA, and management permissions on user (and maybe group) objects. In some cases, the aforementioned wizard might give the AD MA account more permissions than needed. If, for example, MIM should only be able to *create* and *manage* the objects but not *delete* them, we need to adjust the permissions in order to use the least-privilege approach.

Directory replication

When importing (reading) information from AD, it is possible to use what is called **delta**. Delta means we only get the changes since the last time we checked. In order for the MIM Active Directory Management Agent to read only the changes (the delta information in AD), it needs a special permission called **Replicating Directory Changes** at the domain level. If you do not perform this step, you will receive the error "Replication access was denied" when you attempt to read the AD object data. You can read more about this at http://support.microsoft.com/kb/303972.

1. Open up the **Security** tab in the domain (`ad.company.com` for example).

2. You either create a group, if that is how you always do it, or you assign permission to the `SVC-ADMA` account(s). You need to check the **Allow** option for the **Replicating Directory Changes** permission, as shown in the following screenshot:

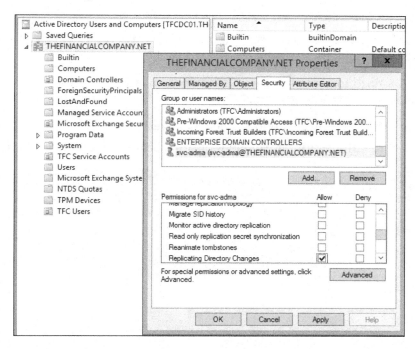

Alternatively, the least-privilege way is to go into the registry, create a DWORD value named `ADMAUseACLSecurity`, and set it to `1`. This will tell the AD Management Agent to use the AD ACL permissions rather than requiring the DIRSYNC permissions. You will need to create the value in `SYSTEM\CurrentControlSet\ Services\FIMSynchronizationService\Parameters`.

Password reset

If you are implementing password synchronization and/or the Self-service Password Reset feature, you will need to assign permissions for that; details about this are given in *Chapter 9, Password Management*.

Creating AD MA

In this segment, we will walk you through the steps for creating the Active Directory Management Agent. We will slowly work through some of the new terms, but trying to discuss every term is a sure way for beginners to get lost in the product. Some of these terms will be explained later on in this book as we start to use more advanced features.

If you are curious to know about some terms right away, you can click on the **Help** button available on all the pages in the wizard.

To begin, you need to log in to your MIM Synchronization server using an account that is a member of the MIMSyncAdmins group:

1. Start MIM Synchronization Service Manager.

2. Select the **Management Agents** tool, and click on **Create** in the **Actions** pane:

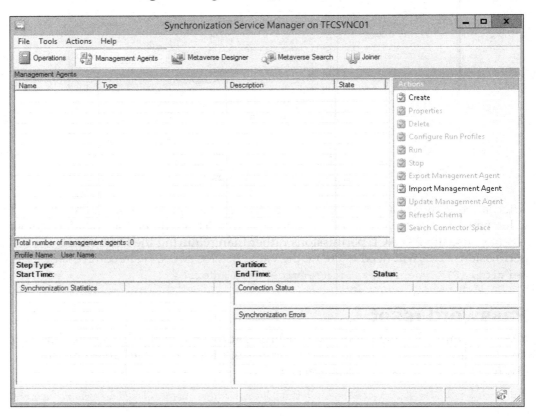

3. Select **Active Directory Domain Services** in the **Management agent for:** drop-down list.

4. Give the MA a descriptive name; at The Financial Company, we simply call it **AD**:

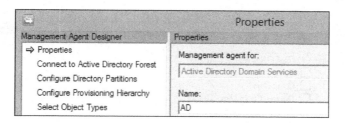

5. The AD MA connects to the Active Directory forest, and not to a specific domain in the forest. We decide later on which domain in the forest to connect to. When connecting to the AD forest, we configure the account used for the connection. We will use the SVC-ADMA account. The **Options...** button allows you to change the default LDAP connection options. It is recommended that you leave the default **Sign and Encrypt LDAP Traffic** option as it is:

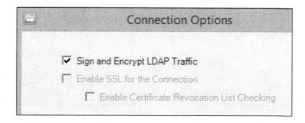

6. In the **Configure Directory Partitions** section, select the domain partition **DC=thefinancialcompany,DC=net**. If you want MIM to use a preferred set of domain controllers, check **Only use preferred domain controllers**, and click on the **Configure...** button to choose the ones you want MIM to use. Specifying a preferred domain controller or domain controllers means MIM will only use those domain controller(s). If you were to specify a single domain controller, and that domain controller is down for maintenance or decommissioned, MIM will need to be changed to add a usable domain controller.

7. The default is to work with the whole domain; but we do not want that, so let's click on the **Containers...** button. In the **Select Containers** dialog, uncheck the domain (top) level, thereby unselecting all the options. Then select the containers you want MIM to manage. In our example, we select the **TFC Users** OU, as seen in the following screenshot:

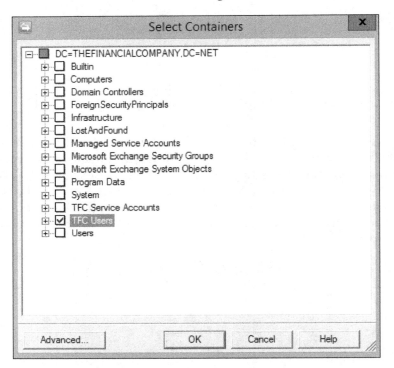

8. On the **Configure Provision Hierarchy** page, we do not need to change anything; just click on **Next**.

Provision Hierarchy means MIM can automatically create a missing OU if needed during provisioning. In our example, if we had configured MIM to provision Active Directory accounts to an OU named TFC User Accounts, which does not exist, it would throw an error. Enabling Provision Hierarchy would mean MIM would create the missing OU. Note that MIM will only create an OU if one is needed for provisioning, and it does not delete OUs.

9. In the **Select Object Types** page, select the object types which you know MIM needs to manage. Keep the defaults, and add only what you need. Do not deselect the default **Container, domainDNS**, and **organizationalUnit** object types, because these are required for MIM to know *where* in AD the objects reside. Do not select object types you have no need for. Initially, The Financial Company has no need for the **contact** object type, so we do not select it. If we need any of these objects in the future, we can change the configuration.

10. Select the attributes that you know you need. Needs will be discussed in the following chapters, and we will make frequent changes to this configuration. If you check **Show All**, it will display your complete AD schema, which includes any custom schema changes you have made. In addition to the Active Directory domain, there are two special attributes, **objectSid** and **sAMAccountName**, which are required if you want users to access the MIM Portal. For our basic demonstration, make sure the following attributes are checked: **department, displayName, employeeID, employeeType, givenName, manager, middleName, name, objectSid, pwdLastSet, sAMAccountName, sn, title, unicodePwd, userAccountControl**, and **userPrincipalName**.

> If, for some reason, we have configured the containers and object types in a way that we can reach objects we are not supposed to manage, we can make a connector filter to make sure these objects are out of scope. We will configure a connector filter in our MIM Service in the next chapter.

11. The join and projection rules will be configured using MIM Service in our environment. So, click on **Next**.

> If you are running only Synchronization Service, or, for some other reason, using non-declarative (classic) synchronization, this is where you will configure your join and projection rules for the AD MA. We will discuss that later in the chapter.

12. Attribute flow will be configured using MIM Service in our environment. So, click on **Next**.

If you are running only Synchronization Service, or, for some other reason, using non-declarative (classic) synchronization, this is where you will configure your attribute flow rules for the AD MA. MIM supports the usage of both declarative and non-declarative attribute flows in your MAs.

13. On the **Configure Deprovisioning** page, there are a few things we need to consider:

    ○ **Deprovisioning** is what happens when an object in the connector space is disconnected from its Metaverse object. We will look into how we can control this later in this book. If you are uncertain, leave the default value as **Make them disconnectors**.

    ○ **Stage a delete on the object for the next export run** is what you will select if you want MIM to delete objects in AD when they are disconnected from the MV. To actually have deletes of users and groups in AD could cause a lot of problems if they occur when they shouldn't. In all cases, when we allow MIM to perform the deletes of objects in a connector space, we need to be very careful.

    ○ The **Do not recall attributes contributed by objects from this management agent when disconnected** checkbox might sometimes be useful if, for example, you are replacing a Management Agent with a new one, and do not want the Metaverse attributes to be deleted in the process.

 Please read Carol Wapshere's article explaining deprovisioning options at http://aka.ms/ FIMDeprovisioning before you start using the options.

If you are doing a non-declarative (classic) synchronization using only Synchronization Engine, and if you are using code to solve some problems, this is where you will configure which DLL contains your code. This is also where you will select the version of Exchange that you will use if MIM is to provision users for Exchange. For now, we will leave this as **No provisioning**.

HR (SQL Server)

The most popular MIM connection is Active Directory, and the second most common connector is SQL Server. For those organizations that do not have identity data in SQL, there are occasions when creating a few SQL tables will assist in your identity management solution.

At The Financial Company, the HR system uses SQL Server as a database, and we will interact with HR using a typical SQL MA. As with Active Directory, we should implement the least-privilege approach when assigning permissions to the account that MIM is using to connect to SQL.

As the HR database (at present) is not supposed to receive any data, just send the data to MIM; we can assign the db_datareader permissions to the SVC-HRMA account:

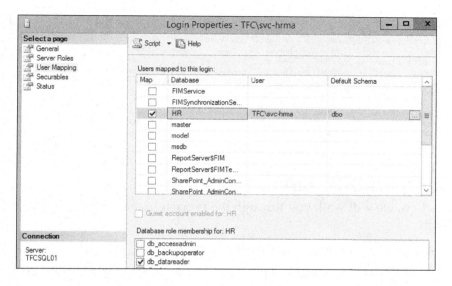

At The Financial Company, the HR data is in a database named **HR**.

If you want to filter what information is made available to MIM in SQL, you can easily do that by creating an SQL view and configuring MIM to read from that view. Just remember that when MIM uses an SQL view to talk to SQL, updates become a little trickier. If you create a complex view for MIM to read, and later on realize that MIM should also be able to update a column in a table, it may not be possible without redesigning the view.

Before we can configure our MA, we need to understand the data source we are connecting to. So, let's take a quick look at how the HR database is built up.

In the HR table (named **HRData**), there is information about our users and organizational units. In the table that follows, note the relation that we have between the column **manager**, which references the object **ID** column.

If the SQL data has this kind of reference information, we will be able to use this to synchronize these to attributes in other CDSs, which also use reference attributes. For example, as the **manager** column in our HR data is a reference value, MIM can easily populate the **manager** attribute in AD, and also reference an attribute pointing to another object in the AD:

ID	objectType	manager	HRType	title	department	firstName	middleName	lastName
10000005	person	NULL	Employee	CEO	Executive	Joe	NULL	Mxyzptlk
10000010	person	10000005	Employee	VP	Executive	David	NULL	Steadman
10000033	person	10000010	Employee	Sales Lead	Sales	Steve	NULL	Gates
10000042	person	10000005	Employee	VP	Executive	Jeff	NULL	Ingalls
10000055	person	10000042	Contractor	Engineer	Engineering	Frank	Howard	Jackson
10000058	person	10000010	Contractor	Sales Associate	Sales	Amber	Nicole	Smith
10000059	person	10000042	Employee	Sr. Engineer	Engineering	Vern	NULL	Rottmann
10000064	person	10000042	Employee	Sr. Technologist	IT	Dave	NULL	Stevens
10000073	person	10000010	Employee	Human Resour...	HR	Melanie	NULL	Young
10000077	person	10000042	Employee	Architect	Engineering	Lincoln	Abraham	Hanks
10000079	person	10000042	Contractor	Developer	IT	Dan	NULL	Petrak
10000081	person	10000010	Employee	Support Engineer	IT	Tim	NULL	Mack
10000083	person	10000010	Employee	Support Engineer	IT	Glenn	NULL	Zay
10000091	person	10000042	Employee	Architect	Engineering	Reagan	Ethel	Thompson
10000093	person	10000010	Contractor	Intern	HR	Chuck	NULL	Morris
10000056	person	10000042	Employee	Developer	IT	Fred	NULL	Jackson

Creating an SQL MA

In this section, we will walk you through the process of creating the SQL MA for the HR system:

1. Start the Synchronization Service Manager.

2. Select the **Management Agents tool**, and click on **Create** in the **Actions** pane:

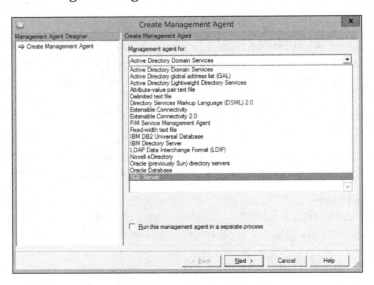

Select the **SQL Server** option in the **Management agent for:** drop-down menu, and give the MA a descriptive name such as **HR**, as seen in the following screenshot:

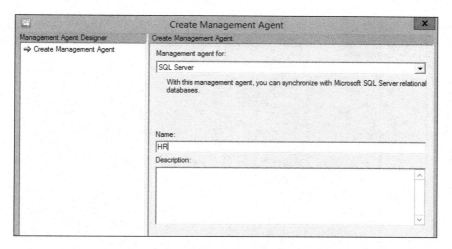

3. As we are using SQL aliases, we use the alias server name **dbHR**. The database is **HR**, and the base table is **HRData**. We are using Windows integrated authentication with the SVC-HRMA account.

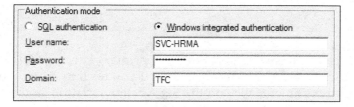

4. Clicking on **Next** should show that the SQL MA has retrieved the schema, the columns, and the database types from the SQL database. This is seen in the next screenshot:

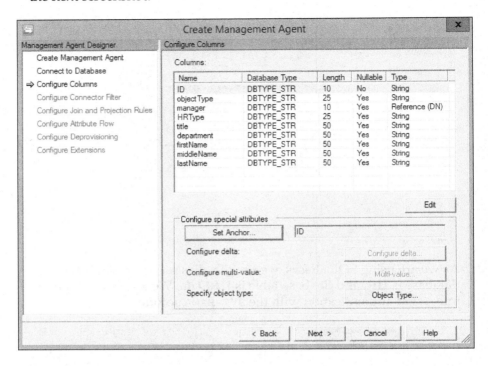

5. In our case, because the ID column is a primary key, the SQL MA automatically sets the ID as an anchor. If you need to modify the anchor in your environment, click on the **Set Anchor...** button, and set the anchor attributes accordingly.

In our example, the anchor attribute consists of a single column in the database that contains an unchanging unique value of each object. By definition, an anchor can be a unique combination of one or more attributes that do not change. Which attribute is to be used as an anchor attribute in each of the CDSs is an important decision to make. The anchor attribute value should *never* change for a specific object; the value should remain the same for the entire life cycle of the object. If the anchor attribute changes, it will be detected as a *delete* of the old object and an *addition* of a new object by MIM when importing information from the CDS.

6. Clicking on the **Object Type...** button allows you to define if the SQL MA only contains one fixed object type, or if the information about object type is stored in a column. It would be better if you can get this information as a column in the view or table. This particular setting can only be configured during the creation of the MA; if you would like to change this later on, you will need to recreate the MA. In our HRData table, we have the object types in the column **objectType**. In order for MIM to detect the possible object types available, the table or view we look at must contain sample data with the possible object-type values.

7. There is one attribute in the list that needs to be edited, as we need to tell MIM that it is of the Reference (DN) type. A Reference (DN) type tells MIM that the data in the column contains the ID value of some other object. Select **Manager**, click on the **Edit...** button, and check the **Reference (DN)** checkbox:

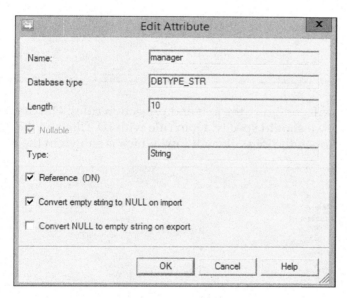

8. If, for some reason, we have configured the table or view used by the MA in a way that we reach objects we are not supposed to manage, we can configure a connector filter to make sure these objects are out of scope. Essentially, MIM asks if there is an attribute criteria that should filter or block the connector space objects from connecting to their respective Metaverse objects (MIM calls this process a join), or if MIM should block a connector space object from creating its own unique Metaverse object (called a projection). In our example, everyone in the HR source system should be provisioned an Active Directory account. Therefore, we keep the defaults of **Filter Type** as **None**, and click on **Next**.

9. We will not configure a connector filter, a way to prevent connection to the Metaverse, so leave it as is:

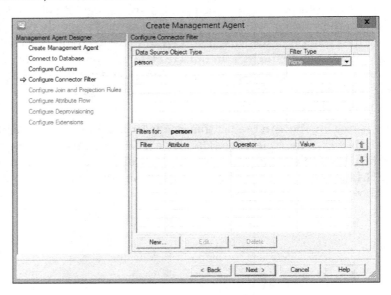

10. Next we will configure the join and projection rules. Our anchor is ID; therefore, we should specify a join rule with ID. Click on the **New Join Rule** button to open the join rule window, which is shown in the next screenshot:

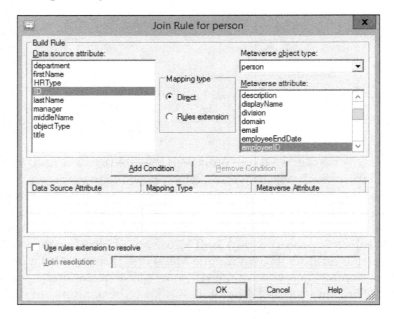

11. Change the **Metaverse object type** to **person**, select **ID** in the **Data source attribute** section, and **employeeID** for the **Metaverse attribute**. Click on the **Add Condition** button, and a non-index join warning message appears, as shown in the following screenshot:

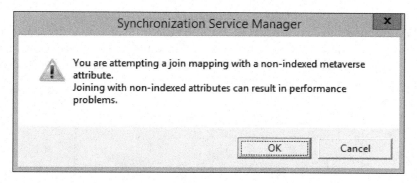

12. MIM warns us that finding a matching **employeeID** value in the Metaverse would be faster if we indexed that attribute. Click on **OK** for now, and we will show you where the attribute index is later in this chapter. Click on **OK** to finalize the ID to the **employeeID** join, and you will be back at the **Configure Join and Projection Rules** step:

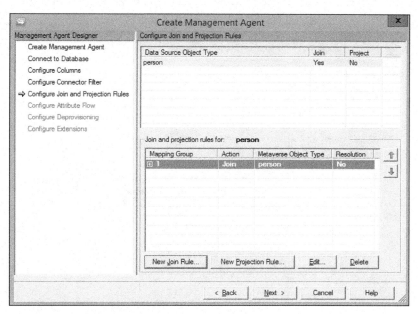

Join rules are especially helpful in disaster recovery scenarios where you need to re-associate objects in systems with the Metaverse. We recommend you have a join rule in every Management Agent where possible.

13. We now need to configure a projection rule. This is one of the easiest things you will do today. Click on the **New Projection Rule** button, and the **Projection** type window will be displayed, as shown in the following screenshot:

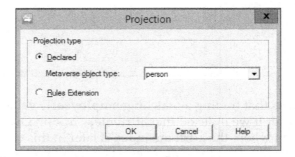

14. Accept the default **person** as **Metaverse object type**, and click on **OK**:

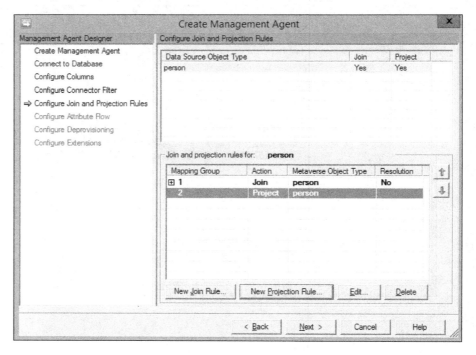

15. Click on **Next** to move on to the next step.

16. We will now configure the attribute flow, that is, mapping attributes in the connector space to attributes in the Metaverse. This means the connector space attribute value can be copied to the mapped Metaverse attribute. In our case, we are mapping the connector space object type **person** (on the left-hand side) to a **person** object type in the Metaverse on the right side. Click on **department** in the **Data source attribute** section on the left-hand side of the screen, and click on **department** in the **Metaverse attribute** (right-hand side). Keep the **Mapping Type** set to **Direct**, and **Flow Direction** set to **Import**. Click on the **New** button to add the mapping. You should see a new attribute flow like the following:

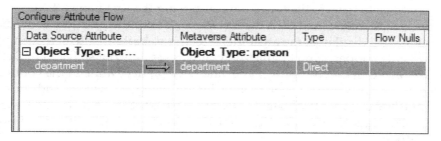

17. Perform the same steps to set up an import attribute flow, as shown in the following screenshot:.

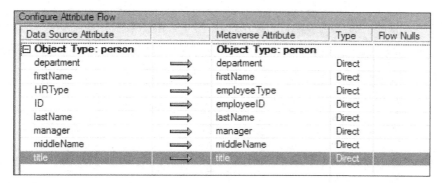

This is a good time to talk about attribute names. Often, people new to identity management will get caught up on connector space attribute names not matching with the same attribute names in the Metaverse. For example, the attribute **HRType** does not exist in the Metaverse. Should you change your HR system, or create a new Metaverse attribute? Ultimately, it is your decision, but there is no reason to re-architect your source and target systems simply because attribute names do not match. In this case, something like **employeeType** effectively has the same function; therefore, it can be used. Non-matching attributes are expected in the identity world, because the systems are disparate. Our advice? Get over it.

18. Let's set up an import attribute flow for our display name. TFC would like identities to have a display name comprising the first name, the first letter of the middle name, and then the last name. Notice that our source system does not have a display name attribute, but we can build it with some simple code. Not a developer? Don't panic! As you will see, it is not so bad. First, click on **Advanced** in the **Mapping Type**, and click on **firstName** in the connector space section on the left-hand side. Hold down the *Ctrl* key, and click on **middleName** and **lastName** to select the other attributes needed to build the display name. In the **Metaverse attribute** section on the right-hand side, click on **displayName**.

19. Click on the **New** button to bring up the advanced window, and change the **Flow rule name** to **displayName**:

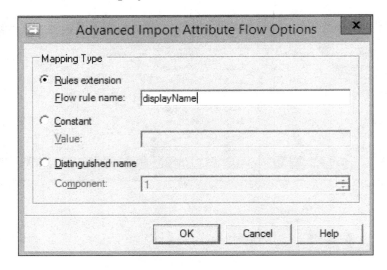

20. Click on **OK**. The screen should now show the advanced import attribute flow, as seen in the following screenshot:

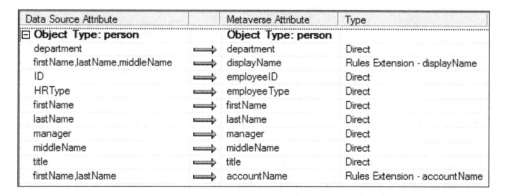

Data Source Attribute		Metaverse Attribute	Type
⊟ Object Type: person		Object Type: person	
department	⟹	department	Direct
firstName	⟹	firstName	Direct
HRType	⟹	employeeType	Direct
ID	⟹	employeeID	Direct
lastName	⟹	lastName	Direct
manager	⟹	manager	Direct
middleName	⟹	middleName	Direct
title	⟹	title	Direct
firstName,lastName,middleName	⟹	displayName	Rules Extension - displayName

21. Add another advanced import attribute flow for **accountName**, as shown in the next screenshot:

Data Source Attribute		Metaverse Attribute	Type
⊟ Object Type: person		Object Type: person	
department	⟹	department	Direct
firstName,lastName,middleName	⟹	displayName	Rules Extension - displayName
ID	⟹	employeeID	Direct
HRType	⟹	employeeType	Direct
firstName	⟹	firstName	Direct
lastName	⟹	lastName	Direct
manager	⟹	manager	Direct
middleName	⟹	middleName	Direct
title	⟹	title	Direct
firstName,lastName	⟹	accountName	Rules Extension - accountName

22. We will complete **displayName** and **accountName** and the rules after we finish the remaining two steps. Click on **Next** to move on to the deprovisioning step.

23. The HR system is a source system that will not have deprovisioning. On the **Configure Deprovisioning** page, we will click on **Next** to keep the default **Make them disconnectors**, and then click on **Next** again.

24. The final step specifies the rules extension name that was auto-calculated as HRExtension.DLL. You could change the name if you want, but we will keep the default for the purpose of this example. This DLL that we will create will contain the coded **displayName** and **accountName** that we want to generate. Click on the **Finish** button to complete the creation of the HR Management Agent. You should now see two Management Agents in the **Service Manager** console: **AD** and **HR**, as shown in the following screenshot:

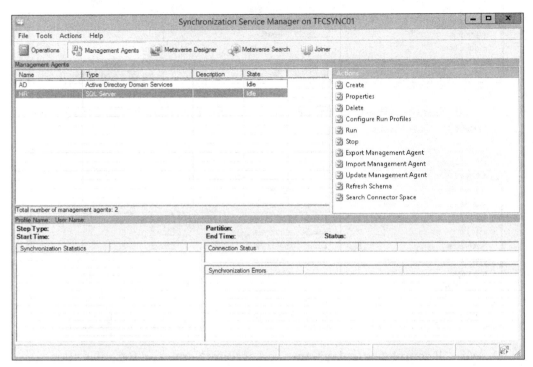

Creating a rules extension

A rules extension supplements the MIM Management Agent, and provides the flexibility for you to build customized rules. We will walk you through a simple (and common) example of building an attribute value from the values of other attributes. TFC wants **displayName** to be **firstName**, first initial of **middleName**, and **lastName**. Follow the steps listed next:

1. Let's begin by right-clicking on the **HR** Management Agent, hovering over **Create Extension Projects...**, and selecting **Rules Extension**:

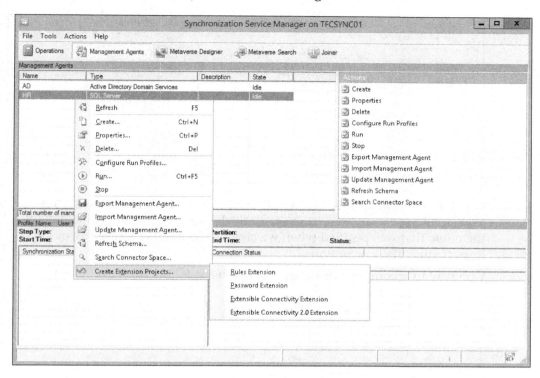

2. The **Create Extension Project** window appears. We will write our rules extension in Visual C# using Visual Studio 2015, and store our source code in C:\SourceCode. If you are also using Visual Studio 2015, choose the highest Visual Studio version shown in your window. Click on **OK** to launch Visual Studio:

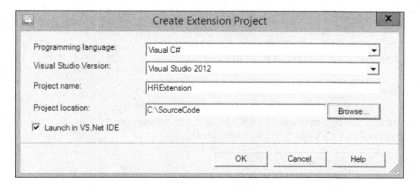

3. The Visual Studio interface gets loaded. Double-click on the `HRExtension.cs` file so that it is opened:

4. Scroll down until you see `IMASynchronization.MapAttributesForImport`. You should see `case displayName:` which matches, and not coincidentally, the name that we specified when we created the **displayName** advanced import attribute flow options.

One way to accomplish our goal is to insert the following code:

```
case "displayName":
string firstName = string.Empty;
string lastName = string.Empty;
if (csentry["firstName"].IsPresent)
{
    firstName = csentry["firstName"].Value;
}
if (csentry["middleName"].IsPresent)
{
    if (csentry["middleName"].Value.Length >= 1)
    {
        middleInitial = csentry["middleName"]
          .Value.Substring(0,1);
    }
}
if (csentry["lastName"].IsPresent)
{
    lastName = csentry["lastName"].Value;
}
mventry["displayName"].Value = firstName + " " +
    middleInitial + " " + lastName;
break;
```

The following is a screenshot of what Visual Studio should now look like:

```
void IMASynchronization.MapAttributesForImport( string FlowRuleName, CSEntry csentry, MVEntry mventry)
{
    switch (FlowRuleName)
    {
        case "displayName":
            string firstName = string.Empty;
            string lastName = string.Empty;
            string middleInitial = string.Empty;

            if (csentry["firstName"].IsPresent)
            {
                firstName = csentry["firstName"].Value;
            }

            if (csentry["middleName"].IsPresent)
            {
                if (csentry["middleName"].Value.Length >= 1)
                {
                    middleInitial = csentry["middleName"].Value.Substring(0,1);
                }
            }

            if (csentry["lastName"].IsPresent)
            {
                lastName = csentry["lastName"].Value;
            }
            mventry["displayName"].Value = firstName + " " + middleInitial + " " + lastName;
            break;
    }
}
```

After the break, we will have another case statement for the **accountName**. Here's one way to handle that:

```
case "accountName":
if (mventry["accountName"].IsPresent)
{
    // Do nothing, the accountName was already generated.
}
else
{
    if (csentry["FirstName"].IsPresent && csentry
      ["LastName"].IsPresent)
    {
        string FirstName = csentry["FirstName"].Value;
        string LastName = csentry["LastName"].Value;
        string accountName = FirstName.Substring(0, 1) +
          LastName;
        string newaccountName = GetCheckedaccountName
          (accountName, mventry);
        if (newaccountName.Equals(""))
```

```
        {
            throw new TerminateRunException("A unique accountName
                could not be found");
        }
        mventry["accountName"].Value = newaccountName;
        }
    }
    break;
```

5. After `IMASynchronization.MapAttributesForImport` and before
    `IMASynchronization.MapAttributesForExport`, add a new
    `GetCheckedaccountName` method like this:

```
string GetCheckedaccountName(string accountName, MVEntry mventry)
{
    MVEntry[] findResultList = null;
    string checkedaccountName = accountName;
    for (int nameSuffix = 1; nameSuffix < 100; nameSuffix++)
    {
        findResultList = Utils.FindMVEntries("accountName",
            checkedaccountName, 1);
        if (findResultList.Length == 0)
        {
// The current accountName is not in use.
            return (checkedaccountName);
        }
        MVEntry mvEntryFound = findResultList[0];
        if (mvEntryFound.Equals(mventry))
        {
            return (checkedaccountName);
        }
// If the passed accountName is already in use, then add an
    integer value
// then verify if the new value exists. Repeat until a
    unique accountName is created.
        checkedaccountName = accountName + nameSuffix.
            ToString();
    }
// Return an empty string if no unique accountName could be
    created.
return "";
}
```

All that this preceding piece of code does is verify whether **accountName** is unique, and if not, add an integer value to the end.

6. Click on **Build**, and then on **Build Solution** to compile the DLL. That's it!

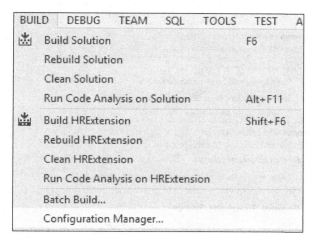

The Metaverse rules extension

There's one more rules extension that we need to create—the Metaverse rules extension. A Management Agent rules extension, such as the HR one we just created, is a DLL that allows us to manipulate data between the connector space and the Metaverse. The Metaverse DLL allows us to manipulate data between connector spaces. In our scenario, we want to push HR data to the Metaverse (this was done by setting the HR Management Agent to **project**), and then from the Metaverse out to AD. Another case to look at the need for a Metaverse rules extension is when you need to specify a one-time or an initial value for one or more attributes. For example, if you were to create an AD object using any other tool, you would need to specify a password. We set our password and any other attributes that only need to be performed once in our Metaverse rules extension. Follow the steps as described next:

1. In the **Management Agents** tool, click on **Tool**, and then on **Options...**. Check **Enable metaverse rules extension**, and click on **Create Rules Extension Project...**:

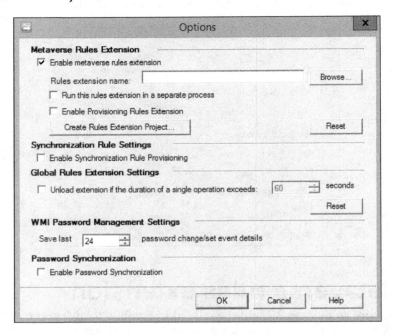

2. Once Visual Studio opens the Metaverse solution, you will want to go to the `Provision` method, and enter the following:

```
void IMVSynchronization.Provision (MVEntry mventry)
{
    ConnectedMA ManagementAgent;
    int Connectors;
    if (mventry.ObjectType == "person")
    {
        ManagementAgent = mventry.ConnectedMAs["AD"];
        Connectors = ManagementAgent.Connectors.Count;
        if (0 == Connectors)
        {
            ProvisionADAccount(mventry);
        }
    }
}
```

3. You can create a new `ProvisionADAccount` method like this:

```
private bool ProvisionADAccount(MVEntry mventry)
{
    ConnectedMA ManagementAgent;
    ReferenceValue dn;
    CSEntry csentry;
    ManagementAgent = mventry.ConnectedMAs["AD"];
    if (mventry["accountName"].IsPresent)
    {
        string ADContainer = "OU=TFC Users,DC
          =TheFinancialCompany,DC=net";
        string accountName = mventry["accountName"].Value;
        string rdn = "CN=" + accountName;
        dn = ManagementAgent.EscapeDNComponent
          (rdn).Concat(ADContainer);
        string password = "Password123$";

// password = "Password123$" means every new AD account
// will have the same password!
//
// A more secure solution would be to do something like
// this:
//
// string password = GenerateRandomPassword();
//
// where GenerateRandomPassword() is a method that
// generates a randomized password.
// We leave this exercise up to the readers as there are
// several examples you can find on the Internet for the
// activity. Note you will need to generate a password that
// is allowed in your AD and meets your business security //
requirements.

        csentry = ManagementAgent.Connectors.
          StartNewConnector("user");
        csentry.DN = dn;
        csentry["sAMAccountName"].Value = accountName;
        csentry["unicodePwd"].Value = password;
        csentry["pwdLastSet"].IntegerValue = 0;
        csentry["userAccountControl"].IntegerValue = 0x0200;
          // Create a normal, enabled AD account.  See KB
            305144.
        csentry["userPrincipalName"].Value = accountName +
          "@TheFinancialCompany.com";
        csentry.CommitNewConnector();
```

```
        return true;
    }
    else
    {
        return false;
    }
}
```

4. Build the solution, then go back to **Tools | Options...** and check **Enable Provision Rules Extension** to allow MIM to fire the provision code you just wrote and compiled:

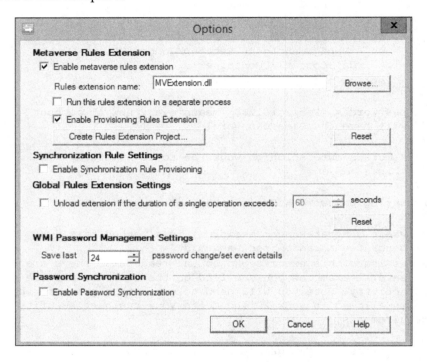

Indexing Metaverse attributes

Remember back when we created our HR Management Agent, and created a join between the HR **ID** attribute and the Metaverse **employeeID** attribute? We received the error "You are attempting a join mapping with a non-indexed metaverse attribute. Joining with non-indexed attributes can result in performance problems." To fix that problem, go to the **Metaverse Designer** tool, click on the **person** object type in the top pane, and click on **employeeID** in the **Attributes** or bottom pane. Next, click on **Edit Attribute**, and check the **Indexed** box, as shown in the following screenshot:

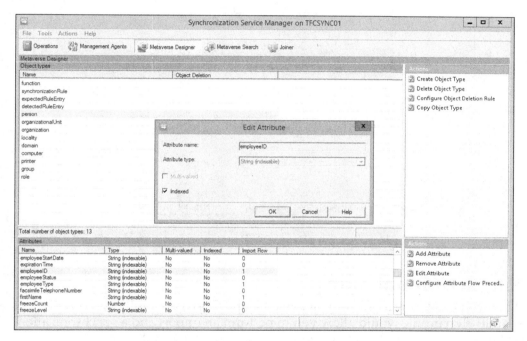

Creating run profiles

In order for Synchronization Engine to do anything useful, we need to create run profiles for each Management Agent, depending on our needs. A run profile is used to tell the MA to import, synchronize, or export the data that it has in its connector space.

This concept is fully explained in the **Help** section of Synchronization Service Manager. In the Management Agents tool, click on the **HR** Management Agent, and then click on **Configure Run Profiles**. Now click on **New Profile**. Then, enter **Full Import**, select **Full Import (Stage Only)**, click on **Next**, keep the default **Partition**, and finally click on **Finish**.

You will need to create a full synchronization run profile called **Full Sync**. For the AD Management Agent, create run profiles for **Export**, **Full Import**, **Delta Import**, and **Delta Sync**:

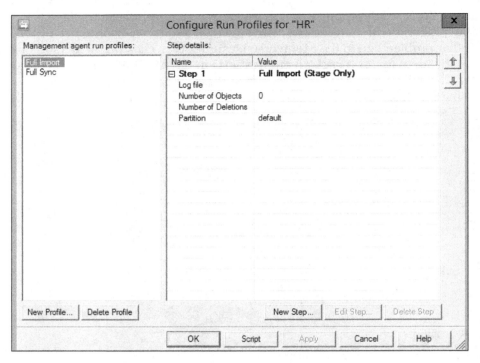

Single or multi step

When you create a run profile, you have the option to use a multi-step one. A multi-step profile would allow you to perform an import and a synchronization within a single step rather than having one import profile and a second synchronization profile. There are three reasons why you should not use multi-step profiles. First and most importantly, you will avoid a known problem where existing disconnector objects from a previous run are not processed. Secondly, the combined import and synchronization profile is scheduled to be deprecated in the future. Finally, you will have finer control when using a single-step profile.

When you configure a run profile with a single step of the type **Delta Import and Delta Synchronization**, a condition can occur in which existing disconnector objects from a previous run are not processed. This condition occurs because the existing objects in the connector space that have not changed since the last run are ignored. Our recommendation is not to use it.

Schema management

Very early on in our MIM deployment, we ran into discussions regarding the need for schema changes in MIM. The default schema is not sufficient, and needs to be modified in almost every case. I will only give a short overview about schema management in this chapter, and will try to explain more in the coming chapters.

MIM Sync versus MIM Service schema

One of the problems with the MIM Synchronization/MIM Service system is that it holds two schemas. We have one schema for the MIM Synchronization Service database and one for the MIM Service database.

Depending on our needs, we change one or both of these schemas. Whether the attributes or objects are required within MIM Service depends on whether or not they are managed using MIM Portal, or used in some policy. If not, we do not need them in the MIM Service schema.

On the other hand, if an attribute or object type is used in a policy within MIM Service, but is never supposed to be synchronized to other data sources, we do not need to change the MIM Synchronization Service schema.

Object deletion in MV

One type of schema configuration that we need to look at in our deployment is object deletion rules in the MIM Synchronization Service database.

Open up the **Synchronization Service Manager** window, and select the **Metaverse Designer** tool; this is where you will configure the MV schema or, if you like, the MIM Synchronization Service database schema.

If you want to select an object type, you can select **Configure Object Deletion Rule** in the **Actions** pane:

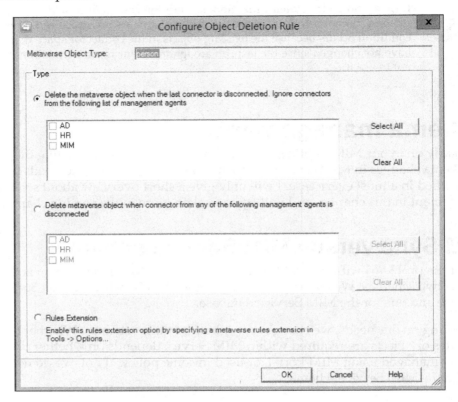

Here we can decide the grounds on which the object should be deleted from the Metaverse.

The settings available in this dialog can be a bit confusing. The top option, to delete the Metaverse object when the last connector is disconnected, means that the Metaverse object will be deleted when all unchecked Management Agents no longer have a connection to the Metaverse. The second option, delete the Metaverse object when connector from any Management Agent is disconnected, means that the Metaverse object will be deleted when any checked Management Agent loses its connection to the Metaverse. In other words, we AND the unchecked items to determine Metaverse object deletion in the first option. In the second option, on the other hand, we OR the checked items to determine Metaverse object deletion. The third option means that you can write code to determine the Metaverse object deletion logic. More information on these options can be found at `http://bit.ly/MIMDeprovisioningOptions`.

The default setting is that a Metaverse object will be deleted when the last connector is disconnected. It is important to understand that an object cannot exist in the MV if it does not have a connector to an object in at least one connector space.

In many projects, object deletion is not meant to happen at all. The idea is that once an object is created within MIM, it should live on and just change its status. That said, every business is different, and with MIM, you have the flexibility of the .NET framework to build a technology solution to meet those business requirements.

Initial load versus scheduled runs

When we first start to import information into Synchronization Engine, it is likely that information already exists in many or all of the connected systems. We might need to create special synchronization rules just for the initial load, which are not used again unless we need to rebuild the data.

At The Financial Company, the basic idea is that users should be imported from the HR system and created in AD. But when we start, there might be existing users in AD, and we would need to connect them using a join rather than provisioning (creating) them in AD. During the initial load, we would therefore turn off provisioning in MIM, import users from both systems, project them into the MV, and join the users existing in both the systems.

Initial load is usually done manually; that is, we manually start the required run profiles for each MA.

If the environment is large, the initial load might take many hours due to the fact that when we export our objects into the MIM Service database using the MIM Service MA, there might be many policies configured in the MIM Service that need to be applied for each object.

There are numerous ways of creating scheduled runs. I will show you a way that does not require any coding or third-party add-ons.

If you look at the run profile that you would like to schedule, there is a **Script** button to create a script. It will generate a VB script, which will start the run profile.

The task scheduler in Windows can then be used to create a schedule to run the script by using `cscript runprofilevbscriptname`. Just remember that the account (network service, for example) running the scheduled task needs to be a member of the `MIMSyncOperators` group in order for it to be allowed to run the MA run profiles.

So far, we have the following requirements in our environment:

1. Import from HR
2. Synchronize the changes
3. Export to AD
4. Verify export to AD

You will need to run a Full Import on the AD and MIM Management Agents to pull in the schema for those systems in order to provision user objects out to them. That is, click on the **AD** MA, click on **Run**, and select **Full Import**. Next, run a Full Import on the MIM MA. Now that you've brought in the schema to those systems, you can run the MAs in order of the data flow, which is as follows:

1. HR MA: Full Import
2. HR MA: Full Sync
3. AD MA: Export
4. AD MA: Delta Import
5. AD MA: Delta Sync

Maintenance mode for production

Initially, while the MIM system is still being developed, we do not need to concern ourselves with someone working in the production environment. But later on, we need to make sure that no one is working in the environment while we import new settings into the production servers.

One way of doing this is to put the servers into *maintenance* mode.

To place MIM Synchronization Service into maintenance mode, ensure that no Management Agents are running; that is, stop all schedules, and make sure that no MAs are running, then deny it access to port 5725. The steps to deny access to port 5725 are as follows:

1. Open Windows Firewall with Advanced Security. In order to do this, follow these two steps:
    1. Click on **Start**, and type Windows Firewall with Advanced Security.
    2. Once the search result appears on the **Start** menu, click on **Windows Firewall with Advanced Security**.
2. In the console tree, click on **Inbound Rules**.

3. In **Inbound Rules**, right-click on the **Forefront Identity Manager Service (Webservice)** rule, and then click on **Disable Rule**.

In order to place MIM Portal into maintenance mode, disable MIM Portal with the following steps:

1. Open Internet Information Services (IIS) Manager: click on **Start**, type `Internet Information Services (IIS) Manager`, and then click on it when the option appears in the **Start** menu.

2. Expand the objects in the console tree until you see **SharePoint – 80**.

3. Right-click on **SharePoint – 80**, click on **Manage Web Site**, and then on **Stop**.

 When you are done importing the new configuration, I recommend that you do some manual testing before putting the system into production again.

Disabling maintenance mode

No change is necessary to bring MIM Synchronization Service out of maintenance mode. If you have scheduled run profiles, you need to start the schedule again, and allow access to port 5725. The steps to allow access to port 5725 are as follows:

1. Open Windows Firewall with Advanced Security.

2. In the console tree, click on **Inbound Rules**.

3. On the **Inbound Rules** page, right-click on the **Forefront Identity Manager Service (Webservice)** rule, and then click on **Enable Rule**.

To return MIM Portal to normal operation, enable MIM Portal using the following steps:

1. Open Internet Information Services (IIS) Manager.

2. Navigate to **SharePoint – 80**.

3. Right-click on the site, click on **Manage Web Site**, and then click on **Start**.

Summary

In this chapter, The Financial Company configured their first Management Agents and prepared the MIM environment for further configuration. Note that one common source of error in a MIM environment is the lack of well-documented processes to make sure the development/test and production environments look the same. Learning and documenting how to move your configuration from development/test to production is vital as the configuration gets more complex. If you take your time to make sure your basic configuration setup is satisfactory, it will save you many hours of troubleshooting later on. If you feel confident that your basic configuration is correct, moving on and making more complex configuration settings will be easier.

In the next chapter, we will look at how to configure MIM Service.

4
MIM Service Configuration

In this chapter, we will look at different pieces of the MIM Service component. You will learn that many of the MIM Service components work hand-in-hand with one another. MIM Service provides a web service API along with a customizable web portal for user and policy management.

Here's what we will discuss in this chapter:

- MIM Service request processing
- The MIM Service Management Agent
- Understanding the portal and UI

MIM Service request processing

The AD and HR (SQL Server) MAs only give the synchronization engine the possibility of talking to these data sources. For MIM to apply codeless logic to the data flow, we need to use a special MA that connects the MIM Synchronization service to the MIM Service interface.

Before we talk about the MIM MA (referred to as the FIM MA by the product), its dependencies, and what is needed to get things flowing through the system, we need to understand some of the technology's mechanics. Before we dive a bit deeper into the request overview, we want to touch upon and remind you about the fact that in FIM/MIM, we have three main phases:

- Authentication
- Authorization
- Action

If you have worked with FIM in the past, you may have seen this graphic many times, but we feel this is an important visualization of the topic discussed:

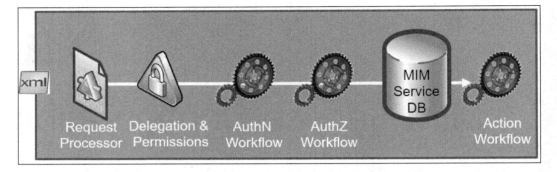

The MIM request pipeline starts with the request object creation, then the Management Policy Rule evaluation. The authentication workflow(s) are next, followed by the authorization workflow(s). Finally, any action workflow(s) are processed which is considered in most cases as the work completed. As a note, any request coming from the synchronization account will bypass all authentication and authorization workflows; only the action workflows would be applied:

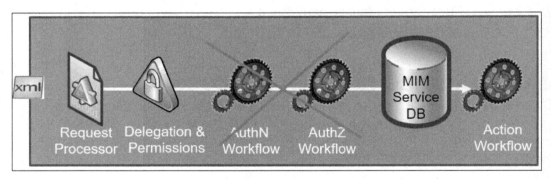

We will communicate with MIM Service using a **request**. A request is essentially a compilation of a set of commands to perform. The set of commands can create, read, update, and delete — or what we call, perform CRUD operations. When we talk about a CRUD operation within MIM Service, we refer to the creating, reading, updating, or deleting operations on data within the MIM Service database. A request can be submitted by a variety of endpoints and could go through a C# service or a web service request to update an object.

The following figure illustrates how different systems can work with MIM Service. On the right-hand side, we have shown that the MIM synchronization engine is making a request to *create* an employee from an HR system. On the far left-hand side, a user uses the Outlook add-in to submit a request to join a distribution group from an e-mail (an *update* operation). At the center of the figure, someone is shown using the MIM portal to *read* distribution list memberships. Lastly, we can have a custom script that makes a request to *delete* a security group because the group no longer has members:

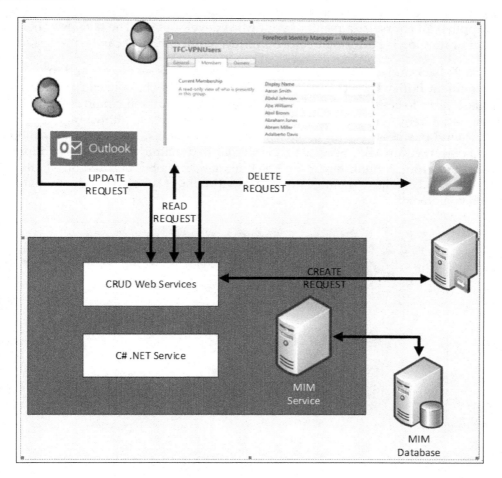

When MIM Service receives data from a client to perform a particular CRUD operation, it follows a sequence of events every time. During this request creation, we will send a request for what we want to do: create, update, read, or delete. When a request is sent, MIM Service will perform an evaluation to determine where the request could end up, thus impacting a set or determining what policy rules will be applied (we will talk about policy rules later in this chapter). Once the evaluation is done, we will send the request back to MIM Service with the actual request key and its policies, informing whether it is permitted and whether there are any authentication or authorization workflows that apply to the particular request. What gets applied, of course, is a result of your MIM development. The takeaway here is that an evaluation is performed before an MIM Service request can be processed.

Let's circle back and explain a few MIM concepts, such as set objects and the **Management Policy Rule (MPR)** object. MPR is an MIM object used to define permissions or to check or apply business logic for the authentication and authorization requirements. An MPR object is configurable to allow you to apply logic around business executions such as action workflows. The set object is another special object within MIM Service that is similar to dynamic distribution groups but without group limitations. A set is a combination of objects based on XPath definitions and can have members from any MIM object type — even the custom objects you create:

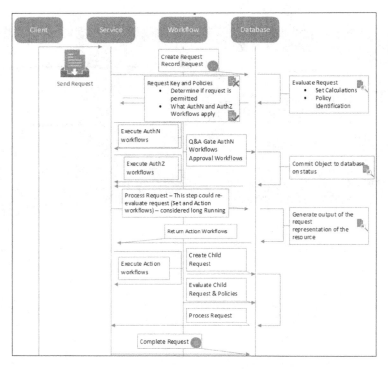

Earlier, we talked about the life cycle of a typical request or its child request. There are six final statuses, three in the precommit and three in postcommit:

- Precommit:
    - ° Denied
    - ° Canceled
    - ° Failed

- Postcommit:
    - ° Completed
    - ° CanceledPostProcessing
    - ° PostProcessing Error

When we look at the request operations, we see that there may be additional data exchanges that the client needs to be aware of. An example is when you view the MIM portal. Rendering the portal is not one simple client call to the service but many calls that make up a single page. The service has to confirm your access type, and then multiple calls are done around objects that you might be a part of. Viewing the MIM portal is a simple example of how the client controls the conversation via a service API between initiating and completion. Understanding the six states of the status allows you to know where in the process the request failed. From a troubleshooting standpoint, you will know whether the failure was a client-side issue, a server-side issue, or both.

It is also important to know that the read operation is not persisted in the MIM Service database, and there isn't an audit trail for this type of activity. The other operations, create, update, and delete, however, persist to the request object and provide an audit trail. Note that the request object stays in the MIM Service database until it is expired and deleted by the system process.

Request processing involves cache tables within FIM/MIM Service. That is, if you were to submit an update request, you would see a stored procedure performing the update. Let's walk through a single update request and take a look at the evaluation and creation of the request:

1. First, we can get the security context of the user by making a request in the SQL profiler trace, as follows:

```
declare @p2 uniqueidentifier
set @p2='7FB2B853-24F0-4498-9534-4E10589723C4'
exec [fim].GetUserFromSecurityIdentifier @SecurityID=0x010500000000000515000000023C72364D8A4558D75830F562040000
select @p2
```

2. Then, we will get the resource type for the request. In this case, it is `person`.

3. Next, we can see the following two built-in accounts:
   - This is the first built-in account:

```
declare @p1 xml
set @p1=convert(xml,N'<v>fb89aefa-5ea1-47f1-8890-abe7797d6497</v>')
exec [fim].GetObjectTypesFromIdentifiers @values=@p1
```

   - This is the second built-in account:

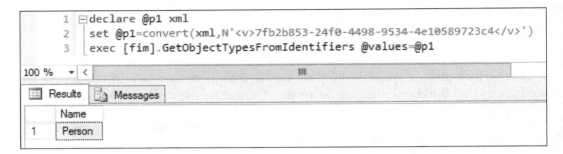

```
1  declare @p1 xml
2    set @p1=convert(xml,N'<v>7fb2b853-24f0-4498-9534-4e10589723c4</v>')
3    exec [fim].GetObjectTypesFromIdentifiers @values=@p1
```

100 % ▼ <   III

	Name
1	Person

4. Next, we will evaluate the request:

```
set @p8=convert(xml,N'<AncillaryParameters><RequestParameter xmlns:xsi="http://www.w3.org/2001/XMLSchema-instance"
xsi:type="CreateRequestParameter"><Calculated>true</Calculated><Target>00000000-0000-0000-0000-000000000000</Target
xsi:type="xsd:string">urn:uuid:fb142efd-1f06-4767-83be-ac407ea49ebb</Value><Operation>Create</Operation></RequestPa
declare @p15 uniqueidentifier
set @p15='A6D15BD4-EE02-4498-B3E1-E7BC23326AE8'
declare @p16 nvarchar(448)
set @p16=N'Update to Person:   ''Built-in Synchronization Account'' Request'
declare @p17 nvarchar(448)
set @p17=N'Person'
declare @p18 datetime
set @p18='2015-09-10 11:32:11.383'
exec [fim].EvaluateNewRequest
@serviceId=2,@servicePartitionId=2,@targetIdentifier='FB89AEFA-5EA1-47F1-8890-ABE7797D6497',@creator='7FB2B853-24F0
Request',@locale=default,@cause='7FB2B853-24F0-4498-9534-4E10589723C4',@requestMarker='AA3DD1F1-8B88-4FC0-9C85-EA18
select @p15, @p16, @p17, @p18
```

5. We can now see the postprocessing phase and update the request status:

```
declare @p4 uniqueidentifier
set @p4='FB89AEFA-5EA1-47F1-8890-ABE7797D6497'
declare @p5 tinyint
set @p5=NULL
declare @p6 smallint
set @p6=10
declare @p7 datetime
set @p7='2015-09-10 11:32:11.583'
exec [fim].ProcessRequest @requestIdentifier='A6D15BD4-EE02-4498-B3E1-E7BC23326AE8'
select @p4, @p5, @p6, @p7
```

6. Then, we will update the request:

```
exec [fim].UpdateRequest
@requestIdentifier='A6D15BD4-EE02-4498-B3E1-E7BC23326AE8',@targetIdentifier='FB89AEFA-5EA1-47F1-8890-ABE
```

7. Lastly, we can see the complete request status:

```
exec [fim].UpdateRequest
@requestIdentifier='A6D15BD4-EE02-4498-B3E1-E7BC23326AE8',@targetIdentifier='FB89AEFA-5EA1-47F1-8890-ABE7797D6497',@displayName
```

The preceding exercise was a simple update to an attribute, but you can imagine how backend processing can get complex quickly if you have multiple management policies and rules. If the system needed to apply an action or authorization, you would have seen such an event during phase 4 followed by multiple actions that we call collateral requests or workflows.

Once a request is in the completed state, MIM Service will query every 10 seconds to request to complete or mark it as completed with an expiration date. This is used for the clearing and purging of system objects.

Let's talk about how the system takes care of expired requests. The system handles the deletion of expired request objects by the SQL Server agent job FIM_ DeleteExpiredSystemObjects, which is scheduled to run once per day. The job can be run multiple times depending on your overall run history. The job of FIM_ DeleteExpiredSystemObjects is to find all the requests with the expiration time that is prior to the current time; gather up all the dependent system objects, such as workflow approvals and approval responses; and then delete these objects from the MIM objects value tables. The process involves multiple tables, scrubs only the data, and leaves object ID behind.

Keep in mind that the FIM_DeleteExpiredSystemObjects SQL agent job will only clean 20,000 expired objects per run. If you happen to have 40,000 expired request workflows and approvals/responses, then it is highly recommended to run this agent job twice or even three times a day.

We know how to clean up expired objects, but how are the expiration date timestamps calculated on the object? The object expiration date time is calculated by a customizable 30-day retention, which can be set up by going to the portal and clicking on **Administration**, then on **All Resources**, and finally on **System Resource Retention Configuration**:

Created Time	Resource Type	Retention Period in Days
11/13/2013 4:14:46 AM	System Resource Retention Configuration	30

There are some things to note about expiration retention. The retention period takes effect on any new requests you make. That is, changing the retention period will not change the retention period of past objects, only that of new ones. To look at the expiration system trends, you would need to look at what the retention period is set to and the objects that are about to expire, as shown in the following SQL script:

```
SELECT COUNT(*) AS NumberOfExpiredRequest,
CONVERT(DATE, ValueDateTime) AS ExpirationDate
FROM fim.ObjectValueDateTime WITH(NOLOCK)
WHERE AttributeKey = 82
AND ObjectTypeKey = 26
GROUP BY CONVERT(DATE, ValueDateTime)
ORDER BY ExpirationDate
```

	NumberOfExpiredRequest	ExpirationDate
1	5	2015-06-22
2	5	2015-06-23
3	5	2015-06-24
4	5	2015-06-25
5	5	2015-06-26
6	5	2015-06-27

In the results of the preceding script, we will see the number of expired requests and the expiration of this request. We now have to look at the expiration retention. Subtract the expiration date (that you see under **ExpirationDate** in the preceding screenshot) from the current date to give you an idea about which day you have a high number of requests per day. Again, this will only go as far back as your agent job is running, or not running in some cases, so if you have a set of 30 days, you should only see 30 days' worth of requests in the expiration date and time.

The management policy

So, how do we apply policies in MIM? Simple, we have a defined object called Management Policy Rule that defines a set of object definitions, conditions, or events that can occur in MIM Service. It is the MPR object that defines the permission and possible mapped workflows. There are two types of MPR:

- **Request-based MPR**: This is based on the CRUD operation discussed earlier (create, read, update, and delete)

- **Set transition MPR**: This performs operations based on the evaluation of the object and its transition into a set or out of a set

Additional reading on the request processing model can be found at `http://bit.ly/MIMrequestProcessing`.

Service partitions

When we talk about service partitions, there can be questions about its impact on the system, such as what the recovery plan for service partitions is, what would happen if one's service dies, and how the recovery would happen. Before we talk about high availability, which will come up in a later section, we need to understand the design fundamentals of MIM Service and how service partitions work. Service partitions were introduced as a way of looking at a particular request coming from a particular endpoint and then tying this request to this service. In our example, we have two MIM Service servers, but during the installation, we gave a single MIM service address `MIMService.thefinancialcompany.net`. Using one service address, we fundamentally changed the way the two servers will behave. Essentially, we put the two servers into a single service partition.

If we had done the default configuration for the two servers, we would have two service partitions called TFCMIM01 and TFCMIM02. By providing an alias for the service partition, we created a central location for both the servers to process requests and workflows:

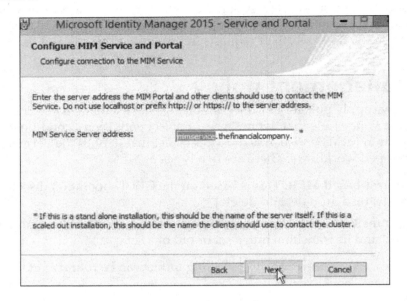

When we look at when a request is made, there is asynchronous processing that ties the request and associated workflows to the service partition ID to be used. For example, a single service partition might have the service partition ID of 2. Partitioning the service would allow you to isolate the work streams so that you can have something similar to a user portal and an admin portal.

The first time MIM Service starts, it registers the server name in the database along with the service partition name that is assigned a global unique ID for each partition. In our example shown as follows, we have one service partition with multiple servers. If there is no server name defined in the MIM Service configuration, then it will use the default server name. That is, if you install MIM Service on two servers without making a configuration change, you would have two service partition names.

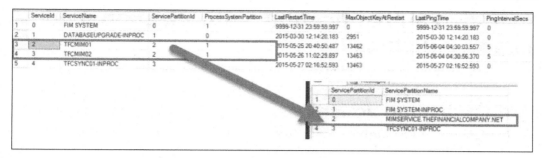

In the preceding screenshot, we can see the configuration database. We have two MIM server services, and they are tied to the service partition ID **2** in the service partition. Note that the **ProcessSystemPartition** column is set to **1** for both, which means all nodes will process any system-related event.

The service configuration settings are customizable and contained in the `Microsoft.ResourceManagement.Service.exe.config` file, as shown here:

```
<resourceManagementClient resourceManagementServiceBaseAddress="mimservice.thefinancialcompany.net" />
<resourceManagementService externalHostName="mimservice.thefinancialcompany.net" />
```

A few other common configuration items are in the following table. You can look at the service configuration file for more configurable settings:

Parameter	Description	Range	Default
postStartupRecoveryRetry IntervalInMilliseconds	Sets the time interval for the process stuck workflow and request objects after a FIM service restart	-1 to max(int)	-1 disables
dataReadTimeoutInSeconds	Database timeout for read operations	0 to max(int16)	58
dataWriteTimeoutInSeconds	Database timeout for write operations	0 to max(int16)	58

Included authentication, authorization, and action activities

We will go over the configuration of the activities as we use them in our scenario.

Authentication activities

All the activities under authentication are explained as follows:

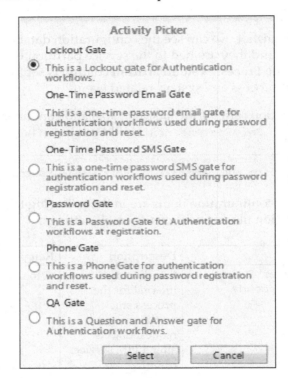

- **Lockout Gate**: The lockout gate is a critical activity to make sure you lock out invalid attempts against a workflow. The lockout gate is typically used with the self-service password reset.

- **One-Time Password Email Gate**: As with the SMS gate, this activity sends a code to a user's registered e-mail address. The gate is configurable to allow a user to register an e-mail or to use an e-mail that comes from a system.

- **One-Time Password SMS Gate**: SMS gate is an API starting point to integrate your SMS service provider to send a code to a user's registered mobile device.

- **Phone Gate**: This is a new gate that was developed to integrate with the phone factor authentication, now known as Azure MFA.

- **QA Gate**: This gate is typically used for the self-service password reset. In this activity, you will define questions, and the user will register answers that will later be used to prove their identity.

Authorization activities

Authorization activities are used to authorize specific requests, such as adding a user to a group or sending an e-mail:

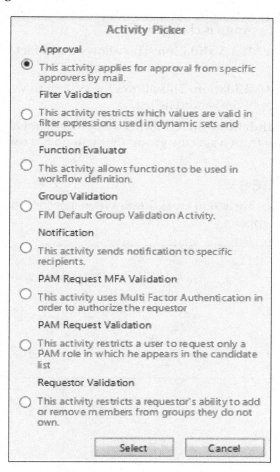

- **Approval**: This allows you to control who is authorizing the request, such as a manager, application owner, or group owner.

- **Filter Validation**: Filter validation is a function that confirms whether a set or group is valid XPath.

- **Function Evaluator**: Function evaluator allows you to format the data pipeline to attributes and objects. Take a look at `http://bit.ly/MIMFunctions` for more information.

- **Group Validation**: This is used to restrict nested group restrictions that are found in AD and cross-forest scenarios.

- **Notification**: A notification is used to send a customizable template e-mail to targets, say, if a group is changed.

- **PAM Request MFA Validation**: This allows multi-factor authorization using Azure MFA.

- **PAM Request Validation**: This allows the system to verify that you are a valid requestor in the candidate list.

- **Requestor Validation**: This confirms that you are not able to add or remove members to or from a specific group that you do not own.

Action activities

The last set of activities are action workflows. When selecting this type of workflow, we can see an option appear:

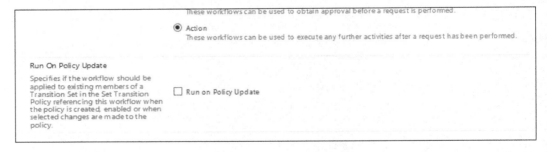

You will then see all the action activities available, as shown in the following screenshot:

- **Active Directory - Add User to Group**: This adds a user to an AD group.
- **Active Directory Password Reset Activity**: This performs a user password reset by doing a WMI call to the synchronization engine.
- **Function Evaluator**: This allows formatting the data pipeline to attributes and objects.
- **Notification**: This is an e-mail generation activity.
- **Synchronization Rule Activity**: This applies a specific sync rule to a user, otherwise known as **Expected Rule Entry** (**ERE**).

Let's focus our attention on the action workflow and **Run on Policy Update**. Failure to understand this single setting has created numerous organizational problems, effectively breaking request processing in the system by generating millions of unnecessary requests.

When you select the **Run on Policy Update** setting, any time you make any change to the management policy rule that this workflow is tied to, the system will reevaluate all targeted objects and run the policy or action against it to verify it is true.

Let's say your manager wants to update the company attribute for all users. To make the change, create a new workflow that fires off an activity to update the company's attribute. Set the workflow to **Run on Policy Update**. Next, create a disabled management policy rule that targets the **All Active People** set. When you enable the MPR object, the policy is considered updated, so the workflow executes against all the users in this set. Future changes to the MPR object will fire off the workflow to everyone again, so you should unselect **Run on Policy Update** when your one-time change is completed. Future accounts that fall into your set criteria will have the company set, but existing accounts will not be (and should not need to be) re-evaluated.

The MIM Service Management Agent

We will make some schema changes as we expand MIM to suit the needs of The Financial Company. There is one attribute that we change in most implementations: the EmployeeType attribute.

Before you start changing the service schema, you should have a look at http://bit.ly/MIMServiceSchema.

 In MIM Service, as in many other products, modifying the schema in the wrong way might stop it from working and require you to do a total rebuild of your environment.

The EmployeeType attribute is commonly used to store information that governs many policies. There is usually a big difference between being a contractor and an employee, for example. And every company has its own values. If you take a look at the earlier part of this chapter, you will see that in the HR database at The Financial Company, there are two different values in HRType for person objects. The values are Employee and Contractor.

If we look at a user in the MIM portal and the values we can assign to the EmployeeType attribute (it is in the **Work Info** tab), we will see that you have three values to choose from: **Contractor**, **Intern**, and **Full Time Employee**. As you can see, this does not match what The Financial Company uses.

This is due to a validation setting on this attribute in the default MIM Service schema. In order to change this, we will look in the MIM portal and go to **Administration | Schema Management**:

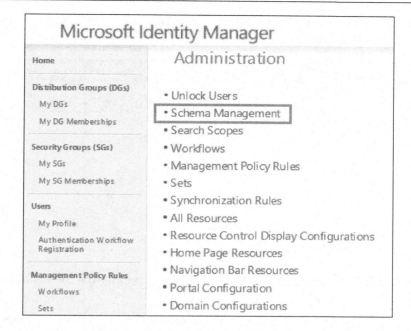

There are three things to manage here: **Resource Types** (often referred to as object types), **Attributes**, and **Bindings**. If you click on **All Attributes** and search for `EmployeeType`, you will find the attribute we are interested in:

In the **Validation** tab, we will find the regular expression controlling the values we can store in this attribute:

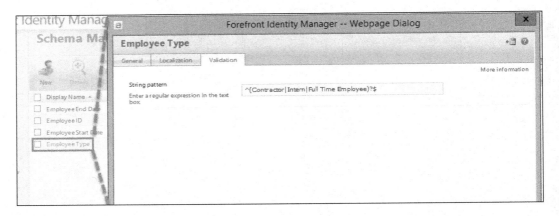

If we change this to `^(Contractor|Employee)?$`, it will match the needs of The Financial Company:

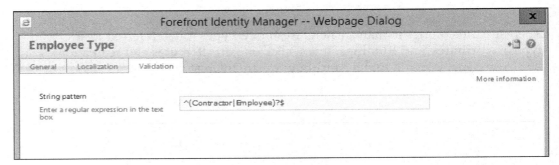

Information about the syntax used for the regular expressions in MIM can be found at `http://aka.ms/FIMServiceSchema`.

This, however, is not enough because we can have one validation on the attribute, but when binding an attribute to a resource type, we can also define this; and for the `EmployeeType` binding to a user resource, this is the case.

In **Schema Management**, click on **All Bindings** and search for EmployeeType. You will find the binding of the **Employee Type** attribute (**1**) to the **User** resource type (**2**):

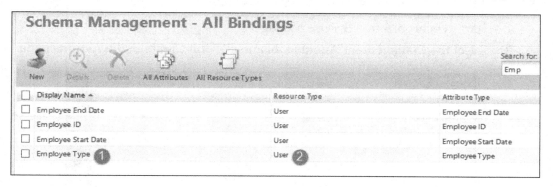

Once again, change the validation setting to ^(Contractor|Employee)?$; this should actually be enough as the binding settings will override the base settings we have on the attribute type itself.

The MIM Service MA

The AD and HR (SQL Server) MA only give the synchronization engine the possibility of talking to these data sources. However, in order for the system to apply its logic to the data flow, we need to have a very special MA connecting the synchronization service to the service used by the portal. In the product, you will see these named FIM Synchronization Service and FIM Service; however, we will refer to them as MIM Synchronization Service and MIM Service to make it consistent with the product branding.

Creating the FIM Service MA

We will now walk you through the steps of creating the FIM/MIM Service MA:

1. Start Synchronization Service Manager.

2. Select the **Management Agents** tool and click on **Create** in the **Actions** pane:

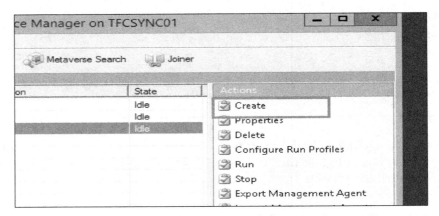

3. Select the **FIM Service Management Agent** option in the **Management agent for:** drop-down list.

4. Give the MA a descriptive name; we will call it **MIM**:

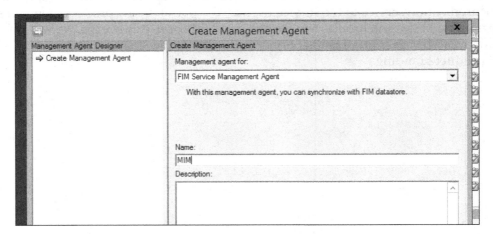

5. Back in *Chapter 1*, *Overview of Microsoft Identity Manager 2016*, we configured SQL aliases, and we will use one of them here. We will enter the server name alias dbMIMService in the **Server** field:

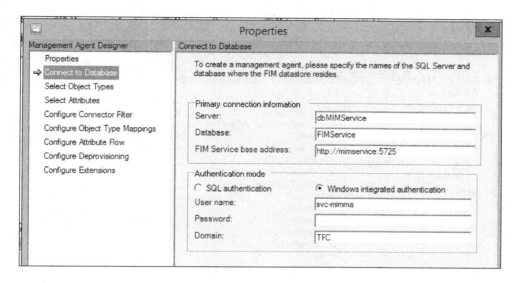

The MIM Service MA will not only connect to the MIM Service database, but also make calls to the MIM web service interface. The default port for this service is 5725, so we will connect to http://mimservice:5725 as the MIM Service base address on the server.

6. Select the object types you know MIM needs to manage:

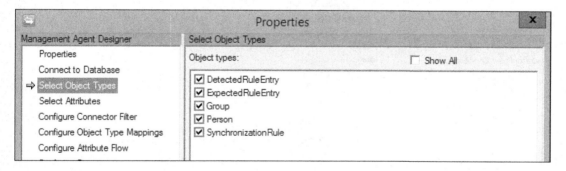

Do not unselect the default object types because they are required for MIM to perform declarative synchronization. If, later on, we add new resource types (objects) to the MIM Service schema, we will need to go back and add them to this configuration.

7. By default, all the predefined attributes are selected. If we add new attributes to the MIM Service schema, we will need to get back here and select them. Giving the MIM Synchronization service access to new objects and attributes in MIM Service is not that straightforward, but we will show you how to do it:

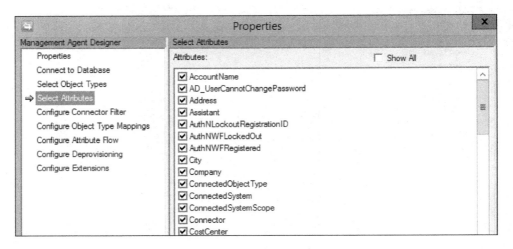

8. We will leave the connector filter as it is for the moment but will return here later to filter some accounts:

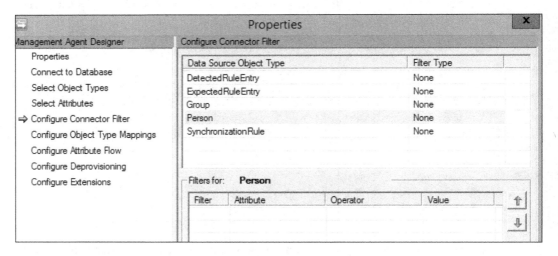

9. We need to tell the MA how to map the object types in the FIM Service schema to the object types in the MV schema. If you have not made any customizations to your schema, it should be *Group: group* and *Person: person*:

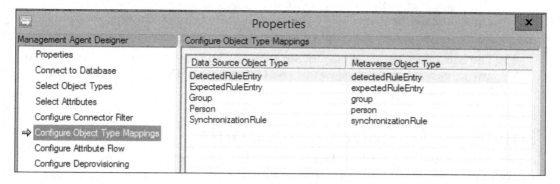

10. We will leave the attribute flow with the default values for the moment, although this is a setting you will frequently come back to and change when you're first setting things up. Note that the **Advanced Mapping Type** option is not available in the FIM Service MA; we can only have direct mappings:

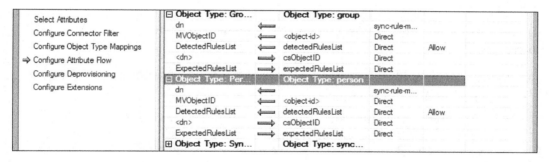

11. We have discussed before the concept of deprovisioning. Go to `http://aka.ms/FIMDeprovisioning` and read it before you start using this option. I suggest you use the default setting to begin with. If you also have the default for **Object Deletion** in the MV schema, the result will be that once an object has made it into the MV/FIM Service database, it will not be deleted. This is because it will always have a connector between the MV and FIM service connector spaces.

12. By now, you might be wondering where the join and projection steps you had seen in the other MAs went. The FIM/MIM Service MA is a little special because it has automatic join and projection rules. As soon as an object appears in the MIM Service or MIM Synchronization service, it will automatically be projected to the other if there is an object type mapping defined. It will also automatically join objects using object ID.

13. The MIM Service MA does not support any rule extensions; we cannot have any advanced attribute flows or use **Determine with a rules extension** in **Deprovisioning Options**.

The MIM MA filtering accounts

In MIM Service, we might have objects that we do not want the Synchronization service to manage. During the first import described in the previous section, you found two users that were created during setup. We never want to have these users in Metaverse.

What we need to do is filter out the installation (administrator) and built-in synchronization user accounts. We can do this by filtering out the GUIDs of these objects.

If you are following this guide, you will have a newly made first import. Follow these steps:

1. Select the MIM Service MA and look at the **Synchronization Statistics** frame.

2. Click on **Adds** in the frame.

3. Click on the first entry and select the GUID after **Distinguished Name**, right-click, and click on **Copy**. The first entry should be the installer account with the GUID 7fb2b853-24f0-4498-9534-4e10589723c4.

4. Click on the **Close** button twice.

5. Open **Properties** for MIM Service Management Agent.

6. Select the **Configure Connector Filter** step and then select **Person** in the **Data Source Object Type** list.

7. Next, click on **New...**.

8. Paste the GUID into the **Value** field and click on **Add Condition**. This will filter the object, where <dn> equals <guid>.

9. Click on **OK** twice to save the Management Agent configuration.

10. Click on **Adds** in the **Synchronization Statistics** frame and repeat the aforementioned steps to filter out the built-in synchronization account (fb89aefa-5ea1-47f1-8890-abe7797d6497) as well.

11. When done, your connector filter should look similar to the following screenshot:

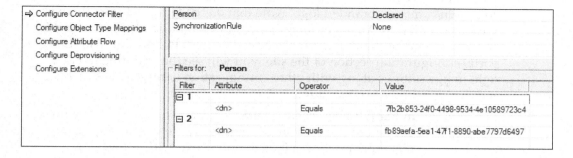

Understanding the portal and UI

Let's look at the basic structure of the portal:

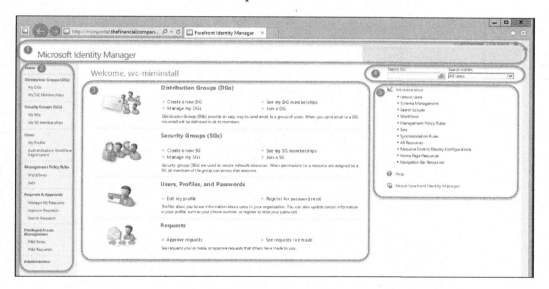

The layout of the MIM portal is broken up into five major sections, as follows:

- **The banner and logo (1)**: This section is typically where you would put your own company branded logo. Note that on the left-hand side, there is a Microsoft Identity Manager image, and on the right-hand side panel, it is grayed out, indicating that it too can be configured. In the administration portal configuration section of the site, you will see the branding left and right image settings along with other configuration items, such as caching and the global time zone setting.

- **The navigation bar (2)**: This section is the vertical menu on the left-hand side and is controlled by navigation bar resources. We will configure the navigation bar later on and take a look at how we can affect this view:

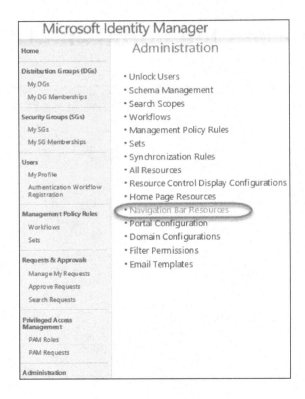

If we look at this area, we will see that **Distribution Groups (DGs)** is a parent item and **My DG Memberships** and **My DGs** are both child items, as in the following screenshot:

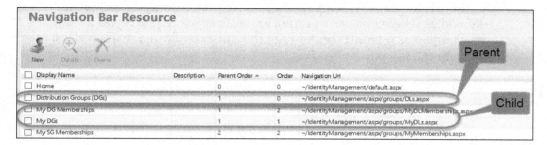

- **The homepage center region (3)**: This area of the site includes text and links that lead the user or the administrator to explore different areas of the portal. To customize the home page area, we will go to **Administration** and then **Home Page Resources**:

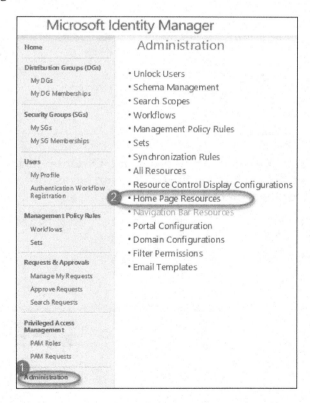

12. **Search scopes (4)**: This is how we can interact with the service to search for defined objects or scoped objects within the system. Items can be customized (added or removed) by looking at **Search Scopes** within **Administration**.

Within **Home Page Resources**, click on **Requests**, and you will see that it is defined as where you can approve requests or see requests you have made. It is defined as region **1** (center region) with parent order **4** and order **0** indicating it is a parent heading:

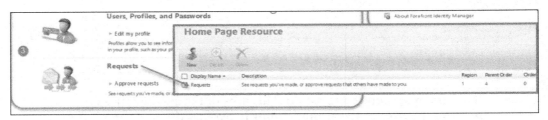

Similar to the previous screenshot, here is an example of the items within **Home Page Resources** for requests:

Display Name ▲	Description	Region	Parent Order	Order	Navigation Url
☐ Approve requests		1	4	1	~/IdentityManag
☐ Requests	See requests you've made, or approve requests that others have made to you.	1	4	0	~/IdentityManag
☐ See requests I've made		1	4	2	~/IdentityManag

We can change **Region, Parent Order**, and **Order** by clicking on **Home Page Resource** and by clicking on the **UI Position** tab as shown in the following screenshot for the **Unlock Users** resource:

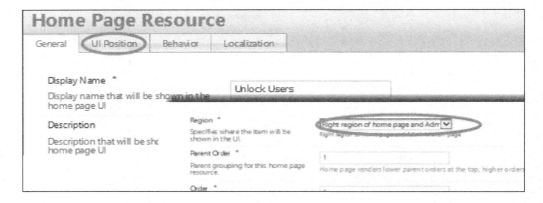

13. **Homepage Right (5)**: This consists of two sections similar to the center region, as follows:

- ° The **Administration** region
- ° The **Help** region

We can change the region, similarly to **Parent Order** and **Order**, by clicking on **Home Page Resource** and clicking on **UI Position**:

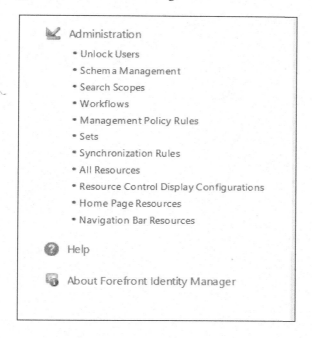

Portal configuration

No matter how many portal servers you have running, the MIM Service will use the global settings of the environment. The global portal configuration provides the capability to change the branding text and the left- and right-hand side images among other things. The default location for all the images is `C:\Program Files\Common Files\microsoft shared\Web Server Extensions\14\TEMPLATE\IMAGES\MSILM2`:

Portal Configuration

| Common Attributes | Extended Attributes |

Branding Center Text
The centered branding text that used by branding control

Branding Left Image *
The left url image that is used by branding control
`~/_layouts/images/MSI`

Branding Right Image *
The right url image that used by branding control
`~/_layouts/images/MSI`

Global Cache Duration *
This time how long the UI configuration element will be kept on the cache
`86400`

Is Configuration Type
This is an indication that this resource is a configuration resource.
☐

ListView Cache Time Out *
Specify the amount of time for the ListView cache to time out and expire.
`120`

ListView Items per Page *
Specify the number of items to show per page in all ListViews.
`30`

ListView Pages to Cache *
Specify the number of pages to cache while retrieving ListView results.
`3`

Navigation Bar Resource Count Cache Duration *
This time how long the UI dynamic counts will stay on the cache before it expired
`600`

Per User Cache Duration *
This time for how long the UI user data will stay on the cache before it expired
`14400`

Time Zone
Reference to timezone configuration
`(GMT-08:00) Pacific Time (US & Canada)`

After the branding text and images, the next setting is the duration of the global cache. **Global Cache Duration** is how long before a user would see a change take effect. This setting is for any changes that have been made, whether you're adding search scopes on any new navigation bar items, home page information, resource control, or others. Restarting IIS overrides this setting or, rather, makes the changes show immediately.

Navigation Bar Resource Count Cache Duration specifies how long the UI dynamic counts will stay on the cache before expiring. Specified in seconds, the default is 10 minutes and is adjustable.

Per User Cache Duration is a combination of settings for the user. The settings include all the UI elements and user's time zone information as it relates to their session information. The cache will be refreshed after the duration expires. Set in seconds, the default is set to four hours.

We have list view settings, too. We have **ListView Items Per Page** and **ListView Pages to Cache**. **ListView Items Per Page** lets you configure how many items or entries are shown in the actual view. By default, the entries are 30. The larger the number, the longer each page will take to load, because every page takes a query to the MIM Service. The larger your cache size, the larger the number of items per page you could have. **ListView Pages to Cache** has a default of three pages (the targeted page and the pages immediately preceding it). Once the three pages are loaded, we would have to go back out to the service to refresh the view.

There are two time zone settings within the portal. One time zone setting is set in the global settings, and another is on each user's profile. The global time zone setting is used if a user does not have a time zone set in their profile.

The navigation bar resource

When creating a custom navigation bar resource, you can specify a display name, which can take up to 448 characters and is mandatory. You can also specify a description that can take up to 400 character values and is optional. Navigation bar resources have **usage keywords**. Usage keywords are special multivalued attributes that customize the view of certain navigation items and are based on the user with permissions set around the user. Every object in the portal allows for localization, too. The **Localization** tab provides all the supported languages that are installed by the language pack. By selecting one of the languages, you can specify how the navigation bar, or even an object, will be displayed or translated.

Search scopes

Not all search scopes can be seen from the drop-down menu. Some of the primary search scopes are listed here:

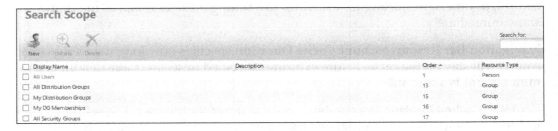

Click on the **All Users** search scope and you will notice several usage keywords. These keywords allow the MIM interface to control what is visible to some or all users. You have the opportunity to even create your own usage keywords for your customizations. A great example can be found at `http://bit.ly/ MIMUsagekeywords`:

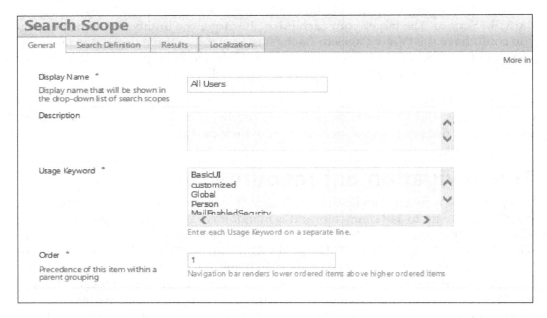

Filter permissions

Filter permissions are different among management policy rules. The permissions allow for the system to query against attributes from an administrative standpoint or even as a non-administrator. This means that we can use filter permissions to enable the attribute to be used for the criteria. If you want one or more attributes to be used for criteria for administrators, then you should click on **Administrator Filter Permission** and add the attribute:

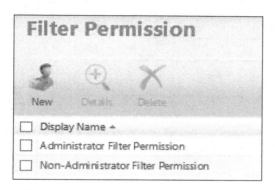

Resource Control Display Configurations

We will explain **Resource Control Display Configurations (RCDCs)** by example. In MIM, we have ways to create new user groups. In the group creation options, you can specify whether the group is a security or distribution group. If The Financial Company wants to adjust the look of creating group resources, user resources, or other resources for that matter, it is done by updating the RCDC. Let's take a look at the following image, which we have broken into several areas. The first area that we want to look at is area **1**, which is called a panel. Every RCDC has a panel and encompasses multiple grouping categories. Area **2** is known as the header grouping. The header grouping has only one control, which controls what is displayed based on the caption and description attribute. The next grouping, area **3**, is displayed in tabs.

Most have one or two tabs, but you can add more based on your business requirements. Just so you know, you can have up to 16 groups to include the header and summary, meaning you can have 14 (**3**) with 1 to 256 controls (**4**). The controls are denoted by a name and can be of four types: UocButton, UocCheckbox, UocDateTimeControl, or UocFileDownload:

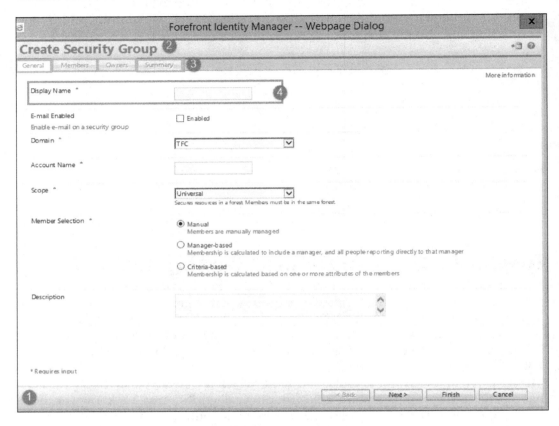

Now that we've gone over the areas, let's talk about modifying RCDCs. Go to the portal, click on **Administration**, and then click on **Resource Control Display Configurations**:

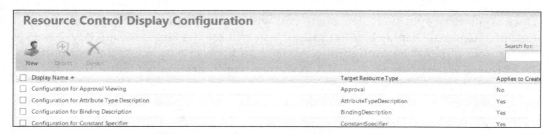

You should see a list of display controls, as shown in the following screenshot:

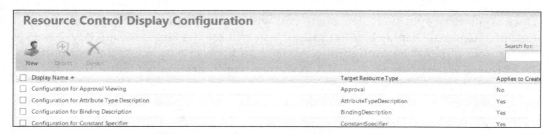

Note that we have several columns. The first column is the display name of your control. In this example, you see **Configuration for Approval Viewing**. The second column specifies the resource targeted for the particular configuration. The next three columns determine when this particular configuration should be applied. The takeaway here is that if you want a different view to edit a resource, then you should modify the edit configuration item and make sure that it applies to editing.

Before editing an RCDC, the very first thing we want to do is make sure that we have a backup. The authors recommend saving the RCDC to a TFS or a secure location, just in case you have to roll back the configuration:

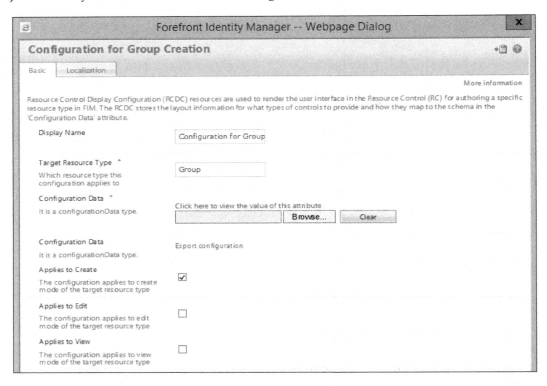

Once you have a specific RCDC open, you will see the display name of our Resource Control Display Configuration. You will see the target resource type and configuration data. The configuration data has a **Browse** button and a **Clear** button. The **Browse** button is how you load in the new configuration file that is modified. Let's first click on the **Export configuration** link and save it to our backup location:

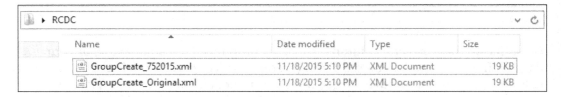

Now that we have an original RCDC, we can copy the file to a new name. Any name works, although putting the date in the name can help with your change management. Next, open the copy in our favorite XML editor, such as Visual Studio or Notepad++. We will use Notepad ++ for this simple configuration change. Later in the chapter, when we go over BHOLD, you will see that we will make some changes to our RCDC to support the configuration for group role-based management:

```xml
<?xml version="1.0" encoding="UTF-8" ?>
<my:ObjectControlConfiguration my:TypeName="UocGroupCodeBehind"
xmlns:xsi="http://www.w3.org/2001/XMLSchema-instance"
xmlns:my="http://schemas.microsoft.com/2006/11/ResourceManagement"
xmlns:xd="http://schemas.microsoft.com/office/infopath/2003">
  <my:ObjectDataSource my:TypeName="PrimaryResourceObjectDataSource" my:Name="object" my:Parameters=""/>
  <my:ObjectDataSource my:TypeName="PrimaryResourceDeltaDataSource" my:Name="delta"/>
  <my:ObjectDataSource my:TypeName="SchemaDataSource" my:Name="schema"/>
  <my:ObjectDataSource my:TypeName="DomainDataSource" my:Name="domain" my:Parameters="%LoginDomain%"/>
  <my:ObjectDataSource my:TypeName="PrimaryResourceRightsDataSource" my:Name="rights"/>
  <my:XmlDataSource my:Name="summaryTransformXsl" my:Parameters="Microsoft.IdentityManagement.WebUI.Controls.Resources.DefaultSummary.xsl"/>
  <my:Panel my:Name="page" my:AutoValidate="true" my:Caption="Caption">
    <my:Grouping my:Name="Caption" my:IsHeader="true" my:Caption="caption" my:Visible="true">
    <my:Grouping my:Name="GroupingBasicInfo" my:Caption="%SYMBOL BasicInfoCaption END%">
    <my:Grouping my:Name="GroupingMembers" my:Caption="%SYMBOL MembersTabCaption END%">
    <my:Grouping my:Name="GroupingCalculatedMembers" my:Caption="%SYMBOL GroupingCalculatedMembersTabCaptionTabCaption END%">
    <my:Grouping my:Name="GroupingOwners" my:Caption="%SYMBOL OwnersTabCaption END%">
    <my:Grouping my:Name="GroupingSummary" my:Caption="%SYMBOL SummaryTabCaption END%" my:IsSummary="true">
      <my:Control my:Name="SummaryControl" my:TypeName="UocHtmlSummary" my:ExpandArea="true">
        <my:Properties>
          <my:Property my:Name="ModificationsXml" my:Value="{Binding Source=delta, Path=DeltaXml}"/>
          <my:Property my:Name="TransformXsl" my:Value="{Binding Source=summaryTransformXsl, Path=/}"/>
        </my:Properties>
      </my:Control>
    </my:Grouping>
  </my:Panel>
  <my:Events>
    <my:Event my:Name="Load" my:Handler="OnLoad"/>
  </my:Events>
</my:ObjectControlConfiguration>
```

Look at the configuration and note that some of the terminology we discussed now makes sense, such as a panel and grouping. The caption name gives you information about the configuration file that you're updating. We see several other groups, such as `GroupingBasicInfo`. When we look at `GroupingBasicInfo`, we see the caption `%Symbol`, which denotes that we are going to look at the section of the localization file that controls the title of this tab. As we navigate down in our grouping, we can see our first control:

```xml
<my:Control my:Name="Name" my:TypeName="UocTextBox" my:Caption="{Binding Source=schema, Path=DisplayName.DisplayName}" my:RightsLevel="{Binding Source=rights, Path=DisplayName}"
my:Description="{Binding Source=schema, Path=DisplayName.Description}">
  <my:Properties>
    <my:Property my:Name="Required" my:Value="true"/>
    <my:Property my:Name="MaxLength" my:Value="128"/>
    <my:Property my:Name="Text" my:Value="{Binding Source=object, Path=DisplayName, Mode=TwoWay}"/>
  </my:Properties>
</my:Control>
```

This control is the first item called `Name` (refer to the value for `my:Name`) and is bound to the display name of the target resource (`Path=DisplayName.DisplayName`). The description (`my:Description`) will be identified by pulling the information off `Displayname.Description` from the schema of the group object:

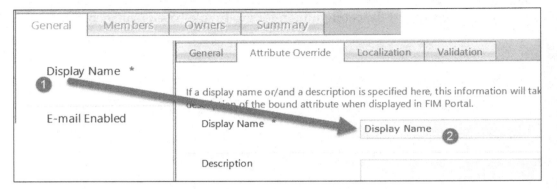

The Financial Company wants to add a field for users and administrators to denote whether a security group should be controlled by the BHOLD role-based access management system that will come online during the implementation. To set the stage for the requirement, we need to create a Boolean attribute and allow administrators to update this field. For now, we will focus on administrators. First, go to **Administration | Schema Management | All Attributes** and add the attribute, as follows:

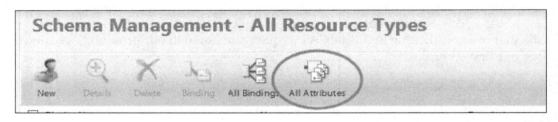

Then, we will click on **New** and create an attribute named BManaged:

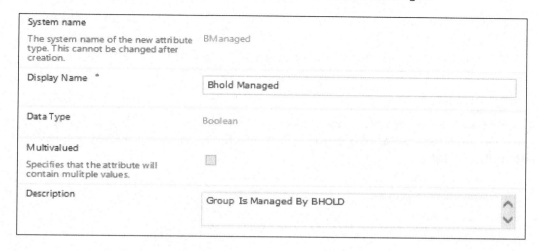

We will now link the attribute to the group object by clicking on **All Bindings** and then on **New** and adding the new attribute binding to the group:

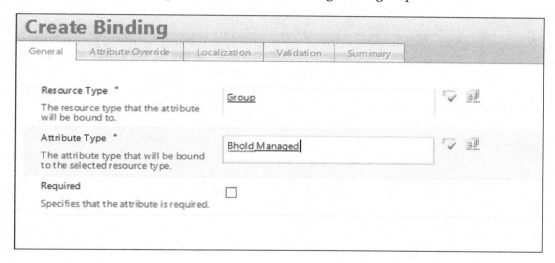

We now need to add the attribute to several MPRs and filter permissions (administrative and non-administrative), as described earlier.

We will add the attribute to the following MPR objects:

- Group management: Group administrators can create and delete group resources

- Group management: Group administrators can read attributes of group resources

- Group management: Group administrators can update group resources

Click on **Management Policy Rules**, find the first MPR object in the preceding list, and click on it. In the **Target Resources** tab, add the attribute to the **Select specific attributes** section:

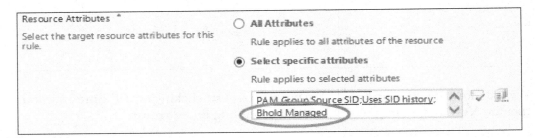

We now need to add this new attribute as something to be seen during the creation of the group that requires updating the RCDC. We have the RCDC open, so now, we need to figure out where we want to add the checkbox for this control. The general page is a great spot for now. Sure, we could add a grouping called BHOLD, but let's keep this simple. When we look at the RCDC, we will know that we want to add a checkbox; therefore, this control type should be `UocCheckBox`. In looking at this control, we need to map the attribute and the control properties, as follows:

```
<my:Control my:Name="BManaged" my:TypeName="UocCheckBox"
my:Caption="{Binding Source=schema, Path=BManaged.DisplayName}"
my:Description="{Binding Source=schema, Path=BManaged.DisplayName}"
my:AutoPostback="true" my:RightsLevel="{Binding Source=rights,
Path=BManaged}">
<my:Properties>
<my:Property my:Name="Text" my:Value="{Binding Source=object,
Path=BManaged, Mode=OneWay}"/>
<my:Property my:Name="Checked" my:Value="{Binding Source=object,
Path=BManaged, Mode=TwoWay}"/>
</my:Properties>
</my:Control>
```

Now that we have edited the XML code, we need to save and upload it. Navigate back to the RCDC and click on **Group Create**. Click on the **Browse** button and select our new configuration file. Click on **OK** to complete the action and then on **Submit**. Once this is committed, you will need to run `IISReset` on the site for the change to take effect immediately. Cache refresh is discussed previously in this chapter if you would like to wait.

Now, we can test. Let's go to **Security Groups (SGs)** | **New**. You should see the new attribute right at the front of the **General** tab, as shown here:

If you were to modify a new or existing group, you would notice that the attribute is not shown. This is because we only modified the RCDC associated with creation, whereas modifying a group uses an RCDC associated with editing. Refer to the following links for additional information on customizing and RCDCs:

- Introduction to configuring and customizing the portal (`http://bit.ly/MIMCustomizeportal`)
- Resource Control Display Configuration XML reference (`http://bit.ly/MIMRCDCXMLRef`)

Custom activities development

Custom activity development is dependent on whether the Microsoft Identity Management workflows meet your business requirements. In most cases, it's not sufficient, so the users have the opportunity to either develop their own activities or use multiple open source libraries. Now, the support stance on custom activities is clear; you develop it, you support it. Again, this is a grey area for Microsoft support, so it would be considered commercially reasonable support if something was found in the reference library that you used to develop the activity.

The Financial Company has a requirement that you have to enter the ZIP code of the user object. This is due to the mobile workforce that is remote across the country. One of the unique requirements is that they want the portal and service to look at this ZIP code and then update the city on the user object. There is no out-of-the-box functionality, so we can use a power show workflow that is open source or develop our own activity.

Let's begin what we need in order to develop our custom activity. First, we need Visual Studio again; any version above 2008 will suffice. But note that if you're using Visual Studio 2012 or 2013, you need to make sure you set the runtime to.NET 3.5 as this is the version of the reference library.

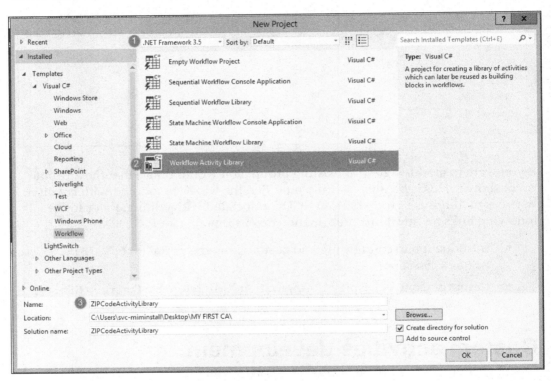

Open Visual Studio and then select **New**. Select **.NET Framework 3.5** and then the **Workflow Activity Library** which is under **Templates | Visual C# | Workflow**. The last item we need to enter is the name of our activity and solution; to set this to a folder on the desktop called MY FIRST CA is only fitting.

The next thing we need to do once we have the project open is add the `Microsoft.ResourceManagement.dll` assembly. This is typically in the default installation location where you installed the Microsoft Identity Manager service:

1. Navigate to **References**, then right-click and click on **Add Reference**.
2. Browse to the reference DLL.
3. Click on **Add**:

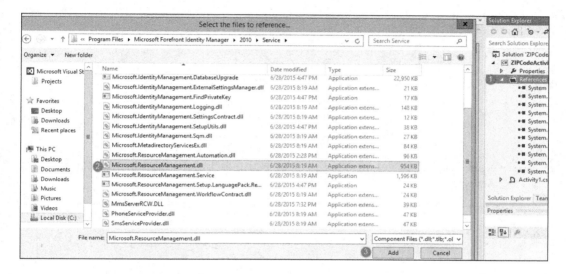

The next thing we need to do is set the application properties. So, in **Solution Explorer**, we will go and click on **ZIPCodeActivityLibrary**. Perform the following steps:

1. Click on **Properties**.
2. In **Assembly name**, we will type `ZIPCodeActivityLibrary`.
3. In **Default namespace**, we will enter `MIM.TFCCustomWorkflowActivitiesLibrary.Activities`:

4. Then, save and close.

5. The next thing we need to do is delete the default `Activity1.cs` and then add a new activity called `RequestZiplookupActivity.cs`:

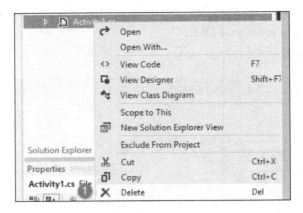

6. Next, we will select our root project, right-click, select **Add**, and finally select **Activity**:

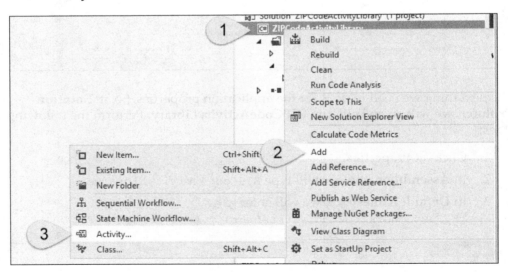

7. In Visual Studio, we do not see the MIM activities in the toolbar, so the first thing we need to do is add these items. Therefore, in the left-hand side of the Visual Studio ELCA item called **Toolbox**, we will go ahead and add a tab and call it **MIM Activities**:

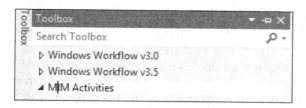

8. So, in Visual Studio 2012, all we need to do now is drag the `Microsoft.ResourceManagement.dll` file into the new tab that we created:

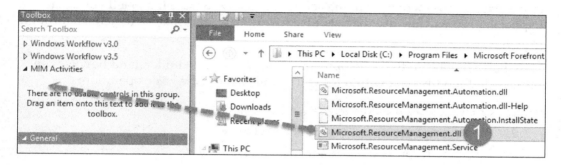

9. Then, you should see the following in our tab:

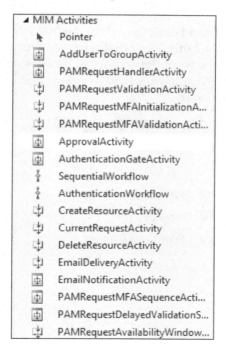

Now that we have our activities in the tab, we can simply drag and drop it to our designer. Now, when we create an activity, no matter what type of activity it is, we always want to make sure that we are designing in a standalone fashion; therefore, we don't want to be dependent on other activities, and we want to have an input and then an output. In our activity, we need to pass in the current request and perform a RESTful lookup. So, again, this will be a separate call to the web service, and we will consume this information and then update the target object. For this, the only property name that we need is the current request; this will give us the object ID and the ZIP code that was entered in the object. Now, this custom activity will not have all the logging that a production activity would require and want; just in case anything goes wrong with the activity, you have a trace file to tell you what happened. We will just use the event log to write our information to help us through the code.

First, before we begin the development steps, you need to understand how we can retrieve and modify data within MIM. The following is the basic operation:

1. Creating resources: `CreateResourceActivity`

2. Reading resources: `ReadResourceActivity`

3. Updating resources: `UpdateResourceActivity`

4. Deleting resources: `DeleteResourceActivity`

5. Enumerating resources: `EnumerateResourceActivity`

More information can be found at `http://bit.ly/MIMCustomActivities`, and it is highly recommended to read this. Now that we have everything set up, we need to create our property item; we want the activity to be self-contained. The first thing we need to do is highlight `RequestZiplookupActivity.Designer.cs`, then right-click, and finally click on **View Code**:

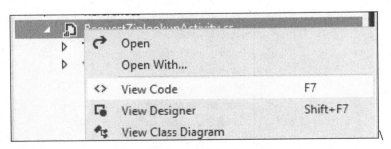

We will add the following code; this will store information about the request:

```
#region Public Workflow Propertiespublic static DependencyProperty
ReadCurrentRequestActivity_CurrentRequestProperty =
DependencyProperty.Register("ReadCurrentRequestActivi
ty_CurrentRequest", typeof(Microsoft.ResourceManagement.
WebServices.WSResourceManagement.RequestType), typeof(MIM.
TFCCustomWorkflowActivitiesLibrary.Activities.
RequestZiplookupActivity));
        /// <summary>
        /// Stores information about the current request
        /// </summary>
        [DesignerSerializationVisibilityAttribute(DesignerSerializati
onVisibility.Visible)]
        [BrowsableAttribute(true)]
        [CategoryAttribute("Misc")]
        public RequestType ReadCurrentRequestActivity_CurrentRequest
        {
            get
            {
                return ((Microsoft.ResourceManagement.
WebServices.WSResourceManagement.RequestType)(base.
GetValue(MIM.TFCCustomWorkflowActivitiesLibrary.Activities.
RequestZiplookupActivity.ReadCurrentRequestActivity_
CurrentRequestProperty)));
            }
            set
            {
                base.SetValue(MIM.TFCCustomWorkflowActivitiesLibrary.
Activities.RequestZiplookupActivity.ReadCurrentRequestActivity_
CurrentRequestProperty, value);
            }
        }
        #endregion
```

The next thing we need to do is bind the public function to `CurrentRequestActivity`. To do this, we need to go to **Toolbar** under the MIM activities, select the `CurrentRequestActivity` activity, and drag it to the designer:

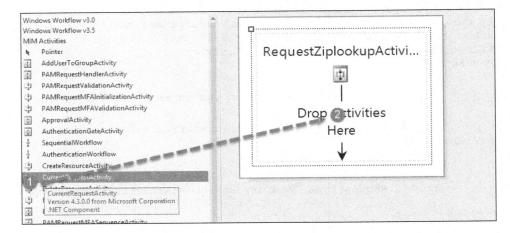

After this is done, we need to link up the public function we created. But first, let's rename `currentRequestActivity1` to `ReadCurrentRequestActivity`. Select **Items** and click on **Properties**:

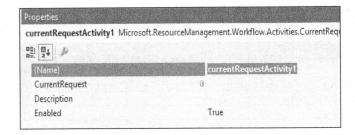

Then, select **Description**:

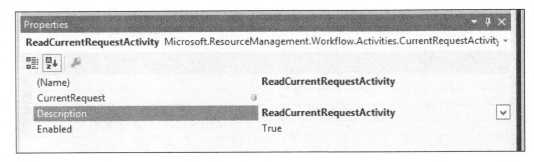

The next item is to link up activities to the function. Simply select **CurrentRequest** and then select the binding to the public function:

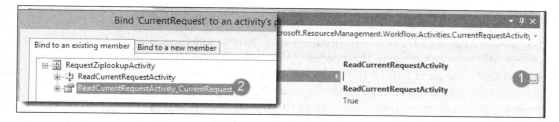

Okay! Now that we have the binding to gather the request from the workflow, we now need to start with the code to be able to run what we are trying to do. So, the next thing we will do is drag the **Code** component from **Windows Workflow v3.0** to the designer:

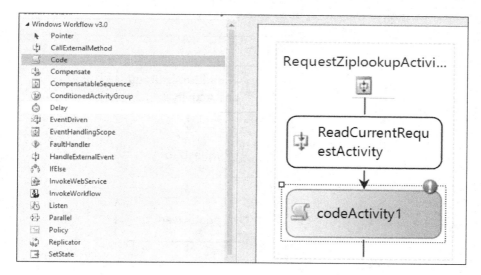

We want to rename it to something related to what we are doing—in this case, `requestzip`. Once renamed, let's go ahead and view code. Once we see this, we want to add a few more references that we want to use:

```
//extra
using System.Collections.Generic;
using System.Collections.ObjectModel;
using System.Diagnostics;
using System.Xml;
```

```
using System.Net;
//MIM References
using Microsoft.ResourceManagement.WebServices.WSResourceManagement;
using Microsoft.ResourceManagement.Workflow.Activities;
```

So, now we need to think about the logic and how to get the ZIP code for the object. We know that we will be passing this workflow if the target object ZIP code is updated. The next part of the code will add several items to help us identify whether the request object has the ZIP code field populated, which, in our case, is PostalCode. The workflow will look at the postal code and at the request object. It will evaluate the request parameters, do a comparison on a case, then create a web service call to a sample web service that we selected, pass the ZIP code, return the city, and finally use update resource to update the city on the object.

Earlier, we added the ReadCurrentRequest activity; now, to put everything in the finalized order, we need to drag and drop and then rename UpdateResourceActivity to UpdateUserCity:

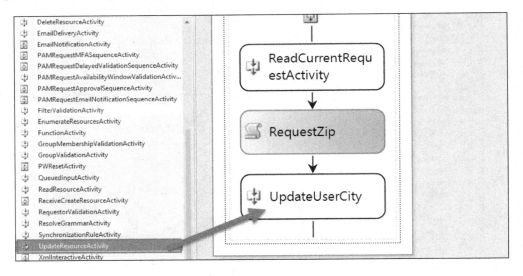

The following is a piece of code that we will use in the requestzip code base in between the try and catch. We have documented what we were doing in the particular area of code; this way, it is easier to follow when reading it:

```
try
        {
            //Get current request from previous activity
            RequestType currentRequest = this.
    ReadCurrentRequestActivity_CurrentRequest;
```

```
                    // Output the Request type and object type
            EventLog.WriteEntry(sSource, ("Request Operation: " +
currentRequest.Operation), EventLogEntryType.Information, 100);
            EventLog.WriteEntry(sSource, ("Target Object Type: " +
currentRequest.TargetObjectType), EventLogEntryType.Information, 100);
            // As UpdateRequestParameter derives from
CreateRequestParameter we can simplify the code by deriving
            // from CreateRequestParameter only.
            ReadOnlyCollection<CreateRequestParameter>
requestParameters = currentRequest.ParseParameters<CreateRequestParam
eter>();
            // Loop through CreateRequestParameters and print out
each attribute/value pair
            EventLog.WriteEntry(sSource, ("Parameters for request:
" + currentRequest.ObjectID), EventLogEntryType.Information, 100);
            foreach (CreateRequestParameter requestParameter in
requestParameters)
            {
                if (requestParameter.Value != null)
                {
                    switch (requestParameter.PropertyName)
                    {
                        //Case statement to focus on the attribute
                        case "PostalCode":
                            string zcity =
lookupzip(requestParameter.Value.ToString());
                            EventLog.WriteEntry(sSource, ("Your
City for Zip Code: " + requestParameter.Value.ToString() + " Is: "
+ lookupzip(requestParameter.Value.ToString())), EventLogEntryType.
Information, 100);


                            // Set the actor ID and the resource
ID again.
                            UpdateUserCity.ActorId = new
Guid(FIMADMIN_GUID);
                            UpdateUserCity.ResourceId =
ReadCurrentRequestActivity.CurrentRequest.Target.GetGuid();


                            // Create a list of
UpdateRequestParameter objects
                            List<UpdateRequestParameter>
updateRequestParameters = new List<UpdateRequestParameter>();

                            // Add the AccountName and DisplayName
we generated as parameters to update on the object
```

```
                                    updateRequestParameters.Add(new
UpdateRequestParameter("City", UpdateMode.Insert, zcity));

                                    // Convert the update parameters list
into an array of UpdateRequestParameter objects and assign it
                                    // to the UpdateParameters property of
the Update Resource Activity
                                    UpdateUserCity.UpdateParameters =
updateRequestParameters.ToArray<UpdateRequestParameter>();

                                    break;
                            default:
                                    EventLog.WriteEntry(sSource, ("       "
+ requestParameter.PropertyName + ": " + requestParameter.Value.
ToString()), EventLogEntryType.Information, 100);
                                    break;
                        }
                    }
                }
                    EventLog.WriteEntry(sSource, (currentRequest.ObjectID.
Value + " Complete"), EventLogEntryType.Information, 100);
                }
                catch (Exception ex)
```

Now, you will notice within the code that we called a private function called `Lookupzip`. This function simply uses a web service reference that points to the selected web service. We query the web service for the ZIP code, the information comes back from a XML node, and that would turn up the selected data that we want, in this case, the city. Now, there could be other scenarios where we could actually return the city, the state, and any other pertinent information that we can apply to the user. As you can see, this has endless possibilities to remove user errors in data entry. Again, this is a simple example, but you can see the value of being able to create your own custom activities that interface with the service.

The full code of `RequestZipLookupActivity.cs` can be found at `http://bit.ly/MIMRequestZipLookupActivity`. This way you can compare whether you're following along and possibly also where you may have missed a step.

Now that we have the code we want in place, we need to set up the UI elements of the activity for the portal. When you load the activity in the MIM portal, you will see three main areas of the title of the activity. The body is where all the controls are at from the activity. Finally, there is the **Actions** button area, which houses the **Save** and **Cancel** controls.

So, getting the controls for the UI element is a bit of a chase, as with the UI elements. The user interface is placed in the global assembly cache and is therefore called by the SharePoint services. To do this, we need to locate the `MicrosoftILMPortalCommonDLLs.wsp` file. This is typically in the default portal location, `C:\Program Files\Microsoft Forefront Identity Manager\2010\ Portal`.

Once you have the file, make a backup and rename it `MicrosoftILMPortalCommonDLLs.cab`. Open the file and let's locate the following DLLs:

Microsoft.IdentityManagement.WebUI.Controls.dll	1,880 KB	Application extension	6/28/2015 9:14 AM
Microsoft.IdentityManagement.WFExtensionInterfaces.dll	32 KB	Application extension	6/28/2015 9:13 AM

Extract the two files of your choice:

Microsoft.IdentityManagement.WebUI.Controls.dll		1,880 KB	Application extension	6/28/2015 9:14 AM
Microsoft.IdentityManagement.WFExt	Extract...	32 KB	Application extension	6/28/2015 9:13 AM
Microsoft.MetadirectoryServicesEx.dll	Copy	84 KB	Application extension	6/28/2015 9:13 AM
Microsoft.ResourceManagement.dll		954 KB	Application extension	6/28/2015 9:13 AM

Then, let's get back to the `Zipcode` activity and add the two DLLs we just extracted. Then, select the solution file and add a new class; we will call this class `RequestZipActivitySettingsPart.cs`. We will then overwrite the default generated code with the following:

```
using System;
using System.Collections.Generic;
using System.Linq;
using System.Text;
using System.Web.UI.WebControls;
using System.Workflow.ComponentModel;
using Microsoft.IdentityManagement.WebUI.Controls;
using Microsoft.ResourceManagement.Workflow.Activities;
using MIM.TFCCustomWorkflowActivitiesLibrary.Activities;

namespace MIM.TFCCustomWorkflowActivitiesLibrary.WebUIs
{
    class RequestZiplookupActivitySettingsPart : ActivitySettingsPart
```

As we need to have this class implement the activity setting, we need to have Visual Studio generate the implementation for us. To do this, we need to select `ActivitySettingsPart`, right-click, and then select **Implement Abstract Class**:

```
class RequestLoggingActivitySettingsPart : ActivitySettingsPart
{

}
```

Refactor

Organize Usings

Implement Abstract Class

We still need to render a UI and will need to add a helper function that allows us to add those UI functions. The code you will need closely matches the logging custom activity found at `http://bit.ly/MIMCALogging`.

We now have the updated data, and we can begin to deploy the custom activity. The next step is critical as in order to deploy the solution, we need to sign it. To do this, we simply need to open the **Properties** window of the solution and then, in the **Signing** area, select **Sign the assembly**:

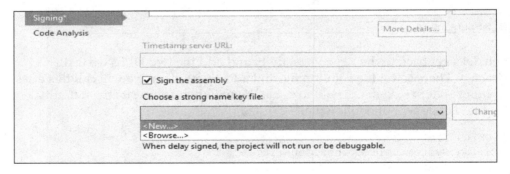

Enter the name of the key file and then unselect the password:

Click on **OK** and rebuild the solution. Now we have the DLL we need to get loaded into the system. If you have multiple MIM services and portals, you will need to load this DLL to all that are participating in workflow processing. We have copied ZIPCodeActivityLibrary.dll to the MY FIRST CA folder on the desktop of the MIM server. We need to load it into the global assembly cache. For this, we will run the following command:

```
PS C:\Users\svc-miminstall\Desktop\MY FIRST CA> .\gacutil.exe /i .\
ZIPCodeActivityLibrary.dll.
```

Once loaded, we need to browse to the assembly folder and gather the following details: public key token, version, and culture of the assembly for configuration in the portal. This can be found on the DLL we loaded on the assembly cache:

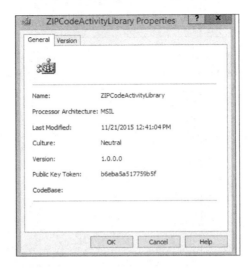

Then, we will enter it in a simple table for later use, as follows:

Public key token	b6eba5a517759b5f
Version	1.0.0.0
Culture	Neutral

Next, we need to restart the Forefront Identity Manager service and perform IISreset on the web service:

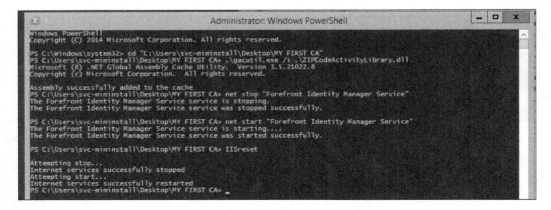

Once we have all this loaded, we need to configure the custom activity. This is done in the portal by going to **Administration | All Resources | Activity Information Configuration** and then clicking on **New**. The following tables outline what we need to add based on the new activity that we developed. Take a look at the following tables:

Common attributes

Attribute name	Value
Description	Activity to request ZIP code information about the current object and update object city
Display Name	Request ZIP code activity

Extended attributes

Attribute name	Value	Notes
Activity Name	MIM. TFCCustomWorkflowActivitiesLibrary. Activities.RequestZiplookupActivity	Must match the activity name in our project (including namespace).
Assembly Name	ZIPCodeActivityLibrary, Version = 1.0.0.0, Culture = Neutral, Public Key Token = b6eba5a517759b5f	The version, culture, and Public Key Values must match the values that are stored in the GAC. You located those values in a previous section of this document.
Type Name	MIM. TFCCustomWorkflowActivitiesLibrary. WebUIs. RequestZiplookupActivitySettingsPart	Must match the name of the class (including namespace) in your project that implements the IActivitySettingsPart interface.
Is Action Activity	Checked	Indicates that the activity can be used in an action workflow.

Once you have entered all this information in, you can click on **Finish** and then restart the MIM Service and do IISreset, as we did earlier when loading the DLL. In some cases, you will see an Access Denied error. If you get any Access Denied errors from the service, you may have forgotten to correct the typo IsAuthoriztionActivity to IsAuthorizationActivity in the built-in MPR object called **Administration: Administrators control configuration related resources.**

Now, we need to go create the workflow for this action item. Create the workflow by going to **Workflows** in the portal and then giving a name such as **Test Zipcode Activity**. Select the **Action** workflow type and then select the new activity. Take a look at the following screenshot:

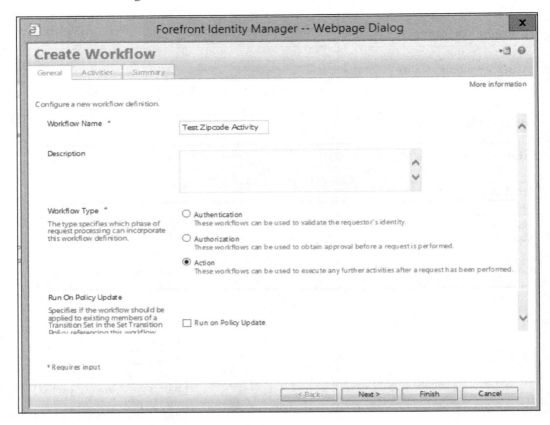

Then, we should take a look at our new custom action activity:

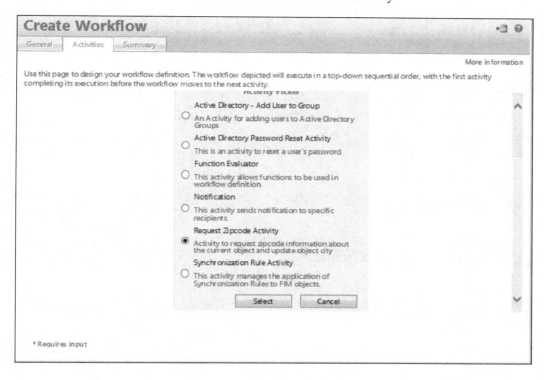

Click on **Select** and then on **Save**; we do not have any custom actions/settings for this workflow:

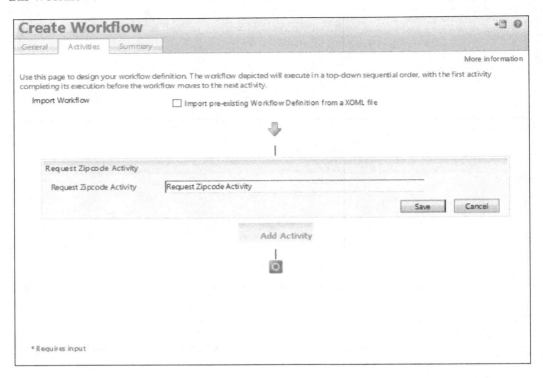

Once we have a workflow created that has our new custom activity in place, we need to create an MPR object that targets any requests—in our case, those coming from administrators that update all the active people in the attribute. We want to focus on the postal code so that our workflow will fire off, look up the ZIP code, and then update the city. The following is a sample screenshot of the MPR object that we created:

Create Management Policy Rule

General Requestors and Operations Target Resources Policy Workflows Summary

Attribute	Value
Action Parameter	PostalCode;
Action Type	Modify;
Action Workflows	Test Zipcode Activity;
Disabled	False
Display Name	_MPR Test Zipcode Activity
Grant Right	False
Management Policy Rule Type	Request
Principal Set	Administrators
Resource Current Set	All Active People
Resource Final Set	All Active People
Resource Type	Management Policy Rule

Now, we have the MPR object created as well as tied to the workflow, which, in turn, is executed when the ZIP code is updated and will return the city that correlates to the ZIP code numbers. Go ahead and test this! I'm going to pick a user and update their ZIP code. Now, our current implementation thus far only has the required attributes populated in the portal, so you'll see in our next few screenshots that we don't have a display name for the user, but for the user to log on, the only things required are the SID of the object, the account name, and the domain. The next few steps will guide and test our custom activity; go to **All Users**, and select the first user that is populated:

1. Select the first user in the list; as you can see, there is **No display name**, so just ignore this as we will go into user management stuff such as the display name later:

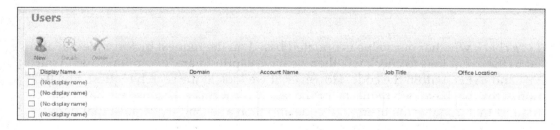

2. Enter the ZIP code:

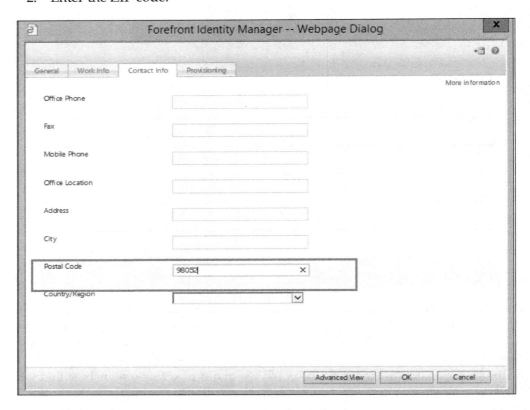

3. Then, click on **Submit**:

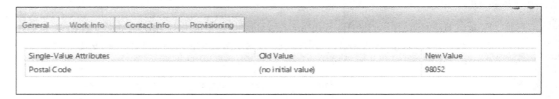

Let's check whether our value is updated based on the request history. We can also go to the event logs to check whether we have captured any exceptions due to our `try` and `catch` within the code. However, if we look at the search request, you'll notice that we have two requests for the single user; this is because we have one request that updates the users' ZIP code and then a secondary request that updates the user because of the custom activity:

Search Requests			
✕ Cancel			
☐ Request Title	Date Submitted ▾	Status	Originator
☐ Update to Person: " Request	11/23/2015 11:53:17 AM	Completed	svc-miminstall
☐ Update to Person: " Request	11/23/2015 11:53:15 AM	Completed	svc-miminstall

Also, if we open the user backup from the users' panel, you can see that the postal code that we populated is present. We can see the city being populated, as well:

City	Redmond
Postal Code	98052

Summary

In this chapter, we looked at many areas of the service and portal. We looked at the request processing, the management policy, and also what included custom activities are; we will use these later on, and in chapters related to user management and group management, this will be important. And, of course, we also discussed self-service password reset.

We looked at the MIM Service Management Agent, the creation of the Management Agent, the default rules that are needed in order to successfully create the Management Agent, and the filtering of the building accounts that is required.

The biggest area of this chapter that we focused on is understanding the portal and UI, as this is fundamental to understanding MIM Service and portal when you run into it issues down the road. We outlined in this chapter the portal configuration, the navigation bar resources, and search scopes, and also discussed filter permissions and a little bit about what an RCDC is. Then, we provided a sample custom activity; while it is simple, it holds great value in understanding what you can do with custom activities to meet your business rules.

The Financial Company is well on its way to having an identity service for its user base that will allow productivity and single identity management across the board.

In the upcoming chapters, we will focus on user management and group management.

5
User Management

User management is the most common goal of identity deployments. Synchronizing user information between different Management Agents and managing user provisioning and deprovisioning will be our primary goals for this chapter. We will show you two different approaches: one using the synchronization engine with its rules extensions, and the second using the MIM portal and its synchronization rules, **Management Policy Rules** (**MPRs**), and workflows.

In this chapter, we will look at the following topics:

- Additional sync engine information
- Portal MPRs for user management
- Configuring sets for user management
- Inbound synchronization rules
- Outbound synchronization rules
- Provisioning
- Managing users in a phone system
- Managing users in Active Directory
- Temporal sets
- Self-service using MIM Portal
- Managing Exchange
- More considerations

Additional sync engine information

In the previous chapters, we have shown you how to configure a Management Agent for SQL, Active Directory, and MIM Portal. We wrote a simple rules extension for the SQL (HR) Management Agent to generate a unique account name, and generated the display name by concatenating two attributes, the first name and last name. A Metaverse rules extension was created to provision objects to the Active Directory connector space. Run profiles were used to copy the data from the HR system to its connector space, into the Metaverse (called a projection), out to the Active Directory connector space (referred to as a provision), and then out to Active Directory.

As we have it now, the Active Directory objects have minimal information: sAMAccountName, userPrincipalName, and a password. The Active Directory accounts are enabled by setting the userAccountControl attribute, and the pwdLastSet attribute is set to 0. Look back at *Chapter 3*, *MIM Sync Configuration*, and you will notice that sAMAccountName, userPrincipalName, unicodePwd, userAccountControl, and pwdLastSet are all specified in the Metaverse rules extension. Does this mean that we have to specify the additional attributes that we have in our HR system in our Metaverse rules extension code? Nope! The attributes we specify in the Metaverse rules extension are only used for provisioning out to one or more connector spaces, meaning that we set those values, upon provisioning, out to the connector space. Another way to look at provisioning in the Metaverse rules extension is to think of it as a one-time set. Once provisioned out to the connector space, we don't modify the attributes in any way. If we need to keep attributes up to date, we need to add some attribute flow rules to our configuration.

Before we begin, why did we select those few attributes in our Metaverse rules extension? First, a few of these attributes are required by Active Directory in order to create an account. Secondly, some attributes should only be set initially, and then left to be managed by the end user or some other team. For example, we almost never want to change someone's logon name (sAMAccountName or userPrincipalName), or their password without their prior knowledge. If the logon names need to be changed (and business rules require them to be changed), we would need to coordinate that change with the end user; otherwise, the end user would have no idea how to log on and work. End-user passwords should be handled directly by the end user, when possible, or by a service desk. We will talk more about passwords later in the book.

Now, let's update our configuration to account for future HR data changes of additional attributes, and enable the flow of potential updated data out to the target systems:

1. Start MIM Synchronization Service Manager.

2. Select the **Management Agents** tool, click on **AD Management Agent,** then click on **Properties**.

3. Click on **Configure Attribute Flow**:

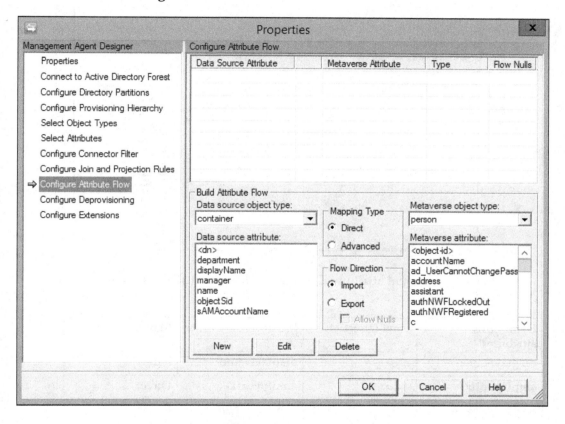

4. In the **Data source object type** drop-down menu, select **user**, and verify that **Metaverse object type** is set to **person**.

5. Verify that **Mapping Type** is set to **Direct** and **Flow Direction** is set to **Export**.

6. In the **Data source attribute** section, click on **department**.

7. In the **Metaverse attribute** section, click on **department**.

8. Click on the **New** button. You should now have a new export attribute flow for **department** in your AD Management Agent, as shown in the next screenshot:

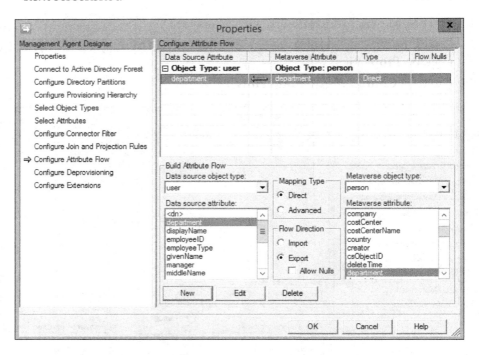

9. Create additional attribute flows for additional attributes, as listed in the following table:

Data source attribute	Flow Direction	Metaverse attribute	Mapping Type
displayName	⟸	displayName	Direct
employeeID	⟸	employeeID	Direct
employeeType	⟸	employeeType	Direct
givenName	⟸	firstName	Direct
manager	⟸	manager	Direct
middleName	⟸	middleName	Direct
sn	⟸	lastName	Direct
title	⟸	title	Direct

10. In the upper **Configure Attribute Flow** pane, click on the first row **Object Type: user** and **Object Type: person** in order to create a new import flow.

11. In the **Flow Direction** section, click on **Import**.

12. In the **Data source attribute** section, click on **objectSid**.

13. In the **Metaverse attribute** section, click on **objectSid**.

14. Click on the **New** button to create a new import attribute flow for **objectSid**.

15. Create another import attribute flow from **sAMAccountName** to the Metaverse attribute **accountName**.

16. In **Mapping Type**, click on **Advanced**, and then click on the **New** button.

17. Choose **Constant**, and enter TFC. Note that TFC is the NETBIOS name for our domain:

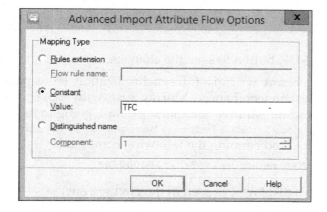

18. The final attribute flow for the AD Management Agent should look like the following:

	Properties		
Management Agent Designer	**Configure Attribute Flow**		
Properties	Data Source Attribute	Metaverse Attribute	Type	Flow Nulls
Connect to Active Directory Forest	⊟ **Object Type: user**	**Object Type: person**		
Configure Directory Partitions	department ⟵	department	Direct	
Configure Provisioning Hierarchy	displayName ⟵	displayName	Direct	
Select Object Types	employeeID ⟵	employeeID	Direct	
Select Attributes	employeeType ⟵	employeeType	Direct	
Configure Connector Filter	givenName ⟵	firstName	Direct	
Configure Join and Projection Rules	manager ⟵	manager	Direct	
⇒ Configure Attribute Flow	middleName ⟵	middleName	Direct	
Configure Deprovisioning	sn ⟵	lastName	Direct	
Configure Extensions	title ⟵	title	Direct	
	sAMAccountName ⟹	accountName	Direct	
	objectSid ⟹	objectSid	Direct	
	⟹	domain	Constant - TFC	

19. Click on the **OK** button to save the changes.

As an aside, before we run a full synchronization, let us peek at one of the objects in the connector space, Murray Sosa, with `employeeID` 10000868, by running an administrative command prompt, going to `Program Files\ Microsoft Forefront Identity Manager\2010\Synchronization Service\Bin`, and running the following command:

`csexport "HR" msosa.xml /f:d="10000868"`

The output is displayed as seen in the next screenshot:

```
C:\Program Files\Microsoft Forefront Identity Manager\2010\Synchronization Service\Bin>csexport "HR" msosa.xml /f:d="10000868"
Microsoft Identity Integration Server Connector Space Export Utility v4.3.2195.0
c 2012 Microsoft Corporation. All rights reserved

[1/1]

Successfully exported connector space to file 'msosa.xml'.
```

Open the XML file in an XML viewer to see just how much information is stored about the object. MIM is able to perform state-based processing of an identity by storing all the information found in the XML file we just created. The complete identity information for a state (the condition of the identity data that MIM has at that time) is called a hologram. MIM keeps a hologram for the data imported into the system, and for the data that would be exported out to a target system. From a performance perspective, MIM uses holograms in order to minimize the amount of data changes it needs to process. For example, if a single attribute value changes on a single object, the MIM engine only needs to make a single attribute update, and not update all the data on the entire object. Holograms also enable us to apply new synchronization logic without retrieving the source data again. More information on holograms and state-based processing can be found in an older Microsoft TechNet article dating back to MIM's origins, but its contents are still valid today. You can refer to this article at `http://bit.ly/ MIMStateBasedProcessing`:

```
<cs-objects>
  <cs-object cs-dn="10000868" id="{5C713698-1C24-E611-8129-00155D026225}" object-type="person">
    <unapplied-export>
      <delta operation="none" dn="10000868">
        <anchor encoding="base64">EAAAADEAMAAwADAAMAA4ADYAOAA=</anchor>
      </delta>
    </unapplied-export>
    <escrowed-export>
      <delta operation="none" dn="10000868">
        <anchor encoding="base64">EAAAADEAMAAwADAAMAA4ADYAOAA=</anchor>
      </delta>
    </escrowed-export>
    <unconfirmed-export>
      <delta operation="none" dn="10000868">
        <anchor encoding="base64">EAAAADEAMAAwADAAMAA4ADYAOAA=</anchor>
      </delta>
    </unconfirmed-export>
    <pending-import>
      <delta operation="add" dn="10000868">
        <anchor encoding="base64">EAAAADEAMAAwADAAMAA4ADYAOAA=</anchor>
        <primary-objectclass>person</primary-objectclass>
        <objectclass>
          <oc-value>person</oc-value>
        </objectclass>
        <attr name="HRType" type="string" multivalued="false">
          <value>Employee</value>
        </attr>
        <attr name="ID" type="string" multivalued="false">
          <value>10000868</value>
        </attr>
        <attr name="department" type="string" multivalued="false">
          <value>Sales</value>
        </attr>
        <attr name="firstName" type="string" multivalued="false">
          <value>Murray</value>
        </attr>
        <attr name="lastName" type="string" multivalued="false">
          <value>Sosa</value>
        </attr>
```

20. Click on the **HR** Management Agent. Then, in the **Actions** pane, click on **Run**, select **Full Sync**, and click on **OK**.

21. In the pane labeled **Synchronization Statistics** on the lower-left side, you should see some changes that have taken place out to the AD connector space, as shown in the following screenshot:

22. Click on the **Export Attribute Flow** hyperlink, and you will see a listing of objects that have been updated in the AD connector space:

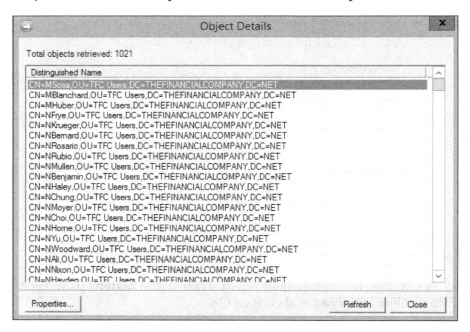

23. Double-click on any object, and click on the **Properties** button to find out what has been changed for that object:

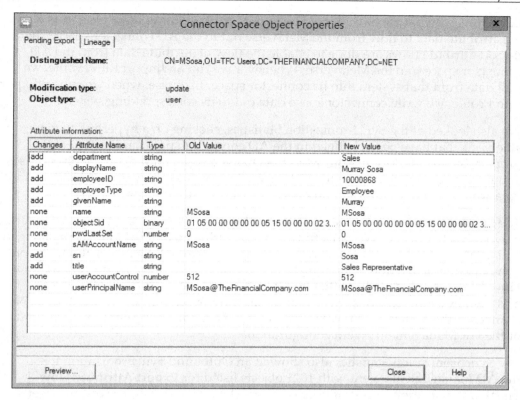

24. You can click on the **Changes** column to sort the attributes that have been changed, or in this case, the attributes that have been added.

25. Click on the **Close** button.

26. Click on the **AD** Management Agent. Then, in the **Actions** pane, click on **Run**, select **Export**, and click on **OK**. You should see 1021 updates.

27. Click on the **Updates** hyperlink in the **Export Statistics** pane on the lower-left side of the screen to open up **Object Details**.

28. Click on an object and look at its properties. Notice that the tab at the top says **Awaiting Export Confirmation**.

29. Click on the **Close** button.

30. Verify that the **AD** Management Agent is selected. Then click on **Run**, select the **Delta Import Run Profile**, and click on **OK**.

Let us review what we have done. The Export attribute flows were created to enable the attribute data to flow from the Metaverse out to the AD connector space. The Import attribute flows are done to enable the flow of attribute data from the AD connector space into the Metaverse. Whenever we run an Import Run Profile, we pull data from that system into its connector space. Likewise, when we run an Export Run Profile, we write connector space data out to its corresponding system.

We also looked at the Synchronization Statistics, clicking on a hyperlink to view all objects that have been changed in the AD connector space, and looked at the property of an object to find out what has changed (been added) on the object. As you may suspect, a change to an existing attribute would show up as Modify, and if data were deleted (cleared) for an attribute, MIM would indicate a Delete.

The Synchronization Statistics can be confusing for beginners, but think of it in terms of what has happened. We ran a full synchronization on our HR Management Agent, and MIM reported zero for almost everything in Inbound Synchronization. The only non-zero item listed under Inbound Synchronization are **1021 Connectors without Flow Updates**, which tells us that no Metaverse changes occurred between our existing HR connector space objects and their corresponding Metaverse objects. No changes in the Metaverse makes sense as we have made no changes to the HR data or the HR Management Agent configuration.

The Synchronization Statistics also showed an Outbound Synchronization for the AD Management Agent with 1021 objects listed for **Export Attribute Flow**. The Synchronization Run Profile can change Metaverse objects, as well as target connector spaces. Therefore, it follows that we have now pushed data in the Metaverse out through those new Export Attribute Flow mappings.

Recall back to when we ran an Export Run Profile for the AD Management Agent, and new attribute data was exported to AD. At that moment, MIM showed **Awaiting Export Confirmation** for our objects, telling us that it needed to verify the changes made to Active Directory. MIM verifies that the write happened by importing what it exported, which is done by running an Import Run Profile — either Full Import or a Delta Import.

As you may have guessed, a Delta Import Run Profile imports only those objects with content that has changed in the connected data source into its connector space. Similarly, a Delta Synchronization Run Profile re-evaluates and applies synchronization rules to objects and attributes that are staged in the connector space and which have changed. Those changed objects and attributes are then synchronized with the Metaverse, or they disconnect from the Metaverse based on defined rules. A Full Import Run Profile imports all objects and attributes from the connected data source into its connector space, while a Full Synchronization Run Profile re-evaluates and applies synchronization rules to all connector space objects, synchronizes with the Metaverse, or disconnects from the Metaverse.

Import and Export Run Profiles are simple enough; they pull data from the source system into its connector space, or push data from the connector space out to the target system. Synchronization Run Profiles are more involved. Let's look at the Run Profile synchronization process a little closer by reviewing the following diagram:

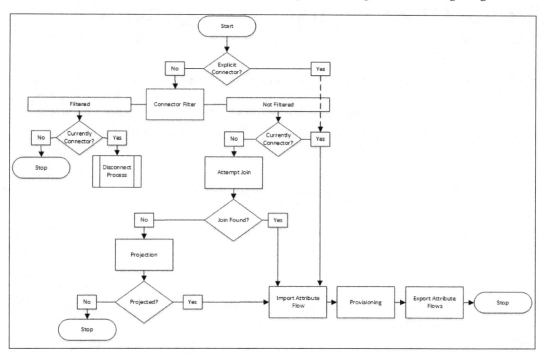

The preceding diagram references some terminology we have not discussed yet. We first look to see whether the object is an explicit connector, and if so, ignore any currently defined or future connector filters. Connector filters were demonstrated back when we configured the MIM Service Management Agent and filtered the administrative account (installation account) and the MIM MA account. An explicit connector can only be created manually by the Joiner Tool, a tool that allows you to forcefully connect a connector space object with a Metaverse object, regardless of your defined rules. The key takeaway here is that when you use the Joiner Tool to go around your defined logic, and forcefully project or join a connector space object to the Metaverse, the synchronization engine assumes you want to ignore any current or *future* logic and keep the connector space object connected to the Metaverse object. The authors suggest avoiding the use of the Joiner Tool as much as possible. Let's now look at how we can utilize MIM Portal to perform user management functions.

Portal MPRs for user management

There are many MPRs in MIM Service that control how user objects can be modified by self-service, administrators, or the synchronization engine.

In many cases, we need to modify the existing MPRs and/or create new ones. Whether we use the existing MPRs or decide to create new ones is something you can decide as you wish. In this book, we will reuse many of the built-in MPRs, and add new ones when needed.

Before we can start our user management, it is a good idea to look at the existing MPRs and try to understand what they do. If we go into MIM Portal, select **Management Policy Rules**, click on **Advanced Search**, and search for **Display Name contains user**, we will get around 26 MPRs (many are regarding group management) in our default setup. Take a quick look at the first page of results in the following screenshot, and you will notice that many are disabled by default:

Select management policy rule that match **all** of the following conditions:		
Display Name contains user		
Add Statement or Add Sub-condition		

Display Name ▲	Action Type	Disabled
Administration: Administrators can delete non-administrator users	Delete	No
Administration: Administrators can read and update Users	Create, Add, Modify, Remove	No
Anonymous users can reset their password	Modify	Yes
Distribution list Management: Users can add or remove any members of groups subject to owner approval	Add, Remove	Yes
Distribution list management: Users can add or remove any members of groups that don't require owner approval	Add, Remove	Yes
Distribution List management: Users can create Static Distribution Groups	Create	Yes
Distribution list management: Users can read selected attributes of group resources	Read	Yes
General: Users can read non-administrative configuration resources	Read	Yes
General: Users can read schema related resources	Read	No
PAM: Administrators control Users and Groups	Add, Create, Delete, Modify, Read, Remove	No
PAM: User can read Pam Roles that he can request	Read	No
PAM: User can read Pam Roles that he owns	Read	No
PAM: User can see PAM requests that he created	Read	No
PAM: Users can create a PAM Request	Create	No
Password reset users can read password reset objects	Read	Yes
Password Reset Users can update the lockout attributes of themselves	Add, Remove, Read	Yes
Security group management: Users can add or remove any member of groups subject to owner approval	Add, Remove	Yes
Security Group management: Users can create Static Security Groups	Create	Yes
Security group management: Users can read selected attributes of group resources	Read	Yes
Security groups: Users can add and remove members to open groups	Add, Remove	Yes

One that is enabled by default is **Synchronization: Synchronization account controls users it synchronizes**, which allows the synchronization account to manage user objects. Let's take a quick look at this one, because it is a common reason why synchronization of users might not work as expected when using Portal synchronization rules. Perform the steps listed here:

1. Click on the link to the MPR, **Synchronization: Synchronization account controls users it synchronizes**, to open up its properties.

   ○ In the **General** tab, we can see that this MPR is of type **Request**, since it deals with a request from the synchronization account to modify a user object:

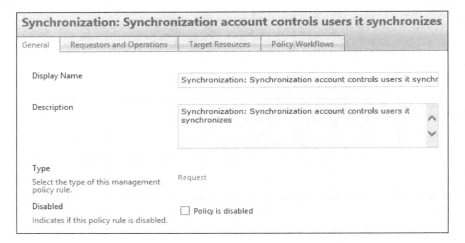

   °   The **Requestors and Operations** tab shows that this MPR is applied when the requestor is **Synchronization Engine,** and the operation is something other than **Read resource**:

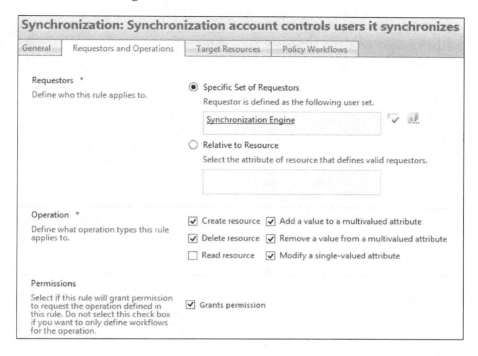

     °   In the **Target Resources** tab, we see that the target in this case is set to **All People**. If you look at the definition of that set, you will see that the criterion is a user object or all user objects. Notice that this MPR does not apply to all attributes, but only a selection of attributes:

 If you change the **All People** set, be aware that this and other MPRs might stop working as expected.

2. If you click on the icon that looks like a stack of papers and perform a blank search, you can get a list of all the attributes. Some of these attributes relate to the user resource, while other attributes are bound to other resources:

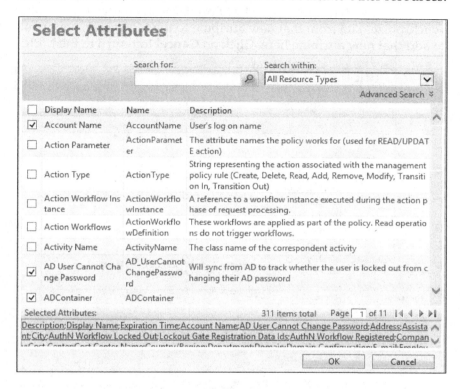

3. On the **Select Attributes** page, in the **Search within:** drop-down menu, select **Users**, and then click on the search icon. You will then see all the attributes bound to user resources, and will be able to select and deselect as you like. If you ever need to extend the MIM Portal schema with a new attribute, and synchronize data from that new attribute to the Metaverse, you would need to add that new attribute here. Click on **Cancel** to return to the MPR:

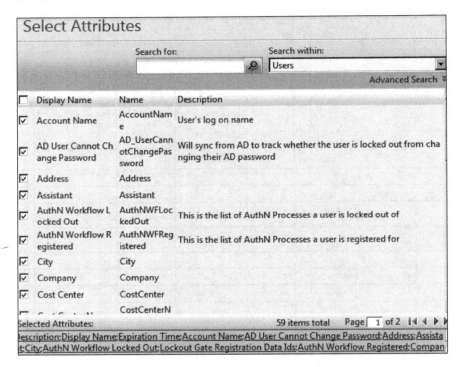

4. In the **Policy Workflows** tab, notice there are no policy workflows triggered by this MPR. That is, there is nothing listed in the **Selected Resources** section of the **Authentication Workflows**, **Authorization Workflows**, or **Action Workflows**:

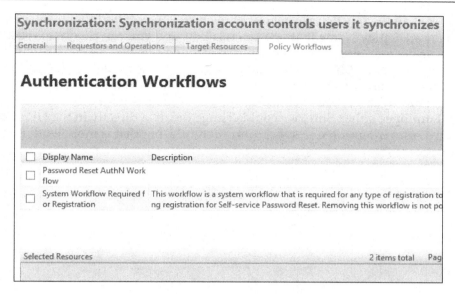

 Remember, any request made by the synchronization engine will bypass authentication and authorization workflows. Only action workflows can be triggered when the requestor is the synchronization engine.

Configuring sets for user management

Organizing objects in MIM Service is done using a set; all MPRs use a set to work.

 Sets are not groups. Sets are only used within MIM Service to organize managed objects, while groups are a type of managed object that can be synchronized with other systems.

It is common to have different employee types managed differently. In order to manage them differently, we would first group them into different sets.

If we look at all the sets that we get out of the box, you will find that many of them have a **Display Name** that you can relate to, and you can choose to reuse them or create your own. There are some predefined sets that we can use, such as **All Contractors** or **All Full Time Employees**. Take a look at the **All Full Time Employees** set, and notice that the criteria specifies a **Full Time Employee**. In our scenario, **Employee Type**, as defined by the HR system, is not **Full Time Employee** but the **Employee** value. Sure, we could change the data directly in the HR system by using a rules extension or a synchronization rule, but that is more work than necessary:

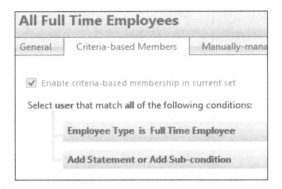

In the **All Full Time Employees** set, we can see that the criterion of the **Employee Type** attribute is **Full Time Employee**; we need to change this to **Employee**:

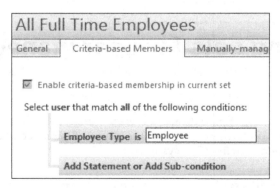

For consistency, we could change the display name of the set to **All Employees**. As we proceed with configuring MIM Service, we will create many new sets.

Inbound synchronization rules

One of the first things we need to do in order to manage users is get some users into MIM Synchronization Service and MIM Service. We can create them using MIM Portal or some other interface, but usually there are existing users in some system that we would like to import. In our example, the HR system is our primary source of users.

Importing will require us to create what is called an inbound synchronization rule. For one external system, such as the HR system, we might have multiple inbound synchronization rules. One reason for that could be that we have multiple object types in one **CDS (Connected Data Source)**, and we can only synchronize one resource type (object) in each rule.

So first of all, we create a synchronization rule to import users from the HR system. Follow these steps:

1. In the MIM portal, go to **Administration | Synchronization Rules | New**.

   When creating synchronization rules, it is a good idea to have some kind of naming standard to make it easier to find the correct rules later on. In our example, we use the syntax *MA ObjectType Direction*, so this one is called **HR Users Inbound**. We tend to create separate synchronization rules for each direction, because it gives us more control. The behavior and settings on inbound and outbound rules are quite different. But, as you will see later in this chapter, we do create rules with both the inbound and outbound directions:

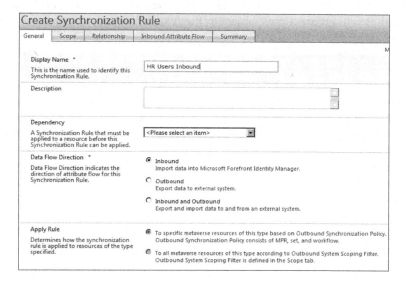

2. In the **Scope** tab, we define the **Resource Type** involved in MIM and in the connector space object for the external system. Remember that we are now looking at the MIM Synchronization Service (Metaverse) schema, not the MIM Service schema:

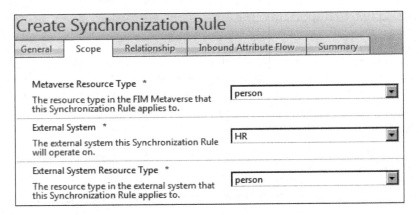

3. In the **Relationship** tab, we define how MIM should try to join the connector space object to the Metaverse object. If you add multiple conditions, the objects have to satisfy all conditions. If you need more complex rules to join the objects, you might need to configure the Management Agent join rules instead. If MIM cannot match objects using the Relationship Criteria, we would, in this case, like MIM to project a new object into the Metaverse. To project, we then need to check the **Create Resource in FIM** checkbox. So, in this example, MIM will first check whether it can match **Relationship Criteria**, and if no match is found, it will create a new object in the Metaverse:

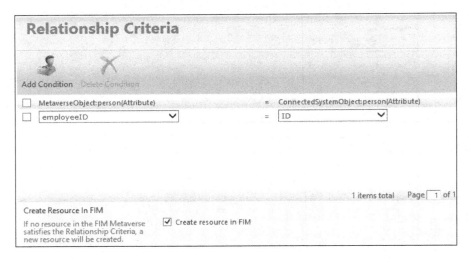

4. Click on the **Inbound Attribute Flow** tab. Notice that we define the attribute flows here, which tells MIM how to flow data from the connector space into the Metaverse. Click on **New Attribute Flow**. In the **Source** tab, select **department**, then click on the **Destination** tab and select **department**. Click on **OK** to save that flow:

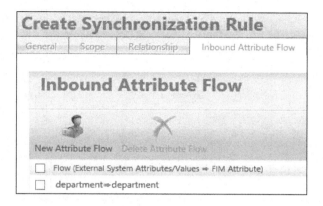

5. Create additional flows as follows:

Source attribute	Destination attribute
firstName	firstName
HRType	employeeType
ID	employeeID
lastName	lastName
manager	manager
middleName	middleName
status	employeeStatus
title	jobTitle

6. The display name will be built using the first name, followed by a space, and then the last name. Click on **New Attribute Flow**. Select **firstName**, and click on **Concatenate Value**. In the second drop-down list, select **String** and enter a space. Finally, click on **Concatenate Value** and select **lastName**:

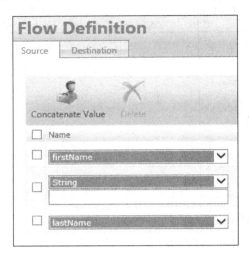

7. Click on the **Destination** tab and select **displayName** for the **Destination** attribute. Click on **OK**:

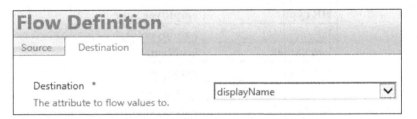

8. When you are done, you should see the following:

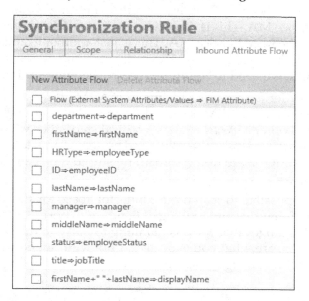

Some important things to note here are as follows:

- A synchronization rule cannot be used directly after creation. We first need to import the new synchronization rule object into the synchronization engine in order to do the synchronization. An easy way is to run Delta Import followed by Delta Sync on the MIM Service MA. The synchronization engine will then associate the new rule with the correct MA — HR in our example.

- It is now possible to use the new synchronization rule. Test it by running a Full Sync on the HR MA. We assume you have already run the Full Import profile. In **Synchronization Statistics**, you will see how many new objects (projections) are projected (created) in the Metaverse.

- ○ Further down in **Synchronization Statistics**, you will see that for each projection, there is also a **Provisioning Adds** option to the MIM Service MA. This is caused by the automatic provisioning happening for the MIM Service MA. This is just another example of the special way the MIM Service MA works. As you will see later, for all other MAs, we need to configure the provisioning for it to happen.

- ○ In order for the users to appear in MIM Portal, we need to run an Export to the MIM Service. Running Export to the MIM Service MA (and other MAs as well) is a critical step, since we will now start to change data in the connected system. To make sure you are not on your way to doing something stupid, you can check what will happen.

- ○ It is possible to search the connector space for **Pending Export**. By doing this and looking at Pending Export, you can verify that the changes that MIM is planning to make in the connected data source are what you expected. If not, you can go back, reconfigure, synchronize again, and check whether Pending Export looks better:

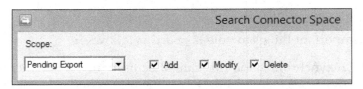

9. After running Export, go into MIM Portal and search for **Users**. If you find users without any data, verify whether your MIM MA is configured as shown in the following screenshot:

	Properties		
Management Agent Designer	Configure Attribute Flow		

Data Source Attribute		Metaverse Attribute	Type	Flow Nulls
⊞ **Object Type: Det...**		**Object Type: dete...**		
⊞ **Object Type: Exp...**		**Object Type: expe...**		
⊞ **Object Type: Gro...**		**Object Type: group**		
⊟ **Object Type: Per...**		**Object Type: person**		
dn	⬅		sync-rule-m...	
MVObjectID	⬅	<object-id>	Direct	
DetectedRulesList	⬅	detectedRulesList	Direct	Allow
AccountName	⬅	accountName	Direct	
DisplayName	⬅	displayName	Direct	
ObjectSID	⬅	objectSid	Direct	
FirstName	⬅	firstName	Direct	
LastName	⬅	lastName	Direct	
Domain	⬅	domain	Direct	
EmployeeType	⬅	employeeType	Direct	
Department	⬅	department	Direct	
JobTitle	⬅	title	Direct	
Email	⬅	mail	Direct	
<dn>	➡	csObjectID	Direct	
ExpectedRulesList	➡	expectedRulesList	Direct	

(sidebar menu items:)
- Properties
- Connect to Database
- Select Object Types
- Select Attributes
- Configure Connector Filter
- Configure Object Type Mappings
- ⇒ Configure Attribute Flow
- Configure Deprovisioning
- Configure Extensions

10. If you did have an issue, you would need to run Full Sync followed by Export for the data to appear in Portal.

You should now understand how the flow of inbound synchronization works at a high level. If you see any strange behavior, go back and look at your attribute flows. One common mistake is to confuse the Metaverse schema with the MIM Service schema. You may create an attribute mapping on your source system (in our case, HR) to flow to one attribute in the Metaverse, and forget to flow that attribute out to a target system, or accidentally choose a Metaverse attribute that is not being populated by a source Management Agent.

During the testing and development of MIM Synchronization and MIM Service, you may find that you need to make frequent changes and synchronizations to verify your configuration. If your test/development environment contains a large number of objects, it might take hours to run a synchronization cycle; therefore, keeping the number of objects in your test/dev environment to a minimum saves time. You should also consider that a good test has enough representative data to verify the configuration. If the production environment data is wildly inconsistent and not represented in test/dev, then all that time you spend in testing may not be beneficial. Also note that it is a good habit to back up your configuration before you make changes, even in your test/dev environment.

Outbound synchronization rules

As you can see, inbound synchronization rules are associated with the connector space MA that we like to import information from. Outbound synchronization is very different! Because of the differences, many people choose not to have Inbound and Outbound Data Flow Direction in the same synchronization rule.

Outbound synchronization rules are associated with each object type (or resource to be consistent with MIM Portal naming conventions). There are two ways to apply an outbound synchronization rule: using an **Outbound Synchronization Policy** or by using an **Outbound System Scoping Filter**:

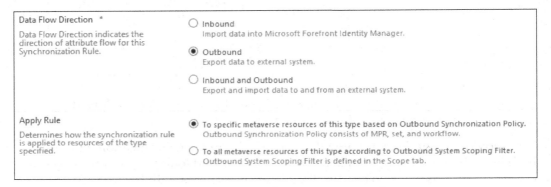

 You can only make this choice during the creation of the outbound synchronization rule. You cannot change it once the synchronization rule has been created.

In some scenarios, you will find that it is useful to have multiple outbound synchronization rules for one external system. In those cases, you might mix the two different ways of associating the rule to the object. You will find one example of this later in this chapter, in the *Managing Exchange* section.

You will quickly find out that using Outbound Scoping Filter is easier and more performant. However, there are limitations when you use this approach for outbound synchronizations. Specifically, it does not automatically deprovision (trigger a delete), or allow you to use workflow attributes (such as generated passwords) in your synchronization rule.

Outbound Synchronization Policy

An Outbound Synchronization Policy associates the users with **Expected Rule Entries (EREs)**. In order for us to do that, we need to create what some people call the configuration triple: a set, a workflow, and an MPR:

- A **set** contains the objects that should have the ERE
- An action **workflow** adds the ERE to the object
- An **MPR** runs the action workflow when the object transitions into the set

If we want to do deprovisioning as well, we would also need an action workflow to remove the ERE, and an MPR that triggers that workflow.

Outbound System Scoping Filter

If we have a very simple scenario, we can use what is called **Outbound System Scoping Filter** to tell MIM which objects to associate the outbound synchronization rule with:

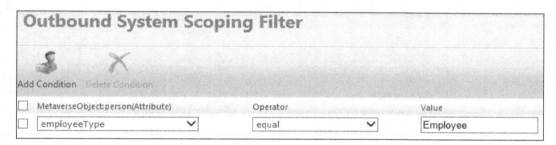

The outbound synchronization rule is where we define the filter. Something very important to remember here is if you add conditions, they are **ANDed**. This means your objects need to match all conditions. We will use **Outbound System Scoping Filter** for the phone system.

Detected Rule Entry

If, for some reason, you would like to know whether an object exists in the external system, you can configure MIM to create a **Detected Rule Entry (DRE)** and associate it with the object.

One reason for this would be that we need to know whether the provisioning is successful, and maybe trigger some actions based on that. For Active Directory, for example, we might use this to trigger the creation of home folders only after a DRE is detected on the user.

We can configure this by adding a small checkbox to our outbound synchronization rule.

If you check **Use as Existence Test** on one of the outbound attribute flows, MIM will create the DRE if it detects a successful export of that value during the next import from the system. The attribute flow that you use should be the one that is populated for all objects. If we synchronize this DRE with MIM Service, we can check the **Provisioning** tab on the object, **User** for example.

In **Detected Rules List**, we will see the DREs that this particular user is associated with:

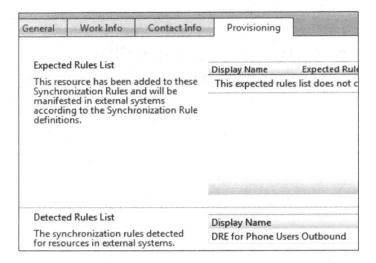

If you plan on using DREs, or would like to understand them better, I suggest you begin by reading http://aka.ms/FIMDRE, where the whole concept of DREs is explained in detail. You will also find some nice examples of how to use them.

Provisioning

Recall that provisioning is when we create new objects in a connector space, using the Metaverse as the source. We enable synchronization rule provisioning in the synchronization engine by running Synchronization Service Manager and selecting **Tools | Options**:

1. Check the **Enable Synchronization Rule Provisioning** checkbox to enable provisioning:

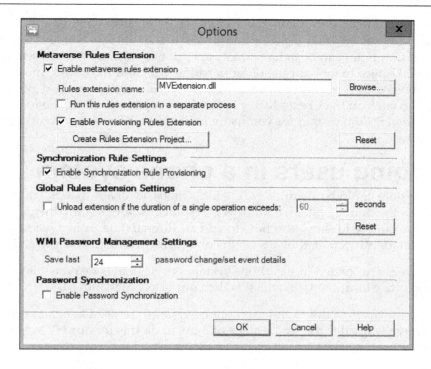

2. To allow provisioning for an outbound synchronization rule, we need to check the **Create resource in external system** checkbox:

Create Resource in External System

If no resource in the external system satisfies the Relationship Criteria, a new resource will be created.

☑ Create resource in external system

Non-declarative provisioning

If you are doing non-declarative classic synchronization using code, you would instead check **Enable metaverse rules extension**, type (or browse for) the name of the DLL files containing your code, and check the **Enable Provisioning Rules Extension** checkbox.

If you are planning on doing non-declarative classic provisioning, you will find plenty of examples on what the code could look like in the Metaverse extension DLL. A good starting point can be `http://aka.ms/FIMMVExtension`. When searching the Internet, make sure to look for the older versions MIIS and ILM, since most examples are from those older versions. Enabling Metaverse rules extension also gives you the ability to click on the **Create Rules Extension Project…** button; the tool will then create a Visual Studio project for you using either VB.NET or C#, as you choose.

Managing users in a phone system

A phone system could be a simple SQL table. The basic idea is that all employees should be in the phone system, and MIM is responsible for creating them. We discuss this simple example to show you how to add additional data from a secondary system to an identity created by a system configured for Metaverse projection.

Once the users are created in the phone system, the system is responsible for entering phone and office location data, which is then imported back into MIM.

To manage the users in this SQL-based phone system, we need to create the MA. Since we have walked through the steps on how to do this for our HR system, we will point out some basics:

1. The Management Agent type would be **SQL Server**, and we give it the name **Phone**. Using an SQL alias of **dbPhone**, we connect to the **Phone** database and the **PhoneData** table containing the phone data.

2. Next, we set the **ID** column as anchor and the **Object Type** as **person**:

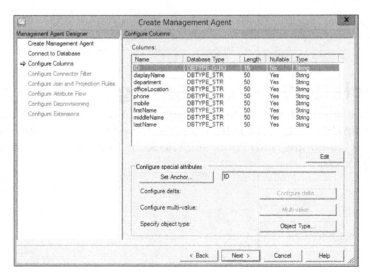

3. MIM will manage the users in the phone system, and will also delete them if they no longer have a connection to MIM. In order for MIM to do that, we select **Stage a delete on the object for the next export run** in **Deprovisioning Options**, as shown in the following screenshot:

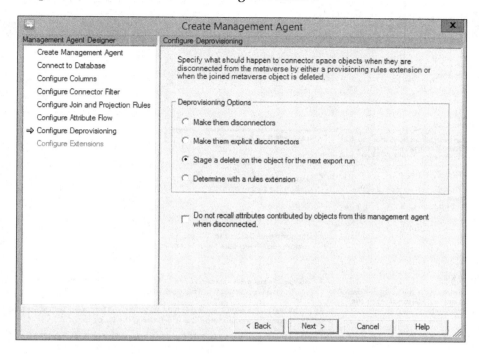

4. After creating the Phone MA, we can go into the MIM portal and create the synchronization rule required for creating users in the phone system and importing the phone related data to MIM.

5. For the phone user's synchronization rule, we choose to do both inbound and outbound in the same rule. To decide which objects to do outbound synchronization for, we use the **Outbound System Scoping Filter** option:

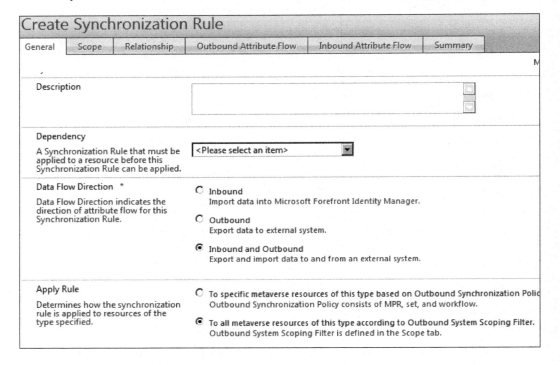

6. We select the resource types in MIM and the phone system, and then define the **Outbound System Scoping Filter**. We create a simple (inclusive) filter, **employeeType equal Employee**, to associate all users matching this filter with the synchronization rule:

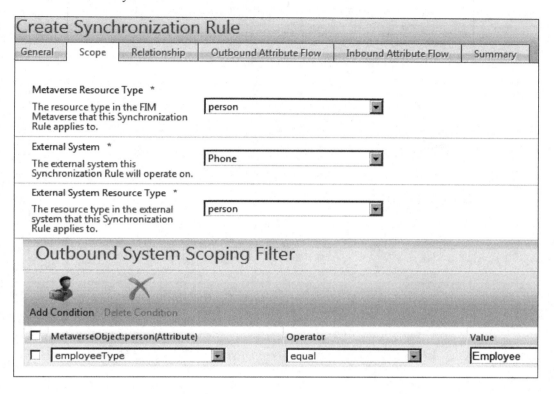

7. To provision users to the phone system, we place a check in **Create Resource in External System**. Configuring **Relationship Criteria** might seem unnecessary here, since MIM is creating the users. But consider a situation where we need to perform a recovery or reestablish our connections. We will need a way to import and join to existing users in the Metaverse:

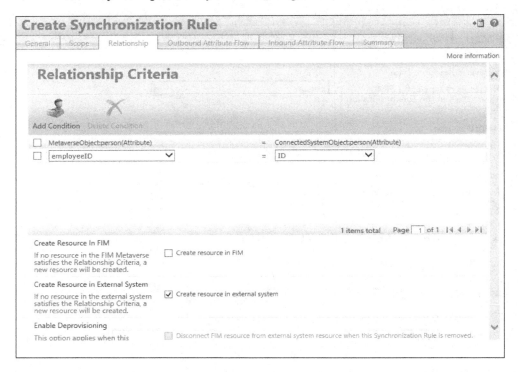

8. Define **Outbound Attribute Flow**. We have chosen to define the **ID** attribute flow as **Initial Flow Only**, and it is not expected to change:

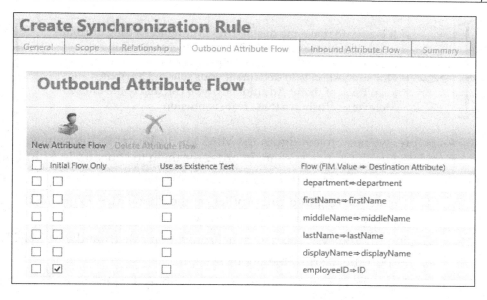

9. **Inbound Attribute Flow** is just as easy as before. Notice how the **mobile** attribute flows to the **mobile** attribute in the Metaverse. In the Metaverse, you have both the **mobile** attribute and the **mobilePhone** attribute to choose from:

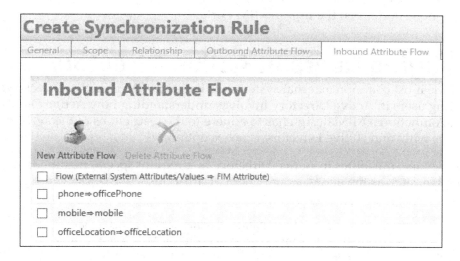

It is easy to make the mistake of selecting the wrong attribute in the Metaverse when configuring synchronization rules, especially when there are multiple attributes to choose from. Our suggestion is to document your selected attributes and keep track of them! Additionally, you can delete the unused Metaverse attributes that create confusion.

10. As before, we need to configure the MIM MA to export the attributes populated by the phone system, in order for them to show up in MIM Portal.

11. You then need to carry out the following steps:

    1. Create the required run profiles on the Phone MA: **Export, Full Import, Full Sync**, and **Delta Sync**.

    2. Import and sync the new synchronization rule from the MIM MA.

    3. Export the users to the phone system.

    4. Have the operators of the phone system update the user object with the relevant data.

    5. Import and sync the new information from the phone system.

    6. Export it to the MIM MA.

12. If all works as it should, you will be able to see the information from the phone system on the user in MIM Portal.

Managing users in Active Directory

One of the most common external systems we have in MIM is Active Directory. Managing users in Active Directory involves understanding how Active Directory works. A functional MIM design has to adhere to the restrictions of the systems it interfaces with, and Active Directory is no exception.

There are some attributes in Active Directory that require special treatment and knowledge, such as the `userAccountControl` attribute.

Note that in our implementation, the idea is that management of normal users in Active Directory is to be made using MIM, but the initial password is set by the users themselves when they visit the security officer's desk to identify themselves and sign a form about account usage. At the desk, there is a small web application where the user can fill in his initial password.

The userAccountControl attribute

The `userAccountControl` attribute is most commonly used in identity implementations to enable or disable a user account. Reviewing `http://support.microsoft.com/kb/305144`, you will find the attribute is a bunch of bit flags. To control it, we need to understand the meaning of each bit and modify the appropriate bits accordingly.

If we would like to create (provision) a normal enabled account, we would set the `userAccountControl` attribute to integer value 512. Once the account is provisioned, however, we would add or subtract bit flags, but never set the attribute value directly, because we can inadvertently remove account information. For example, let's say an account that requires smart cards needs to be disabled. The `userAccountControl` integer value for such an account for would be 262656. If you were to simply set the `userAccountControl` attribute to 514, you would remove the fact that the account required smart cards. Instead, you should add 2 bits to the existing value in `userAccountControl` to disable the account. For this account, the integer value would be 262658, and in other accounts, the value could be something else.

`ACCOUNTDISABLE` is the flag we need to modify in order to enable or disable a user account. To do this, we have to use the **BitAnd** and **BitOr** functions in our synchronization rules:

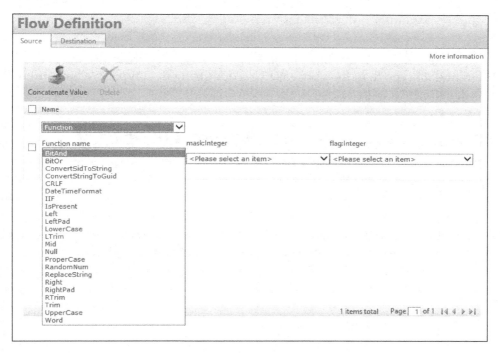

BitAnd and **BitOr** are just two of the built-in functions we can use in our synchronization rules. We will not give you a complete description of each function in this book, because they are well described on the Microsoft TechNet site.

Once you understand the functions, using `CustomExpression` is usually a little easier to use, because you can copy and paste the function directly into the text box.

This could then end up with an expression such as the following:

```
IIF(active,IIF(IsPresent(userAccountControl),BitAnd(922337203685477580
5,userAccountControl),512),IIF(IsPresent(userAccountControl),BitOr(2,u
serAccountControl),514))
```

In this example, we have added a Boolean attribute active to the schema, and the value of that attribute controls whether the Active Directory account should be enabled or disabled. We also check whether `userAccountControl` has a value or not. If it has an existing value, we modify the bit flags; otherwise, we set it to the standard value of 512 or 514. If you wonder where the value 9223372036854775805 came from, it is the maximum value of the 64-bit signed integer, 9223372036854775807, minus 2.

A deeper explanation and more information on this can be found at `http://social.technet.microsoft.com/wiki/contents/articles/how-to-enable-or-disable-accounts-in-active-directory-domain-service-using-fim.aspx`.

`userAccountControl` is just one of many Active Directory attributes that have a different data type than the very easy Unicode string data types we have been working with, such as `givenName`, `sn`, and `displayName`.

Provisioning users to Active Directory

Creating users in Active Directory requires two attributes to be present:

- `sAMAccountName`
- `dn`

The dn (distinguished name) attribute tells MIM where in Active Directory to put the user, and `sAMAccountName` is the login name we use for Active Directory.

One special attribute in Active Directory is `unicodePwd`; this can be used to set the initial password of a user, and this attribute can only be used with Initial Flow Only. You cannot use a synchronization rule to set `unicodePwd` to change the password on the user after it has been created.

Let's walk through the very basic way of provisioning users to AD using EREs (Outbound Synchronization Policy). This involves creating the following:

- A synchronization rule
- A set
- A workflow
- An MPR

Synchronization rule

We start by creating the outbound synchronization rule:

1. When working with Active Directory, I almost always separate the outbound and inbound synchronization. So, we create a synchronization rule with **Outbound** as **Data Flow Direction**, and select the resources based on the **Outbound Synchronization Policy** for the **Apply Rule** option:

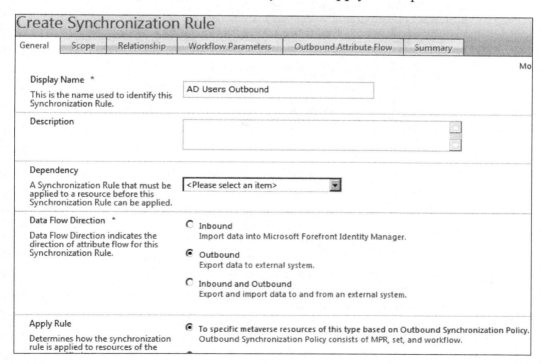

2. The resource types are **person** in the **Metaverse Resource Type** and **user** in the **External System Resource Type**:

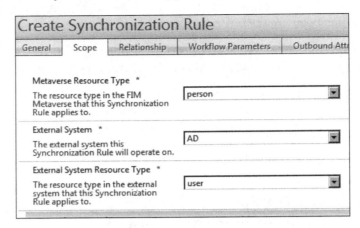

3. We check **Create resource in external system** to enable provisioning. Since you are doing an outbound-only rule, and the plan is that MIM should create all users in AD, it is easy to forget **Relationship Criteria**:

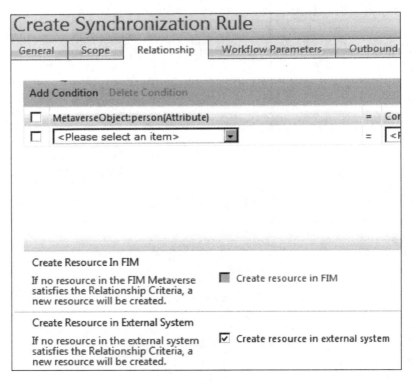

4. If you forget **Relationship Criteria**, you will get an error reminding you to configure it, as seen in the following screenshot:

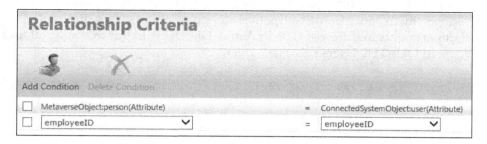

5. In this example, we have no **Workflow Parameters**. But in many cases, an MIM deployment has some custom workflows that will give parameters to use in your synchronization rule. A typical example in this case, when doing AD provisioning, would be a custom workflow creating the initial password:

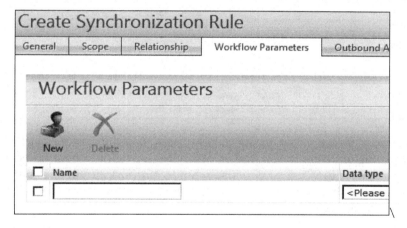

6. When defining the attribute flow for AD, there are many times when the built-in functions are useful. This example shows how the **Distinguished Name (DN)** is built. The DN is often also dependent on things such as department, since many companies store user objects from different departments in different OUs in Active Directory. In our example, all users are in **OU=TFC Users**:

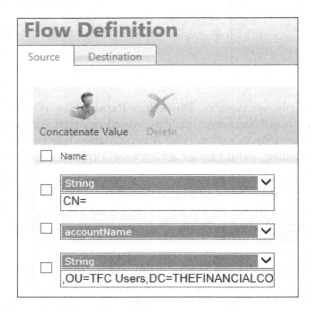

7. To provision users to AD, the dn attribute flow should be marked **Initial Flow Only**. However, if you also want to support moving or changing the dn attribute of the user, you need to add the same flow without the **Initial Flow Only** checkbox:

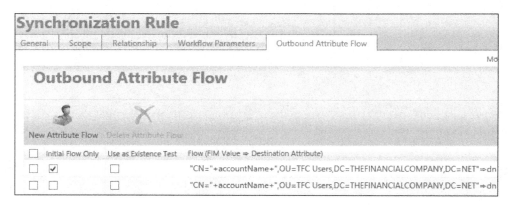

Creating the set

We then need to create the set that contains the users we would like to provision to AD. This is done as follows:

1. Before we start to create a set, we need to decide its purpose and content. That way, we can give it a descriptive name. Since MIM contains a large number of out-of-the-box sets, we have seen some businesses prefix their own sets with something to make them easier to find and distinct from the built-in ones:

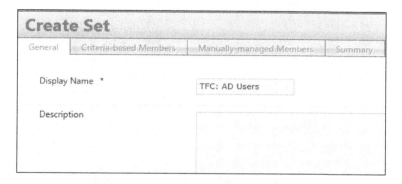

2. The set used to determine who should have an account in Active Directory is usually based on some criteria. Here, the criterion is that **Employee Type** is either **Employee** or **Contractor**. Try keeping your criterion as simple as possible; otherwise, troubleshooting set membership can become quite problematic. Use the **View Members** button to verify that you've got the correct content in your set:

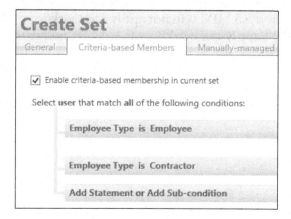

Setting up the workflow

We need a workflow to add the synchronization rule as an ERE on the user:

1. We need a workflow of type **Action** that is used to add the **Outbound Synchronization Rule** to the user objects. We will name it **TFC: Add AD Users Outbound**:

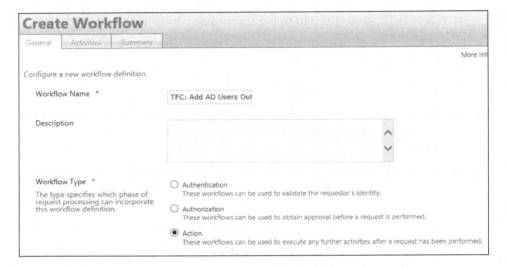

2. There is a vital checkbox on the **General** tab called **Run on Policy Update**. This is required if you have users that are already members in a set that you would like to apply the workflow on. This will be clear when we do the MPR, but basically what we will say is that MIM should run this workflow when users become part of the set. For existing members, that event has already occurred, so MIM will not apply the workflow. Checking this box will make MIM apply the workflow to existing members, which is normally not needed:

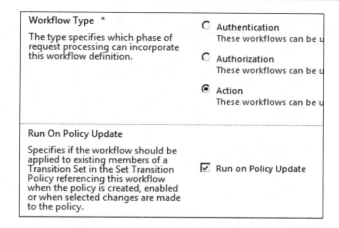

 Enable **Run on Policy Update** only when you must reapply the workflow to all applicable objects whenever the MPR is changed. Keep it off (unchecked) in all other circumstances.

3. In the **Activities** tab, in this case, select the **Synchronization Rule Activity** option. In rare cases, you might also want this workflow to do more than one activity, such as sending a notification:

4. Select the synchronization rule and the action to perform. In this case, it is the **AD Users Outbound** synchronization rule; select **Add** for the **Action Selection** option:

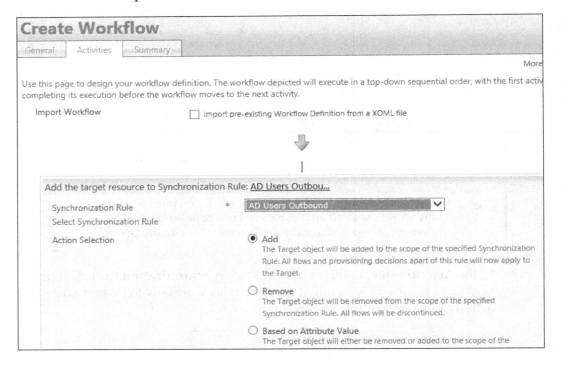

Creating the MPR

Finally, we need to create the MPR that will trigger the workflow:

1. Once again, since there are many built-in MPRs, I recommend using some kind of prefix to distinguish your own. The **Type** for this MPR is **Set Transition**. This means it will trigger due to some object entering or leaving a set:

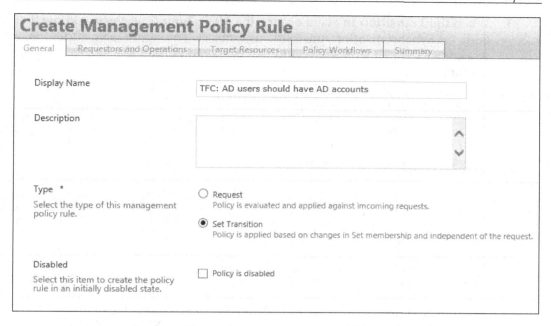

2. The set we are interested in is our newly created one, containing the users we would like to have in AD. This MPR should get triggered when there is a **Transition In** event, that is, when someone becomes a member of this set:

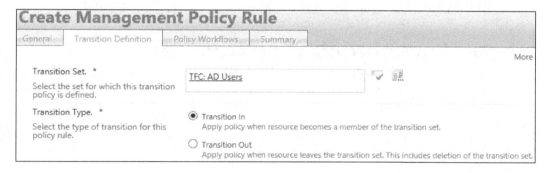

3. When the **Transition In** event occurs, the MPR should run the workflow that adds the synchronization rule to the user object. You might have additional workflows defined that you would like triggered in this case, such as sending a notification:

Create Management Policy Rule

General | Transition Definition | Policy Workflows | Summary

Action Workflows

	Display Name	Description	Run On Policy Update
☑	TFC: Add AD Users Outbound		No

4. After creating the MPR, you can look at a user in MIM Portal. On the **Provisioning** tab, you will see that you have a new ERE in the **ERL (Expected Rules List)** with a status of **Pending**, since we have not run any synchronization yet. If you run a cycle of synchronizations, you will be able to verify that the users have been created in Active Directory, and the status of the ERE on the user in MIM Portal will then change to **Applied**.

Inbound synchronization from AD

Depending on what we would like to do, there are some attributes required in MIM that AD can provide. In order for a user to be able to log in to the MIM portal or authenticate against MIM Service using some other client, the MIM Service DB requires three attributes:

- `AccountName`
- `Domain`
- `ObjectSID`

In MIM Service, the combination of `Domain` and `AccountName` has to be unique. In this context, `Domain` is the NetBIOS name of the Active Directory.

If you, like The Financial Company, have a single-domain forest, you can import `Domain` as a constant. If you have a multi-domain forest, you need to add some logic to get the correct `Domain` value.

In order to import `userAccountControl`, we extended the Metaverse schema with a new attribute named `userAccountControl`.

The **Attribute type** for `userAccountControl` is **Number**, and we will store the decimal value of the attribute:

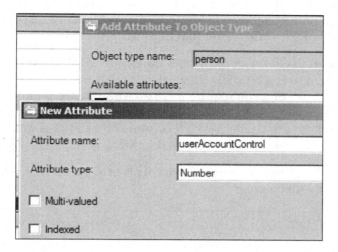

Inbound Attribute Flow might look like the following:

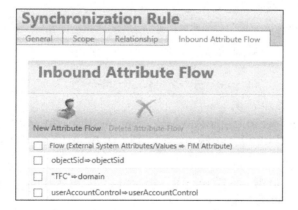

You should also verify whether you are configured to export the required attributes, `AccountName`, `Domain`, and `ObjectSID`, to MIM Service in order for the user to be able to log in to Portal.

Temporal sets

In many situations when we manage users, we are working with time-dependent actions.

For example, we might state that a user should be disabled in Active Directory the day his/her employment ends, but should be deleted from AD 30 days after the end of their employment. How do we do that in MIM?

First of all, we need to get the employment dates into MIM. Usually, we get them from the HR system. It is a bit tricky to work with date/time attributes, since localization and formatting can require us to do some troubleshooting before we get it right. You will very likely end up using the built-in `DateTimeFormat` function when importing date/time data from HR or some other source, and converting it to the *yyyy-MM-ddTHH:mm:ss.000* format used in MIM.

We then create what is called a **temporal set**. This is just a normal set, but we use a criterion that is time-dependent:

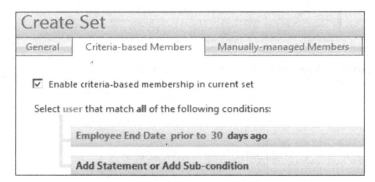

We can then use this set to trigger an MPR that modifies an attribute, such as the active attribute I used in my previous example, or an MPR that triggers some workflows.

In the MIM Service DB, there is an SQL job that evaluates these temporal sets once a day; the default time is 1 AM. If that is the time at which you also have some backups or run profiles scheduled, you should consider changing the schedules to avoid conflicts:

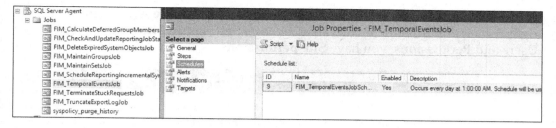

Self-service using MIM Portal

For users to be able to log in to the MIM portal and authenticate to MIM Service, we need three attributes populated for the user: `AccountName`, `Domain`, and `ObjectSID`.

But even if we have populated these attributes in MIM Service, and a standard user tries to log in to the portal (`https://MIMPortal/IdentityManagement`), the person will get the message shown in the following screenshot:

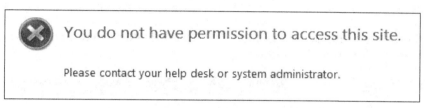

Why? Well, because there is no MPR enabled by default to allow users to access MIM Portal and/or MIM Service. The MPRs required to allow access to users are disabled by default. We just need to enable them in order for users to have access.

The MPRs we need to enable are as follows:

- **General**: Users can read non-administrative configuration resources
- **User management**: Users can read attributes of their own

Moreover, if you look back, you might recall that we had some options during installation talking about user access as well. There was a checkbox that said **Grant Authenticated Users access to the MIM Portal Site**. If you forgot to allow that during setup, don't panic. This setting is only to allow SharePoint access, and we can fix this now if we forgot to do so earlier.

If you start MIM Portal as the administrator, you will find **Site Actions** in the upper-right corner, and from there you can access **Site Settings**. In **Site Settings**, below **Users and Permissions**, you have **Site permissions**:

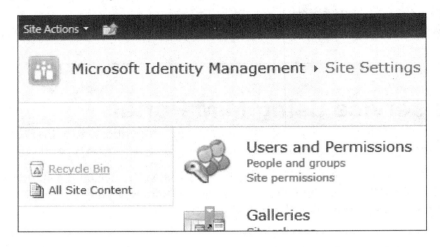

Follow that link into **Permissions** and add **Authenticated Users** with **Read** permissions, as shown in the following screenshot:

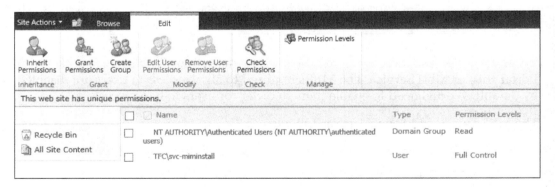

After fixing the MPRs and verifying that users have SharePoint permissions, the user will be able to access Portal:

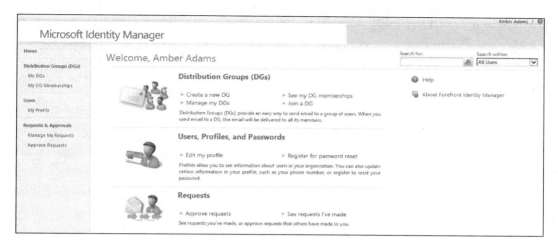

Compared to the view that the administrator has, the user's view is quite limited. If the user tries to do something, they will find that they are unable to do anything except look at some of their own attributes. They cannot modify anything, or see any other users. For that to be possible, we need to enable some other MPRs, and maybe configure new ones in order for the user to be able to work in the portal.

Managers can see direct reports

Let's walk through the creation of a new MPR allowing managers to read information about their direct reports:

1. This MPR is of type **Request**. If you are going to use MIM for self-service, you will likely end up with quite a few MPRs. Make sure you give them good descriptive names, and also a good description so that it will be easy to understand the purpose just by looking at them in the future:

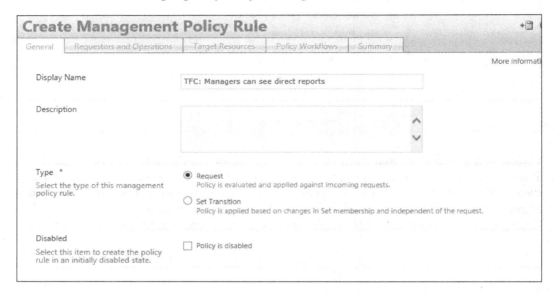

2. You will now start to see the beauty of using MIM to manage users. We can define the **Requestor** as **Relative to Resource**. What we are saying is that the **Requestor** should be the user referenced in the **Manager** attribute of the user that we try to look at or modify. The **Operation** in this case is just **Read resource,** but you can easily see how a similar MPR might allow a manager to modify some attributes as well. Finally, we need to check **Grants permission**:

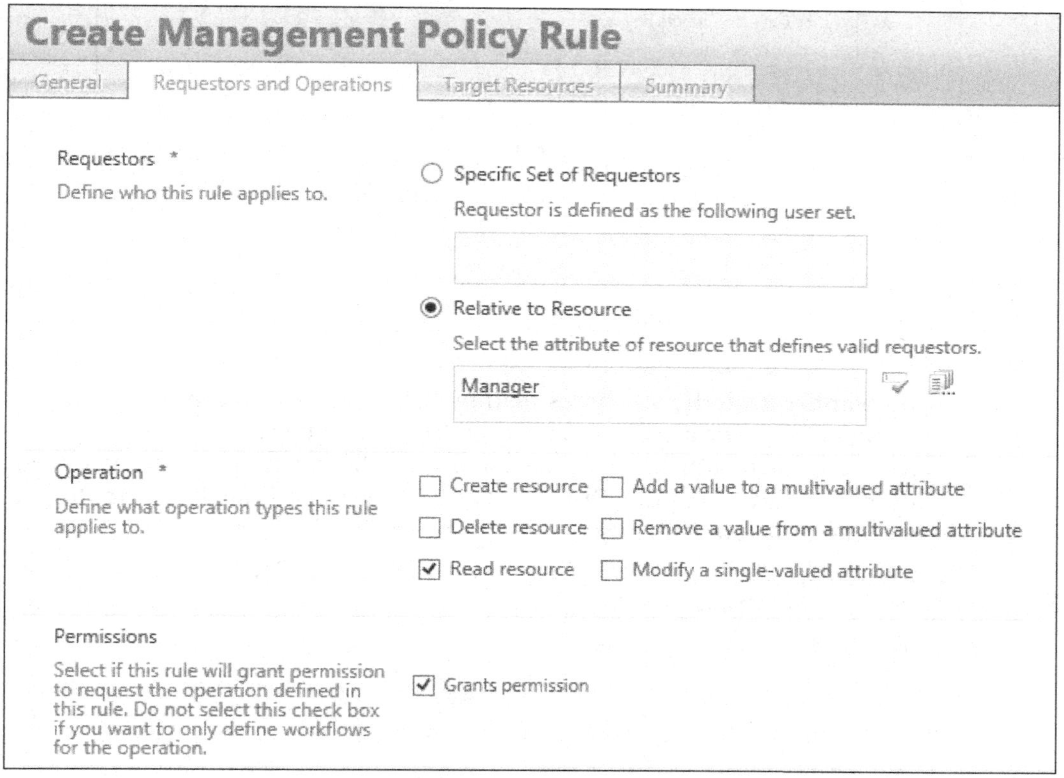

Create Management Policy Rule

| General | Requestors and Operations | Target Resources | Summary |

Requestors *

Define who this rule applies to.

○ Specific Set of Requestors

Requestor is defined as the following user set.

◉ Relative to Resource

Select the attribute of resource that defines valid requestors.

Manager

Operation *

Define what operation types this rule applies to.

☐ Create resource ☐ Add a value to a multivalued attribute

☐ Delete resource ☐ Remove a value from a multivalued attribute

☑ Read resource ☐ Modify a single-valued attribute

Permissions

Select if this rule will grant permission to request the operation defined in this rule. Do not select this check box if you want to only define workflows for the operation.

☑ Grants permission

3. The target resource in this case could be **All People**, or some other set containing the users we want the managers to see. In this case, we allow the managers to see all the attributes of their direct reports:

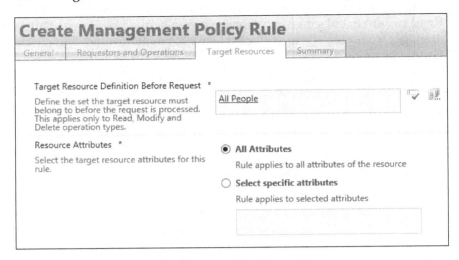

4. If you want to limit the attributes read by managers in this example, just select **Select specific attributes** and type (separated by semicolons) — or search and select — attributes in the list of available attributes. Just remember that you will have to update this MPR as soon as there is a new attribute you would like the managers to see:

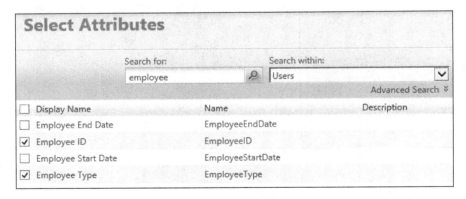

5. The result of this MPR will be that when a manager searches for users in MIM Portal, they will only find themselves and any of their direct reports.

Allowing users to manage their own attributes

Another typical scenario is that we want users to manage some attributes of their own. This could, for example, be information such as a mobile phone number.

In order for this to work, we need to create a new MPR that gives the users permission to change selected attributes. This MPR is of type **Request**. If you are going to use MIM for self-service, you will likely end up with quite a few MPRs:

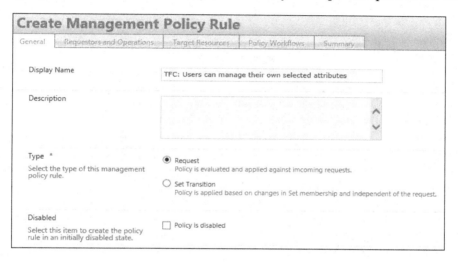

6. This time, we set the **Requestor** as **Relative to Resource**, based on **Resource ID**. This is the same as saying self. We want to allow **Modify a single-valued attribute**. If you are to allow the users in this scenario to manage a multi-value attribute, you will need to also allow both adding and removing a value in multi-valued attributes:

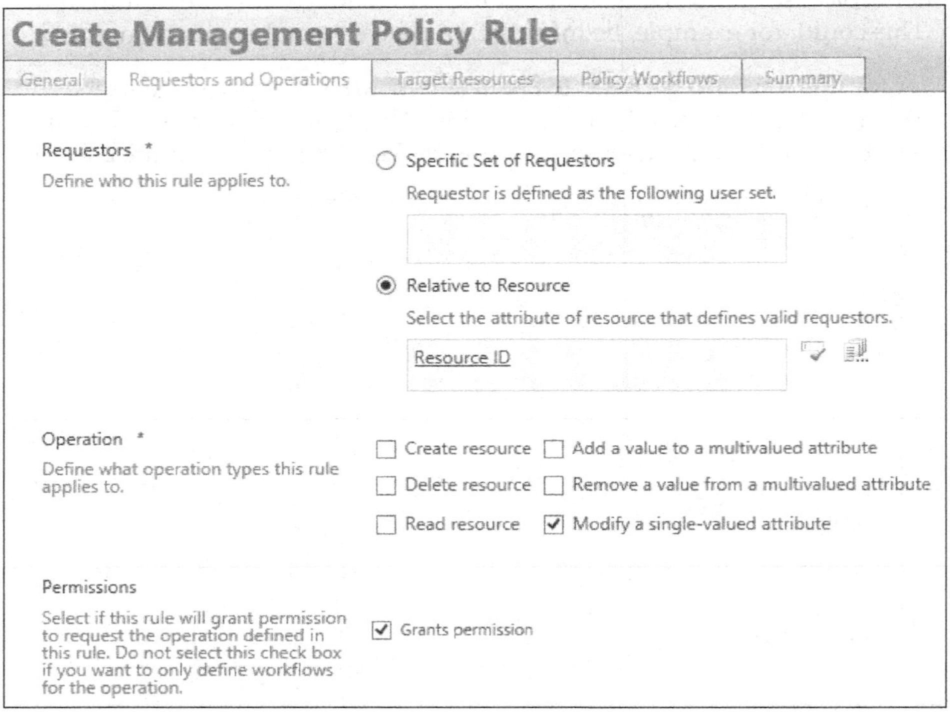

7. If you would like, say, only contractors to have this ability, you could set the target to **All Contractors** rather than **All Users**. And in this case, when we talk about modifying, we always define the attributes. You should not allow administrators to modify **All Attributes**:

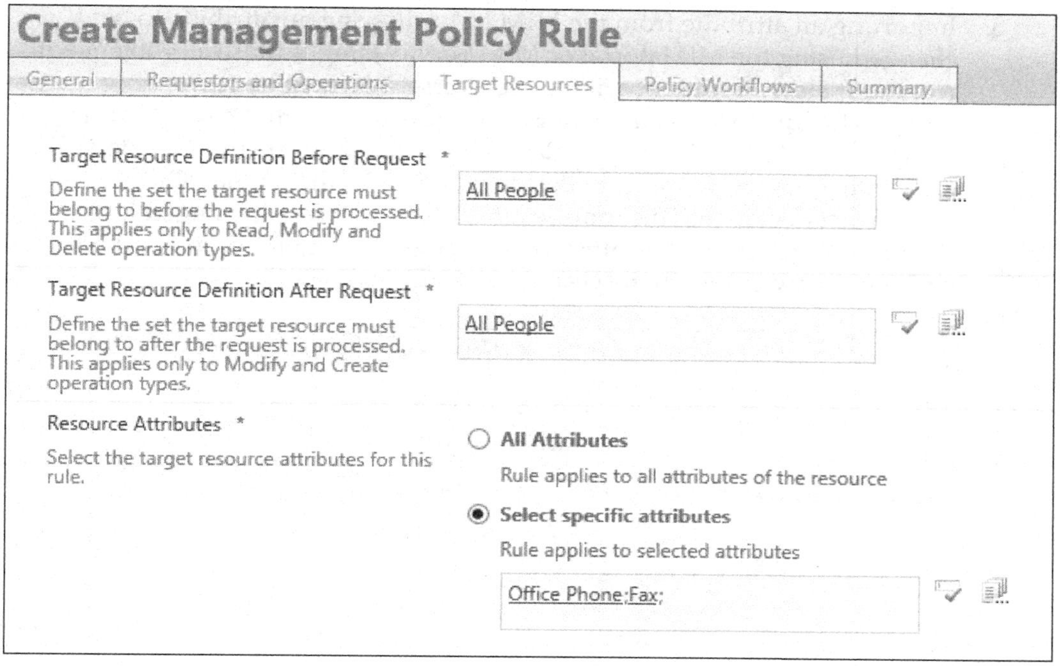

Create Management Policy Rule

General | Requestors and Operations | Target Resources | Policy Workflows | Summary

Target Resource Definition Before Request *

Define the set the target resource must belong to before the request is processed. This applies only to Read, Modify and Delete operation types.

All People

Target Resource Definition After Request *

Define the set the target resource must belong to after the request is processed. This applies only to Modify and Create operation types.

All People

Resource Attributes *

Select the target resource attributes for this rule.

○ **All Attributes**

Rule applies to all attributes of the resource

◉ **Select specific attributes**

Rule applies to selected attributes

Office Phone;Fax;

For some scenarios, you might want to also kick off some workflows as the request is made. It could, for example, be an authorization workflow requesting that the change be approved by a manager before being applied, or maybe an action workflow sending a notification to the user about the change.

8. Importing an attribute from the MIM MA (allowing an attribute to be changed using the MIM portal or MIM Service) might cause a problem with **Attribute Flow Precedence** in the Metaverse. We need to decide how we are going to handle this. In our example, we now have both the MIM Service and the phone system trying to populate the **mobile** attribute in the Metaverse. If a conflict occurs, we need to decide who will be the winner. Or maybe, we can just decide that the **mobile** attribute is no longer managed by the phone system, remove the attribute from the inbound flow, and add it to the outbound flow in the Phone system synchronization rule:

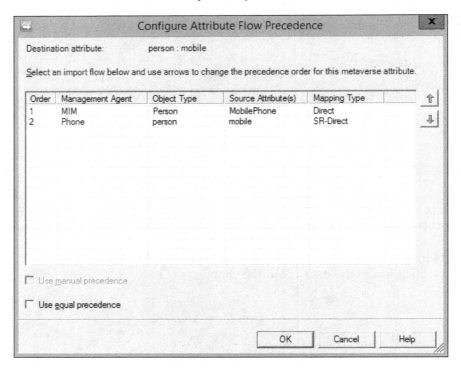

The authors suggest avoiding the use of the **Use equal precedence** setting. Checking that box would mean the last writer wins, meaning multiple systems associated with the attribute can overwrite one another within the Metaverse. From an operational perspective, if you were to use an equal precedence attribute to trigger a workflow, and the systems had different values, you would see the workflow re-trigger every time a synchronization is performed. Microsoft has announced that equal precedence will eventually be removed from the product, so you might as well not use it.

Managing Exchange

When managing users, we usually also find that we need to manage e-mail settings, or even e-mail systems. Microsoft Exchange is a common on-premises enterprise e-mail system.

In order for MIM to also manage Exchange, there are some configuration settings and permissions required. Microsoft documentation recommends you to add your AD MA service account to the **Recipient Administrators** role group. However, you can eliminate unnecessary privileges by being more granular. Please see `http://bit.ly/MIMExchangeRecipient` for more information. There are no drawbacks, so please consider granting your service accounts the least privileges they need.

In order for us to manage the attributes used and required by Exchange, we will need some knowledge about Exchange. There are, for example, multiple types of recipients to deal with.

At The Financial Company, they have decided that all employees should have a mailbox (recipient type: `UserMailbox`) but contractors should be mail-enabled users (recipient type: `MailUser`). Each recipient type requires a different set of attributes configured for them to work.

Exchange 2007

Wow, you're still using Exchange 2007? If you are, it is required that you install the management tools for Exchange 2007 on the MIM Synchronization Service server. MIM will use the Exchange PowerShell tools to tell Exchange to update the recipient information.

On the **Configure Extensions** page of the Active Directory MA, select **Exchange 2007** for the **Provision for** option. Optionally, you can also configure the **RUS** (**Recipient Update Service**) server that MIM should use.

Exchange 2010 and later

Managing Exchange 2010 and later does not require any extra installation of tools on MIM, unless you consider PowerShell 2.0 as extra.

On the **Configure Extensions** page of the Active Directory MA, select **Exchange 2010** for the **Provision for** option, even if you are using a version of Exchange beyond 2010:

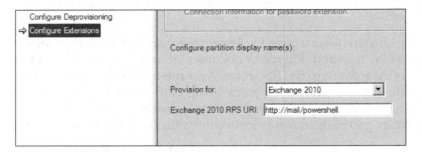

You also need to configure which **CAS (Client Access Server)** MIM should use to make the remote PowerShell call to update the recipient.

Synchronization rules for Exchange

We will create a synchronization rule for employees, and another one for contractors. These rules will work in addition to the general Active Directory synchronization rule responsible for creating the users in Active Directory.

First we need to add some attributes to the AD MA. The attributes listed next are a sample. In reality, you might manage more attributes, or like to import more Exchange-related attributes.

We have added the following:

- `homeMDB`
- `mail`
- `mailNickname`
- `mDBUseDefaults`
- `msExchHomeServerName`
- `targetAddress`

In this example, we create two separate outbound synchronization rules: one for employees that should get mailboxes, and one for contractors that should be mail-enabled users.

Mailbox users

The rules for mailbox users use **Outbound System Scoping Filter**, where **employeeType** equals **Employee**:

Outbound System Scoping Filter

Add Condition   Delete Condition

MetaverseObject:person(Attribute)	Operator	Value
employeeType ⌄	equal ⌄	Employee

The attributes required to create a mailbox user are as follows:

- homeMDB
- mailNickname
- msExchHomeServerName

As you can see, I do not set `ProxyAddresses`. This is because at The Financial Company, the generation of e-mail addresses for mailboxes is the responsibility of Exchange.

The tricky part is to find the `homeMDB` and `msExchHomeServerName` values that we need to use. Your Exchange admin should be able to provide them for you.

In our example, the following strings are mapped:

String value	Destination attribute
CN=TFCEX01,CN=Mailbox Database 1760172488,CN=Databases,CN=Exchange Administrative Group (FYDIBOHF23SPDLT),CN=Administrative Groups,CN=First Organization,CN=Microsoft Exchange,CN=Services,CN=Configuration,DC=THEFINANCIALCOMPANY,DC=NET	homeMDB
/o=First Organization/ou=Exchange Administrative Group (FYDIBOHF23SPDLT)/cn=Configuration/cn=Servers/cn=TFCEX01	msExchHomeServerName

It is required to have the `Email` attribute in the MIM Service database populated if we are to use any workflows relying on e-mails.

To get this information into MIM, we can add a flow of the `mail` attribute in AD (this usually contains the primary e-mail address of the user when you are using Microsoft Exchange as the e-mail system), and add `mail` to the `Email export` attribute flow in the MIM Service MA.

Mail-enabled users

The rules for mail-enabled users use **Outbound System Scoping Filter**, where **employeeType** equals **Contractor**:

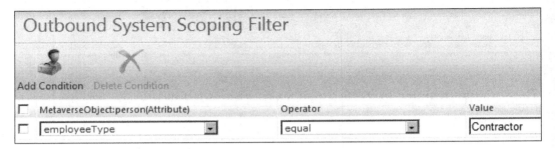

The **Outbound Attribute Flow** option required to create a mail-enabled user in Exchange 2010 is shown in the following screenshot:

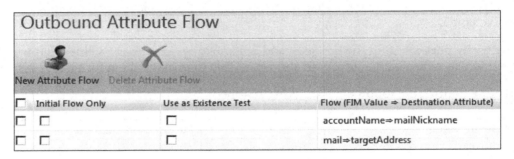

More considerations

It would be pretentious to think that anyone knows the right identity management approach for your organization without fully understanding the challenges and goals associated with your business processes and your technology. For some organizations, user management is defined as periodically updating a few attributes, while other organizations have a more evolved identity solution, and one or more actions will trigger multiple accounts to be provisioned, updated, or deprovisioned. Generally speaking, the authors agree that user management should strive to aggregate, manage, provision, deprovision, and synchronize changes.

MIM aggregates information into unique objects in the Metaverse. Thus, a user can have a single object representation for all their identities throughout the organization. In other words, the system that is authoritative for each piece of identity information builds a representation that we call a Metaverse object.

MIM is designed to interact with systems using Management Agents and/or with MIM Portal workflows. There's nothing stopping you from running scripts and custom applications outside the MIM synchronization engine and portal, of course (and this is how many perfectly working solutions have been implemented), but keep in mind that you will lose aggregation and centralized user management at the expense of operational complexity.

One of the first user management questions people ask, and maybe you're wondering this too, is whether attribute flows should be done using Portal Synchronization Rules or through the synchronization engine Management Agents. The question gets controversial too, because some architects lean very strongly towards one way or the other. Here are a few things to consider:

- Portal Synchronization Rules are great when mappings can be done using the built-in functions, but you will be forced to write code if you need anything beyond those functions.

- Some organizations may feel more comfortable using the built-in functions over code, especially if they do not have developers on staff.

- Using the Outbound Synchronization Policy means you will have ERE objects to synchronize in addition to your other objects using those synchronization rules. Your synchronization-run profiles, specifically full synchronizations, will be undoubtingly longer using OSPs than using synchronization engine attribute mappings with comparable rule extensions.

Summary

In this chapter, we have seen how the power of MIM allows you to manage identities out of the box, although some things require customization. We suggest building the basic, easier pieces first, and work on more advanced pieces in phases.

Before touching the MIM product, you will need to decide where the required unique attributes, such as `AccountName`, first-time password, and possibly things like e-mail address, are to be created.

We have also seen how easy it is to implement basic self-service using MIM Portal, which allows you to delegate some administration to the users themselves.

In the next chapter, we will extend this to groups, and look at how MIM can be used to enhance your group management.

6
Group Management

Once you have user management in place, it is usually time to start looking at group management. In many MIM implementations that we have done, group management capability has been the key reason for choosing MIM. Yet, in order to manage groups, we need to also have the users, who are supposed to be members, managed by MIM.

In this chapter, we will look at the following topics in depth:

- Group scope and types
- Modifying MPRs for group management
- Creating and managing distribution groups
- Managing groups in AD
- Installing client add-ins

Group scope and types

We need to understand how groups in MIM work, and since Active Directory is so common, we will use that as a comparison.

Active Directory

If you go into AD and create a group, you are asked about **Group scope** and **Group type**.

This selection will end up in the attribute called `groupType` in AD. This is a bitmask attribute stored in Active Directory, as described in the following table (as well as at `http://bit.ly/GroupTypeFlags`):

Value	Description
1 (0x00000001)	Specifies a group that is created by the system. If you look at AD in the `CN=Builtin` container, you will find groups with this flag set.
2 (0x00000002)	Specifies a group with global scope.
4 (0x00000004)	Specifies a group with domain local scope.
8 (0x00000008)	Specifies a group with universal scope.
16 (0x00000010)	Specifies an `APP_BASIC` group for Windows Server Authorization Manager.
32 (0x00000020)	Specifies an `APP_QUERY` group for Windows Server Authorization Manager.
2147483648 (0x80000000)	Specifies a security group. If this flag is not set, then the group is a distribution group.

As with the `userAccountControl` attribute on user objects, we need to make sure that we manage this attribute using bit handling.

However, the bit for the Security group is 2^{31}, and the rule is that if the value of a 32-bit integer is larger than $2^{31} - 1$, subtract 2^{32} (which is 4,294,967,296). The value of the `groupType` attribute for a universal security group becomes:

2,147,483,656 - 4,294,967,296 = - 2,147,483,640

Here *2,147,483,656* is *2,147,483,648 (Security)* + *8 (Universal)*.

So what we then end up with is the following table describing the values we need to set in AD for the `groupType` value for each group scope and type:

Group scope/type	groupType value
Universal Distribution Group	8
Global Distribution Group	2
Domain Local Distribution Group	4
Universal Security Group	-2,147,483,640
Global Security Group	-2,147,483,646
Domain Local Security Group	-2,147,483,644

If you have to change these values using MIM, you might need to consider whether you are required to do a bit operation, or whether you can just change the values. Today, there is a tendency towards creating only universal groups, and therefore, changes of the scope are rare. In AD, we also need to remember that there are rules controlling the group types that a given type of group can have as members. This is another reason for creating universal groups.

Group scope and type in MIM

In MIM, however, the service schema for groups looks quite different.

In MIM, we not only have the scope and type, but also need to look at other attributes.

Type

If you look at the schema in MIM, you will find that the group type can be **Distribution**, **Security**, or **MailEnabledSecurity**:

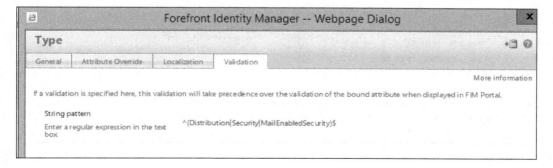

This means that if we need to import a group from AD into MIM, we need to check the bits of the `groupType` attribute, and set the type in MIM accordingly.

It might look similar to the following statement in our inbound synchronization rule:

```
IIF(Eq(BitOr(63,groupType),63),"Distribution","Security")
```

The preceding statement does not, however, take care of groups that might be mail-enabled security groups. If we use the MIM portal to create a **MailEnabledSecurity** group, it will require us to also fill in the **E-mail Alias**:

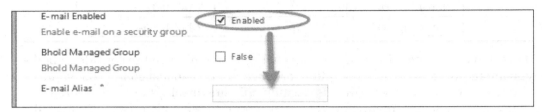

In AD, this is represented by `mailNickname` if you are running Microsoft Exchange as the e-mail system.

Scope

Scope is very similar to the corresponding setting in AD. If you look at the MIM schema, you will find that scope can be **DomainLocal**, **Global**, or **Universal**:

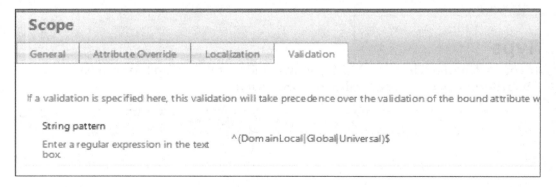

So, if we are to import groups from AD, we need to check the bits for scope in the AD `groupType` attribute when importing groups.

So the inbound synchronization rule that we use to import groups from AD might contain something similar to the following:

```
IIF(Eq(BitAnd(2,groupType),2),"Global",IIF(Eq(BitAnd(4,groupType),4),"
DomainLocal","Universal"))
```

As you can see, we need to use the bit operating functions to check the bits, rather than checking the value of the `groupType` attribute.

Member selection

When you try to create a group using MIM Portal, you will be asked about **Member Selection**:

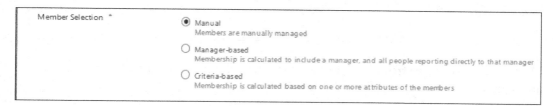

Depending on what we choose here, there are a few attributes involved. **Member Selection** does not correspond to just one attribute, but will affect several.

In MIM, we have two types of groups when it comes to membership selection. They can be **Manual** (static) or **Criteria-based** (dynamic); **Manager-based** is just a special case of **Criteria-based** selection.

Manual groups

If you choose **Manual**, the Boolean attribute `MembershipLocked` will be `false`. This also means that if we want to import groups with memberships from AD or some other source, we need to set this to `false`.

When creating a manual group, we also get the opportunity to set **Join Restriction**:

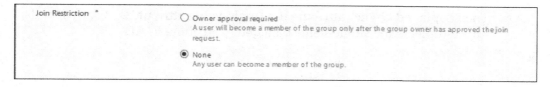

The **Join Restriction** selection corresponds to an attribute called `MembershipAddWorkflow`. If we look in the MIM schema, we will see that this attribute can have three values—**None**, **Custom**, and **Owner Approval**:

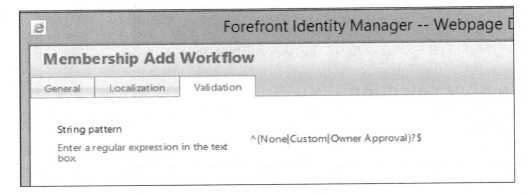

If we import a group from an external system, such as AD, the attribute `MembershipAddWorkflow` should be set to `None`.

 Keep in mind that when a request is made from Synchronization Service using the Built-in Synchronization account, the authorization workflow step is skipped.

Hence, as authorization workflows are skipped when requests come from Synchronization Service, we cannot have **Owner Approval** on a group managed by an external system through Synchronization Service.

In order for us to use **Owner Approval**, we also need to configure the owner.

In MIM, there are two owner attributes: **Owner** and **Displayed Owner**:

- The **Owner** attribute is used for **Owner Approval** workflows. This is a multi-value attribute that lets us define multiple owners that can approve the request.
- The **Displayed Owner** attribute is a single-value attribute that corresponds, for example, to the single-value `managedBy` attribute in AD.

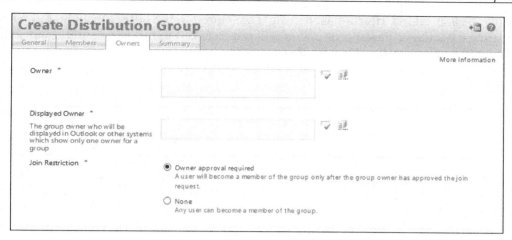

 Typically, **Owner** and **Displayed Owner** have the same value in MIM.

Manager-based groups

Manager-based is essentially a **Criteria-based** (dynamic) group. The difference is that when creating manager-based groups, the wizard in MIM will only ask you for **Manager**. This type of group is very useful, since it gives us a way to allow a manager to have a group that reports to him/her directly:

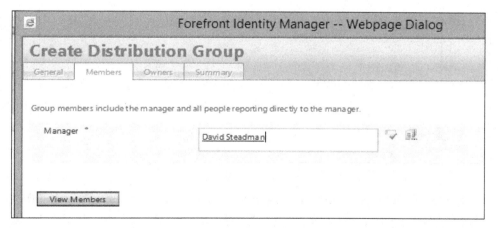

The result is that `MembershipAddWorkflow` is set to `None`, and `MembershipLocked` is set to `true`.

The criteria used in **Criteria-based** groups are stored in the **Filter** attribute. But when creating a **Manager-based** group, you will not be asked to fill in the criteria, since the filter will be generated automatically:

Filter	
A predicate defining a subset of the resources.	xmlns="http://schemas.xmlsoap.org/ws/2004/09/enumeration">/Person[(Manager = '1def1245-ec1f-4179-9998-4d725fbb1463') or (ObjectID = '1def1245-ec1f-4179-9998-4d725fbb1463')]</Filter>

In the previous example, **Filter** defines that members should all be **Person** objects, where **Manager** is the selected manager, or the **Person** object itself is the selected manager.

Criteria-based groups

A **Criteria-based** group is the most flexible version. Here you have the power to decide what the criteria for membership should look like.

As with **Manager-based** groups, MembershipAddWorkflow is set to None and MembershipLocked is set to true. But here, you will have to define **Filter** yourself:

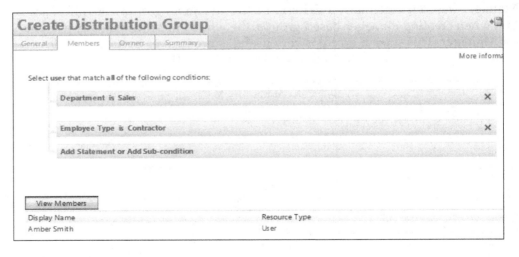

In complex scenarios, you might not even be able to define the criteria using the wizard, but will instead open up the advanced properties of the group and manually edit the **Filter** attribute.

Your criteria could contain some time references like the ones in the following screenshot:

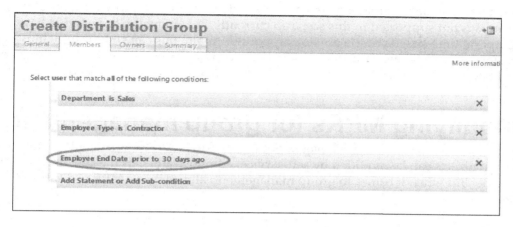

The **Temporal** attribute of the group object is checked:

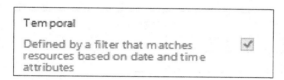

Please remember that temporal groups are only recalculated every 24 hours (by default) around temporal sets, depending on the SQL job, as covered in *Chapter 5, User Management*.

A new feature that was introduced in a later version of Forefront Identity Manager 2010 R2 is **Deferred Evaluation**. Deferred evaluation is used to eliminate the evaluation of the group in real time to hold the evaluation for a later time. This improves performance when dealing with large groups:

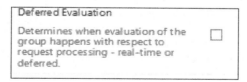

This setting can be enabled globally under the system configuration setting by default. But when you enable this feature, there are two limitations that you need to understand. First, the group would not be calculated in real time. Nested groups is not supported in this scenario currently. Additionally, groups that have temporal time-based criteria are not supported. Again, this can significantly improve performance when we talk about groups, but you need to understand the impact and limitations when considering enabling this feature on large group objects.

Modifying MPRs for group management

There are less than a dozen **Management Policy Rules** (**MPRs**) that control how group objects can be modified by self-service, administrators, or the synchronization engine. But when it comes to group management, almost every MPR is disabled by default:

☐ Distribution list management: Owners can update and delete groups they own	Modify, Delete, Add, Remove
☐ Distribution list Management: Users can add or remove any members of groups subject to owner approval	Add, Remove
☐ Distribution list management: Users can add or remove any members of groups that don't require owner approval	Add, Remove
☐ Distribution List management: Users can create Static Distribution Groups	Create
☐ Security group management: Owners can update and delete groups they own	Modify, Delete, Add, Remove
☐ Security group management: Users can add or remove any member of groups subject to owner approval	Add, Remove
☐ Security Group management: Users can create Static Security Groups	Create
☐ Security groups: Users can add and remove members to open groups	Add, Remove

To start with, let's take a look at the distribution groups.

The Financial Company only wants employees to be able to create *static* distribution groups. The following steps will be required to allow that:

1. Enable and change the MPR **Distribution List management: Users can create Static Distribution Groups**. The MPR allowing the creation of this type of group is **Distribution List management: Users can create Static Distribution Groups**:

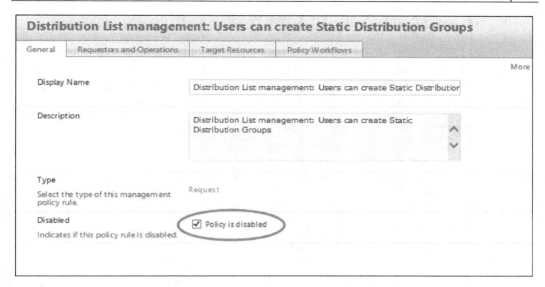

2. The set called **All Active People** is the default value of **Requestor**. We need to change that to **All Employees**, or confirm that we have employees only:

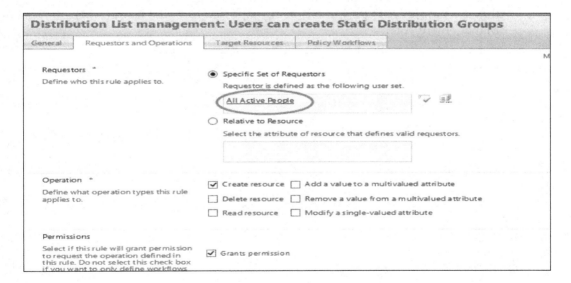

3. Lets navigate over to the **All Active People** set and update the MPR to confirm that it only contains employees. As a note, we need to make sure we have all the attributes on the users to make sure that the filters work. In *Chapter 5, User Management*, we may have updated the attribute flow from the Metaverse. But we would want to confirm this, just in case, by selecting **EmployeeType** and flow the attribute to the MIM service:

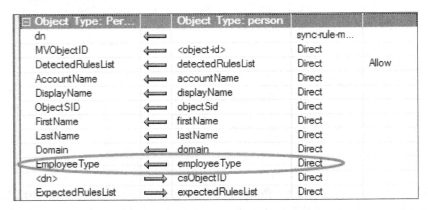

4. Update the set filter to only include **Employee** now that we have confirmed that the **EmployeeType** value is being exported from the MIM (FIM) Management Agent:

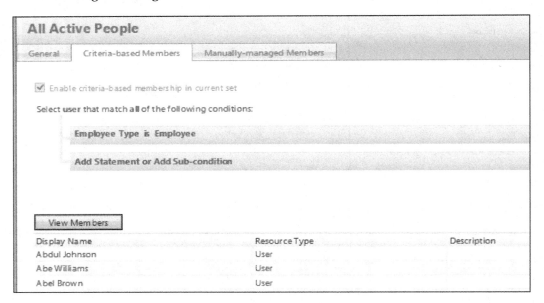

5. In order for users to be able to add themselves and owners to approve the requests, we need to also enable the following MPRs:

   ° Distribution list management: Owners can read attributes of group resources

   ° Distribution list management: Owners can update and delete groups they own

   ° Distribution list management: Users can add or remove any members of the groups, subject to owner approval

   ° Distribution list management: Users can add or remove any members of groups that don't require owner approval

   ° Distribution list management: Users can create Static Distribution Groups

   ° Distribution list management: Users can read selected attributes of group resources

Managing groups in AD

After looking at the groups and the types, we need to first bring the existing groups into MIM portal before we make it authoritative for group creation and management, so that all groups will be static in terms of membership. As discussed earlier, we now need to consider the `groupType` attribute in AD. We also need to consider whether we have different needs depending on the group type.

At The Financial Company, they have decided that MIM should not delete security groups once created in AD. This is a common approach, since deleting a security group—and thereby its **SID (Security ID)**—might cause dramatic events if the group is used for some kind of permission. Recreating a group with the same name will not recreate the SID, and will not fix the permissions.

On the other hand, when talking about distribution groups, we want MIM to be able to delete them. The owner might want to delete it, and will use the MIM portal interface to do so. Or, it could be that we have a policy stating that distribution groups where the owner has left The Financial Company and no new owner has been assigned should be deleted.

Before we begin to import or even export the groups, we need to make sure we have all the attributes needed from AD all the way from the Metaverse to MIM. First, let's select the attribute in the Active Directory Management Agent:

After selecting the object type to group, we need to select the attributes that we need to import. They are as follows:

- `displayName`
- `groupType`
- `managedBy`
- `member`
- `sAMAccountName`

Seeing The Financial Company, we are only bringing in from the AD so we would import via the sync rule from ADMA only, and then export flow in the FIM MA, as depicted in the following screenshot:

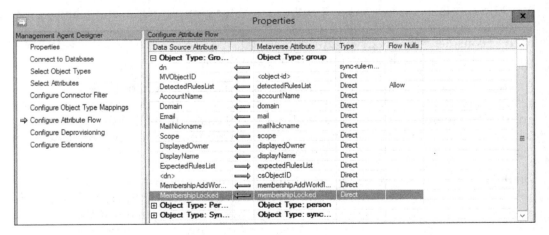

Once we complete the setup of the TFC environment, they will have groups managed in MIM and AD.

Security and distribution groups

The next area to tackle is creating groups from the portal. In the previous section, we were concerned with importing them from AD to get the baseline. Now we want the portal to be the authoritative source for creating groups and controlling membership.

Synchronization rule

In an effort to limit the ERE into the system, we can use a synchronization rule based on Inbound and Outbound System Scoping filters. The following screenshot shows what this synchronization rule might look like:

 In the previous and current versions, we see an all-in-one type of data flow rule. In our opinion, not using this type of rule is highly recommended since it might create an issue in rare cases such as sync rule fragmentation. If you have a combined rule, there is a chance that fragmentation occurs on both in and out flows.

1. We will not scope the inbound rule, but when you are looking to scope a rule, we would use that as a reminder that this scoping filter is an inclusion filter. Unlike the sync engine that uses exclusion type rules, the attributes in this filter must exist in the Metaverse:

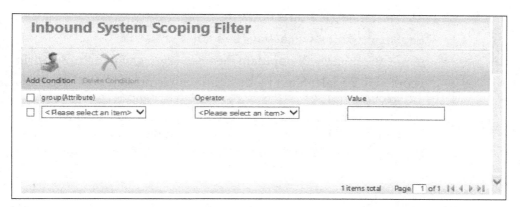

2. The next screen would be for setting the object join criteria. To be able to rejoin, in case we lose the connector to AD, we set up a **Relationship Criteria**. The `objectSid` attribute can be used, since these are only security groups. For added relationships, we will also use the `accountName` and `mail` attributes. To create the group in AD, we check the **Create resource in FIM** box:

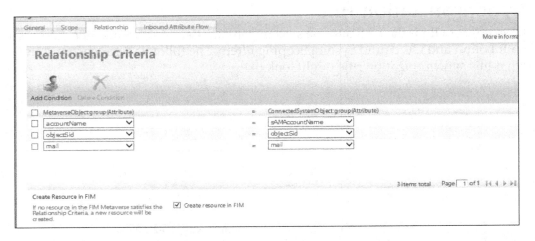

3. For the inbound flows, we need to be able to create the object in MIM Service and Portal. The following are the minimal attribute flows required for importing and for reverse joining criteria:

   ○ `DisplayName` is a direct flow

   ○ `Type` is an expression based on the group importing: `IIF(Eq(BitOr(14,groupType),14),"Distribution","Security")`

   ○ `Mail` is a direct flow

   ○ `Member` is a direct flow

   ○ `mailNickname` is a direct flow

   ○ `membershiplock` will always be set to `false`

   ○ `OwnerApproval` will populate the `membershipAddWorkflow` attribute

   ○ `Scope` will be calculated by the following expression: `IIF(Eq(BitAnd(2,groupType),2),"Global",IIF(Eq(BitAnd(4,groupType),4),"DomainLocal","Universal"))`

   ○ `Domain` will be static `"TFC"`. If we had multiple domains, we could use the SID to determine the domain. See Step 6 in the guide at `http://bit.ly/MIMSyncrules`:

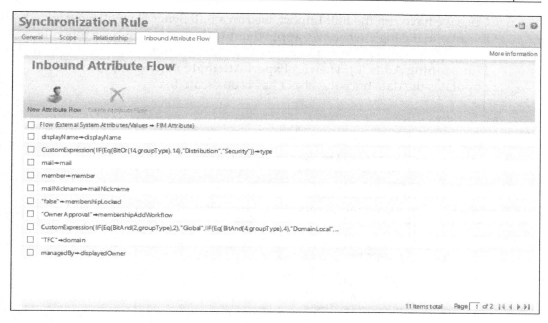

4. Now we just need to import the Sync Rule using the Full Import and Full Sync from the MIM/FIM MA:

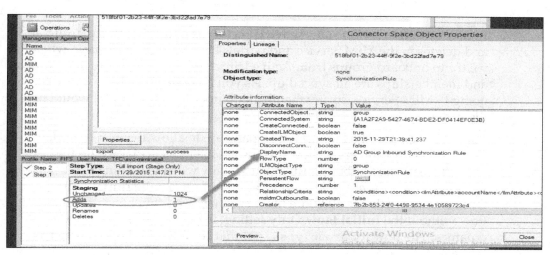

5. Then we can run the Full Import, and sync on the ADMA. This is a requirement, as we need to apply the new rule to every object in the connector space to confirm that it applies.

6. Once we have run the Full Import, we run a Full Sync. The Full Sync is the area in the logic where we apply the rule. In our case, we see this rule being applied and projected to the Metaverse (**1**), and then we see the four **Provisioning Adds** (**2**). Then an **Export Attribute Flow** is applied, which populates the data once the object has been created:

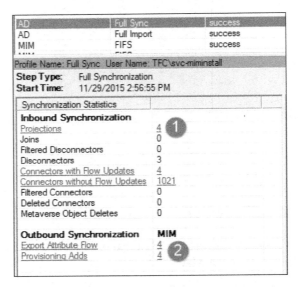

7. In the current setup thus far, Active Directory is authoritative for group add and deletes in the MIM Service and portal. This is a typical scenario when we try to onboard groups from Active Directory, and make sure that groups and memberships are all synced up. As you have seen, we have only exports going to MIM Service, so any membership updates in the portal would be discarded.

8. The next steps for The Financial Company are to allow the user to update the membership and create new groups via the MIM portal. To do this, we will create the Outbound Rule that we saw when managing users in *Chapter 5, User Management*—it is required to select the **Initial Flow Only** setting for the dn attribute flow. We then need the same attribute flow without the **Initial Flow Only** setting, in case we want to support renames. The flow for groupType is not that complex, and is expressed as follows: `"IIF(Eq(type,"Distribution"),IIF(Eq(scope,"Universal"),8,IIF(Eq(scope,"Global"),2,4)),IIF(Eq(scope,"Universal"),-2147483640,IIF(Eq(scope,"Global"),-2147483646,-2147483644)))"`

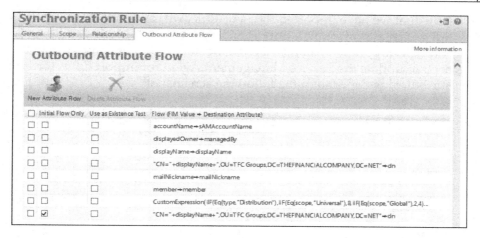

9. If we synchronize after creating this rule, we will get **Pending Export** to AD for the security or distribution groups that we created in the MIM portal:

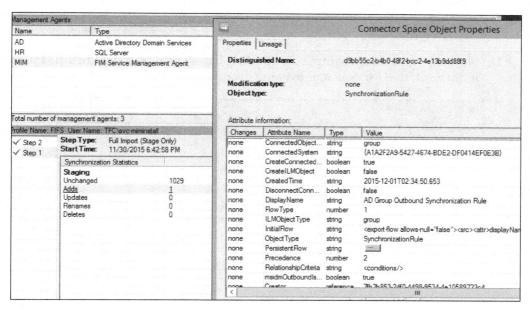

10. Now that we have imported the Sync Rule, we can test this rule by creating a test group, running a Full Import and Sync on the FIM MA, and then Export and Full Import Sync on the Active Directory MA. But before we do this, we need to update the Service Management Agent for import flows for group attributes, as depicted in the following screenshot:

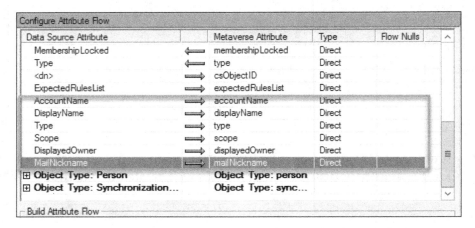

11. Now we can create a sample distribution list. In this example, the MIM portal is authoritative for new and existing groups:

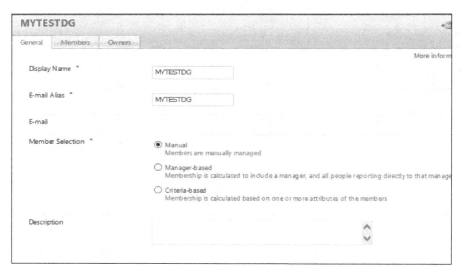

A few paragraphs later, we will discuss how we can make updates to AD and MIM for group memberships.

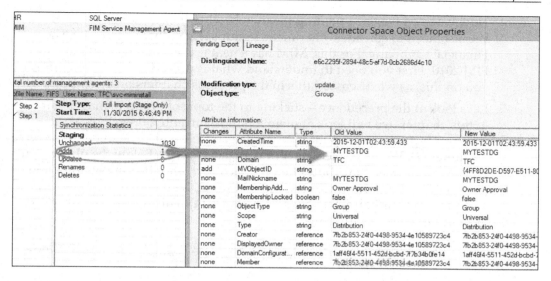

12. We see pending **Adds** to AD for our group when running a Full Import and Sync of the MIM MA:

13. Then we can do an export to AD for this group, followed by a confirming import:

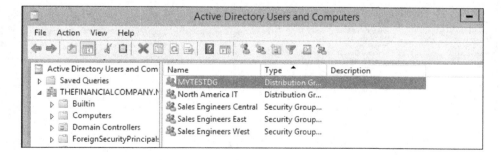

14. Now we need to start updating the membership in MIM and the portal. We also need to consider other memberships from other sources for The Financial Company. For this, MIM has a neat feature that was released in FIM 2010. First you need to understand what is **precedence**; we will refresh you on this, as we discussed this in the previous chapters on sync engine.

15. Let's look at the precedence — sticking to the topic of group management in this chapter, we will look at membership. Currently, if we look at membership, we open up the sync engine console and click on the **Metaverse Designer (1)**. We then select the group object type (**2**). Below the object, you will see all the listed attributes tied to this object, and the import flows and information about the attributes. We will select the **member** attribute (**3**), and click on **Configure Attribute Precedence (4)**. This screen tells us what is authoritative for the attribute:

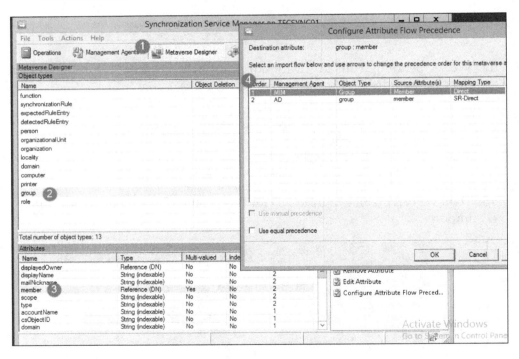

16. Take a look at the preceding screenshot. Currently the MIM Management Agent is authoritative for the `member` attribute, and then AD is secondary. This means that the `member` attribute in AD would get overwritten to whatever is in the MIM Service database. If nothing is present, and if we imported from AD, then the AD values would take precedence, because they are next in line. This works in most scenarios, such as HR and other related configurations. But for The Financial Company, we want to have two master sources of data and merge them at the center. If we set the `member` attribute to equal and look at the object in the Metaverse, we see the merger, as shown in the following screenshot:

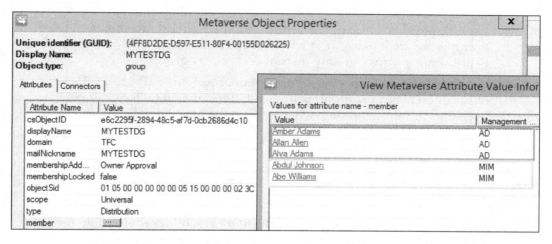

17. So, staying on this topic, let's look at a single value. With a single value attribute, equal precedence is last one wins. For example, if we update `displayName`, it would look something like this for a typical run of the Management Agents:

    ○ **MIM**: Sets `displayName` to `MYTESTDG`

    ○ **Active Directory**: Sets `displayName` to `MYNEWTESTDG`

    ○ **MIM**: Sets `displayName` back to `MYTESTDG`

18. In the next step, let's say, for instance, we did a run on the Active Directory MA out of band. This could be due to troubleshooting. Well, not taking into account a single value attribute, all `displayName` would be overwritten to the AD MA. Again, in this case, we would not see any effect, because the `displayName` was imported first. But to give you a scenario, let's say you disable a value from HR and then you import from an equal precedence source; you could disable or enable account based on that data.

19. The next step, then, is to look at the settings of the AD MA. If we set **Deprovisioning Options** to **Stage a delete on the object for the next export run**, the objects disconnected from the Metaverse will be deleted in AD on running the next export.

As you can see, this is a setting on the MA and will apply to all object types, not just the distribution groups. If you are concerned about MIM accidently deleting other object types, you can solve this in three ways, which are as follows:

- Use the **Determine with a rules extension** setting. This would require you to create a rules extension project and write a few lines of code. Read more about this option, and more on deprovisioning, at http://aka. ms/FIMDeprovisioning. This is the option we would recommend in the example we are looking at. It would require about five lines of code to delete distribution groups but only disconnect security groups.

- Use the **Make them disconnectors** option, configure MIM to send a notification about the group being ready for deletion to, for example, the Exchange admins, and they will carry out the actual deletion of the group.

- Narrow down the permission used by the account that is used by MIM to access AD.

The set we can use for provisioning, in this case, is the built-in set called **All Distribution Groups**.

If we need to have a difference in synchronization rules or deprovisioning behavior for different distribution groups, we would have to create our own sets.

To support deprovisioning based on some criteria, we need to use a set using that criteria. The **All Distribution Groups** set might otherwise trigger MIM to provision the group again.

Our custom set could look something like the following screenshot:

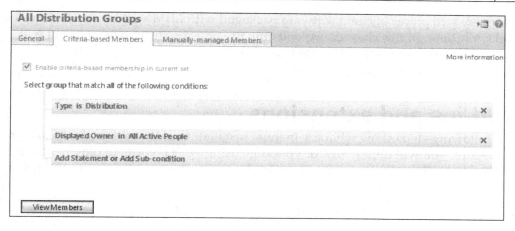

This set, shown in the preceding screenshot, will contain all the distribution groups, where **Displayed Owner** is in the set **All Active People**.

The set **All Active People**, in turn, might look something like the following screenshot:

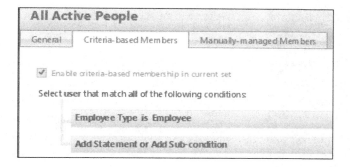

We can now satisfy a policy saying that distribution groups in AD must have an active employee as owner; otherwise, they should be deleted from AD.

Installing client add-ins

It is now time for the client add-ins to be installed to be able to have your users manage from Outlook. If you are using some approval workflows in your user management, you might have a need for the add-ins earlier in your implementation.

There are two pieces of client software packaged with MIM—add-ins and extensions, and CM Client. In this chapter, we will only use add-ins and extensions, and will leave CM Client for *Chapter 10, Overview of Certificate Management*, where MIM CM and smart card management are discussed.

Add-ins and extensions

The following steps show what the manual installation of the add-ins looks like, but in practice, you will deploy the MSI package using your favorite deployment tool, and manage all the settings using group policies. Read more about your options at `http://aka.ms/FIMAddIn`.

To install manually, locate your MIM 2016 media, and follow the ensuing steps:

1. The add-ins and extensions are available in multiple languages. Be aware that there are both x64 and x86 versions. Run `setup.exe` as administrator on the client:

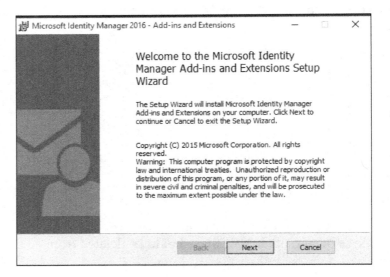

2. After some default steps concerning licensing agreements and some other stuff, you will need to decide what to install. The only actual choice is if you are using Outlook, and would like to install **MIM Add-in for Outlook** or not. Note that we will not select the PAM client, as we will cover that in a later chapter. We will also cover password resets in *Chapter 9, Password Management*:

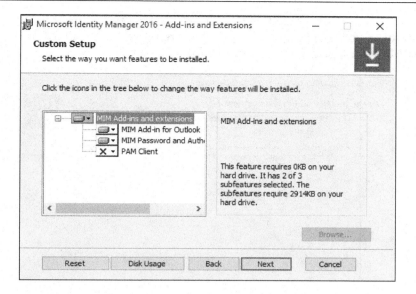

3. The MIM Portal Server address is the hostname, not the URL, that the client should use. The MIM Service account e-mail address is the address used by MIM Service when sending e-mails to clients. It is a good idea to make sure your MIM Service account has a good display name around this for users to know who the e-mail is coming from:

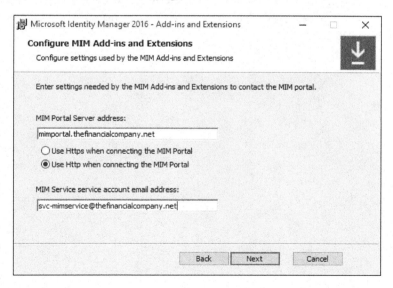

4. Enter the hostname used by the client to talk to MIM Service. Do not add a protocol such as `http` or `https`. If you are using the standard port `5725` for MIM Service, you do not need to add it:

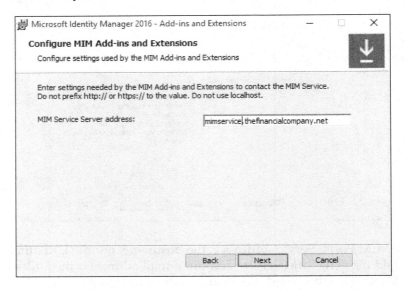

5. When asked about the URL for the Intranet Password Registration portal, you are requested to actually enter the complete URL with both protocol and hostname. We know this setup interface is not 100% consistent in its behavior:

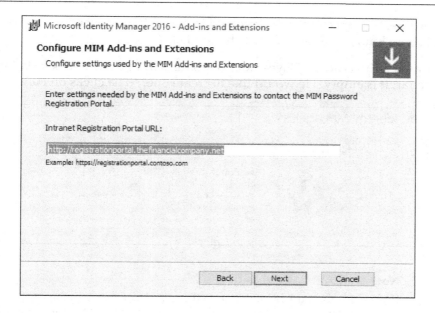

6. After finishing the installation, you are required to reboot before you can start using the client.

In this chapter, we will only discuss the Outlook add-in. In *Chapter 9*, *Password Management*, we will take a look at how to use the self-service password reset support, which we also installed at this point.

Creating and managing distribution groups

After allowing employees to create distribution groups earlier, we can now see what they would look like from a user's perspective.

There are different parts and steps involved in managing distribution groups. Let's start with how John creates a new distribution list:

1. David (who is an employee) logs on to the MIM portal, and selects **My DGs**. So far, it is empty. He would like to create one, so he clicks on **New**:

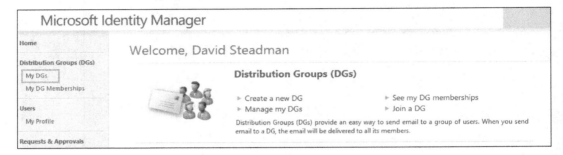

> **Note**
>
>
>
> If your users are unable to log in to the portal, confirm that the `accountName` and `Sid` are populated with domains. Also confirm that the following two MPRs are enabled:
>
> - General: Users can read non-administrative configuration resources
> - User management: Users can read attributes of their own

2. He gives his new group a display name, **Hunters**, and an e-mail alias, **Hunters**. A good description is always useful so that others can decide whether this is a group they would like to join:

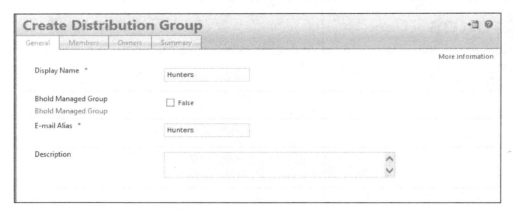

3. David will automatically be added as the first member, and he is given the chance to add others as well, at this point:

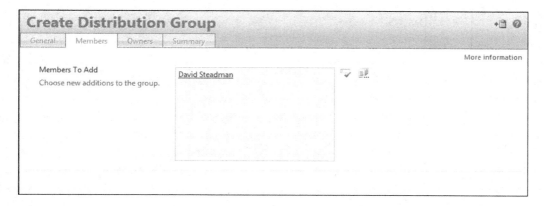

4. David, as the creator, will automatically be set as **Owner** and **Displayed Owner** of this group. David has also chosen that he wants to approve join requests:

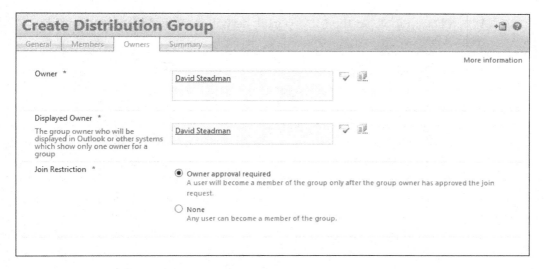

5. In the **Summary** page, David can verify his settings before submitting the request:

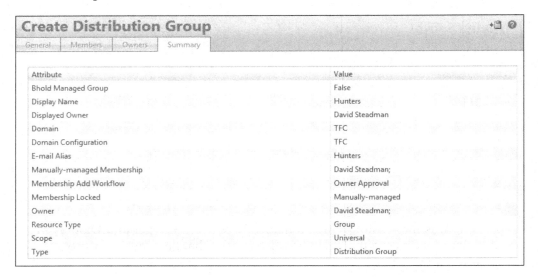

6. When David looks at the MIM portal, he will now find his new group in **My DGs**:

After creating the group, there might be users that would like to join the group. At The Financial Company, they have a consultant, Jeff, who likes to hunt and would like to be part of this distribution group. Let's see how Jeff can use the MIM portal to join the group.

7. Jeff logs on to MIM Portal and searches for distribution groups using the keyword **Hunter**. He finds David's **Hunters** group, selects it, and clicks on **Join**:

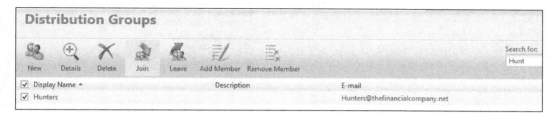

8. When he submits the request, he will see in **Status** that his request is **Pending approval**. Remember, David decided to choose **Owner Approval** for this group:

What happens now is that MIM will wait for David to approve the request. The MPR triggered by Jeff's request to join the group is also configured to send David this request as an e-mail, making it possible for David to use the Outlook add-in installed on his computer to approve or reject this request.

With the Outlook add-in installed, he can approve or reject the request directly from the **Preview** pane in his Outlook window:

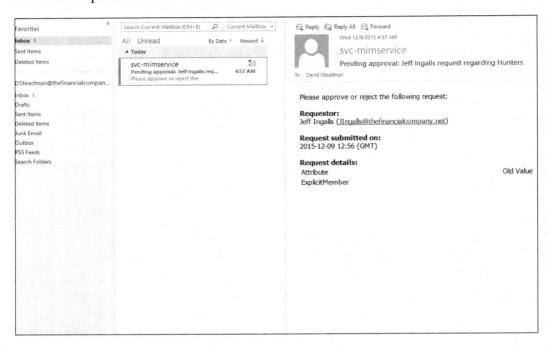

In the e-mail sent back to MIM Service, David can give a reason (not required) for his approval (or rejection), and the text entered in the **Reason** field will, in that case, be part of this request:

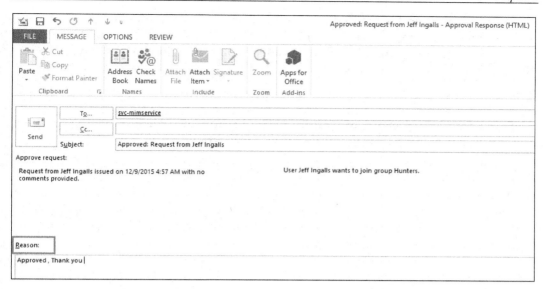

If he did not choose the available Outlook add-in, he could go to the MIM portal to approve or reject the request there instead:

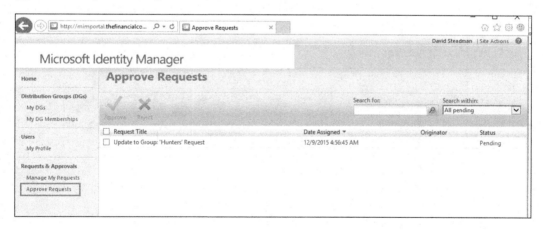

Having Exchange and using Outlook are by no means required in order to work with self-service group management like this. The difference is that you would have to use MIM Portal for approval. In those cases, it would be a good idea to change how the e-mail templates used by MIM look so that they include a link to MIM Portal.

The e-mail template used is the one configured in the MPR triggered by this event.

The MPR **Group management workflow: Owner approval on add member** triggers the authorization workflow **Owner Approval Workflow**:

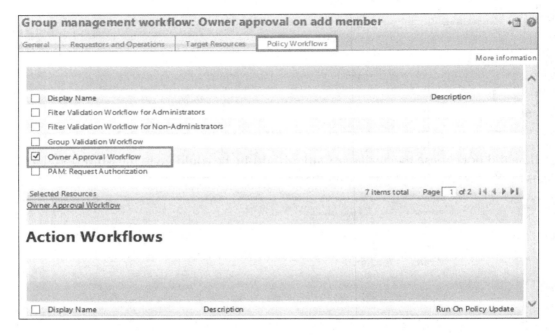

If you look into that workflow, you will find some settings that you might want to change, but you will also find the e-mail templates used by MIM for the different steps in this workflow:

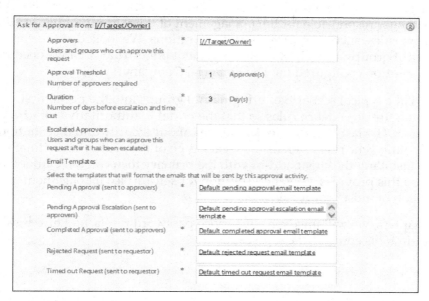

You can change these templates, or create a new one and use that in your workflow. If you are changing the built-in, default e-mail templates, be aware that they might be used in other workflows as well.

 We recommend that you create your own e-mail templates, and use them instead of modifying the built-in ones.

Another risk in modifying the built-in e-mail templates is that future updates and service packs might reset your changes.

Summary

The group management features we have in MIM give us the capability to work with both static and dynamically defined groups. Another great capability is that we make the owner responsible for the management of these groups, but can still define the business rules, such as approvals and expirations. We looked at the various types and scopes of groups, as well as the management policy rules that we need to enable to get the solution configured for The Financial Company.

We looked at a typical scenario of bringing AD groups into the portal first, then flipping the precedence rules so that the portal is authoritative for group management. The last thing we looked at was about security and distribution groups creating sync rules, versus the legacy type of flow rules. Then, finally, we dove into installing the client add-in with the primary focus on the Outlook plug-in. You can see this provides a detailed solution for self-service management and the configuration of most group scenarios.

In later chapters, we will uncover self-service password resets, and also how the client add-in tools enhance the reset capability.

7
Role-Based Access Control with BHOLD

Role-based access control is handled by **Microsoft Identity Manager (MIM)** 2016 using the BHOLD suite, which enables organizations to define roles, and to control access based upon those roles. Although we will touch upon most of the relevant topics, this chapter will not be too in-depth, as it takes time and slow steps to understand all the concepts in BHOLD. We will use the synchronization knowledge that we gained while creating MA and the FIM service knowledge to create sync rules to support the basic **Role-based access control (RBAC)** implementation. The analytics and model loader will not be discussed, as it can take a lot of time to go through all the knobs and switches. The core focus will be the core components that make BHOLD a valuable addition.

In this chapter, we will cover the following topics:

- Role-based access control
- Installation
- **Access Management Connector (AMC)**
- Attestation
- Reporting
- MIM/FIM integration

Role-based access control

When we talk about RBAC, the first thing that comes to mind are security groups and the managers or owners of the security groups. Now, in the discussion around role-based access, we also use the term discretionary access control, also known as RBAC. But when we look at RBAC, we typically see a lot of security groups in a one-to-one relationship between the organizations and the security groups. This can be okay and manageable for a small organizations, but as the organization grows, these memberships of the groups become really hard to manage, and also to monitor who has access to what. The following image is a classic depiction of this challenge:

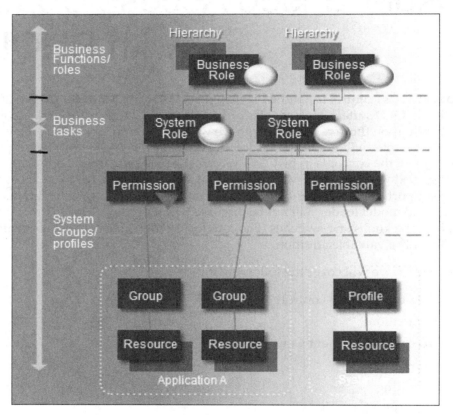

So, how does an organization look at this problem? Most organizations use the MIM Service and Portal, but this only helps in automating processes in the groups; it does not solve the overall problem— it just mitigates it. This is where role-based access with BHOLD comes in. We will also talk about privileged access management, but that solves a different problem. In this case, we have many security groups and many users, so let's first start at the problem.

The first thing that needs to be done is to take a holistic view of the organization. Some folks call this an audit, but in reality, this is just a system-wide or organizational-wide review in terms of who has what and who needs what?

This is not an installation that will solve all your problems — it takes time and manpower to begin addressing the problem. Like with any prolonged problem, there is no simple medication, or surgery, or even a quick fix.

So let's take a look at the The Financial Company. The company can be broken down into many different roles — managers, sales, engineers, and so on. We have a multitude of resources that need to be accessed and certain permissions, whether it is the HR staff that needs access to the SQL HR database, or simply to corporate records. Again, the systems can be broad, but in reviewing your role-based access strategy, you will begin to understand your organization's access control needs.

Now, when we talk about RBAC, we also talk about some of the features that BHOLD brings around this terminology. One of those is **separation of duties (SoD)**. SoD is a common practice in the security field that, by definition, means that one user should not hold all the keys to the kingdom. So BHOLD brings SoD to light when you're planning your role-based access strategy. One example of this is that The Financial Company makes a lot of transactions through a payments system, so one separation of duty strategy is allowing only one set of folks to initiate the payment, and then have another set of people to authorize the payment. RBAC allows the enforcement of this type of policy rather than giving one user full control to authorize and initiate the payment. With **Privilege Access Management (PAM)**, this takes a whole new level of authorization where you can have just-in-time authorization for your highly critical assets. Again, the Microsoft Identity Suite offers many tools that an organization can use to include many of the modules that come with BHOLD. Building your strategy using this technology will help you implement the best solution for your organization.

BHOLD role model objects

When we talk about the BHOLD role model, we need to understand that we have to define the organizational roles, map the users to the roles, and then also map the permissions to the roles. This is a process that can take some time, and all of these connect to five types of objects within the BHOLD role model. We will outline these objects as The Financial Company is reviewing its role-based model.

Organizational units

Organizational units (orgunits) in BHOLD are the principal foundation to organizing users within the BHOLD role model. When you create a user in BHOLD, you have the option to tell BHOLD what orgunits the user is a part of—so, planning this fundamental layout is important. In most organizations, this might match what their organizational structure looks like in Active Directory, but do not confuse this with Active Directory. BHOLD orgunits should be designed around the organization's business policy. Again, it could match Active Directory, but you need to do the underlying work in discovery to meet the needs of your organization.

Let's take a look at the The Financial Company. The OU structure of The Financial Company is flat—essentially, it is one organizational unit that contains all the users. So right from the start, we know that we have to build our organizational structure for BHOLD. Now one good thing in BHOLD is that you can have multiple organizational strategies. You could have an orgunit for your corporate business, and then also plan your strategy around research and development projects, that is, special projects. The following image depicts the high-level organizational structure of The Financial Company. Again, this is very high level, but we can work with this.

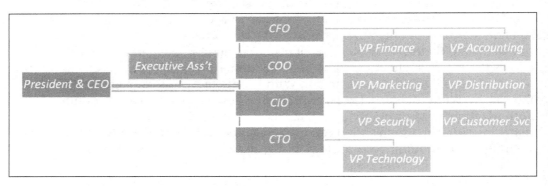

Let's take this a step further. We know that the CFO has a VP for finance and a VP for accounting. Under these, we can outline all the positions that roll up to the vice presidents, which roll up to the Chief Financial Officer within The Financial Company. In the next image we've outlined the positions of the compliance manager, the accounting manager, and, of course, the AR manager and the AP manager. There could be multiple managers as the company grows, and more roles are needed.

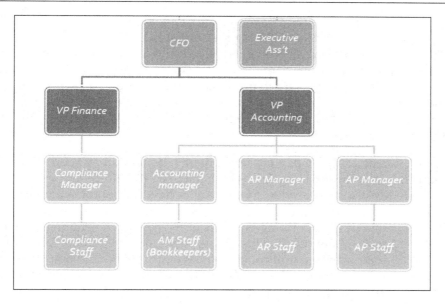

Now, this is where you think about the bigger picture, and—could there be a need for multiple people? The Financial Company is a fairly large company, but its organizational structure, from a business standpoint, is very small. However, the CFO is aware that they are bringing in multiple managers, who will, in turn, manage several regions. This is an important piece of information, as you are working through the organizational unit's structure for a long term. With some input from the CFO, we can now determine that we need to break apart the business into regions— this will allow for SoD by region.

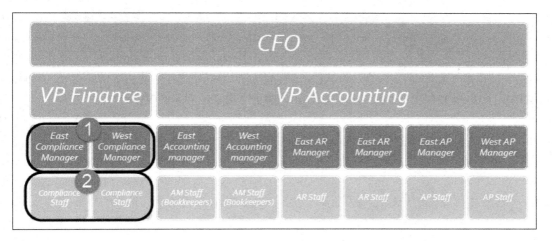

As you can see in the preceding image, we only took a portion of the business to start a development process of outlining the core objectives of the business and what they plan to do in the future. This enabled us to build an organizational structure that will meet the business needs in the future as well as the present. This does take time however, and it is important to understand that trying to do everything at once might not be the best plan. Break it down into areas of the business. As you saw, The Financial Company started out with the finance department, because that is their area of highest priority.

We've given you an example of a possible organizational unit structure, but do not limit yourself just to the business side. There may be other areas that you need to address using RBAC. For example, if you want to have an organizational structure for all your project management needs, such as on-boarding new projects, this doesn't have to just be the operating business of the core organizational structure. You can have one-to-many relationships like you see depicted in the following image. To add organizational units once you have come up with your plan, you can use the BHOLD Core web portal or the BHOLD model generator. More information on the model loader can be found at http://bit.ly/MIMBHML.

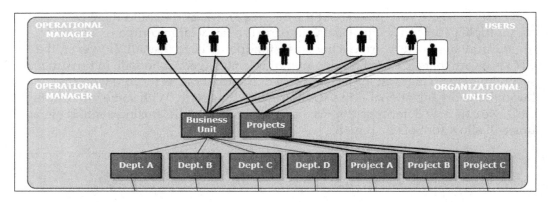

The orgunit has several settings around roles, the users tied to that orgunit, as well as the supervision roles. The following is a sample image of the orgunit:

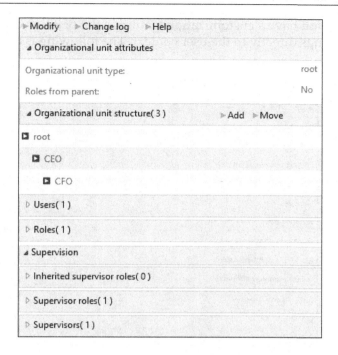

Users

As we discussed in the preceding section, orgunits are probably the core guiding factor when we are looking at a role-based model. We know that when we create users, they have to be assigned to the org unit or units. Again, users can be assigned to multiple units, thereby allowing the organization to assign the role to the orgunit, and then allowing the user that is assigned to pick up the role.

You do have the option to suspend a user, but this doesn't mean that you will delete it—it may just imply that the user went away on medical leave, or there may be a business policy that requires to suspend users that go on travel. But in any case, you can suspend a user, which, in turn, revokes all role assignments for that particular user. Once reactivated, it would restore all the permissions granted by that user's role.

Users can be created one by one using the BHOLD Core web portal, or they can be imported just like our organizational units by the model generator loader or the Access Management Connector from the Synchronization service.

Like the orgunit, you have a customization feature in the BHOLD Core web app to apply or add settings directly to the user context. The following is an example view of this:

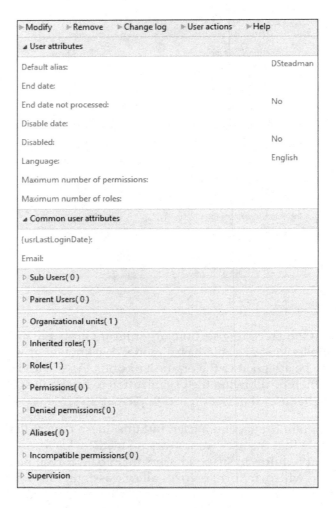

Roles

Roles are the foundation of the RBAC model. In most cases, roles will never be provisioned to the target application unless that application uses its own roles to define permissions. Roles are typically assigned by the organizational unit which the user would be a member of, or by assigning the role directly to the user. In BHOLD, we have inheritable role, proposed role, and effective role.

When a role is assigned to the parent organizational unit, it can be constructed as inheritable and proposed—this means that the role is available for users on request. If the role is constructed as inheritable, but effective, it means that the role would be automatically applied to any user within the organizational unit.

In addition to this, a role can also be activated for the user based on the user attributes. This is called **attribute-based authorization (ABA)**. You can find more about ABA at `http://bit.ly/MIMBHConcepts`.

A role within BHOLD has a few customizable settings. While some limit the number of permissions and the number of sub-roles, others limit the policies and organization units, as seen in the following screenshot:

Permissions

A permission in BHOLD is a collection of all the authorizations that were imported from multiple target applications. These include all the Active Directory security permissions, or third-party permissions—within BHOLD, these are called permissions. Now these permissions map from the Access Management Connector with an object type of group. It is critical to understand this concept, because most systems that you connect to may refer to this as another system type. A case in point is that you might have a system that is called a role, but then you have to map it from that application to the synchronization engine, and then back to the BHOLD permission. The following screenshot is an example of what we are talking about:

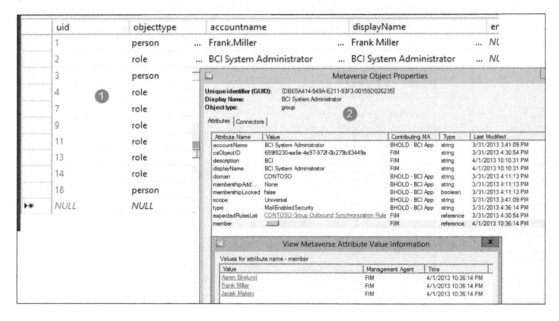

In the example given in the preceding image, we have a SQL database (**1**) that has a role object and a person. This is not an Active Directory, but an application that is used by the business, and it is a core essential application for The Financial Company. As you can see, when we bring it into the synchronization engine, it is brought in as group (**2**). Then once it's in the sync engine, it will be created in BHOLD Core as a permission. So it is easy to get confused, but to draw those variants, any connected system or application, whether it's a role or a permission such as an Active Directory, will always be a group type within the synchronization engine.

Like other objects in BHOLD, you can look at the permission, and the application and roles that the permission is tied to, and modify them accordingly (except the application, which is a hard connection). But most other settings can be updated, as seen in the following screenshot:

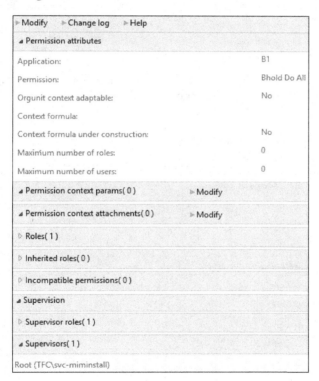

Applications

Applications are connected to a permission. When you create a permission within BHOLD, associated applications can be created within BHOLD Core directly, or when you create the permission from BHOLD or the Access Management Connector. Just as an example, the following screenshot shows one of the BHOLD permissions. You can see that it's defined the application as **B1** by default. When you install BHOLD Core you're going to see the **B1** application tied to multiple permissions:

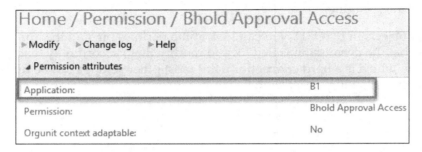

An application is a critical object, as it is where you see all the permissions, and also the stewards. We will uncover what the steward role is in the *Attestation* section of this chapter:

Other advanced features

We touched upon the basic features of RBAC within BHOLD, but we will not to stop there, as there are some advanced BHOLD features that are very important when you're looking at your RBAC model.

The first feature that we will look at is cardinality. Cardinality, in general, is a business rule for that particular role. An example is that you can configure a role limit around the maximum number of sub-roles, or maybe, the maximum number of permissions that can be linked to a role, and you can also configure a permission limit for the maximum number of roles that can be linked to a permission.

The second feature is what we've discussed earlier, that is, SoD. This allows the business to define and prevent users from gaining access to and performing actions that should not be performed by one single individual. In the example we gave earlier, it was all was about initiating it, and then processing. The SoD would prevent this from happening by defining incompatible permissions.

Context-adaptable permissions (CAPs) are another feature that can be applied to applications, permissions, organizational units, and, of course, users. CAPs are a great way to define how the permission is to be applied. For instance, in some examples found online, permissions are granted based on whether the users are a full-time employee or a contract employee. This is, again, the inclusion filter, so by defining if they are part of one group or another, the permission would be automatically applied. This is a great way to have granular permissions based on the current status of the user.

We've already mentioned the feature that is called ABA or attribute-based authorization. Now this is an enablement functionality that allows you to define whether a particular role is activated when all the rules or thresholds apply. This eliminates the need to actively put them as proposed roles for the user. Instead, if the user already meets all the rules, then you can simply apply the actual role without any user intervention or requests. This feature is fine, but there's one thing that you need to know—even if you have any role that passes all variables, you may also have a cardinality setting. For example, if you have a cardinality setting saying you can only apply this role to users within the organizational unit, the cardinality rule wins; therefore, only using it would actually get the role.

Finally, we arrive at our last advanced feature, which is flexible attribute types. Again, this is a great way to extend the attribute-based authorization for users or organizational units, and even for role attributes. Like other components within the Microsoft Identity Suite, you can add attributes to fit your organizational requirements.

Installation

Now that we've gone over some of the core definitions of the BHOLD suite, we are going to start the installation of BHOLD and its modules. In this section, we will just install it, and then we will go into a bit more detail as we continue.

So, let's set the stage. We currently have the MIM service and Synchronization service installed. Now we need to implement a BHOLD Core server for The Financial Company. In going through and looking at the requirements of BHOLD Core, we see that we need a minimum of 3 GB RAM and 30 GB of storage, depending on our deployment size. All the software requirements have been documented for us at `http://bit.ly/MIMBHCoreInstall`.

One thing to note is that when we install BHOLD Core, we should make sure that we are logged in as the `svc-miminstall` account. The reason for this is that when we get to the integration component, the installer will look for the currently logged-in user in the B1 database. So, the first thing we need to do is to create the B1 user account, and to make sure that it is set up as per the requirements document.

We are installing BHOLD Core on a separate server. The integration components will be installed on the MIM Service and Portal.

We have created our service account and a group, and then added the service account to the group:

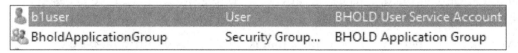

If the user is not a member of the group, then you will get the error shown in the following screenshot during the installation:

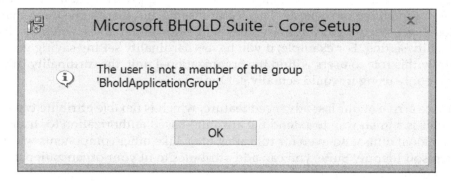

Like the other installations back in *Chapter 1*, *Overview of Microsoft Identity Manager 2016*, with the MIM service and sync, we will use an alias to install BHOLD. Please run `cliconfg`. Then add the **Server alias** as `dbMIMBhold`:

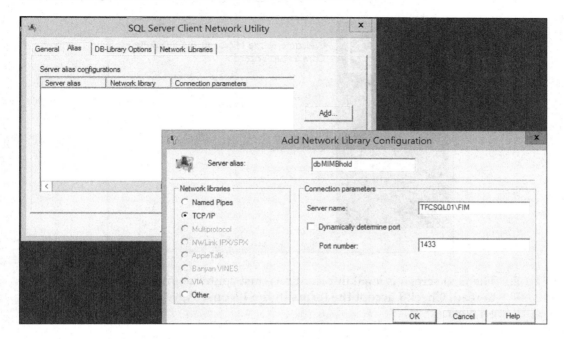

BHOLD Core and other components

We will log in to BHOLD as `svc-miminstall` if you have not already done so, and then begin the setup:

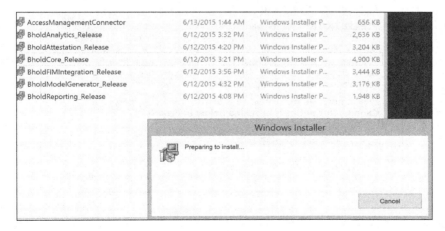

1. Click on **Next** to continue the installation, as shown in the following screenshot:

2. The next screen is legal information—just continue unless you feel the need to read. Check **I accept the terms in the License Agreement**, and then click on **Next**.

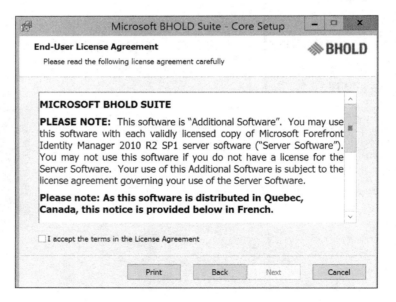

3. Select all the services to install:

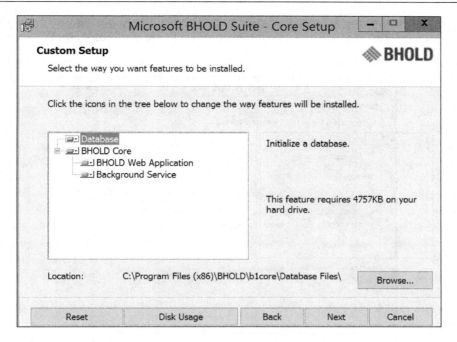

4. In the next screen, fill in the account details and domain information, and then click on **Next**:

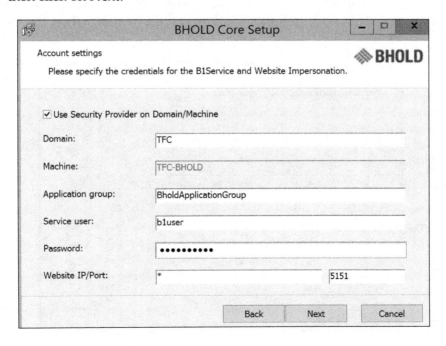

5. In the following screen, we will define the **Database Server** and **Database Name** (note that we are using the previously created alias), then click on **Next**:

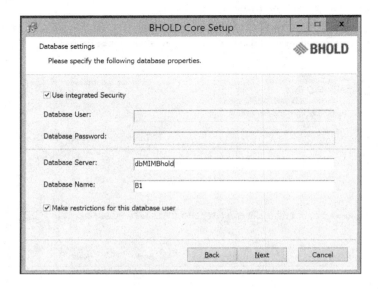

6. Installation will now begin. During installation, the database will be created, and user accounts will be configured. The `svc-miminstall` account will be designated as the local root account, and the `B1` user will be the service account:

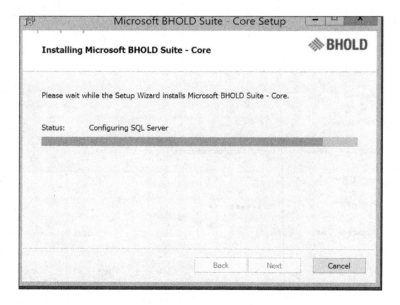

7. Once the installation is complete, we can open the BHOLD website, which looks like the following screenshot:

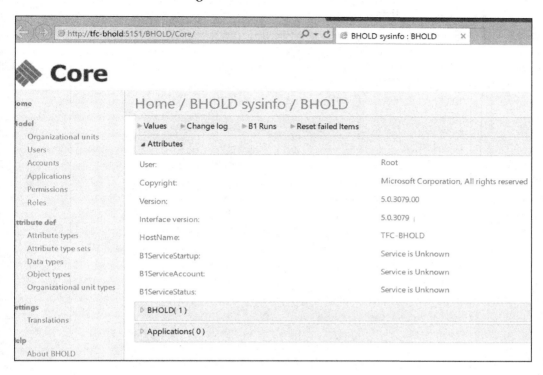

8. Now that the site is up, click on **Values**, which will display the page of configuration options. Definitions of these settings can be found at `http://bit.ly/MIMBHReg`:

Home / BHOLD attributes / BholdAttributes	
▶ Modify ▶ Done	
▷ BHOLD system attributes	
(usrsystemPoliciesMode):	Role policies are evaluated on USER*ROLE instances
bholdDomain:	
bholdGroup:	BholdApplicationGroup
bholdUser:	b1user
bholdDirectory:	C:\Program Files (x86)\BHOLD\b1core\
bholdAuthentication:	WindowsPasswords
webServer:	TFC-BHOLD:5151
webName:	BHOLD
webDirectory:	C:\Program Files (x86)\BHOLD\b1core\Web
NTLogSources:	
NoHistory:	
MoveorgunitToSameorgtype:	
ServiceInterval:	10
Number of logrecords visible:	10
Database version:	5.0.3079.0
Days between ABA run:	01
Start hour of ABA run:	01
OrgUnit Supervisor Role Inheritance:	Y
System Cardinality:	Y
Logging:	Y
SystemQueue Processing:	Y
Start applications during creation:	N
Default application interval:	60

You have now completed the BHOLD Core installation. The other modules, such as Attestation, are simple, and we will run those installations on the TFC-BHOLD server. The final step is to install the FIM/MIM Integration component—one of the most powerful tools to be integrated into the BHOLD RBAC solution. As a note, we are installing all the components on the BHOLD Core so that we can look at its capabilities. In a production environment, we would not recommend loading the model loader.

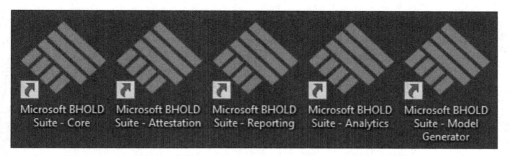

MIM/FIM Integration install

The first step is to confirm that you are logged in to the MIM Install account (svc-miminstall). This account must have local administrator and service administrator permissions, and must be present within the B1 database.

1. Before you start the installation, please run the following command, which precludes the SharePoint module on 32-bit application pools:

    ```
    appcmd.exe set config -section:system.webServer/globalModules/
    [name='SPNativeRequestModule'].preCondition:integratedMode,bitne
    ss64
    ```

2. Launch the installer, and click on **Next**:

3. Check **I accept the terms in the License Agreement**, and then on **Next**:

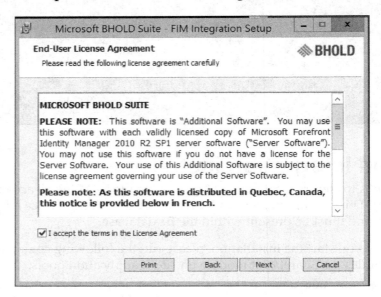

4. Select all components, then click on **Next**:

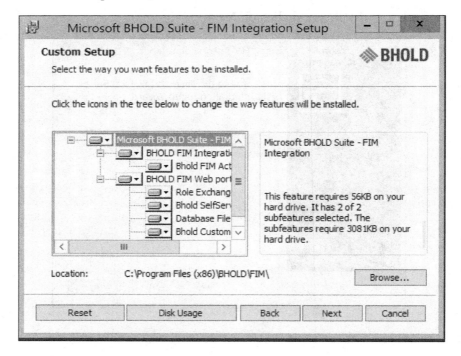

5. Then we will define the user for connection to and from the FIM MIM (integration into the BHOLD Core):

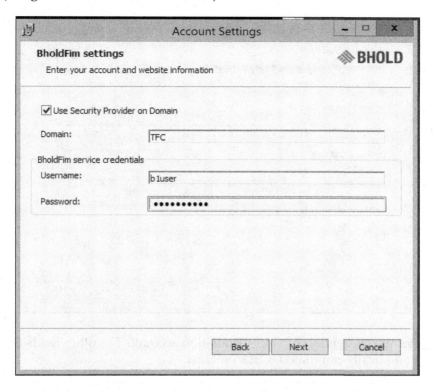

6. Next, define the database server — in our case, we will use the same alias as the MIM Service. Then click on **Next**:

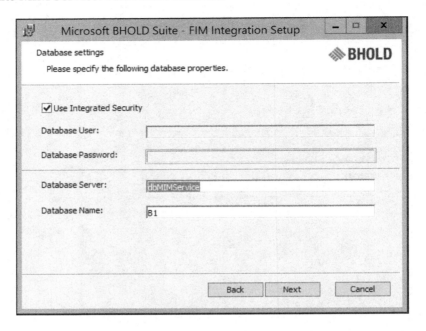

7. Enter the credentials of your installation account. The other fields should be automatically populated. Click on **Next**:

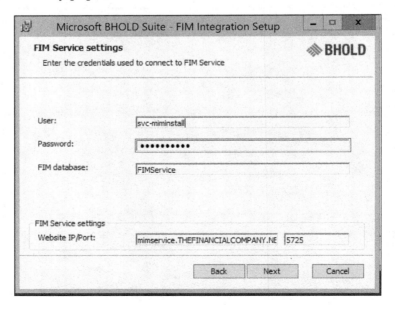

8. This is an important step. Define the BHOLD Core user. You should also enter the IP of the Core server (not the machine name), and then click on **Next**:

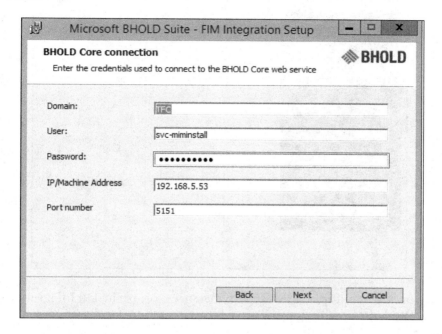

9. Click on **Install** to begin the installation:

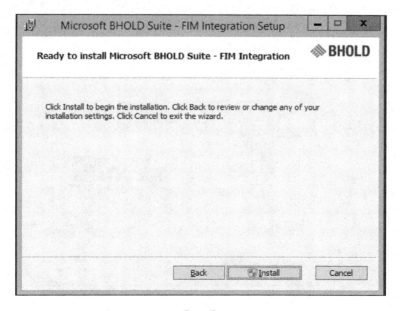

10. Click on **Finish**:

11. If you have multiple MIM Service instances, please install Integration components on all required servers (minus the customizations, as they were already performed on the primary server):

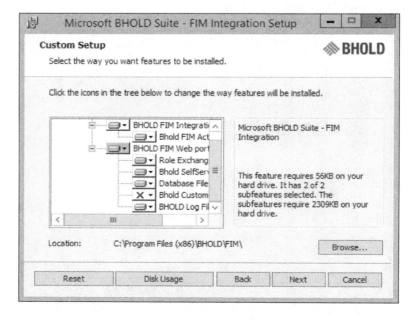

Once the installation is complete, you will see new navigation controls and objects within the service and portal site. We will go over them, and show you what they are used for.

The last step is to install the Access Management Connector on the synchronization engine.

Patching

Patching the BHOLD system is not like installing most patches. You must uninstall and reinstall every component, and target the existing B1 database.

Access Management Connector

For Access Management Connector, we will be creating the users and orgunit dynamically. We will also use the **Resource Control Display Configuration** (**RCDC**) modification, mentioned earlier in the chapter, for permissions:

1. The first step is we need to define our orgunit structure as we defined it earlier in our example. For this, we will create a simple table:

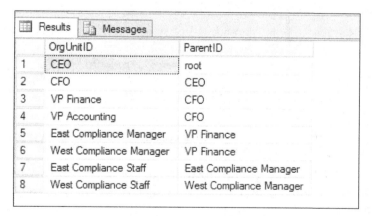

2. Next we will create an SQL Management Agent to bring in this structure. Now, if this data was already present, we could have created a view to dynamically get this OU structure as follows:

```
SELECT DISTINCT 'TFC' AS OrgUnitID, 'root' AS ParentID

FROM            [FIMSynchronizationService].dbo.mms_metaverse WITH
(NOLOCK)

UNION ALL
```

```
SELECT DISTINCT CONVERT(nvarchar(50), department) AS OrgUnitID,
'TFC' AS ParentID
FROM              [FIMSynchronizationService].dbo.mms_metaverse WITH
(NOLOCK)
WHERE             employeetype IS NOT NULL
UNION ALL
SELECT DISTINCT CONVERT(nvarchar(50), employeetype) + '-' +
CONVERT(nvarchar(50), department) AS OrgUnitID, department AS
ParentID
FROM              [FIMSynchronizationService].dbo.mms_metaverse WITH
(NOLOCK)
WHERE             employeetype IS NOT NULL AND department IS NOT NULL
```

This would render the following table dynamically. Pretty cool, yeah?

	OrgUnitID	ParentID
1	TFC	root
2	Executive	TFC
3	Sales	TFC
4	Engineering	TFC
5	IT	TFC
6	Financial	TFC
7	HR	TFC
8	Contractor-Engineering	Engineering
9	Contractor-IT	IT
10	Contractor-Sales	Sales

3. OK, back to the task at hand—after creating the table with our OU, we will hook it up with the SQL MA.

    Navigate back to the Synchronization engine, and create a BHOLD_ORG MA using the generic SQL MA. We will be using the same steps as done previously in this chapter.

4. We will be using the table above called bholdou within the HR database.

5. Please be sure to install the latest connector, documented at http://bit.ly/ MIMConnectorHist.

6. Before we create the connector, we need to add a reference attribute in the MIM Synchronization engine; we will use the object type `organization`.

    Follow these steps:

    1. Click on **Metaverse Designer**.
    2. Click on **organization**.
    3. Click on **Add Attribute**.
    4. Click on **New attribute**.
    5. Enter the **Attribute name** as `ParentID`, **Attribute type** as `Reference (DN)`, and click on **OK**:

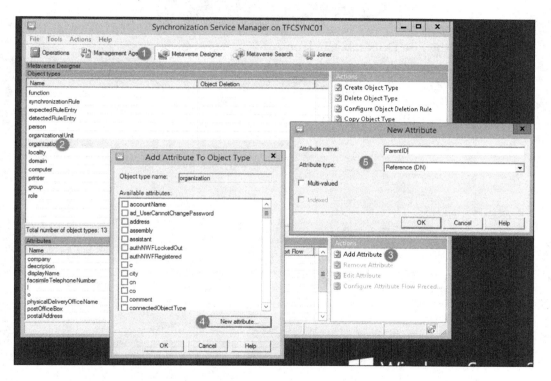

Creating the ODBC connection file

The generic SQL connector uses ODBC to connect to the remote server. First we need to create a file with the ODBC connection information as follows:

1. Start the ODBC management utility on the synchronization server:

2. Select the **File DSN** tab. Click on **Add**:

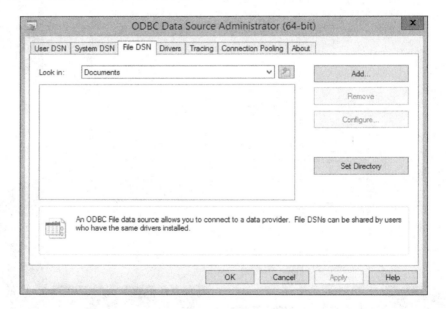

3. The SQL Service Native Client 11.0 will work fine, so select it and click on **Next**:

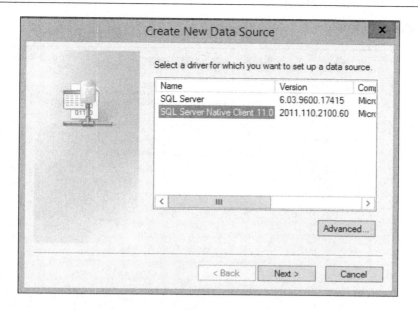

4. Give the file a name, such as BHOLDORG. We will save this to the ODBC folder on the root drive:

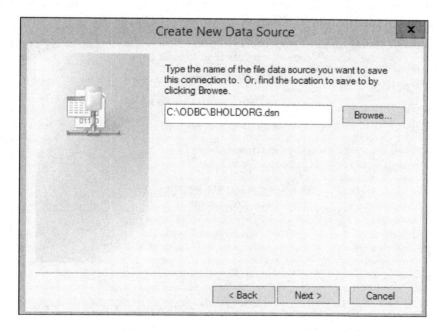

5. Click on **Finish**:

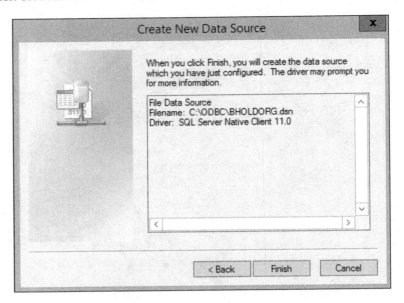

6. Time to configure the connection. Give the data source a good description, and provide the name of the server running SQL Server:

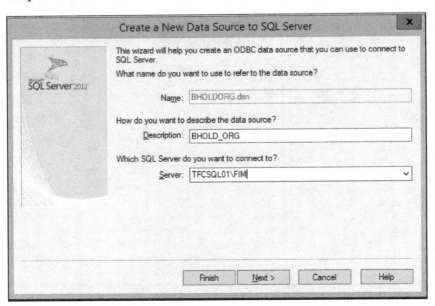

7. Select how to authenticate with SQL. In this case, we will use Windows Authentication:

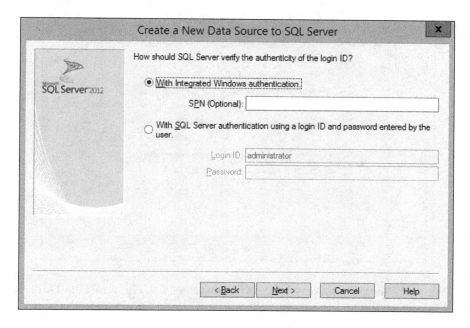

8. Provide the name of the HR database as HR:

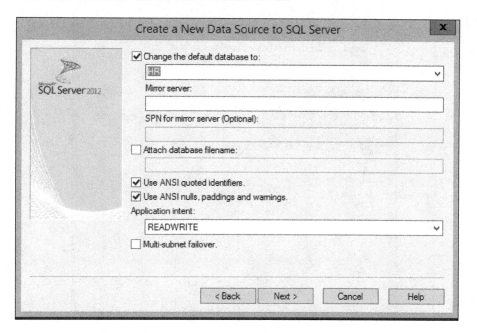

9. Keep everything default on the following screen. Click on **Finish**:

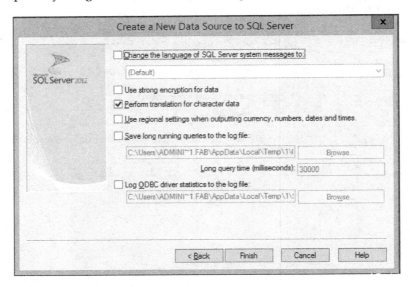

10. To verify that everything is working as expected, click on **Test Data Source**. Make sure the test is successful:

11. The ODBC configuration file should now be visible in **File DSN**:

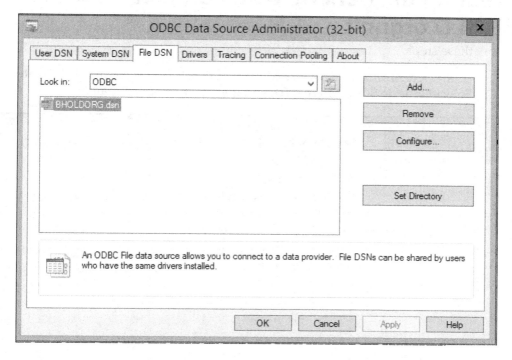

As we now have the file, we need to, and can start creating the connector.

Creating the generic SQL connector for the BHOLD orgunit

Follow these steps:

1. In the Synchronization Service Manager UI, select **Connectors** and **Create**. Select **Generic SQL (Microsoft)**, and give it a descriptive name:

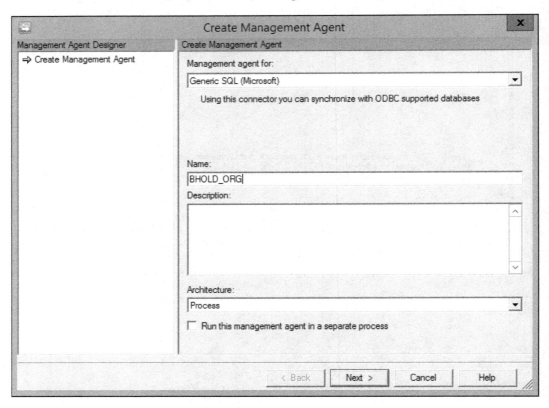

2. Find the DSN file that you created in the previous section, and upload it to the server. Provide the credentials to connect to the database:

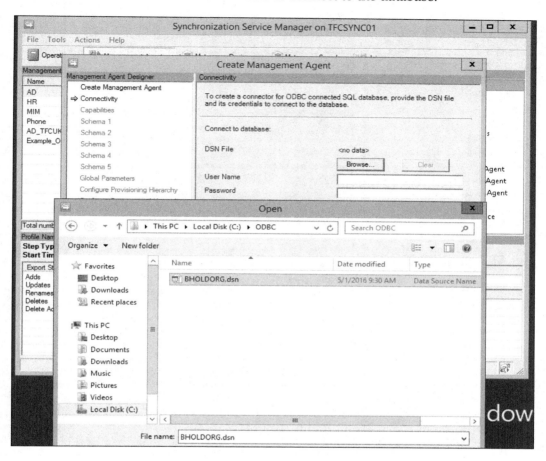

3. In this walkthrough, we will make it easy for you and say that we only have one object type [bholdou]:

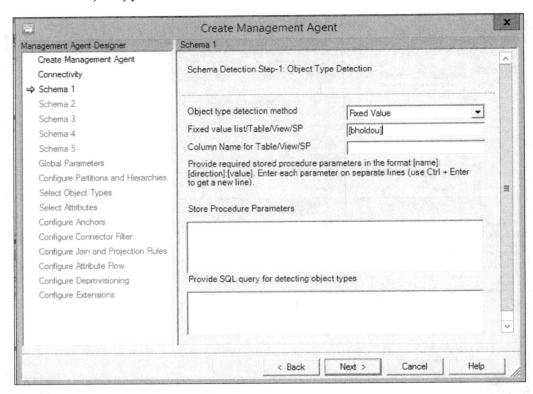

4. To find the attributes, we want the connector to detect those by looking at the table itself. If the object type is a reserved word in SQL, we need to provide it in square brackets []. As a general rule, we plan to use [] so that we do not have to investigate all the reserved words. For a list of all the reserved keywords, there is a good read at http://bit.ly/SQLReservedKeywords:

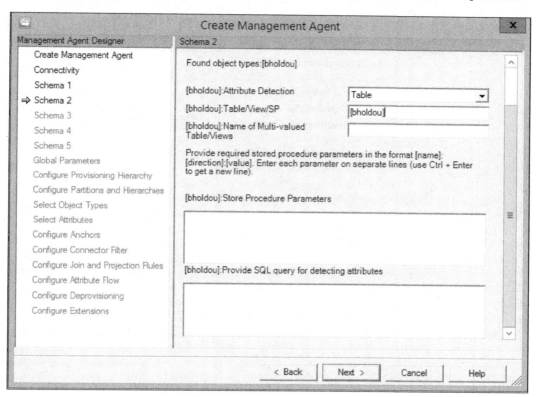

5. It's time to define the anchor attribute and the DN attribute. For bholdou, we will use OrgUnitID:

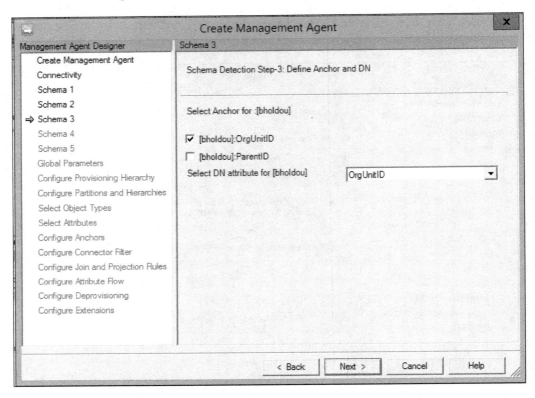

6. Not all attribute types can be detected in an SQL database (for example, the reference attribute type in particular). For **ParentID DataType**, we will update the value to **Reference**, and then select **ImportOnly**:

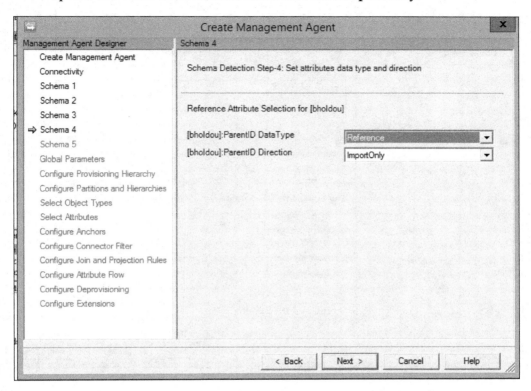

7. On the **Global Parameters** page, select **None** in **Delta Strategy**. Also type in the date/time format as `yyyy-MM-dd HH:mm:ss`:

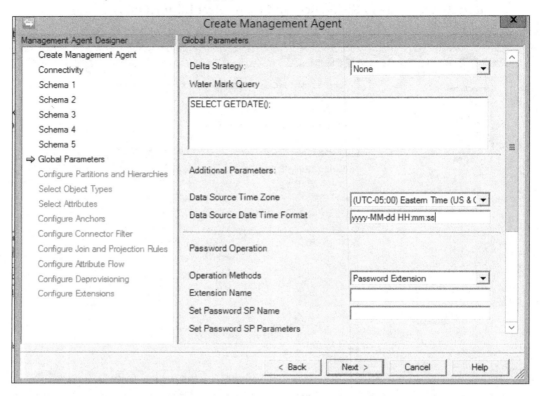

8. On the **Configure Partitions** page, select the `bholdou` object type.

9. For **Select Object Types** and **Select Attributes**, select the `bholdou` object type and all attributes.

10. In the **Configure Join and Projection Rules** screen, create a join mapping from `OrgUnitID` to `organization`, and then a projection:

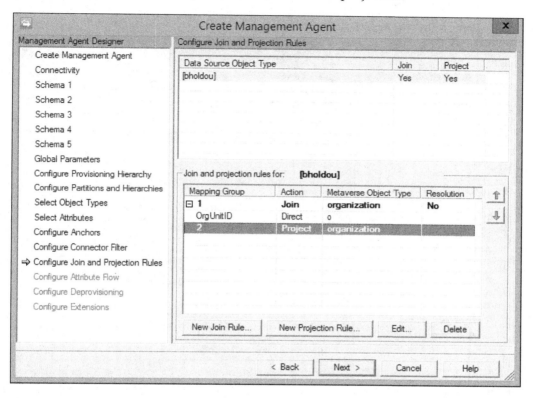

11. On the **Configure Attribute Flow** page, define the inbound flow as follows. Then click on **OK**:

OrgUnitID --> displayName

OrgUnitID --> o

ParentID --> ParentID

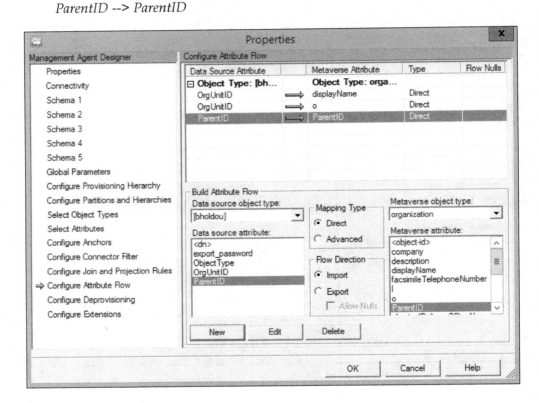

Creating run profiles

To create run profile follow this steps:

1. In the Synchronization Service Manager UI, select **Connectors**, and then **Configure Run Profiles**. Click on **New Profile**. We will start with Full Import.

2. Select the type **Full Import (Stage Only)**.

3. Select the partition **OBJECT=[bholdou]**.

4. Select **Table** and type [bholdou]. Scroll down to the multi-valued object type section, and enter the data as seen in the following screenshot. Click on **Finish** to save the step:

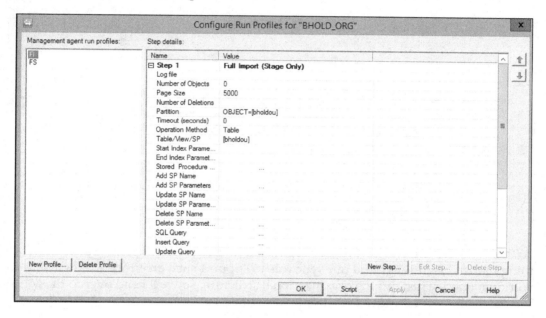

5. Finally, do the same for the Full Sync profile.

Creating a BHOLD connector and sync rules

Now that we've created our generic SQL Management Agent, we will go and run the Full Import and then Full Sync. Once this is done, we will go ahead and go to **Metaverse Search** to see our organization that we've imported and its references. So, now we've built our hierarchy within the sync engine. If we want to add more, we can simply go to our base table and modify accordingly. These updates would be directed into the BHOLD Core once we have built our synchronization rules.

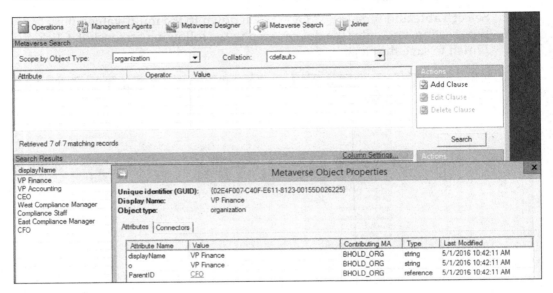

So this is the first step of getting our organizational structure in place. The next thing that we need is to build our sync role to support such an effort. The first step is working, and we just did the organizational structure, so we'll head over to the MIM service in a bit, and create a synchronization rule.

Before we can create the sync role, the BHOLD Access Management Connector needs to be installed and configured. We have already installed this, so now we just need to create the connector. Just like we did with the generic connector, go to **Actions** in the synchronization engine, and click on **Create**:

1. In the Synchronization Service Manager UI, select **Connectors** and **Create**. Select **Access Management (Microsoft)**, and give it a descriptive name:

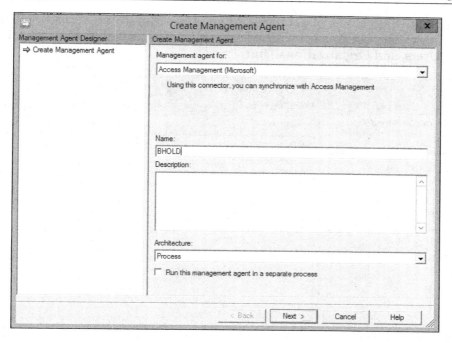

2. Enter the credential information for the service account `bluser`:

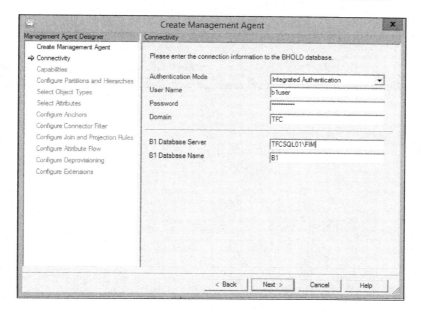

3. Next, select all the object types. As you can see in the next screenshot, the AMC does not connect with roles; it only connects with permissions (**Group**), **Users**, and **OrganizationalUnit**:

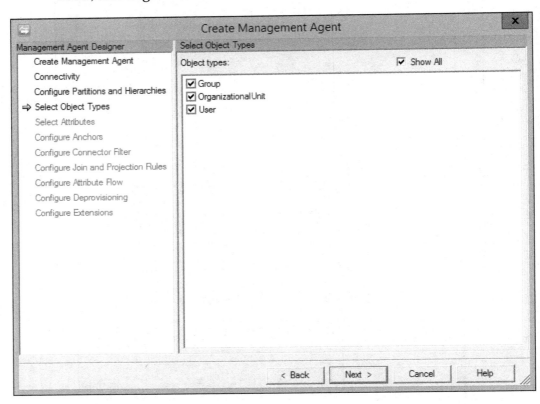

4. Select all the attributes listed, and click on **Next**:

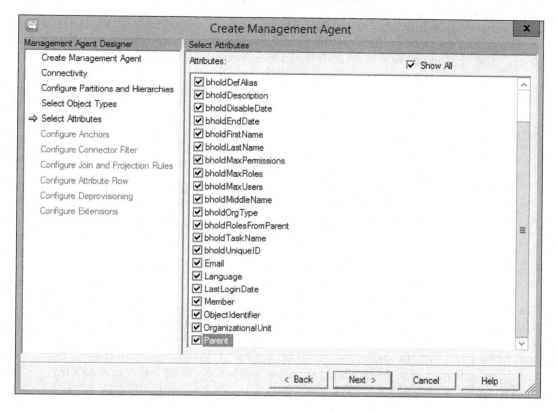

5. In the next several screens, select all default settings, and click on **Finish**.
6. Now create the Full Import and Full Sync run profiles, and run them.

We have completed the installation of the Access Management Connector. Now the next step is: we need to create our synchronization rules in the service and portal. The first sync rule that we will create will synchronize the orgunit with the BHOLD database. We are not detailing out the synchronization rule step-by-step—we will just go ahead, and show you what it looks like in the following screenshot:

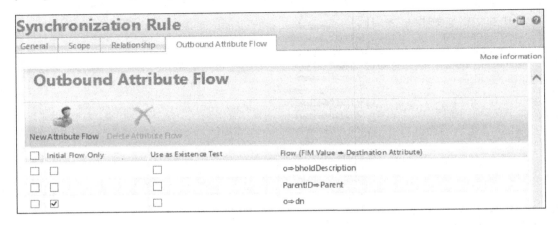

The next step, after we create the synchronization rule, is to run a Full Import, and then a Full Sync on the MIM/FIM Service Management Agent. This will bring in the synchronization rule that we created for the BHOLD orgunits. Next, we will run a Full Sync on the BHOLD_ORG Management Agent. This will trigger the synchronization rule to fire off, and then we will see pending exports ready for provisioning adds and EAF.

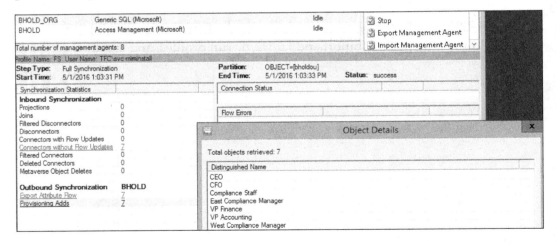

Next we will move on to provisioning the adds. Once this is done, we will go ahead and open up the BHOLD Core web interface, and we should see the orgunit tree:

BHOLD	E	success	5/1/2016 1:06:40 PM	5/1/2016 1:06:54 PM
BHOLD_ORG	FS	success	5/1/2016 1:03:31 PM	5/1/2016 1:03:33 PM
BHOLD_ORG	FI	success	5/1/2016 1:02:45 PM	5/1/2016 1:02:50 PM
BHOLD	FI	success	5/1/2016 1:00:53 PM	5/1/2016 1:00:58 PM
MIM	FIFS	success	5/1/2016 12:58:18 PM	5/1/2016 1:00:12 PM
BHOLD_ORG	FS	success	5/1/2016 10:42:11 AM	5/1/2016 10:42:11 AM
BHOLD_ORG	FI	success	5/1/2016 9:54:08 AM	5/1/2016 9:54:12 AM
HR	Full Import	success	4/30/2016 1:52:54 PM	4/30/2016 1:53:06 PM
MIM	FIFS	success	4/30/2016 1:52:34 PM	4/30/2016 1:54:07 PM
Example_ODS	FI	success	4/19/2016 6:06:05 AM	4/19/2016 6:06:15 AM
Example_ODS	FI	stopped-extension-dll...	4/19/2016 5:25:28 AM	4/19/2016 5:25:33 AM
Example_ODS	FI	stopped-extension-dll...	4/19/2016 5:18:02 AM	4/19/2016 5:18:07 AM
Example_ODS	FI	stopped-extension-dll...	4/19/2016 5:15:14 AM	4/19/2016 5:15:17 AM
Example_ODS	FI	stopped-extension-dll...	4/19/2016 4:54:28 AM	4/19/2016 4:54:33 AM
MIM	FIFS	success	4/19/2016 4:35:41 AM	4/19/2016 4:37:48 AM
AD	Export	success	4/16/2016 9:02:06 AM	4/16/2016 9:02:07 AM
AD	Full Sync	completed-sync-errors	4/15/2016 6:26:15 PM	4/15/2016 6:27:10 PM
AD	Delta Import	success	4/15/2016 6:25:16 PM	4/15/2016 6:25:36 PM

Profile Name: E User Name: TFC\svc-miminstall

Step Type:	Export			
Start Time:	5/1/2016 1:06:40 PM	Partition:	default	
		End Time:	5/1/2016 1:06:54 PM	Status: success

Export Statistics			Connection Status	
Adds	7			
Updates	6		Export Errors	
Renames	0			
Deletes	0			
Delete Adds	0			

As expected, the organizational units appeared as they should, from the parent all the way down to the east/west compliance manager:

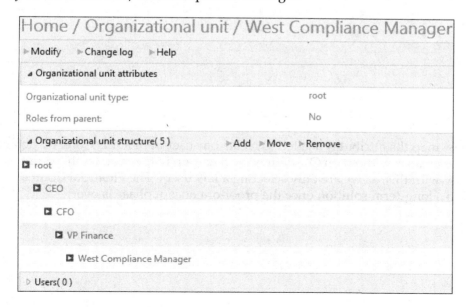

The next synchronization rule that we will implement will be for the users. Since now we are testing this solution, we are not going to import every single user at the moment, but be selective about the users we want to bring in. We will use attributes to define the scope of the synchronization rule. We will create an attribute on the `person` object within the synchronization engine, called `BHOLD_enabled` like we did earlier for the organization, and with the MIM Service attribute description that is already present. We will use this as a trigger mechanism to provision selective users to BHOLD Core. We now begin to create our sync rule for BHOLD users, as shown in the following screenshot:

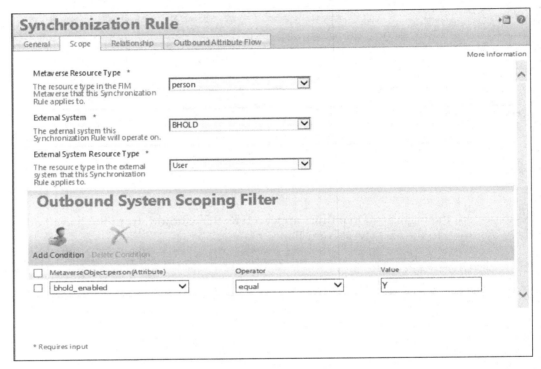

Then we map the attributes needed to create our user in BHOLD Core. By default, any user created without an OU defined will end up in the root. At this point, we are okay with this, as we are only selecting a few users. The Financial Company will develop a long-term solution once the proof-of-concept phase is over:

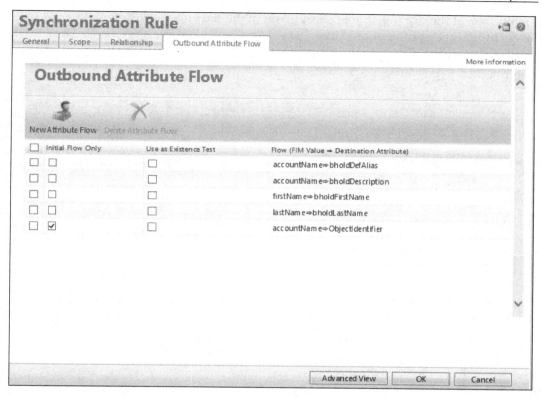

Now let us plan our tree of users for BHOLD Core. We need to have the CFO and the financial VP, and then the east/west compliance managers:

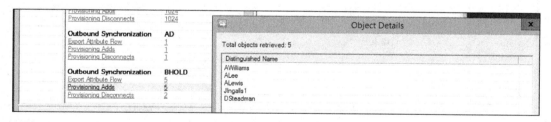

If you look at the organizational chart given in the next image, you will see how the users fit into the organizational tree:

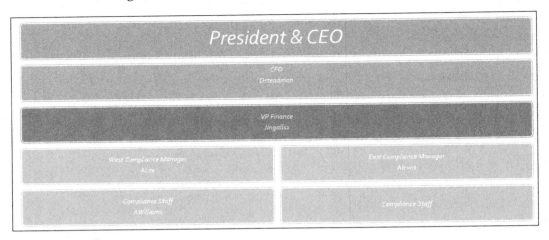

We will not go through and map the users to the organizational chart manually. As you can see in the following screenshot, `DSteadman` is mapped to the CFO orgunit:

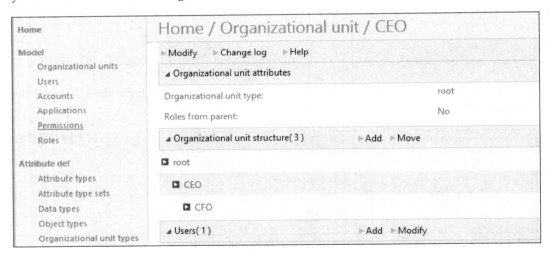

As discussed earlier, users can be mapped to multiple orgunits. We will map the rest of the users, and then create our roles and permissions as an example so that we can see how the RBAC basically works. To set the stage, we need to create the permissions for our application. In this case, the permissions are based on The Financial Company's CFO.

We will have a total of five roles for the group. We will also have five permissions with this, and will comply with the following tables:

Roles

Role	Orgunit	Inherited/proposed
cforolef1	VP finance	Inherited
cforolef2	West compliance	
cforolef3	East compliance	
cforolef4	East and west compliance staff	Inherited
cforolef5	East and west compliance staff	Proposed linked

Permission Mapping

Permission	Role	Incompatible permission	Application
cfoperm1	cforolef1		CFO_Payroll
cfoperm2	cforolef2	cfoperm3	CFO_Accounts
cfoperm3	cforolef3	cfoperm2	CFO_Accounts
cfoperm4	cforolef4		CFO_Invoice
cfoperm5	forolef5		CFO_Invoice

Now, for The Financial Company, we will create the roles manually by going to **Home | Roles | Add** (like you see in the following screenshot). You can also use the model loader to load up roles. With the model loader, you can map the role to an OU as well. In our case, we are simply testing out the RBAC solution before making a huge project, that is, we are looking for proof-of-concept:

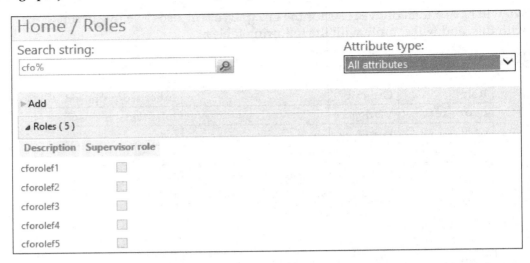

Now we need to create the permission and an application. For this, we've already created the `bmanaged` attribute earlier in the book. Now we'll go through the same steps to create an indexed attribute called `BApplication`. This attribute will help us to dynamically define the attribute that the permission is tied to. In most cases, we would have audited the company and found all the applications and permissions that were tied. Then we would have a set number of apps to do a drop-down box or pre-populate all the permissions with this value:

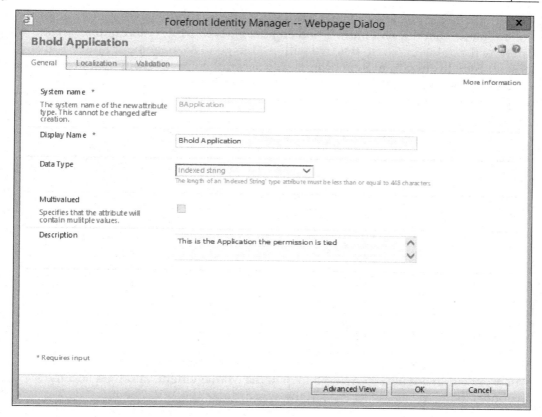

To add the new attribute, we will go to **Schema Management | All Attributes**, and then click on **Add**. This attribute will be an indexed string attribute, like you see in the preceding screenshot. After this, you will need to tie the attribute to the group in the same manner, by clicking on **All bindings**, and then on **New**.

As with the `bmanaged` attribute, we need to add this attribute to the management policy rule so that the synchronization engine, FIM/MIM Agent, can detect it and we can flow the value in. To do this, we will need to go to **Management Policy Rules**, look for **Synchronization: Synchronization account controls group resources it synchronizes**, and add the two BHOLD attributes that we will be using to manage the permission and group. We have detailed this in the following screenshot:

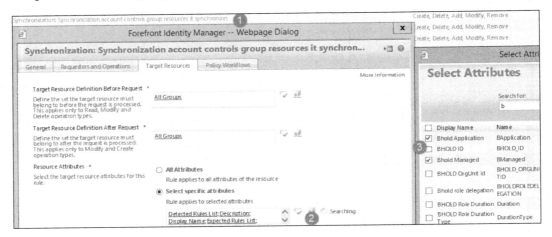

Now that we have both attributes, we need to add two attributes to the synchronization engine. We will go to **Schema Management**, and then add the attributes to the `group` object type in the synchronization MV schema:

- `bhold_application`: **String (indexable)**
- `bhold_managed`: **Boolean**

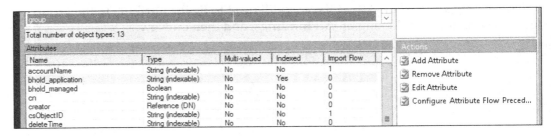

Next let us go to the FIM/MIM Management Agent. In order to see the new attribute, we need to refresh the schema. Once refreshed, we will select the attributes shown in the following screenshot:

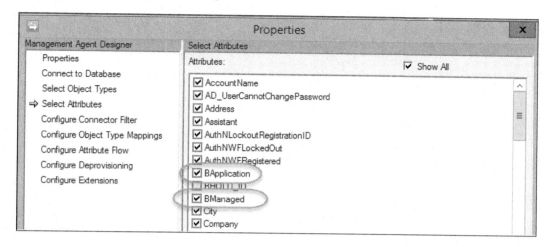

Once you've selected the attributes, we will configure the attribute flow for inbound only on the `group` object:

Now select **OK**, and then run Full Import and Full Sync on the FIM Service Management Agent. Now that we have this in place, let's go back to the portal, and add the security group permission based on the chart we created earlier, with the owners set as Jeff and David:

Display Name ▲	Bhold Application
cfoperm1	CFO_Payroll
cfoperm2	CFO_Accounts
cfoperm3	CFO_Accounts
cfoperm4	CFO_Invoice
cfoperm5	CFO_Invoice

Now we have to create our security groups, but before we can do that, we need to create a sync rule based on whether the `Bmanaged` attribute is checked. Like we did earlier, navigate over to **Synchronization Rules**, and then click on **New**:

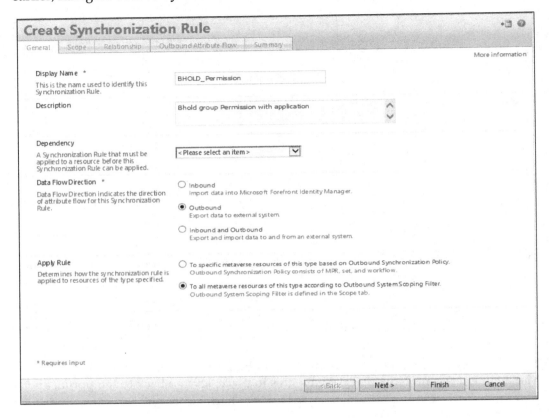

Click on **Next**, and then set **Metaverse Resource Type** as group and **External System Resource Type** as **Group**, and then **External System** as BHOLD. For the outbound system scoping filter, we will use our **bhold_managed** Boolean. Then click on **Next**:

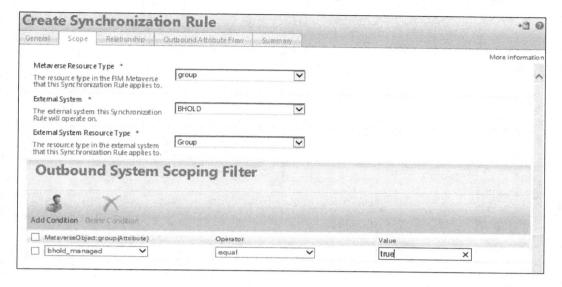

The next screen will be **Relationship Criteria**. For this, we will choose **accountName** and **bholdTaskName**. We will also check the **Create resource in external system** option:

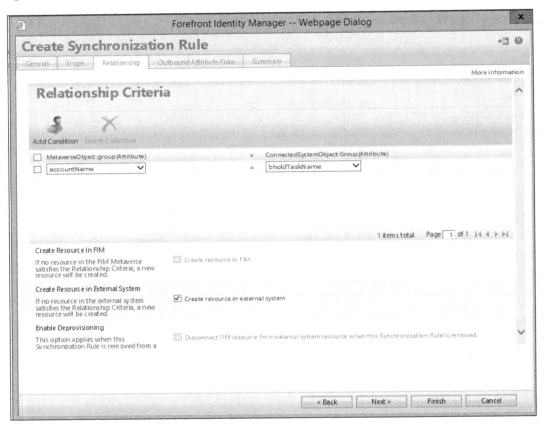

For the **Outbound Attribute Flow** we will have only a few mappings—with only one initial flow as you can see in the following screenshot. Click on **Finish**.

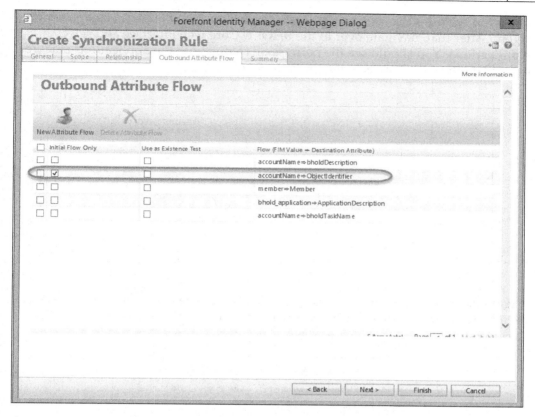

Once this is done, we will go ahead to the Management Agent for FIM/MIM, and complete a Full Import and Full Sync. Once we do the Full Sync, we will be able see the newly imported sync rules as well as permissions. We will also be able to see the five permissions as provisioning adds to the BHOLD Management Agent, as seen in the following screenshot:

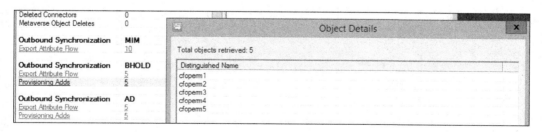

Once you see the staging export, go ahead and export the BHOLD Management Agent. After that, navigate over to the BHOLD Core web interface and select **Applications**. You should see the permissions along with the applications that we defined on the permissions in the previous step:

If you select one of the applications, you will also see the permissions in the stewards for that application—for example, you will see two permissions listed with **CFO_Accounts**:

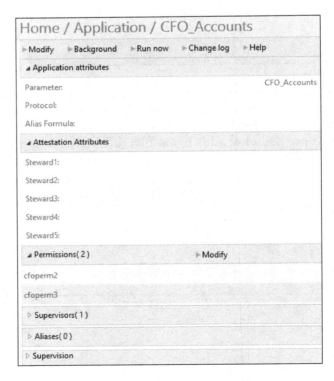

Now that we have the **CFO_Accounts** account's **Permissions** section open, go
ahead and click on **cfoperm3**. Now this is where we are actually going to set up the
incompatible permission. We want the permission to be incompatible with **cfoperm3**
and vice versa so that once we click on it, we will see the details for the permission.
You will also see a menu selection called **Incompatible permissions**. Click
on **Modify**:

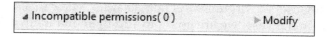

Once you click on **Modify**, you will see a UI that will have a drop-down menu
for applications in attribute types. Go ahead and select **CFO_Accounts** for the
application, and click on the search box. You should only see one permission in this
case—**cfoperm3**. Next to this permission, you'll see two **Add** buttons. One is **Link
Mandatory**, and the other is **Link Overrideable**.

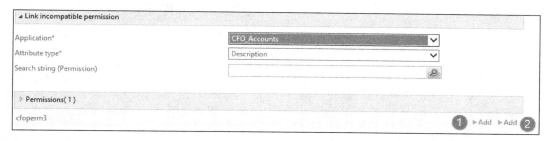

The **Link Mandatory** button defines that this permission will always be incompatible
with the linked incompatible permission. The **Link Overrideable** button means that
this incompatible permission can be overridden with approving authority.

In our case, we are going to click on the **Link Mandatory** button; we do not want this
permission to be overwritten writable with the incompatible permission:

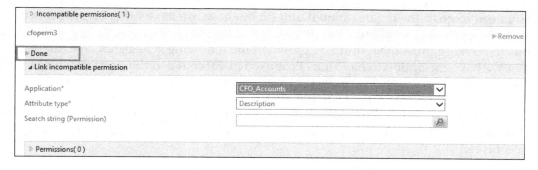

Now that we've gotten the incompatible permissions defined, let's go ahead and apply the permissions to a role. We will only do one of these for now, as an example, and will let you finish up the rest based on the chart in the table given earlier.

To do this work, map the `cforolef1` to the VP finance orgunit. This can be done simply by clicking on the role, navigating to the organizational unit's search string. Then click on **Add**, followed by **Done**. It is pretty easy to map orgunits to roles—it is just like mapping users to orgunits. As noted earlier, you can also do this with the model loader, but in our case, we are going to add them manually:

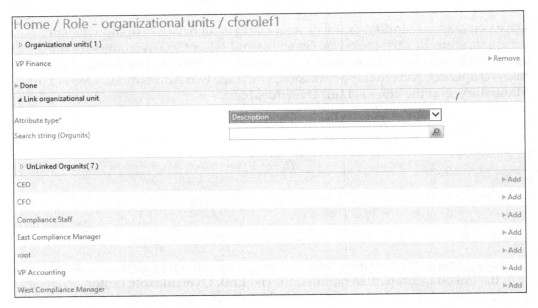

Now we will add the rest of the roles to the organizational units in the same manner based on the chart given earlier. Adding a proposed role is a bit different than just selecting the role, and then clicking on the organizational unit. For a proposed role, you need to go to the organizational unit (in our case, we have the east compliance staff and the west compliance staff that we need to add to `cforolef5`). We will add this to both organizational units, as shown in the following screenshot. We can see that we have the option to have it as **Proposed** or **Effective** in the drop-down box. For the relation type, we also have the option for the child to inherit this role. This means that if we create organizational units underneath the east compliance staff, they would have this as a proposed role as well. The next option you will see is the **Duration type**, which, in this case, can be defined as free or hours/days; we will select **free**:

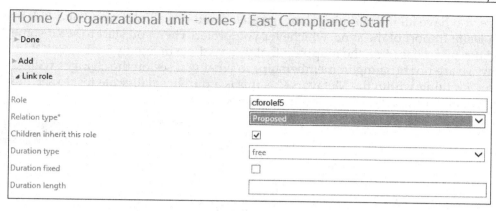

As the final step, we need to map the users to this. By default, the user was created in the root organizational unit, and as we know, we need to move these users. Now the great thing about BHOLD is that a user can be a part of multiple organizational units. Therefore, you can see the flexibility of multiple OU hierarchies, and then multiple RBAC roles based on projects or based on other business classifications that need to be managed by RBAC and the BHOLD Core.

To add a user, simply click on the user, then click on **Modify** next to the organizational units, and select the appropriate organizational unit. We will do this for all the users listed in the earlier chart:

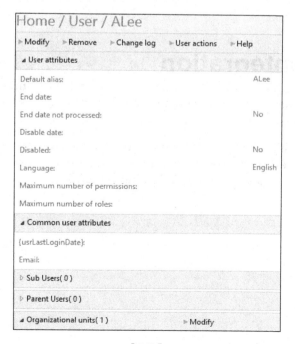

Once you have all the mapping done, go ahead and run a Full Import and Full Sync or a Delta Import of the sync, whichever you prefer. Then you start to see if some updates occur based on the mapping that you've done manually within BHOLD. Now we are not bringing in membership, so what you see on the changes will affect anything within the Metaverse, as this is a purely small-scale test to see the functionality of BHOLD Core and its components:

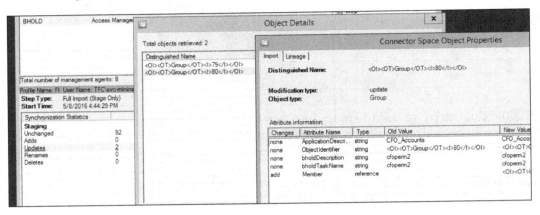

Before we begin with the integration, we need to set up role approval for the next simulation. We followed the guide at the following link to assign a role approvers role for the `cforole5` role. More in-depth information can be found at `http://bit.ly/MIMBHOLDApproval`.

MIM/FIM Integration

The Integration module is one of the lengthy and beneficial components of BHOLD Core. It allows the users to interface with the RBAC module, as they can click on the BHOLD Self Service portal.

With the light role model defined, you can see how it is coming together when you go to the **BHOLD Self Service** link. As a user, you have the capability to enroll in proposed roles, as you can see in the following screenshot:

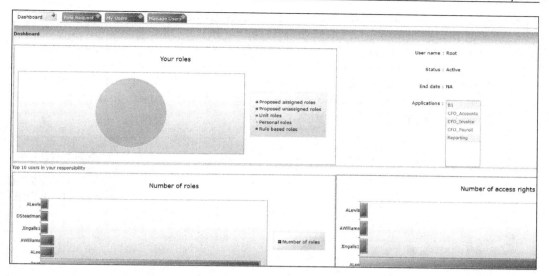

Roles without any approvers are deemed as auto approved. Take the case with AWilliams — we will submit a request for cforole5. So let's select and submit the request as follows:

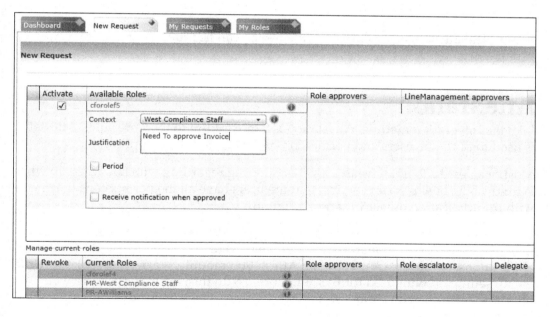

After a short while, you will see the screen refresh, and the `cforole5` assigned to `AWilliams`. If we performed a Delta Import on the BHOLD Management Agent, you will see this update occur. We see one update with the `member` attribute being updated. Again, with role approval, you can automate the traction making the role manager responsible for approving the role. Line managers are approvers only for the orgunit that they manage. Now you can look at the other users that we created to see how the invalid permission works:

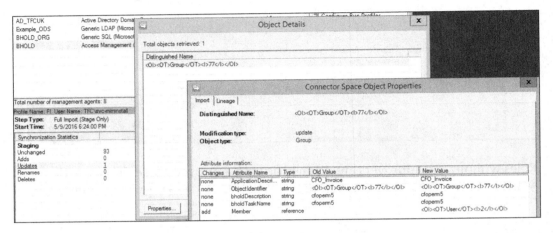

A complete introduction to BHOLD Integration can be found at `http://bit.ly/MIMBHAdmin`.

Attestation

Like the Integration module, Attestation is a nice add-in to the Core suite. Attestation is used to *verify* the users and permissions of an orgunit or an application.

Most businesses do not have this level of auditing regarding who has access to what. With this, the business can confirm that the users have all the permissions they need with the application owner to steward signoff.

Let's take The Financial Company as an example. We have the user `ALee`, who is the manager of the east compliance staff. But we need to do a complete audit of all the applications. Before we can set up the Attestation module, we need to make sure the e-mail setting is configured for BHOLD Core. To do this, log in to the Core web user interface. Then click on **Home**, and then on **Values**. Click on **Modify**, and fill in the appropriate setting for e-mail:

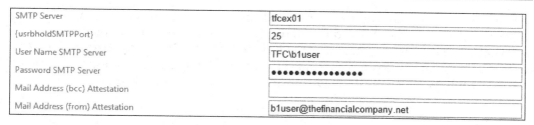

SMTP Server	tfcex01
{usrbholdSMTPPort}	25
User Name SMTP Server	TFC\b1user
Password SMTP Server	••••••••••••••••
Mail Address (bcc) Attestation	
Mail Address (from) Attestation	b1user@thefinancialcompany.net

Next, after launching the Attestation Campaign's shortcut on your screen, you will notice **Campaign Definition**. This lists all the ongoing campaigns currently in the system.

The **Notification** item is how you can customize the e-mail going to the steward or to the campaign owner. A list of the placeholder tags can be found at `http://bit.ly/ MIMBHattestation`:

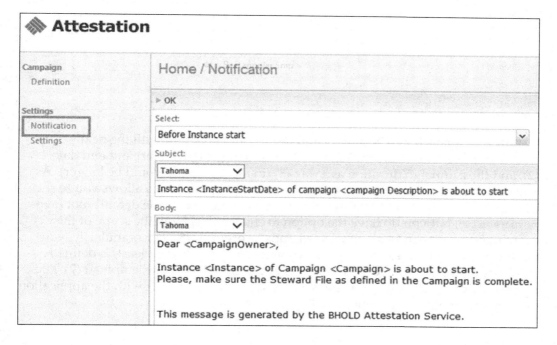

An application can have up to five stewards. In our case, for testing, we will only assign TFC\ALee as the steward for all the applications. To do this, you can open the application in BHOLD Core, and apply it directly or via the model loader. We will not discuss the model loader, as it is far too in-depth for the current topic. As you can see in the following screenshot, adding an application steward is pretty easy:

So now let's go back to Attestation, and define our campaign with the next screenshot. We will define the name of the campaign (**1**), the start and end date (**2**), and the campaign duration as 1 day (**3**) (in most cases, it would be longer). As you can see, we have an option to have a recurrent option—this allows you to set this up on a yearly cycle. Next we will leave the owner (**4**) to the default root (svc-miminstall), but you do have the option to change this. Now the scope of the campaign context can be all or selected apps or orgunits (**5**). For granularity, you have the options to attest permissions or users (**6**). Last, but not least, is defined stewards. In this, you have the options as application based or file upload (**7**). File upload is a nice option if you want to run a separate audit—not with the application owners, but another department:

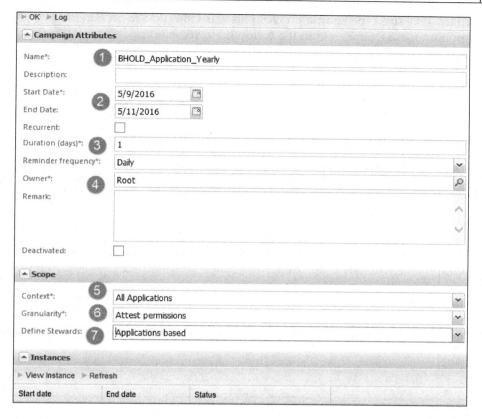

Once you are happy with your selections, click on **OK** at the bottom of the screen. You will notice that an instance (as seen in the next screenshot) is created. If not, confirm that the service is running:

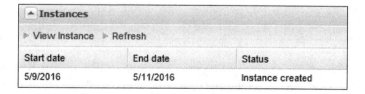

Now that we've fired the campaign, your steward should see an e-mail saying that his campaign is due, as shown in the following screenshot:

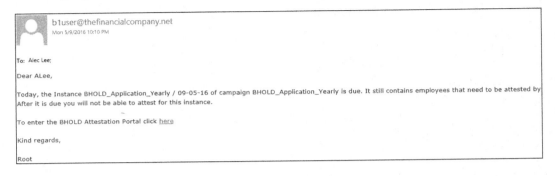

Make sure that before your steward clicks on the link, you have given them the correct rights in BHOLD Core. If not, they could receive something like the following:

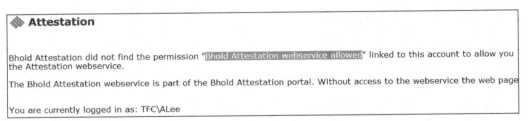

Now that we have given the correct permission to the stewards, they can begin the process of verifying the campaign and permission select view on our campaign.

In this view, the steward is required to select **Responsible** or **Not Responsible**. If **Not Responsible** is selected, the campaign owner is responsible for reassignment. Then what you will see is the account and the access right assigned to the user. We will approve all but AWilliams, and click on **Deny**:

Once done, we can confirm the selections. Then we navigate back to the Attestation Module as the campaign owner, and select **View**. We will then see that ALee is at 100% for all his assigned users:

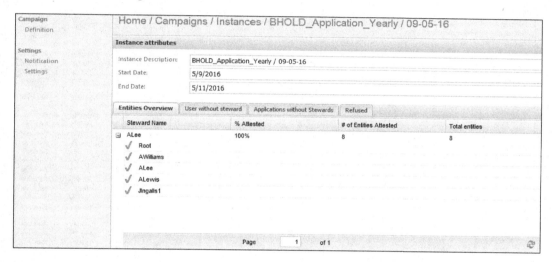

Now, once the campaign is completed, the permission confirmed as approved or denied will take effect. In the next section, we will go over the Reporting module, which brings this information to light.

For more information on the Attestation module, you can go to http://bit.ly/ MIMBHAT.

Reporting

Like MIM Reporting and Hybrid Reporting, the BHOLD Reporting module is a completely separate reporting mechanism. The reports in BHOLD are all based on the BHOLD RBAC solution. The core of the reports focuses on the controls within, such as the top 10 permissions for roles and users. There are many reports that come standard and out of the box to fit your organizational needs. If not, you can simply create a custom report as well, through the reporting interface.

Reports

▸ Expand All   ▸ Collapse All

Reports per category	Owner				
◢ Attestation					
Application manager worklist	Custom	Run	XLS	Modify	Remove
Attestation overview	Custom	Run	XLS	Modify	Remove
Attested users per campaign	Custom	Run	XLS	Modify	Remove
Unattested users	Custom	Run	XLS	Modify	Remove
◢ Controls					
Basic statistics	BHOLD	Run	XLS	Modify	Remove
Top 10 Permissions for roles	BHOLD	Run	XLS	Modify	Remove
Top 10 permissions for users	BHOLD	Run	XLS	Modify	Remove
Top 10 permissions for users by department	BHOLD	Run	XLS	Modify	Remove
◢ Inward Access Control					
Role supervisor By Role	BHOLD	Run	XLS	Modify	Remove
◢ Logging					
History	BHOLD	Run	XLS	Modify	Remove
history - Last Month	BHOLD	Run	XLS	Modify	Remove
Model History - Last Quarter	BHOLD	Run	XLS	Modify	Remove
Model History - Last week	BHOLD	Run	XLS	Modify	Remove
Model History - Last year	BHOLD	Run	XLS	Modify	Remove
Model History - Today	BHOLD	Run	XLS	Modify	Remove
Orgunit activity	BHOLD	Run	XLS	Modify	Remove
Orgunit Activity this month	BHOLD	Run	XLS	Modify	Remove
Role Activity this month	BHOLD	Run	XLS	Modify	Remove
Role History	BHOLD	Run	XLS	Modify	Remove
User history	BHOLD	Run	XLS	Modify	Remove
◢ Model					
Active accounts	BHOLD	Run	XLS	Modify	Remove
Applications, Roles and Permissions	BHOLD	Run	XLS	Modify	Remove
Employees or Users by role	BHOLD	Run	XLS	Modify	Remove
Role supervisors by role	BHOLD	Run	XLS	Modify	Remove
Roles without permissions	BHOLD	Run	XLS	Modify	Remove
Roles without users	BHOLD	Run	XLS	Modify	Remove
Unassigned permissions	BHOLD	Run	XLS	Modify	Remove
Unassigned Roles	BHOLD	Run	XLS	Modify	Remove
Users by Department	BHOLD	Run	XLS	Modify	Remove
Users by Role	BHOLD	Run	XLS	Modify	Remove
Users with Active Permissions and Application	BHOLD	Run	XLS	Modify	Remove
Users with Roles and active permissions	BHOLD	Run	XLS	Modify	Remove
Users without email address	BHOLD	Run	XLS	Modify	Remove
◢ Statistics					
Organizational units with amount of users	BHOLD	Run	XLS	Modify	Remove

When looking at the report, like the Attestation report, you can see who approved it, and then report to your security department about the time it was approved as well:

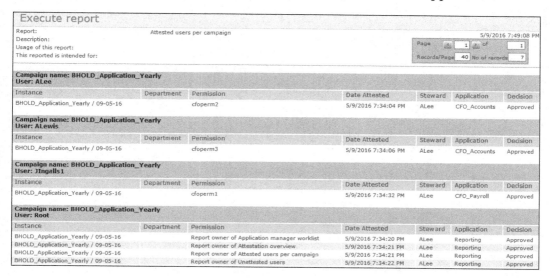

Summary

In this chapter, we took a look at role model objects (organizational units or users), their roles, and the permissions that are applied to the roles. We also explained the concept of applications, and grouping of permissions that are applied underneath that application. We looked at some other advanced features, such as SoD, that is, incompatible permissions. We ran through the installation of the Core modules, explained how to define the organizational unit, and also how to bring that information into the BHOLD Core for consumption. Next we uncovered creating the BHOLD connector and utilizing the Integration module. We touched upon the Attestation module and how it can help an organization. Finally, we looked at the Reporting module and the reports it provides for an organization to use.

In the next chapter, we will take a look at Privilege Access Management—a new feature in the Microsoft Identity 2016 suite.

8
Reducing Threats with PAM

Privileged Access Management (PAM) is a new component that was not included with the previous versions of the product. With PAM, user access is controlled through role requests that grant access for a specific period of time. This means end users in your corporate environment no longer require permanent membership in groups you've configured as security sensitive. Additionally, group membership requests can either be autoapproved or require approval.

In this chapter, we will cover the following topics:

- Why deploy PAM?
- PAM components
- How does it work?
- System requirements
- Considerations
- Our scenario
- Installing PAM and its requirements
- User experience
- PAM in the MIM service
- The sample PAM portal
- Multi-factor authentication

Why deploy PAM?

Many large-scale cyber attacks on business enterprises today focus on gaining administrative privileges. Hackers use various attack techniques such as "Pass-the-Hash" and e-mail "phishing" to try to gain access rights. If people use poor practices, such as making their day-to-day account a domain administrator, then a hacker's job is easier. The root problem, as described in *Microsoft's Best Practices for Securing Active Directory*, is that enterprises need to "eliminate permanent membership in highly privileged groups" and "implement controls to grant temporary membership in privileged groups when needed." MIM does just this, eliminating permanent membership of elevated groups by implementing a time-sensitive control over access. You can read more about Pass-the-Hash and securing Active Directory at `http://bit.ly/SecuringAD`.

PAM components

There are a few components that make PAM work, which are as follows:

- **Active Directory management forest**: A management forest is used to manage the existing forest(s) via one-way trust. Customers who already have a secured management forest, sometimes called a "red" forest, can use this management forest for PAM. If you only have a single forest, you need to create a new management forest.

- **PAM Client**: This is a PowerShell cmdlet or custom solution that uses the PAM REST API, such as the open source PAM API portal we will discuss later.

- **MIM service**: This is used as the PAM request and approval pipeline.

- **MIM database**: This holds MIM resources (objects), attributes, and requests.

- **PAM services**: These are the PAM REST API, PAM component service, and PAM monitoring service.

- **PAM REST API**: This is only used by a custom PAM client and provides a mechanism for PAM interactions such as roles, requests, request approvals, and session operations.

- **PAM component service**: In Windows 2012 R2 deployments, this is a Windows service that looks for requests that are expired and removes the shadow account from the SID History-enabled group residing in the trusted domain. It interacts directly with Active Directory and not with the MIM service. The PAM component service is unnecessary in Windows 2016 server deployments.

- **PAM monitoring service**: This is a Windows service that reads the corporate forest(s) and duplicates specific changes that are done in the corporate forest(s) to the privileged forest or to the MIM service.

 The MIM Synchronization service is not needed or used by PAM.

How does it work?

We can summarize the end user interaction in four steps, as follows:

1. After PAM is deployed, a user in one of the corporate forests (for us TFC), will request the role activation (some sort of elevation) of a secondary account that resides in a managed domain. If the request is performed via the PowerShell cmdlet, then a call is made directly to the MIM service, whereas if a custom PAM client is used, then the call is made to the REST API first, which interacts with the MIM service.

2. If the role request requires approval, then we will wait for approval. In Windows 2012 R2 deployments, once approved or autoapproved, the MIM service account (in the management forest) adds the end user's secondary account (in the management forest) to a shadow group (in the management forest). The SID of the sourced TFC group will be in the shadow group's SID History. Note that we did not change the membership of any TFC groups; however, you will see the shadow group membership change.

3. The person then authenticates and works with the account that is granted time sensitive privileges, which could be 30 minutes or whatever is defined in the role. If we were to look at the Kerberos group membership of the elevated account (in the management forest), it would have membership of the corporate group and the shadowed group.

4. After the role request expires, the account (in the management forest) is removed from the shadow group (in the management forest) by the PAM component service account in Windows 2012 R2 deployments. As already noted, the PAM component service is not used in Windows 2016 deployments and is handled by the server directly without the need for an extra MIM PAM service.

If the PAM component removes group membership in the management domain, what does the PAM monitor service provide? The PAM monitor watches the account state as well as five Active Directory attributes. For the state, the PAM monitor checks to see whether the account is disabled, locked, or deleted and will synchronize the states with their corresponding PRIV accounts:

- The `ACCOUNTDISABLE` flag of `userAccountControl`, which specifies whether the account is enabled or disabled

- The `LOCK_OUT` flag of `ms-DS-User-Account-Control-Computed`, which specifies whether the account is locked out.

The PAM monitor additionally synchronizes the `sAMAccountName`, `domain`, `phoneNumber`, and `mail` attributes.

If `TFC\JIngalls` has a PAM user account named `PRIV\Priv.JIngalls`, when the `TFC\JIngalls` Active Directory account is disabled, the PAM monitor service account will disable `PRIV\Priv.JIngalls`. The same applies when the TFC account is locked out or if one of the attributes listed before changes. Further, if the `TFC\Jingalls` account is deleted, `PRIV\Jingalls` will be deleted:

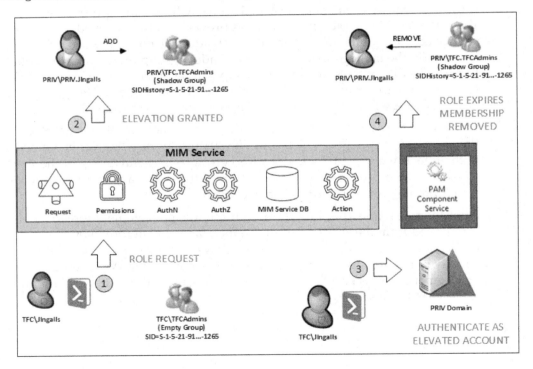

The expiration of the **access elevation** does not use temporal resources, as in the MIM portal. For Windows 2012 R2 deployments, PAM request expiration is handled by a new component called the PAM component service. The Windows 2016 server has built-in mechanisms to handle request expiration. In our example, we will use PowerShell to do this, although a custom client could be used to handle PAM requests and approvals too. Also, note that the PAM clients and the PAM REST API talk directly to the MIM service. The PAM clients could be in the privileged forest or in the corporate forest(s) as long as the clients can communicate to the MIM service (ports `5725` and `5726`), which exists in the privileged forest.

System requirements

PAM requires a management forest of Windows 2012 R2 or above, called a bastion forest, which is trusted (one-way trust) by the existing corporate forest(s). The bastion forest must be highly secured and well managed, which is why a new forest is recommended.

 Microsoft's *Best Practices for Securing Active Directory* is a must read. Find it at `http://bit.ly/SecuringAD`.

If you already have a secured management forest, then it can be utilized for PAM, and a new management forest is not needed. More information on PAM with an existing Active Directory forest can be found at `http://bit.ly/MIMPAMWithExistingDomains`.

If you do not already have a management forest, you may be wondering why Microsoft requires another forest for PAM. There are two reasons: firstly, a new forest will be free from malicious activity, and secondly, a new forest will help restrict access in the existing corporate forest(s). Basically, we can get the best out of our existing forest(s) by assuming the worst and creating a new forest to control or regain control.

In our example, the TFC (corporate) domain trusts the PRIV (bastion) single-domain management forest. In your existing corporate forest(s), the domain controllers must run Windows 2003 or higher. The MIM, PAM component, and PAM monitoring services, along with SQL and SharePoint 2013 Foundation with SP1, will be installed on a server of Windows 2012 R2 or higher, joined to the PRIV domain. The MIM synchronization engine and MIM portal are not required:

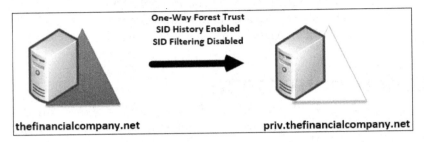

Considerations

Microsoft's PAM deployment considerations are well documented and can be found at http://bit.ly/PAMDeploymentConsiderations. We will highlight the key points.

As already mentioned, PAM helps mitigate attacks on accounts that have permanent membership in elevated groups. PAM is not an all-inclusive component that will mitigate every security-related issue. Consider one security situation in which end users have administrative access to their own workstations. It may seem harmless enough, but security software such as antivirus, antimalware, and firewall can be turned off or removed, and new (potentially malicious) software can be installed. Once malicious software is installed on a workstation, an attacker only needs to find a way to elevate access to gain control over the entire domain or forest. Not logging into untrusted workstations with an elevated account, such as a domain administrator, has been best practice in security for years and is helpful, but you can do better. Consider joining **privileged administrative workstations (PAW)** to the PRIV domain. PAW are workstations that are specifically hardened and done in a secure way, for example, only using verified media when installing the operating system, using full disk encryption, secure boot, and a host firewall and restricting USB ports, to name a few. Basically, assume there's a breach, secure the system, and follow best practices when installing and using the workstation. You can read more about PAW at http://bit.ly/PAWDocs.

Microsoft recommends implementing the bastion environment's administrative privileges in tiers and is an adaptation of the Biba and Bell-LaPadula model for data integrity and mitigating privilege elevation.

Kenneth J. Biba describes his model in his 1975 paper *Integrity Considerations for Secure Computer Systems*, available at `http://bit.ly/BibaModel`. A paper on Bell-LaPadula can be found at `http://bit.ly/BellModel`.

Accounts, workstations, applications, and critical services are classified into one of four privilege tiers, which determine the impact to the organization. For example, a standard user account would be in a lower tier and criticality than an enterprise administrative account. Take a look at the following table:

Tier	Description	Examples
0	Domain/forest administrator	Enterprise admins, schema admins, domain admins, account operators, backup operators, `BUILTIN\Administrator`, special system objects such as `AdminSDHolder`, accounts that have write or full permission on tier 0 accounts, domain controller's OU, OU containing tier 0 objects, group policies linked to a tier 0 OU, applications and services running on domain controllers.
1	Server administrator (access to non-domain controller servers)	Servers joined to the domain and workstations where tier 1 accounts log in, accounts with write or full permission to tier 1 objects, OU containing tier 1 objects, group policies linked to a tier 1 OU, applications and services running on non-domain controller servers.
2	Workstation administrator	Workstations joined to the domain and accounts that can manage those workstations that are not in tier 0 or 1, OU containing tier 2 objects and group policies linked to a tier 2 OU, applications and services running on workstations.
3	Normal user	A non-privileged user without administrative access to tier 0, 1, or 2.

With regard to the bastion forest, its management functions and applications should be limited as much as possible and decided before it is implemented. Your goal should be building a forest with the smallest attack surface possible. The systems joined to the bastion forest should be self-contained, meaning they should not receive any software or services from the existing environment, such as software distribution, DNS, backup software, and time services.

Consider the availability of all bastion forest services or at least how issues can be mitigated within your organization's service level agreement. Deploying at least two Active Directory Domain Services domain controllers and installing the SQL server and the MIM service on multiple systems is recommended. Microsoft suggests configuring all bastion forest systems to automatically install security updates.

Our scenario

TFC management is concerned with the TFC\JIngalls account, owned by Jeff Ingalls, and is subject to malicious internal and external attacks due to its permanent membership in the TFCAdmins group. The TFCAdmins group grants access to several highly confidential shares and servers. TFC management likes to utilize PAM to eliminate the permanent membership of the TFCAdmins group, mitigating risk while still allowing Jeff to do his job.

To validate our PAM deployment works, Jeff will gain access to an NTFS-secured file through a PAM request. In the past, he could open up the file directly, but under PAM, he will need to perform an extra request step before he can access the file. To set up the scenario, a folder named TOPSECRET on the TFCWIN10 workstation will have NTFS permissions applied to only allow access to members of the TFCAdmins group. Once PAM is deployed, the TFC\JIngalls account will not be in the TFCAdmins group. Yet, through PAM, Jeff will be able to access a file named Salaries.txt that resides in the TOPSECRET folder just as he did before, without needing to be permanently in the TFCAdmins group:

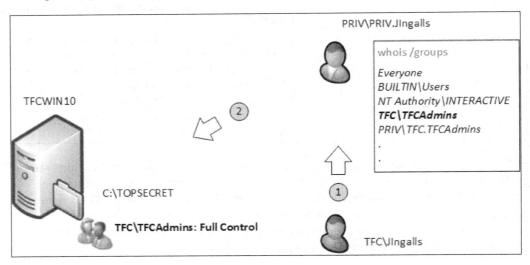

Preparing TFC

We will follow the published TechNet article *Configuring the MIM Environment for Privileged Access Management,* available at `http://bit.ly/MIMPAMInstall`, to allow you to have a secondary reference that may update over time. We will walk through the installation and provide the hints we've learned. For the remainder of the chapter, we will refer to the existing corporate single-domain forest as TFC and the bastion single-domain forest as PRIV. If you happen to have a multiple-domain corporate forest, PAM will only require a single-domain forest. You will see how this works later in the chapter.

Before we dive into the installation of PAM, we need you to make sure you have the most recent update of MIM 2016 and PAM components installed. You can find the most recent updates at `http://bit.ly/MIMUpdates`.

The Windows requirements for PAM are listed in the following table:

	TFC forest	**PRIV forest**
Forest functional level	Server 2003 or higher	Server 2012 R2 or higher
Domain functional level	Server 2003 or higher	Server 2012 R2 or higher
Client OS requirements for PAM PowerShell client	Windows 7 or higher	N/A

We will begin by preparing TFC. There are minor configuration items within TFC, but each item is critical to the setup of PAM.

On a TFC domain controller, TFCDC01, create a new group, TFC$$$, that will be used to support auditing. This special group is required, or PAM will fail. This step is unnecessary in Windows 2016 server deployments:

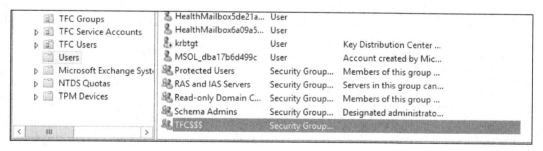

In your environment, the name of the group must be the NETBIOS name of the domain followed by $$$. The group must be a domain local security group. Do not add members to the group. Adding members to the group will make the SID History migration fail. You can read more about SID History migration at `http://bit.ly/ MIMSIDHistoryMigration`.

From PowerShell, type the following command:

```
Import-module ActiveDirectory

New-ADGroup -name 'TFC$$$' -GroupCategory Security -GroupScope
DomainLocal -SamAccountName 'TFC$$$'
```

Next, we can configure auditing by running Group Policy Management in the TFC domain and edit **Default Domain Controllers Policy**.

 Configuring auditing is only a requirement for Windows 2012 R2 deployments.

Go to **Computer Configuration | Policies | Windows Settings | Security Settings | Local Policies | Audit Policy**. Then, enable **Success, Failure** on **Audit account management** and **Audit directory service access**:

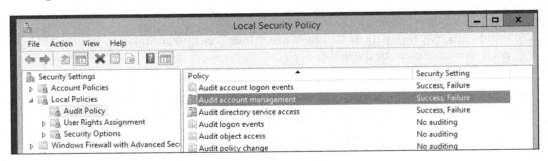

Apply the new group policy settings on TFCDC01 by typing the following:

```
gpupdate /force /target:computer
```

In some rare conditions, the group policy may not reflect the interface, and we ran into this problem just once in our lab. To be sure the setting is correct, run the Auditpol tool. You can do this by typing the following command and verifying that the policy has **Success and Failure** settings:

```
auditpol /get /category:"Account Management","DS Access"
```

```
C:\>auditpol /get /category:"Account Management","DS Access"
System audit policy
Category/Subcategory                           Setting
Account Management
  User Account Management                      Success and Failure
  Computer Account Management                  Success and Failure
  Security Group Management                    Success and Failure
  Distribution Group Management                Success and Failure
  Application Group Management                 Success and Failure
  Other Account Management Events              Success and Failure
DS Access
  Directory Service Changes                    Success and Failure
  Directory Service Replication                Success and Failure
  Detailed Directory Service Replication       Success and Failure
  Directory Service Access                     Success and Failure
```

After the domain group policy is updated, we can configure registry settings on
TFCDC01 for SID History migration. Again, this is only needed for Windows 2012 R2
deployments. For Windows 2012 R2, SID History migration is required to create the
special privileged access management group(s). We will need to reboot the domain
controller after making the registry change. In your environment, run the following
PowerShell command on the domain controller that holds the PDC Emulator role:

```
New-ItemProperty -Path HKLM:SYSTEM\CurrentControlSet\Control\Lsa -Name
TcpipClientSupport -PropertyType DWORD -Value 1
```

```
Restart-Computer
```

```
Administrator: Windows PowerShell
PS C:\> New-ItemProperty -Path HKLM:SYSTEM\CurrentControlSet\Control\Lsa -Name TcpipClientSupport -PropertyType DWORD -Value 1

TcpipClientSupport : 1
PSPath             : Microsoft.PowerShell.Core\Registry::HKEY_LOCAL_MACHINE\SYSTEM\CurrentControlSet\Control\Lsa
PSParentPath       : Microsoft.PowerShell.Core\Registry::HKEY_LOCAL_MACHINE\SYSTEM\CurrentControlSet\Control
PSChildName        : Lsa
PSDrive            : HKLM
PSProvider         : Microsoft.PowerShell.Core\Registry
```

To verify that our PAM installation works, create an Active Directory security group (this can be Domain Local, Global, or Universal) called TFCAdmins on TFCDC01, and add TFC\JIngalls to the group. On TFCWIN01, a computer joined to TFC, create a folder named TOPSECRET with a file called Salaries.txt. Set the NTFS permissions of the folder and its contents to full control for the TFCAdmins group and remove all other permissions. The security of the folder should look something similar to this:

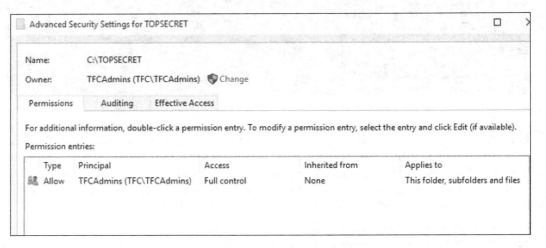

We will now log in as TFC\JIngalls and verify that the file within the folder can be opened:

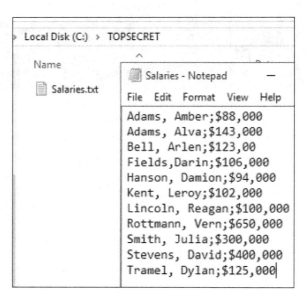

Preparing PRIV

As already mentioned, the single-domain PRIV forest has to be a Windows 2012 R2 forest or that of a higher functional level, and Windows 2012 R2 or a higher domain functional level.

On the new PRIV domain controller, PRIVDC01, we will create new MIM-related service accounts, as shown here. Note that we will be using the same naming convention and password as in the TechNet article at http://bit.ly/ MIMPAMInstall:

```
Import-Module ActiveDirectory
$sp = ConvertTo-SecureString 'Password1' -asplaintext AsPlainText -Force
New-ADUser -SamAccountName MIMMA -name MIMMA
Set-ADAccountPassword -identity MIMMA -NewPassword $sp
Set-ADUser -identity MIMMA -Enabled 1 -PasswordNeverExpires 1
New-ADUser -SamAccountName MIMMonitor -name MIMMonitor -DisplayName
MIMMonitor
Set-ADAccountPassword -identity MIMMonitor -NewPassword $sp
Set-ADUser -identity MIMMonitor -Enabled 1 -PasswordNeverExpires 1
New-ADUser -SamAccountName MIMComponent -name MIMComponent -DisplayName
MIMComponent
Set-ADAccountPassword -identity MIMComponent -NewPassword $sp
Set-ADUser -identity MIMComponent -Enabled 1 -PasswordNeverExpires 1
New-ADUser -SamAccountName MIMService -name MIMService
Set-ADAccountPassword -identity MIMService -NewPassword $sp
Set-ADUser -identity MIMService -Enabled 1 -PasswordNeverExpires 1
New-ADUser -SamAccountName SharePoint -name SharePoint
Set-ADAccountPassword -identity SharePoint -NewPassword $sp
Set-ADUser -identity SharePoint -Enabled 1 -PasswordNeverExpires 1
New-ADUser -SamAccountName SqlServer -name SqlServer
Set-ADAccountPassword -identity SqlServer -NewPassword $sp
Set-ADUser -identity SqlServer -Enabled 1 -PasswordNeverExpires 1
New-ADUser -SamAccountName BackupAdmin -name BackupAdmin
Set-ADAccountPassword -identity BackupAdmin -NewPassword $sp
Set-ADUser -identity BackupAdmin -Enabled 1 -PasswordNeverExpires 1
New-ADUser -SamAccountName MIMAdmin -name MIMAdmin
```

```
Set-ADAccountPassword -identity MIMAdmin -NewPassword $sp
Set-ADUser -identity MIMAdmin -Enabled 1 -PasswordNeverExpires 1
```

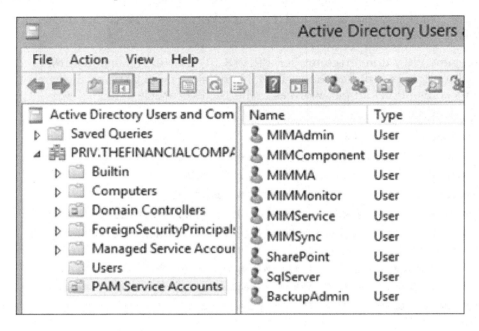

There are a few differences between what we've written here and the TechNet article:

- We used a single quote instead of a double quote when specifying the password. We did this in case you want to use a $ character in your password.

- We created an MIMMA account even though a Management Agent is not used for PAM. We listed it here to match with the TechNet article; however, you do not need to create the MIMMA account in your environment as it is only used during an installation check. Another account could be used instead of the MIMMA account without any issues.

- We omitted the creation of the MIMSync account as PAM does not require the Synchronization service.

Once the accounts are created, we will configure auditing and log-on rights on the PRIV domain. This step is required for Windows 2012 R2 deployments, so don't skip it. On the PRIV domain controller, go to **Group Policy Management** and edit **Default Domain Controllers Policy**. In **Default Domain Controller Policy**, go to **Computer Configuration | Policies | Windows Settings | Security Settings | Local Policies | Audit Policy**. Enable **Success and Failure** on **Audit account management** and **Audit directory service access**. Then, close **Default Domain Controllers Policy**.

We will now secure the service accounts. Take a look at this quick reference table for what we need to do. You can skip the next paragraph if you already know how to make these settings:

Group policy	Policies	Policy	User
Default Domain Policy	User Rights Assignment	Deny log on as a batch job	PRIV\MIMComponent
Default Domain Policy	User Rights Assignment	Deny log on as a batch job	PRIV\MIMMonitor
Default Domain Policy	User Rights Assignment	Deny log on as a batch job	PRIV\MIMService
Default Domain Policy	User Rights Assignment	Deny log on through Remote Desktop Services	PRIV\MIMComponent
Default Domain Policy	User Rights Assignment	Deny log on through Remote Desktop Services	PRIV\MIMMonitor
Default Domain Policy	User Rights Assignment	Deny log on through Remote Desktop Services	PRIV\MIMComponent

To modify the log-on rights, edit the **Default Domain Policy**; go to **Computer Configuration | Policies | Windows Settings | Security Settings | Local Policies | User Rights Assignment**. On the **Details** pane, right-click on **Deny log on as a batch job** and select **Properties**. Click on the **Define these Policies Settings** checkbox; then, click on **Add User or Group**; in the **User and group names** field, type PRIV\ MIMMonitor; PRIV\MIMService; PRIV\MIMComponent, and finally, click on **OK**. Click on **OK** to close the **Deny log on as a batch job** option's **Properties** window. On the **Details** pane, right-click on **Deny log on through Remote Desktop Services** and select **Properties**. Click on the **Define these Policies Settings** checkbox; then, click **Add User or Group**; in the user and group names, enter PRIV\MIMMonitor, PRIV\ MIMService, and PRIV\MIMComponent; and then, click on **OK**. Close the **Default Domain Policy** and **Group Policy Management** windows.

Apply the new group policy settings on the domain controller by typing the following:

```
gpupdate /force /target:computer
```

As we did in the TFC domain, run the Auditpol tool and confirm that the settings are applied, as follows:

```
auditpol /get /category:"Account Management","DS Access"
```

```
C:\>auditpol /get /category:"Account Management","DS Access"
System audit policy
Category/Subcategory                        Setting
Account Management
  User Account Management                   Success and Failure
  Computer Account Management               Success and Failure
  Security Group Management                 Success and Failure
  Distribution Group Management             Success and Failure
  Application Group Management              Success and Failure
  Other Account Management Events           Success and Failure
DS Access
  Directory Service Changes                 Success and Failure
  Directory Service Replication             Success and Failure
  Detailed Directory Service Replication    Success and Failure
  Directory Service Access                  Success and Failure
```

Next, configure the registry settings needed for SID History migration on PRIV DC. The PowerShell command is the same as we performed earlier, as follows:

```
New-ItemProperty -Path HKLM:SYSTEM\CurrentControlSet\Control\Lsa -Name
TcpipClientSupport -PropertyType DWORD -Value 1
```

On the PRIV domain controller, which hosts DNS, we will add a conditional forwarder to thefinancialcompany.net, specifying the IP address of a TFC domain controller hosting DNS. Launch PowerShell and type the following command:

```
Add-DnsServerConditionalForwarderZone -name "thefinancialcompany.net" -
masterservers 192.168.5.10
```

In DNS Manager, you should see that the conditional forwarder has been created, as in the following screenshot:

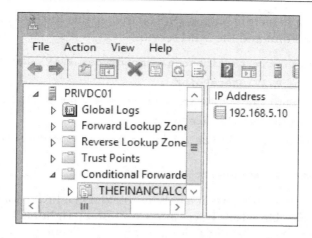

We will now add three A records to reference three PAM services. In TFC, we will add `pam`, `pamservice`, and `pamapi` host records. Take a look at the following table:

Record type	Host	Description
A	pam	SharePoint site
A	pamservice	MIM Service endpoint
A	pamapi	PAM REST API endpoint

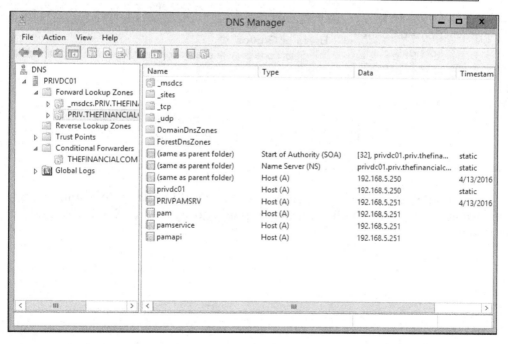

Next, create **Service Principle Names (SPNs)** that enable the Kerberos authentication to be used by SharePoint and the MIM service:

```
setspn -S http/pam.priv.thefinancialcompany.net PRIV\SharePoint

setspn -S http/pam PRIV\SharePoint

setspn -S http/pamapi.priv.thefinancialcompany.net PRIV\SharePoint

setspn -S http/pamapi PRIV\SharePoint

setspn -S FIMService/pamservice.priv.thefinancialcompany.net PRIV\
MIMService

setspn -S FIMService/pamservice PRIV\MIMService
```

Configuring the Active Directory delegation is next. On a PRIV domain controller, run **Active Directory Users and Computers**, right-click on the **PRIV. THEFINANCIALCOMPANY.NET** domain, and select **Delegate Control**. On the **Selected users and groups** tab, click on **Add**. Then, in the **Select Users, Computers, or Groups** popups, type `MIMComponent; MIMMonitor; MIMService`, and then click on **Check Names**. After the names are underlined, click **OK**:

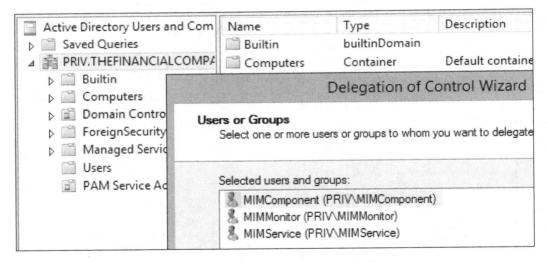

Now, click on **Next**. In the list of common tasks, select **Create, delete, and manage user accounts** and **Modify the membership of a group**, and click on **Next** and then on **Finish**:

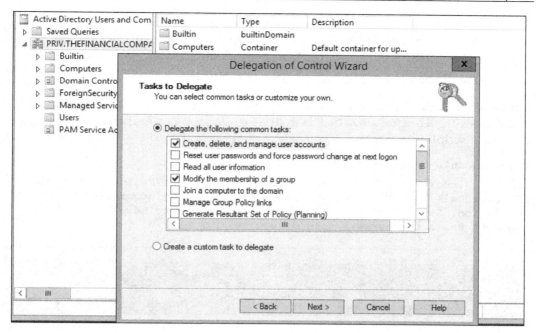

Delegate **MIMAdmin** a custom task to **This Folder** with **General Permissions** and add **Read**, **Write**, **Create All Child Objects**, **Delete All Child Objects**, **Read All Properties**, **Write All Properties**, and **Migrate SID History**. Click on **Next** and then on **Finish**.

Delegate the **MIMAdmin** a custom task to **This Folder** of only **User** objects, and in the permission list, select **Change password** and **Reset password**. Click on **Next** and then on **Finish**. Close **Active Directory Users and Computers**. Reboot the PRIV domain controller for all the SID History changes we made to take effect.

Preparing the PAM server

On the PAM server that is joined to the PRIV domain, we will perform the following tasks:

1. Install the web server (IIS) and application server roles, the .NET framework's features, the Active Directory module for PowerShell, and additional features required by SharePoint.

2. Configure the local security policy and grant access.

3. Configure IIS.

4. Now, install SQL 2008 R2 with SP3, SQL Server 2012 with SP2, or SQL Server 2014 with SP1 and assign the SQL permission.

5. Install SharePoint 2013 Foundation with SP1.

Let's start with the first task and install IIS and the required features. Assuming our Windows 2012 R2 installation disk is in drive D:, launch PowerShell and run the following script:

```
Import-module ServerManager

Install-WindowsFeature Web-WebServer, Net-Framework-Features, rsatRSAT-
AD-PowerShell, Web-Mgmt-Tools,Application-Server, Windows-Identity-
Foundation, Server-Media-Foundation, Xps-Viewer -includeallsubfeature
-restart Restart -source Source D:\sources\SxS
```

Next, we configure the PAM server's local security policy to allow the service accounts to run as services. Go to **Administrative Tools** and run **Local Security Policy**. In **Local Policies**, click on **User Rights Assignment**. Update the rights as shown in the following table:

User Right	Account
Log-on as a service	PRIV\MIMMonitor
	PRIV\MIMService
	PRIV\SharePoint
	PRIV\MIMComponent
	PRIV\SQLServer
Deny access to this computer from the network	PRIV\MIMMonitor
	PRIV\MIMService
	PRIV\MIMComponent
Deny log on locally	PRIV\MIMMonitor
	PRIV\MIMService
	PRIV\MIMComponent

User Right	Account

Deny log on as a batch job	(These accounts were set by the Default Domain Policy)
	
	`PRIV\MIMMonitor`
	
	`PRIV\MIMService`
	
	`PRIV\MIMComponent`

Deny log on through Remote Desktop Services	(These accounts were set by the Default Domain Policy)
	
	`PRIV\MIMMonitor`
	
	`PRIV\MIMService`
	
	`PRIV\MIMComponent`

In **Control Panel**, go to **User Accounts** and click on **Give others access to this computer**. The PAM product group suggests that you add four members to the local administrators group: MIMAdmin, SharePoint, MIMService, and MIMComponent.

Configuring IIS is next. Allow applications to use Windows Authentication mode by launching PowerShell and running the following commands:

```
iisreset /STOP
```

```
C:\Windows\System32\inetsrv\appcmd.exe unlock config /
section:windowsAuthentication -commit:apphost
```

```
iisreset /START
```

Open the `C:\Windows\System32\inetsrv\config\applicationHost.config` file in Notepad and change Windows Authentication's `overrideModeDefault` from `Deny` to `Allow`. The line should then look similar to this:

```
<section name="windowsAuthentication" overrideModeDefault="Allow" />
```

```
<sectionGroup name="authentication">
    <section name="anonymousAuthentication" overrideModeDefault="Deny" />
    <section name="basicAuthentication" overrideModeDefault="Deny" />
    <section name="clientCertificateMappingAuthentication" overrideModeDefault="Deny" />
    <section name="digestAuthentication" overrideModeDefault="Deny" />
    <section name="iisClientCertificateMappingAuthentication" overrideModeDefault="Deny" />
    <section name="windowsAuthentication" overrideModeDefault="Allow" />
</sectionGroup>
```

Save the file and recycle IIS once more by running the following commands:

```
iisreset /STOP
```

```
iisreset /START
```

We are now ready to install SQL. Log on as MIMAdmin, and from an administrative command prompt, install SQL using the following command:

```
.\setup.exe /Q /IACCEPTSQLSERVERLICENSETERMS /ACTION=install /
FEATURES=SQL,SSMS /INSTANCENAME=MSSQLSERVER /SQLSVCACCOUNT="PRIV\
SqlServer" /SQLSVCPASSWORD="Password1" /AGTSVCSTARTUPTYPE=Automatic /
AGTSVCACCOUNT="NT AUTHORITY\Network Service" /SQLSYSADMINACCOUNTS="PRIV\
MIMAdmin"
```

While logged in as PRIV\MIMAdmin, we will install SharePoint 2013 Foundation with SP1 prerequisites, and then the complete installation. To install the prerequisites, extract the `Sharepoint.exe` file by running the `SharePoint /extract:C:\APPS\PAM\SPS` command.

Then, type the `.\prerequisiteinstaller.exe` command:

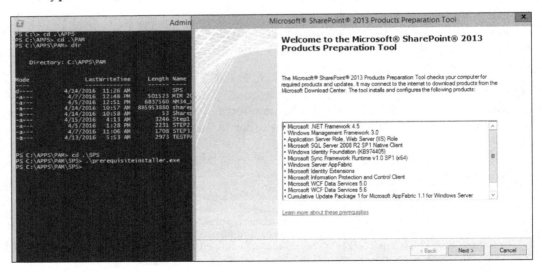

While we are on the topic of prerequisites, it may have been our bad luck, but during the prerequisite installation, we had an issue while installing AppFabric. The server would fail at installing AppFabric, we would reboot and reattempt the installation, and we would fail with the same error code 1603. We were able to work around the problem by removing the `PSModule` entry in System Environment Variables. To do this, go to **My Computer**, right-click on **Properties**, and on the **Systems** page, click on **Advanced System Settings**, on the **Advanced** tab, and then on **Environment Variables**. Remove the entry; then, when the AppFabric installs, re-add the `PSModule` path entry. The path should look similar to this: `C:\Windows\system32\ WindowsPowerShell\v1.0\Modules;c:\Program Files\AppFabric 1.1 for Windows Server\PowershellModules`.

After the prerequisites are installed, the system will need to be restarted. SharePoint should report back that all prerequisites are installed, as in the following screenshot:

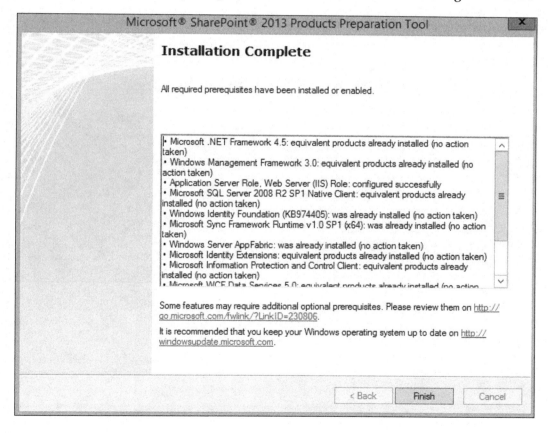

Next, we will run `.\setup.exe` and work through the configuration wizard. In configuration wizard, enter the local PAM server name, PRIVPAMSRV, with the PRIV\SharePoint service account:

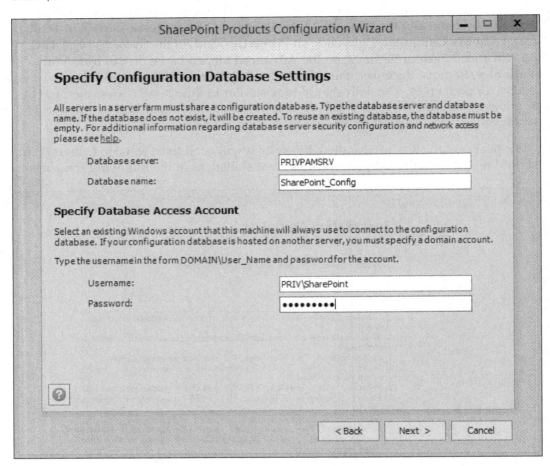

Keep the defaults for the rest of the wizard:

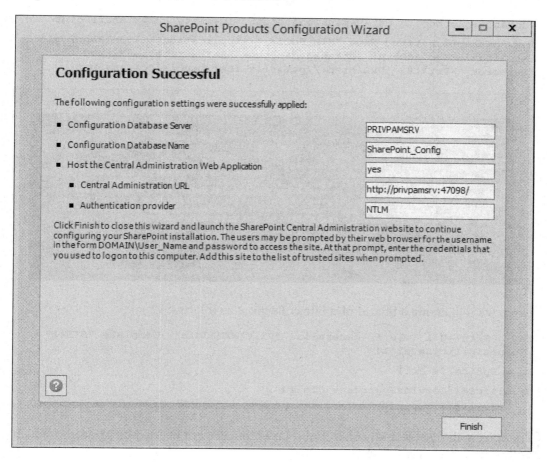

In SharePoint 2013 Management Shell, run the following script:

```
$dbManagedAccount = Get-SPManagedAccount -Identity PRIV\\SharePoint

New-SpWebApplication -Name "MIM Portal" -ApplicationPool "MIMAppPool"
-ApplicationPoolAccount $dbManagedAccount -AuthenticationMethod
"Kerberos" -Port 82 -URL http://pam.priv.thefinancialcompany.net
```

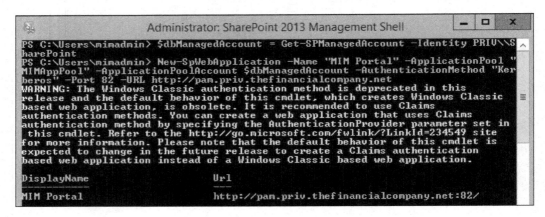

Next, we will create a SharePoint Site collection, as follows:

```
New-SPSite -Url $w.Url -owneralias "PRIV\MIMAdmin" -Template "STS#1"
-CompatibilityLevel 14

$s = SpSite($w.Url)

$s.AllowSelfServiceUpgrade = $false

$s.CompatibilityLevel
```

Then, we will disable a few SharePoint tasks that are not needed by MIM and which will cause issues if not disabled:

```
$contentService = [Microsoft.SharePoint.Administration.
SPWebService]::ContentService;

$contentService.ViewStateOnServer = $false;

$contentService.Update();

Get-SPTimerJob hourly-all-sptimerservice-health-analysis-job | disable-
SPTimerJob
```

```
Administrator: SharePoint 2013 Management Shell                    _  □  X

PS C:\Users\mimadmin> $w = Get-SPWebApplication http://pam.priv.thefinancialcomp
any.net:82
PS C:\Users\mimadmin> New-SPSite -Url $w.Url -owneralias "PRIV\MIMAdmin" -Templa
te "STS#1" -CompatibilityLevel 14

Url                                                      CompatibilityLevel
---                                                      ------------------
http://pam.priv.thefinancialcompany.net:82               14

PS C:\Users\mimadmin> $s = SpSite($w.Url)
PS C:\Users\mimadmin> $s.AllowSelfServiceUpgrade = $false
PS C:\Users\mimadmin> $s.CompatibilityLevel
14
PS C:\Users\mimadmin>
PS C:\Users\mimadmin> $contentService = [Microsoft.SharePoint.Administration.SPW
ebService]::ContentService;
PS C:\Users\mimadmin> $contentService.ViewStateOnServer = $false;
PS C:\Users\mimadmin> $contentService.Update();
PS C:\Users\mimadmin>
PS C:\Users\mimadmin> Get-SPTimerJob hourly-all-sptimerservice-health-analysis-j
ob | disable-SPTimerJob
PS C:\Users\mimadmin> _
```

At this point, you should be able to open Internet Explorer, connect to `http://` `pam.`
`priv.thefinancialcompany.net:82`, and log in as `PRIV\MIMAdmin`. Add the site to
your local intranet. In Windows Services, make sure the SharePoint Administrative
service is running before continuing with the next section.

Installing PAM

Installing the PAM server components on PRIVPAMSRV is done by launching the
administrative command prompt and running the **Service and Portal** installation:

Choose to select the **Privileged Access Management** component under **MIM Service** and the **MIM Portal.** Even though the portal is not required, we are installing it to easily show you the new PAM resources (objects) made within the service:

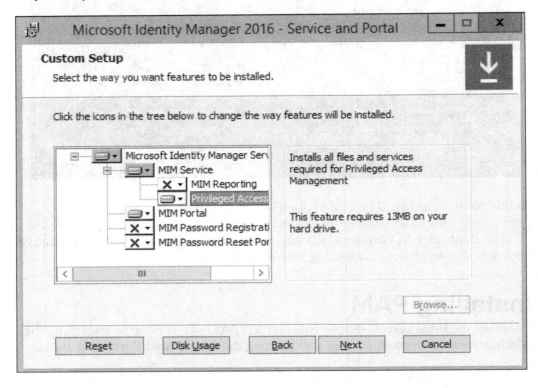

For the MIM database connections, enter the database server name, PRIVPAMSRV, and keep the database name, FIMService (the default name), and select **Create a new database**:

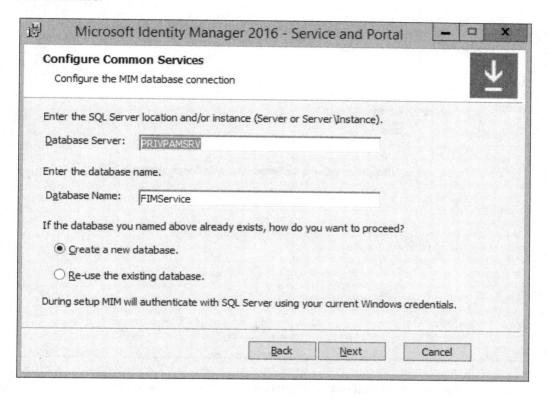

Enter the FQDN of your e-mail server and select the options appropriate to your environment. In our example, we will use `localhost` and click on **Next**:

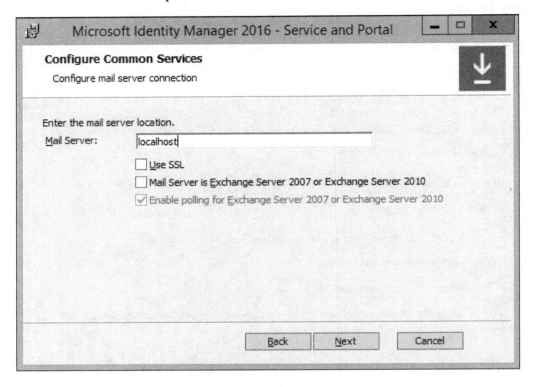

Click on **Generate a new self-issued certificate** and then on **Next**. Enter the MIM service account information, as follows:

- **Service Account Name**: MIMService
- **Service Account Password**: Password1
- **Service Account Domain**: PRIV

- **Service Email Account**: `MIMService@priv.thefinancialcompany.net`

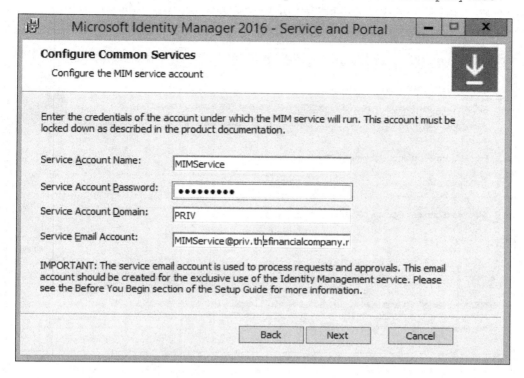

Click on **Next** to move on to a dialog about the synchronization service.

 Remember that you do not need to and should not install the MIM Synchronization service in the PRIV domain.

Keep the default name for the synchronization server name, PRIVPAMSRV, and enter PRIV\MIMMA (or any other existing account) for the MIM Management Agent account.

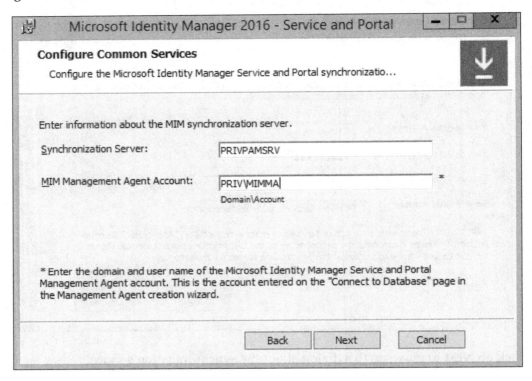

You will receive an error that the synchronization service was not found or is not running. Don't panic; this error is expected. Click on **Next** to move past the error:

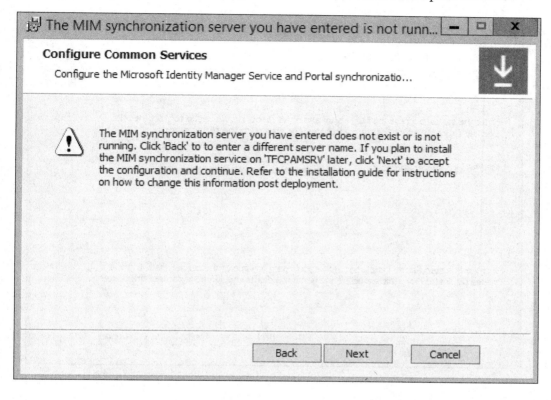

Next, we will enter the MIM Service server address as `pamservice.priv.` `thefinancialcompany.net`:

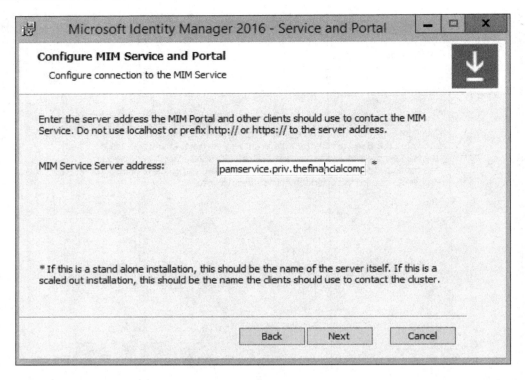

We will now enter the SharePoint site collection URL, `http:// pam.priv.`
`thefinancialcompany.net:82`:

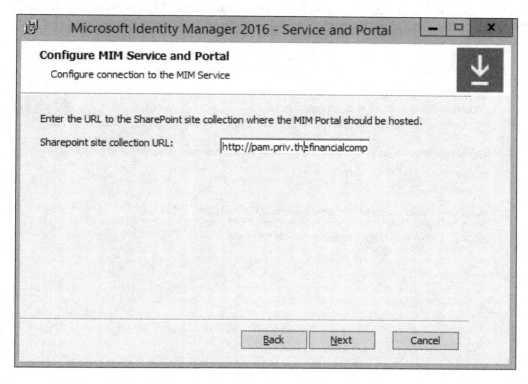

Click on **Next**. Leave the **Registration Portal URL** blank and click on **Next**. The next step is to configure security changes required by the setup. Select the boxes to **Open ports 5725 and 5726 in firewall** and to **Grant authenticated users access to the MIM Portal site**; then, click on **Next**:

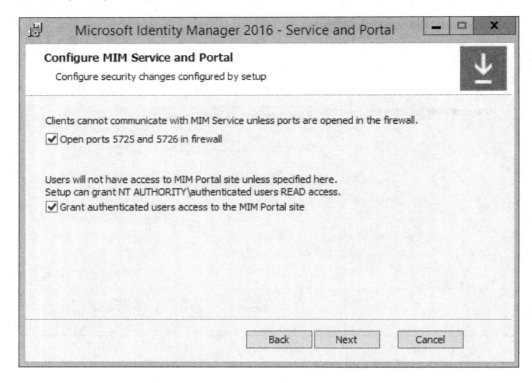

Configuring the PAM REST API is next. Enter the hostname `pamapi.priv.thefinancialcompany.net` and specify an unused port number. We will use port `8086`:

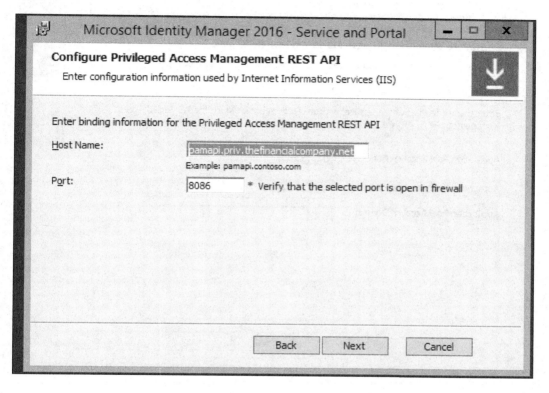

Click on **Next**. We will now define the application pool account that should be used for the REST API. We will use PRIV\SharePoint for the application pool account:

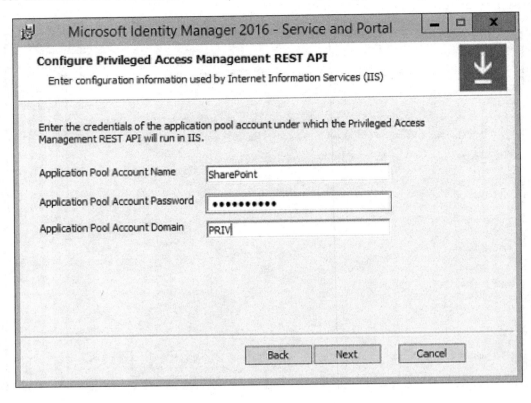

You will receive a warning that the SharePoint account is not secure in its current configuration:

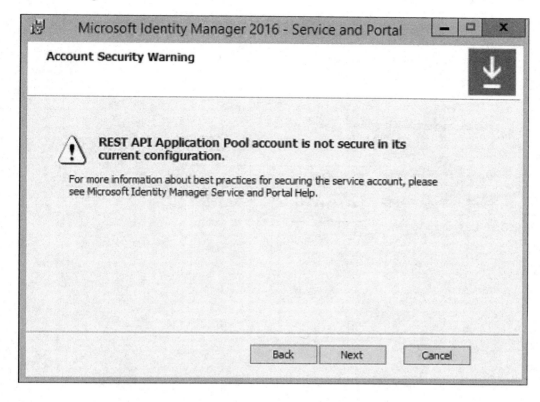

The Microsoft product group has confirmed that this is an expected warning.

We will now specify the PAM component service account and use the MIMComponent account for our component service account:

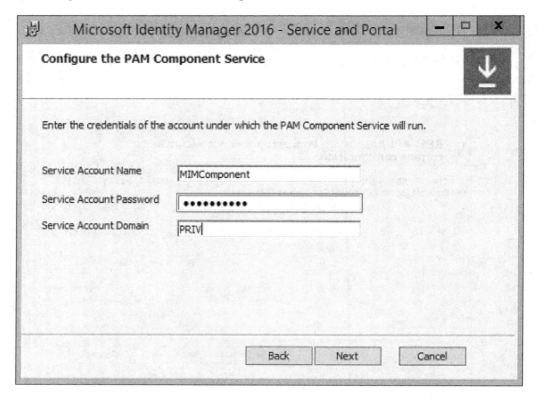

We will now specify the PAM monitoring service account. We will use `MIMMonitor`:

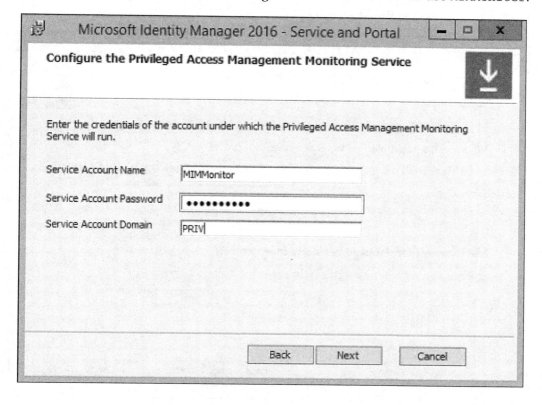

Click on **Next** through the section on **Password Portals** as we do not install password registration or reset in the PRIV domain:

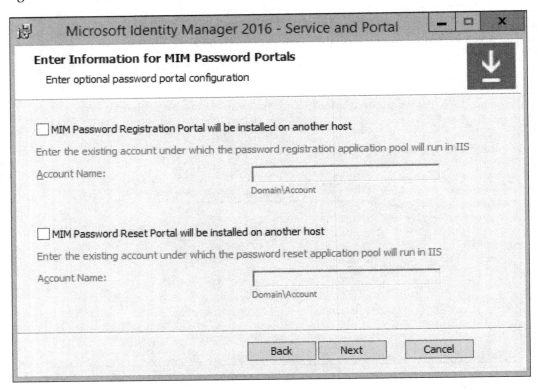

Click on the **Install** button to begin the PAM installation. You will need to restart the PAM server after the installation is complete. After a reboot, launch Internet Explorer, browse to `http://pam.priv.thefinancialcompany.net:82/IdentityManagement`, and verify that the site is loading. If you are prompted to log in, authenticate as PRIV\MIMAdmin.

In Internet Explorer, add `http://pam.priv.thefinancialcompany.net` to the local intranet zone.

 Look forward to additional browser support in a future update. At the time of this writing, additional browser support is in **Customer Technical Preview (CTP)**.

Run **Windows Firewall with Advanced Security**, click on **Inbound Rules**, and make sure that **Forefront Identity Manager Service (STS)**, which is TCP port 5726, and **Forefront Identity Manager Service (Webservice)**, which is TCP port 5725, are listed:

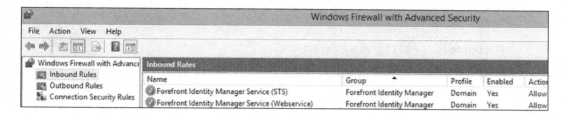

Create a new rule for the REST API. Select **Port** and **TCP** and enter 8086.

Installing PAM PowerShell cmdlets

On a workstation TFCWIN10 joined to the corporate domain (priv. thefinancialcompany.net, not our thefinancialcompany.net management domain), we will install the PAM PowerShell cmdlets. On TFCWIN10, we will go to the MIM installation media in the add-ins and extensions, select our platform (x32 or x64), and run setup.exe:

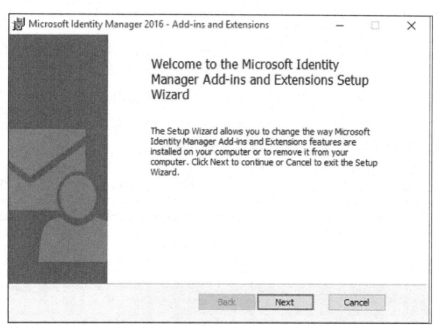

Assuming that you have been following along and have already installed Outlook and password extensions, you will select a **Change** install. Install the PAM client, and at **Configure MIM PAM Service Address**, enter the **PAM Server Address** `pamservice.thefinancialcompany.net` with **Port** 5725:

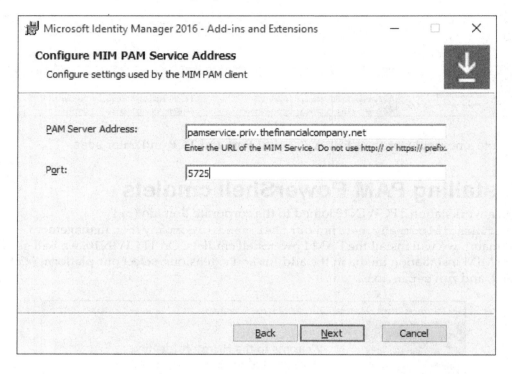

The PAM client installation requires a reboot when complete.

DNS, trust, and permissions

For the corporate forest, `thefinancialcompany.net`, to trust the management forest, `priv.thefinancialcompany.net`, the TFC domain controllers need to find the PRIV domain controllers. Verify that you have a forward lookup zone for `priv.thefinancialcompany.net` or create a conditional forwarder to `priv.thefinancialcompany.net`:

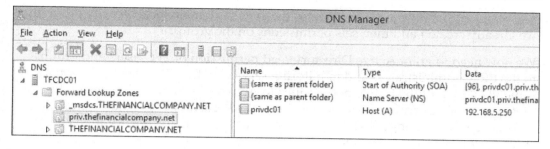

We will now establish the trust. From the PAM server, PRIVPAMSRV, run these three PAM PowerShell commands. When prompted for credentials, enter the credentials for the TFC domain administrator account, such as `TFC\Administrator`, as follows:

```
$ca = get-credential

New-PAMTrust -SourceForest "thefinancialcompany.net" -Credentials $ca

New-PAMDomainConfiguration -SourceDomain "TFC" -Credentials $ca
```

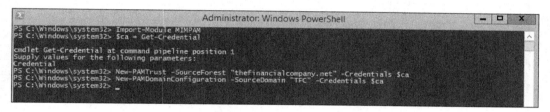

 The `New-PAMTrust` cmdlet uses the FQDN of the source forest, whereas the `New-PAMDomainConfiguration` cmdlet uses NetBIOS of the source domain!

The `New-PAMTrust` cmdlet creates a trust relationship among the PAM domain, PRIV, and our corporate domain TFC, as well as configuring one-way trust to enable SID History and disable SID filtering. That is, the single `New-PAMTrust` cmdlet performs the following three `netdom` commands:

```
netdom trust thefinancialcompany.net /domain:priv. thefinancialcompany.
net /userO:tfc\administrator /passwordO:Pa$$w0rd1! /add

netdom trust thefinancialcompany.net /domain:priv.thefinancialcompany.net
/EnableSIDHistory yes /userO:TFC\administrator /passwordO:Pa$$w0rd1!

netdom trust thefinancialcompany.net /domain:priv.thefinancialcompany.net
/Quarantine no /userO:TFC\administrator /passwordO:Pa$$w0rd1!
```

`New-PAMDomainConfiguration` creates the `TFC$$$` domain local security group that we already created and then sets permissions on the group.

We now need to grant Active Directory read permission of TFC users and groups to the PRIV administrators and monitoring service. In the TFC domain, log on as someone with administrative permissions to Active Directory, right-click on the **thefinanancialcompany.net** domain and select **All Tasks | Delegate Control…**. When prompted, change to the `priv.thefinancialcompany.net` location and enter `PRIV\Domain Admins` and `PRIV\MIMMonitor`:

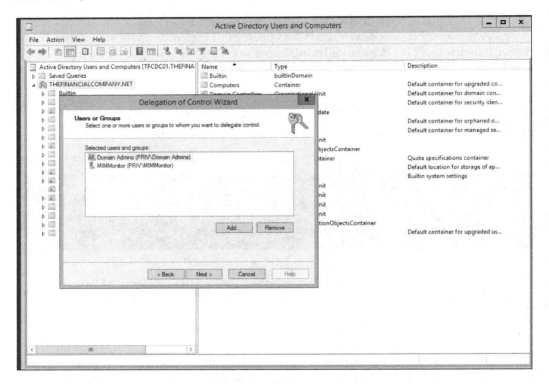

Click on **Next**, and when prompted for the tasks to delegate, select **Read all user information**, as follows:

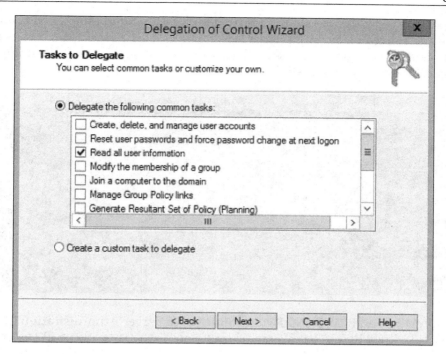

Click on **Next** and then on **Finish**.

Privileged groups, users, and roles

We're almost done with the setup of PAM. From the PAM server, PRIVPAMSRV, run a quick test and make sure that the trust and configuration is set up correctly. In a PowerShell command window, type the following commands and enter the credentials of a TFC domain administrator when prompted:

```
Import-Module MIMPAM

$ca = Get-Credential

Test-PAMTrust -SourceForest "thefinancialcompany.net" -Credentials $ca

Test-PAMDomainConfiguration -SourceDomain "TFC" -Credentials $ca
```

The `Test-PAMTrust` cmdlet should respond with `True`. If it does not, you need to remove and re-create your trust. The `Test-PAMDomainConfiguration` cmdlet should respond that SID History is enabled, SID filtering is not enabled, and the domain local security group `TFC$$$` exists:

```
                                      Windows PowerShell
PS C:\Users\mimadmin> import-module MIMPAM
PS C:\Users\mimadmin> $ca = get-credential # Any TFC domain admin account works here

cmdlet Get-Credential at command pipeline position 1
Supply values for the following parameters:
Credential
PS C:\Users\mimadmin> Test-PAMTrust -SourceForest "thefinancialcompany.net" -Credentials $ca
True
PS C:\Users\mimadmin> Test-PAMDomainConfiguration -SourceDomain "TFC" -Credentials $ca
SID history is enabled for this trust.

The command completed successfully.

SID filtering is not enabled for this trust. All SIDs presented in an
authentication request from this domain will be honored.

The command completed successfully.

The group TFC$$$ exists.
```

On the PAM server, PRIVPAMSRV, install **Remote Server Administration Tools (RSAT)**. Windows 10 RSAT tools can be found at `http://bit.ly/Win10RSAT`.

We are now at the part where we will create an Active Directory shadow group, PAM user, and PAM role. Log in to PRIVPAMSRV as PRIV\MIMAdmin and run the following PowerShell commands:

```
Import-Module MIMPAM

Import-Module ActiveDirectory

$ca = get-credential -UserName TFC\Administrator -Message "Enter any TFC
Domain Admin credentials here"

$pg = New-PAMGroup -SourceGroupName "TFCAdmins" -SourceDomain
thefinancialcompany.net -SourceDC TFCDC01.thefinancialcompany.net
-Credentials $ca

$sj = New-PAMUser -SourceDomain TFC -SourceAccountName jingalls

$jp = ConvertTo-SecureString 'Pass@word1' -asplaintext -force

Set-ADAccountPassword -identity priv.jingalls -Reset -NewPassword $jp

Set-ADUser -identity priv.jingalls -Enabled 1

Add-ADGroupMember "Protected Users" priv.jingalls

$pr = New-PAMRole -DisplayName "TFCAdmins" -Privileges $pg -Candidates
$sj
```

If you look at the PRIV Active Directory domain, you should see a shadow group and user account in the **PAM objects** organizational unit, as shown in the following screenshot:

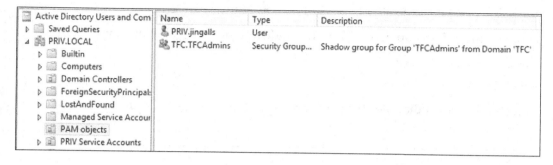

To take a sneak peek behind the scenes, run the following command:

```
Get-ADGroup -Identity TFC.TFCAdmins -Properties SIDHistory
```

Then, run this command:

```
Get-ADGroup -Server TFCDC01.thefinancialcompany.net -Identity TFCAdmins
```

Note that the SID History value of the first command matches that of the SID value of the second command.

User experience

On the corporate TFC Active Directory, remove TFC\jingalls from TFC\TFCAdmins. We will now walk through how the end user, Jeff Ingalls, will use the PAM PowerShell cmdlets to request access into the TFCAdmins group and access the TOPSECRET folder.

Log in as TFC\jingalls to the workstation TFCWIN10, which is joined to the TFC domain, and verify that the TOPSECRET folder containing Salaries.txt cannot be accessed:

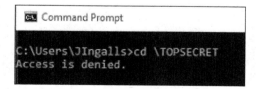

Next, run the following command:

```
runas /user:priv.jingalls@priv.thefinancialcompany.net powershell
```

Enter the password for the `priv.jingalls` account: `Pass@word1`.

A new window will open. In this new window, enter the following commands:

```
Import-module MIMPAM
Get-PAMRoleForRequest
```

You should see all the roles that Jeff can request. In this case, it's just one: the
`TFCAdmins`.

```
Windows PowerShell
Windows PowerShell
Copyright (C) 2015 Microsoft Corporation. All rights reserved.

PS C:\Windows\system32> Import-module MIMPAM
PS C:\Windows\system32> Get-PAMRoleForRequest


Role ID                       : f54d1629-bd77-4621-96ce-d11e047571ea
Display Name                  : TFCAdmins
Description                   :
TTL                           : 01:00:00
Available From                :
Available To                  :
MFA Enabled                   : False
Approval Enabled              : False
Availability Window Enabled   : False
```

Now, enter the following commands:

```
$r = Get-PAMRoleForRequest | ? { $_.DisplayName -eq "TFCAdmins" }
New-PAMRequest -role $r
```

```
PS C:\Windows\system32> $r = Get-PAMRoleForRequest | ? { $_.DisplayName -eq "TFCAdmins" }
PS C:\Windows\system32> New-PAMRequest -role $r


Request ID       : 9ffd69d0-630a-474c-b0ff-44272d02203d
Creator ID       : 9666f60a-e41d-49a4-b6c2-b910c917e632
Justification    :
Creation Time    : 2/24/2016 8:19:17 PM
Creation Method  : PAM PowerShell
Expiration Time  :
Role ID          : f54d1629-bd77-4621-96ce-d11e047571ea
Requested TTL    : 01:00:00
Requested Time   : 2/24/2016 8:19:15 PM
Request Status   : Scheduled
```

We will close the window and launch a new PowerShell window using the following command:

```
runas /user:Priv.JIngalls@thefinancialcompany.net powershell
```

In this new PowerShell window, we will run whoami /groups:

```
Windows PowerShell
Windows PowerShell
Copyright (C) 2015 Microsoft Corporation. All rights reserved.

PS C:\Windows\system32> whoami /groups

GROUP INFORMATION
-----------------

Group Name                                           Type              SID                                            At
=================================================== ================ ============================================== ==
Everyone                                             Well-known group S-1-1-0                                        Ma
BUILTIN\Users                                        Alias            S-1-5-32-545                                   Ma
NT AUTHORITY\INTERACTIVE                             Well-known group S-1-5-4                                        Ma
NT AUTHORITY\Authenticated Users                     Well-known group S-1-5-11                                       Ma
NT AUTHORITY\This Organization                       Well-known group S-1-5-15                                       Ma
LOCAL                                                Well-known group S-1-2-0                                        Ma
PRIV\Protected Users                                 Group            S-1-5-21-601488432-12090359-4268133313-525     Ma
PRIV\TFC.TFCAdmins                                   Group            S-1-5-21-601488432-12090359-4268133313-1168    Ma
Authentication authority asserted identity           Well-known group S-1-18-1                                       Ma
Mandatory Label\Medium Mandatory Level               Label            S-1-16-8192
```

The output shows that the user PRIV\priv.jingalls belongs to the TFC.TFCAdmins group.

Using the PRIV\priv.jingalls account, you should be able to access the file as expected. Try it out!

PAM in the MIM service

PAM installed some new objects in the MIM service. Let's take a look at three new objects: PAM roles, PAM requests, and another object called PAM configuration that provides a configurable PAM setting interface. If you were to open up the MIM portal on PRIVPAMSRV, which again is optional, you will immediately see PAM roles and PAM requests, as follows:

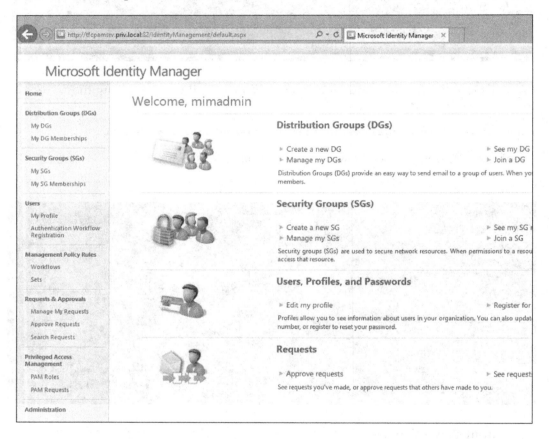

If you were to click on the **PAM Roles** link, you would see an interface to create a new PAM role and delete and see the details of existing PAM roles. Here's the window to create a new PAM role:

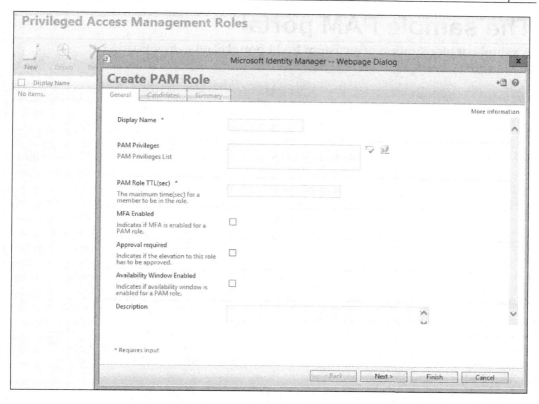

- **Display Name**: This is the display name of the role.
- **PAM Privileges**: This is the security group(s) associated with the role.
- **PAM Role TTL (sec)**: This is the maximum number of seconds before the role expires and the privileges are removed.
- **MFA Enabled**: If checked, this requires the user to use Azure **multi-factor authentication (MFA)**. We will discuss this concept later in the chapter.
- **Approval required**: This indicates whether elevation to this role needs to be approved.
- **Availability Window Enabled**: This indicates if availability window is enabled for a PAM role.
- **Description**: This is an optional text string that describes the role.

The sample PAM portal

A sample demonstration of a custom PAM portal can be downloaded at
`http://bit.ly/CustomPAMPortal`.

Unzip the `Privileged-Access-Management-Portal\src` folder to `\Program Files\Microsoft Forefront Identity Manager\2010\Privileged Access Management Portal` and create a `web.config` file, as shown in the following screenshot:

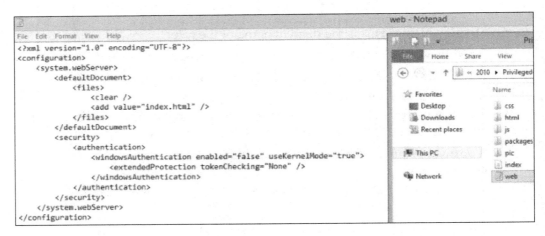

As we have seen throughout this book, the MIM product still uses the old branding name of **Forefront Identity Manager** (FIM) in some of its services, folder paths, and portal dialog boxes.

Next, create the IIS application pool, create a new IIS website with a name (**1**), then browse (**2**) and select the `C:\Program Files\Microsoft Forefront Identity Manager\2010\Privileged Access Management Portal` folder (**3**), and specify port `8090` (**4**). Lastly, click on **OK** (**5**). Take a look at the following screenshot:

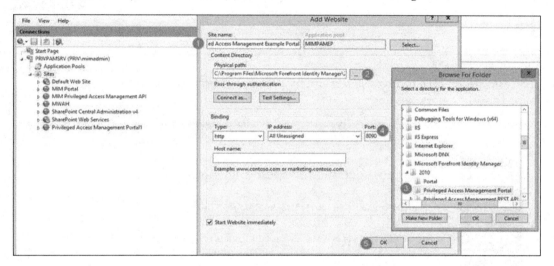

If you try to create the website via PowerShell's `New-Website` cmdlet, you will find that the site will throw a server `500` error. The issue is documented in the blog post found at `http://bit.ly/MIMportal500`.

In the \Privileged-Access-Management-Portal\js folder **(1)**, find the utils.js file **(2)** and open it in Notepad **(3)**. Change the PAM API URL to pamRespApiURL: http://pamapi.priv.thefinancialcompany.net:8086/api/pamresources/.

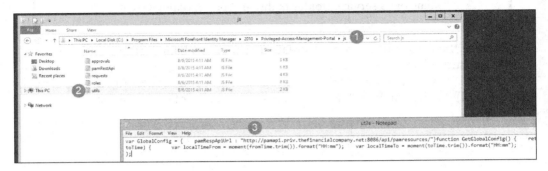

You should be able to browse the site by pointing a browser to http://pam.priv. thefinancialcompany.net:8090:

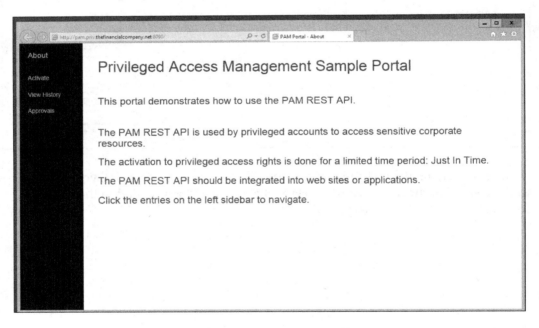

Multi-factor authentication

As in the MIM service, the PAM workflow activity supports **MFA**. To start this setup, we will need to first create our multi-factor authentication providers. Log in to the Azure portal at `https://portal.azure.com`:

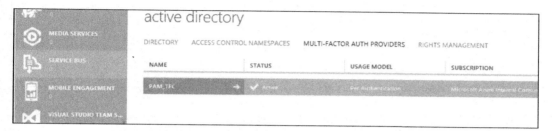

Once created, navigate to the provider and download the SDK. The SDK is located on the left-hand side of the screen, as you see here:

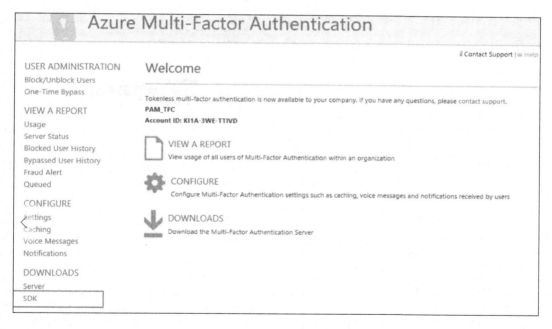

Then, copy the ZIP file to the PAM/MIM Service server. The ZIP file contains key material used to authenticate to Azure, so keep it secured. Once copied, open the ZIP file, and you will see a pf folder. Open the `pf_auth.cs` file with Notepad:

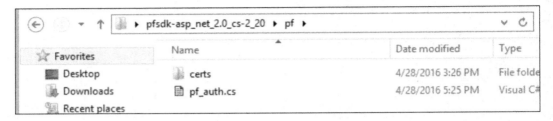

Copy `LICENSE_KEY`, `GROUP_KEY`, and `CERT_PASSWORD` to the `mfasetting.xml` file. If you've kept default while installing the MIM service, the `mfasetting.xml` file is located at `C:\Program Files\Microsoft Forefront Identity Manager\2010\ Service`.

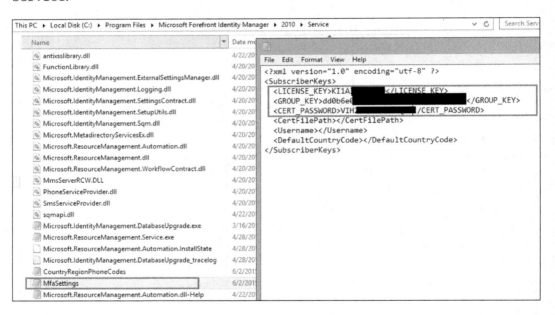

Once you have the settings entered and saved, create a folder in the directory called `MfaCerts` and then copy the `p12` cert to this directory from `pf\certs`. Also, update `mfaSettings CertificatePath` with the full location and filename:

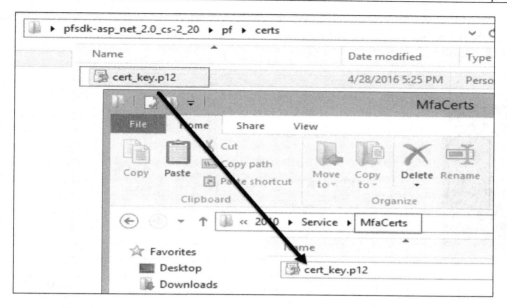

You are now ready to configure a PAM user with a phone number. Update Jeff's phone number to be used with PAM with the following command:

```
Set-PamUser (Get-PAMUser -SourceDisplayName 'Jeff Ingalls')
-SourcePhoneNumber XXXXXXXXXX
```

Here, XXXXXXXXXX is the phone number, including the area code, as you can see here:

```
PS C:\Windows\system32> Set-PAMUser (Get-PAMUser -SourceDisplayName 'Jeff Ingalls') -SourcePhoneNumber 130182█
```

Next, set the PAM role to enable MFA by entering the following command:

```
Set-PAMRole (Get-PAMRole -DisplayName "TFCAdmins") -MFAEnabled 1
```

```
Set-PAMRole (Get-PAMRole -DisplayName "TFCAdmins") -MFAEnabled 1
```

That's it! When Jeff requests a role that is MFA-enabled, we will confirm and validate that it is him. Note that the sample web interface will also show you if a role is MFA-enabled:

Microsoft's latest Azure MFA details can be found at `http://bit.ly/MIMPAMMFA`.

Summary

In this chapter, we discussed why privileged access management is important, its components, and how it works. We gave you the component requirements and walked you through installing the module and verifying its functionality by demonstrating how an end user would perform a request. Considerations, installation of the sample, the custom PAM portal, and setting up multi-factor authentication was also discussed. Did we miss anything? You bet! Explore the official TechNet documents for PAM at `http://bit.ly/MIMPAMTechNet`.

In the next chapter, we will cover how MIM can help your organization save end user time, money, and frustration by setting up self-service password reset and password synchronization. Even though password management such as PAM is an option, we believe you will find it an invaluable enterprise service.

9
Password Management

By now, we have a functional MIM system that is able to manage our users, groups, and do a little self-service. It is now time to look at one of the features of MIM that many customers believe is the most cost saving one.

The feature is **self-service password reset** (**SSPR**), and it allows users to reset their own passwords, which helps in minimizing the frustration, and the time and money spent in contacting an IT help desk. We save ourselves a helpdesk call, and allow the user to be productive again, quicker. A big win for everyone!

In this chapter, we will cover the following topics:

- SSPR background
- Installing SSPR
- Enabling password management in AD
- Allowing MIM Service to set passwords
- Configuring MIM Service
- The SSPR user experience
- SSPR lockout
- Password synchronization
- Password Change Notification Service

SSPR background

Let's assume Amber Adams has forgotten her AD password, and therefore, she is unable to authenticate properly to MIM. So, the solution that SSPR provides is to validate (authorize) the user.

Using SSPR, Amber can make an anonymous request for MIM to reset the password of the user account AAdams. In order for that to happen, we tell MIM to try to figure out who the requestor is. We add an authentication (AuthN) workflow, which gives Amber a chance to prove her identity. If the AuthN workflow proves to MIM that the requestor is indeed the user AAdams, it will allow Amber to reset her password.

Two built-in ways to allow people to verify their identity are the **Question and Answer (QA)** gate and the **One-Time Password (OTP)** gate. If you have Azure, you can configure multi-factor authentication to use MIM's new **Phone** gate too.

QA versus OTP

There are two different ways of doing SSPR—Question and Answer and One-Time Password. QA means that a user can reset their password by giving the correct or the same answers to a number of configurable questions that the user was presented with during registration of this service. OTP is a solution where we distribute a one-time code to the users by SMS or e-mail. The user then uses that code to reset their password.

Installing self-service password reset

SSPR has two major components: the password registration portal, where answers to questions are registered by users, and the password reset portal, where those same answers need to be supplied in order for MIM to reset the password. We will install SSPR on a new server like many medium to large organizations do, although you can install the SSPR components on the same MIM portal server that we used in the previous chapters:

1. Run the MIM Service and portal installation, select the **MIM Password Registration** and the **MIM Password Reset Portal** components, and click on **Next**:

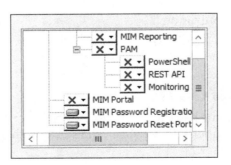

2. The next dialog box requires an account name, password, hostname, and port for the registration portal. We will use the service account TFC\SVC-MIMSSPR, the registration host name register.thefinancialcompany.net, with the standard port 80. Click on **Next**:

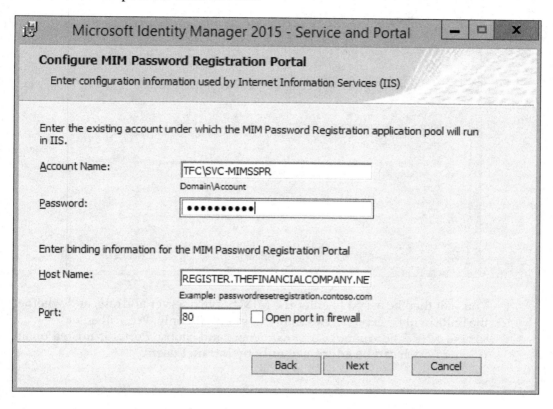

3. You will receive a message that the deployment is not secure in its current configuration—essentially, telling us that we should use SSL. Click on **Next**:

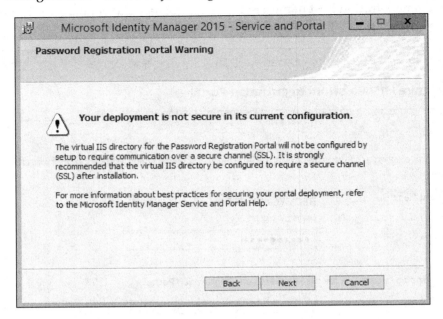

4. You will then be asked to enter the MIM Service server address, and whether the SSPR will be exposed externally or internally only. We will enter `mimservice.thefinancialcompany.net`, and choose **Portal is hosted on an IIS site which can be addressed only by intranet users**:

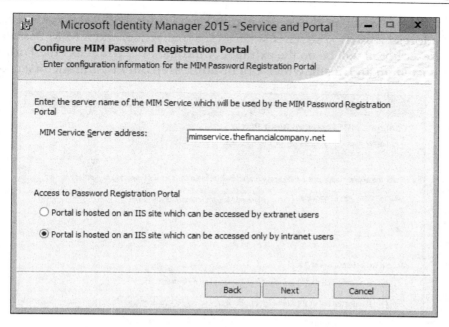

5. We now need to configure MIM Password Reset Portal. Use the same service account, `TFC\SVC-MIMSSPR`, the registration host name of `reset.thefinancialcompany.net`, and the standard port `80`. Click on **Next**:

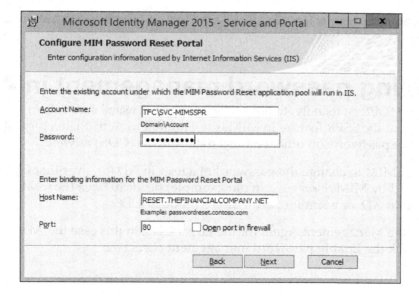

6. Click on **Next** past the secure warning, and enter the MIM Service server address, `mimservice.thefinancialcompany.net`, and if MIM Password Reset Portal will be on the extranet or intranet. We will select the **Portal is hosted on an IIS site which can be addressed only by intranet users** option:

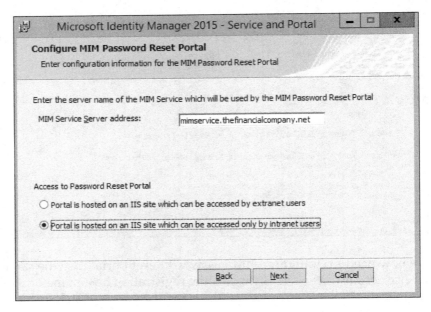

The components are now installed. Let's now look at how the registration and reset portals work.

Enabling password management in AD

The goal for SSPR is, usually, to reset the password of users' accounts in Active Directory, but the SSPR feature in MIM is not limited to Active Directory, and can be used to reset passwords in other **connect data sources** (CDS) as well.

In order for MIM to change the password of a user in AD (or any other CDS), the account used by MIM (`svc-adma` in our example) needs to have the reset password permission in AD, or a similar permission in another CDS:

1. In the Management Agent for the target CDS, in this case the AD, we need to check the **Enable password management** checkbox:

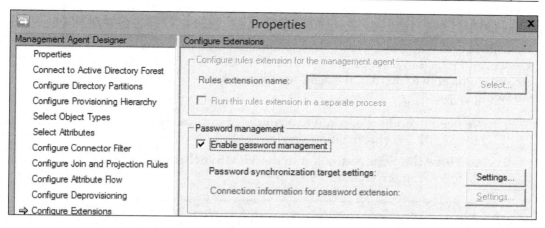

2. If we then look at the settings, we can make some adjustments, as shown in the following screenshot:

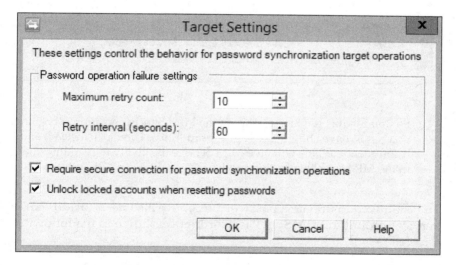

 The **Unlock locked accounts when resetting passwords** option is not enabled by default. It is up to your security team to determine if this setting is right for you. The authors have seen organizations that have this setting enabled as well as disabled.

The Management Agent for AD is now ready for SSPR.

Allowing MIM Service to set passwords

The MIM Service account will be the account that calls the MIM Synchronization service, and tells it to reset the password in AD. But in order for the MIM Service account to be able to do that, we need to assign it some permissions with the following steps:

1. We need to add the account to a couple of groups created during installation of the MIM Synchronization service.

2. Add the MIM Service account to the **MIMSyncBrowse** group, as shown in the following screenshot:

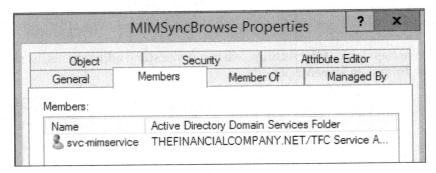

 By default, this is a local group on the MIM Synchronization server, but you might have chosen to use groups in Active Directory instead, and is recommended. This will give MIM Service the ability to read information in the MIM Synchronization service.

3. To be allowed to initiate a password reset, we also need to add the MIM Service account to **MIMSyncPasswordSet**, as shown in the following screenshot:

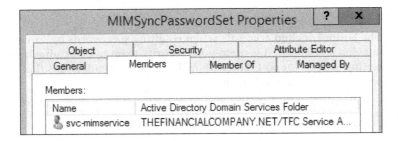

The call from MIM Service to the MIM Synchronization service to do a password reset is made using **Windows Management Instrumentation (WMI)**. This, in turn, means that we need to give MIM Service the WMI permissions as well. Because we have, in our example, separated MIM Service and the MIM Synchronization server, it will be remote WMI calls that demand a few extra steps. A few of these steps can be ignored if the services are running on the same server. You will need to make these changes if/when you separate the services.

4. On the Synchronization server, run **Microsoft Management Console (MMC)**, and add the **WMI Control** snap-in, as seen in the following screenshot:

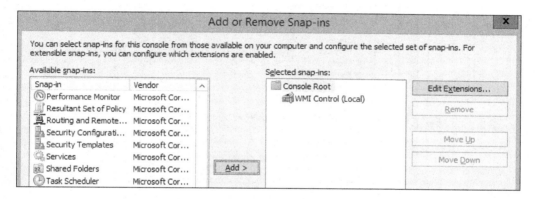

5. Right-click on **WMI Control (Local)**, and select **Properties**:

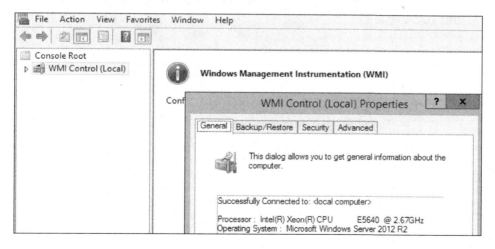

6. In the **Security** tab, expand the **Root** namespace, and select the **CIMV2** namespace. Then click on the **Security** button at the bottom:

7. Add the MIM Service account, and assign the **Enable Account** and **Remote Enable** permissions. This will allow the MIM Service account to connect to this namespace:

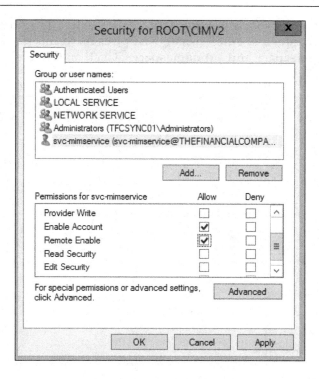

8. But we need to give access to subnamespaces as well. Click on the **Advanced** button.

9. In the advanced security settings for CIMV2, select the entry with the MIM Service account, and edit it. Change **Applies to:** from **This namespace only** to **This namespace and subnamespaces**. Click on **OK** a few times to save your settings:

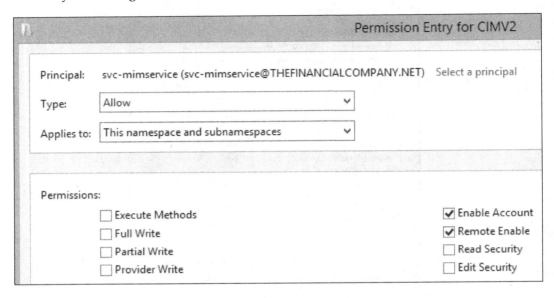

As we have separated the servers, we also need to allow WMI calls through the firewall in the MIM Synchronization server.

10. Navigate to **Control Panel | System and Security** and click on the **Allow an app through Windows Firewall** link:

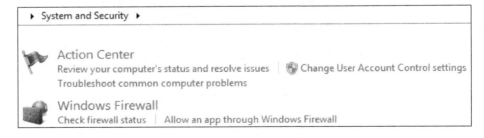

11. In the **Allowed apps and features** setting, check the **Windows Management Instrumentation (WMI)** program:

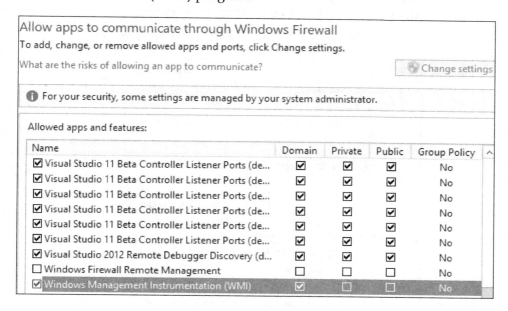

This can be done using GPOs, if that is your preferred way of managing the local firewall on your servers. When allowing WMI to communicate through the firewall, it will create a firewall rule. If you would like to narrow down the IP addresses allowed to use the remote WMI, you can do so by modifying that rule.

The MIM Synchronization groups are assigned some DCOM permissions during setup, but we need to make some adjustments in order for SSPR to work. The following are steps to achieve this:

12. Add the **Component Services** snap-in in the MMC (in the MIM Synchronization server), and click down to **My Computer**. Right-click and select **Properties**, then click on the **COM Security** tab:

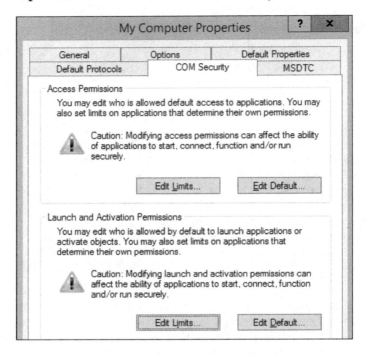

13. Click on **Edit Limits** in the **Launch and Activation Permissions** section and add the **Local Launch** and **Remote Launch** permissions to the **MIMSyncPasswordSet** group:

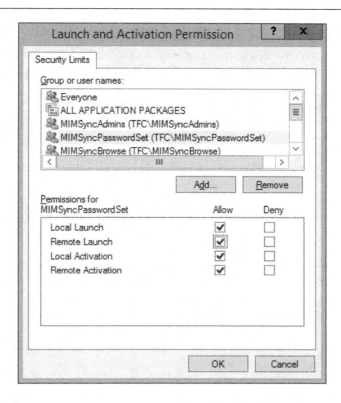

Now the MIM Service account has the permissions required to make the calls to the MIM Synchronization service to tell it to reset the password in the target CDS (AD).

Configuring MIM Service

SSPR is not enabled by default in MIM Service, so we need to enable some MPRs and configure some sets and workflows. The next section will outline what is needed to get this working.

Password Reset Users Set

The default MPRs around SSPR use a predefined set called **Password Reset Users Set**. If you look at the criterion for that set, you will find that it applies to all users:

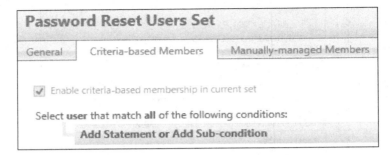

Allowing SSPR for all users is usually more extreme than most organizations allow. In our situation, we will allow SSPR for all employees:

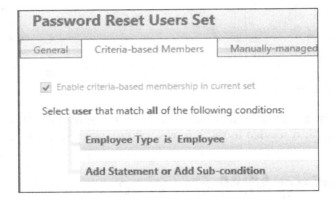

We have now defined users for whom we would like to use the SSPR feature.

Password Reset AuthN workflow

As we discussed earlier, we need to have at least one authentication workflow in our SSPR implementation. The default one is called **Password Reset AuthN Workflow**. The default activity used in this workflow to authenticate the users is the QA gate:

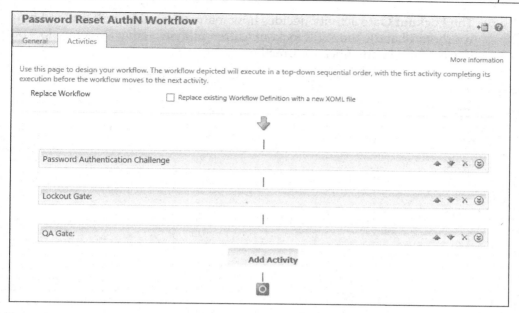

There are also some activities to support the SSPR feature; we will look at those now:

- The **Password Authentication Challenge** activity is used during registration and will force the user to re-enter their current password during the registration process:

- The **Lockout Gate** activity decides how many tries a user will get, and how we should handle the SSPR lockout (different than Active Directory lockout) if users fail to authenticate correctly:

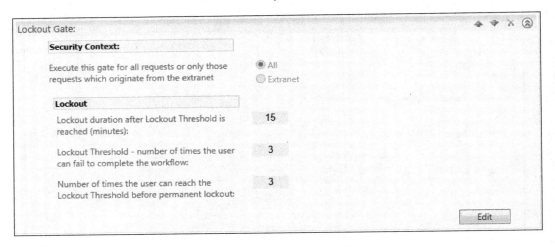

 In the previous screenshot, note that the **Security Context:** activity is, by default, set to **All**, meaning both intranet and extranet users. More information on security context can be found at `http://bit.ly/MIMSSPRSC`.

Configuring the QA gate

Finally, the QA gate activity needs to be configured with the following steps:

1. As with **Lockout Gate,** the **Security Context:** section is, by default, set to **All** (both intranet and extranet):

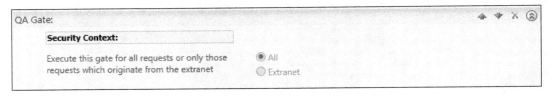

2. We need to decide how many questions to ask, and how many questions the users are required to answer:

Step 1 - Question Settings

Enter the total number of questions for this gate:	3
Number of questions displayed during registration:	3
Number of questions required for registration:	3
Number of questions randomly presented to the user:	3
Number of questions that must be answered correctly:	3
Allow duplicate answers:	☐
Answer constraint:	^.{4,}$
Message to user that describes uniqueness and answer text constraints:	Each answer must contain at least four characters, and no two answers may be the same.
Terse inline error message to user for answers that violate uniqueness or text constraints:	Answer is duplicated or has less than four characters.

Note that the default value of **Answer constraint** requires the answer to contain at least four characters. You may need to change this if you, for example, ask a question such as favorite car, as the answer BMW will not work. The duplicate check and answer constraints, added back in FIM 2010 R2, were added to prevent users from answering the same response for all questions.

3. We now need to define the question pool to be used by the QA gate. There are many thoughts on what a good question is, although there is an agreement that the question should allow someone to prove their identity, while not being likely to be easily guessed by other people. Social media and Internet search engines make this task challenging, but our advice is to seek input and/or approval from your security and legal teams to make sure you are not violating federal or state rules or laws.

Consider these four subjects when evaluating gate questions: unforgettable, non-dynamic, all-encompassing, and secure. In other words, the user should be able to easily remember their challenge answer, questions should not lead users to enter answers that could change over time, questions should be applicable to everyone, and not be guessable by others. A question such as *Enter a personal PIN (4 digits)* is easy to forget, and asking people the name of their significant other (or their pet) are typically easily guessable with a little social media searching.

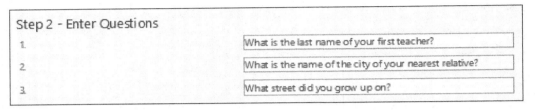

4. Finally, we need to set the compatibility level. As the dialog describes, choosing **Allow** enables duplication of answers. We will keep the default:

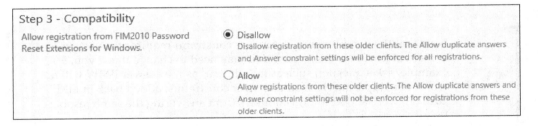

The OTP gate

If we do not want the QA gate, or if we need to support more ways (two-factor authentication) of resetting passwords, we can use the OTP gate included in MIM.

If you click on **Add Activity** in the workflow, you will get the following page:

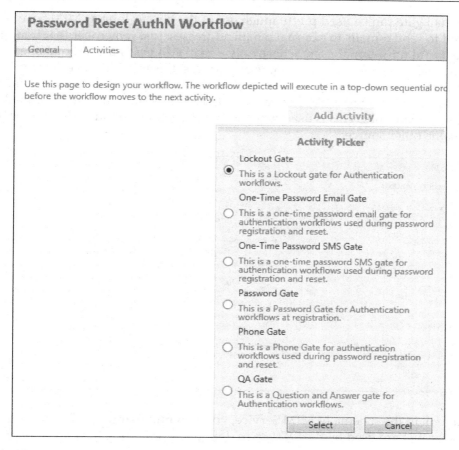

As you can see, there are two OTP gates—one is **One-Time Password Email Gate** and the other is **One-Time Password SMS Gate**.

The e-mail gate can be used pretty much out of the box, as long as MIM Service is allowed to send e-mails to external e-mail addresses. Just remember that it might not be useful for internal users whose only e-mail address is the internal one. For external users, such as consultants or partners, this might be an easy way of implementing SSPR. During registration, the users will provide the e-mail address they want to use for SSPR. As you can see, there is an option to have the e-mail address as read-only. This is used when MIM will get the e-mail address to be used from some other source:

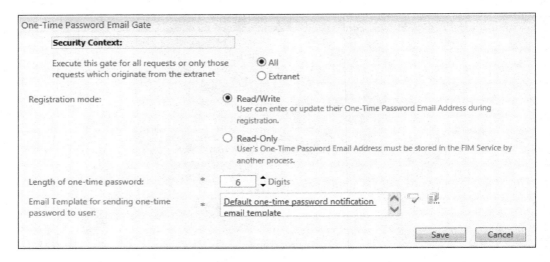

If you look in the schema of MIM Service, you will find that there is a special set of attributes that are used by the OTP gates. If you are providing the e-mail address used for the e-mail gate, or the mobile phone number used by the SMS gate, you need to make sure the values are stored in the **One-Time Password Email Address** and **One-Time Password Mobile Phone** attributes respectively:

The OTP attributes are *not*, by default, allowed to be managed by the synchronization engine or by users, if that is what you want. You will need to change the MPRs to make this work, and they are defined at `http://bit.ly/MIMSSPRDeploy`.

The SMS gate has almost the same settings as the e-mail gate, but requires some additional coding to take place, as we need to compile the DLL files that MIM should use to send the SMS. If you go to `http://bit.ly/MIMOTP`, you will find an example of how to create the `SmsServiceProvider.dll` file. You will need a provider to send the SMS too:

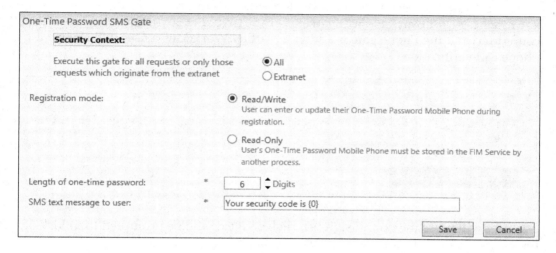

The SMS solution varies depending on how you are calling your SMS provider. We suggest looking at your SMS provider's documentation on how to programmatically call their endpoint using .NET code.

The Phone gate

The Phone gate is a feature new to MIM SSPR, and allows users to verify themselves with a phone call via Azure Multi-Factor Authentication. To use the Phone gate, you will need to configure Azure MFA, and change the Password Reset AuthN Workflow to use the Phone gate. To configure it, you will need to configure a new MFA in Azure and add the `LICENSE_KEY`, `GROUP_KEY`, and `CERT_PASSWORD` to the `MFASettings.xml` file in `\Program Files\Microsoft Forefront Identity Manager\2010\Service\`. In the `<CertFilePath>` of the `MFASettings.xml` file, you will need to point to the path and filename of a local copy of your Azure certificate key; by default, it must be placed in the following location: `C:\Program Files\ Microsoft Forefront Identity Manager\2010\Service\MfaCerts`. Once it is configured and the Phone gate is added to AuthN Workflow, a user will receive a phone call verification:

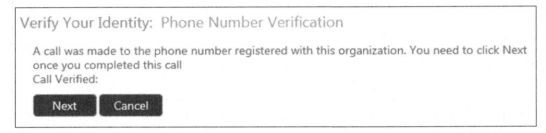

The user will press the pound sign (#), click on **Next**, and be prompted to unlock or reset their password, as shown later in the chapter.

Require re-registration

If. for some reason, you would like users to re-register to the SSPR — the reason could, for example, be that you have redesigned all your questions in the QA gate — you need to check the little **Require Re-Registration** box in the **Password Reset AuthN Workflow** page. This will prompt the users to register again:

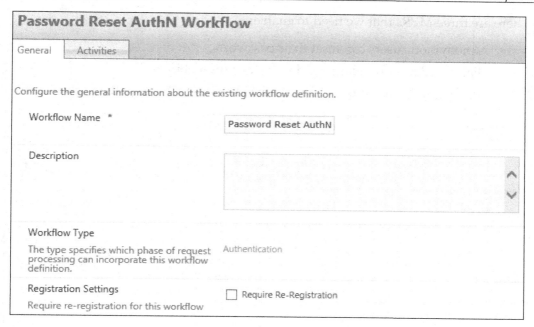

SSPR MPRs

Now that we have decided the set and the gate that we want to use, we need to enable and configure the relevant MPRs to get the SSPR started.

There are three MPRs that we need to enable:

- Anonymous users can reset their password
- Password reset users can read password reset objects
- Password Reset Users can update the lockout attributes of themselves

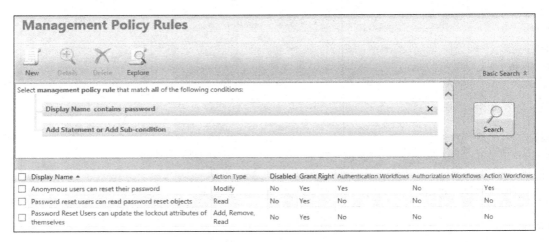

The first one, **Anonymous users can reset their password**, is the one that does the trick. It will fire off Password Reset AuthN Workflow, which we talked about earlier, and the Password Reset Action Workflow that will do the actual reset.

If we haven't done it before, we also need to enable the following MPRs:

- User management: Users can read attributes of their own
- General: Users can read non-administrative configuration resources

The SSPR user experience

The best user experience is installing the MIM client add-ins and extensions. As soon as we enable the MPRs, and a user who is a member of the Password Reset Users set logs onto their computer (which also has the MIM add-ins and extensions installed), a browser window connecting to the Password Registration portal will open.

If you choose not to install the client add-ins, users can access the Password Registration portal manually. The experience is similar, but using the add-ins and extensions will probably increase the number of users actually taking time to register, as they will be automatically prompted to do so.

If we used the FQDN for the Password Registration portal URL, we should make sure that the URL is in the local intranet zone of the client so that IE can use Integrated Authentication. To get a good experience with MIM, I recommend adding `*.thefinancialcompany.net` to the local intranet zone. Like some of the other windows, the password registration window references MIM's predecessor FIM 2010 R2:

1. First the user has to prove that they know the current password. This is the Password Authentication Challenge activity, which we have in our workflow, kicking in:

2. The user is then asked to answer the questions we configured in the QA gate activity. If the QA gate is configured with five questions, but is only supposed to ask three; the three questions asked are randomly picked from the five:

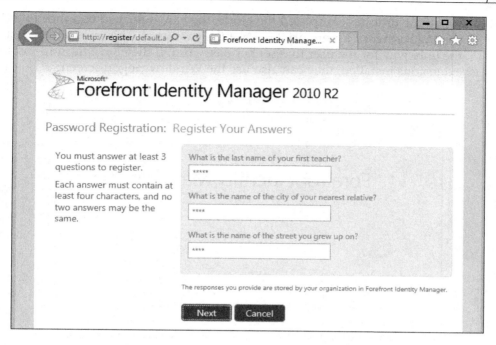

3. If we also used the OTP e-mail gate, the user might also be asked to register the e-mail address to be used for the OTP:

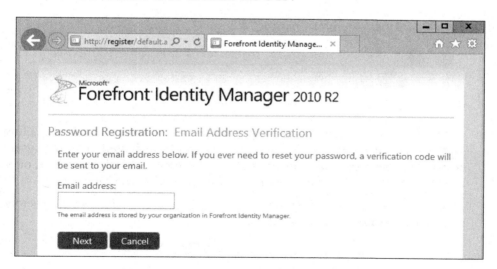

4. When the user has completed the guide, they are informed that they might use the Password Reset portal to reset the password. This is, however, not the only way for the user to reset her password. If they have the add-ins and extensions installed, they can also use the Windows logon screen.

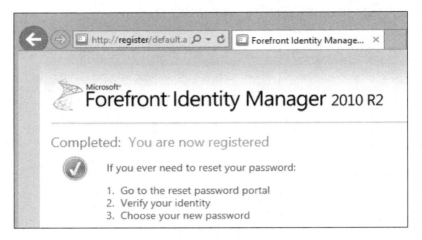

5. If a user who is not a part of the Password Reset Users set tries to manually access the Password Reset Registration portal, they will be duly notified that they are not authorized to register:

6. What happens when the user forgets his or her password? There are a few options: the user could utilize the add-in extensions installed on the system, access the Password Reset portal from some internal kiosk computer, or maybe, have the Password Reset portal published to the Internet.

   If add-in extensions are installed on the system, the Windows logon screen will have a **Forgot your password?** link:

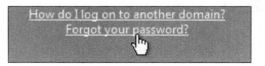

7. The next prompts will look the same whether the add-in extensions or the SSPR portal is being used. We'll walk you through the portal experience for SSPR configured for the default QA gate. The user will be prompted for their account information:

8. The QA gate questions are answered:

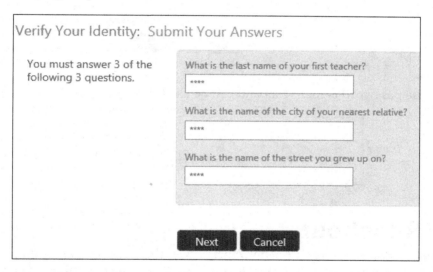

9. There's a new feature in MIM that was not present in the previous versions of the product: the user can select to unlock the account or reset the password. Selecting **Account Unlock: Keep Your Current Password** and clicking on **Next** will unlock the account. Otherwise, a new password can be entered, and the user can use that new password right away:

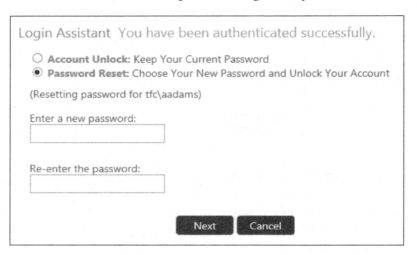

10. The password is then reset and can be used:

SSPR lockout

Look back at Password Reset AuthN Workflow in the **Lockout Gate** settings where the lockout duration, lockout threshold, and number of times until permanent lockout are set:

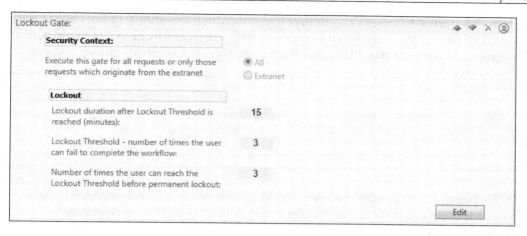

The settings specify that the workflow can fail **3** times. The user can answer one or all of the questions incorrectly, and have the workflow fail once (one failure count):

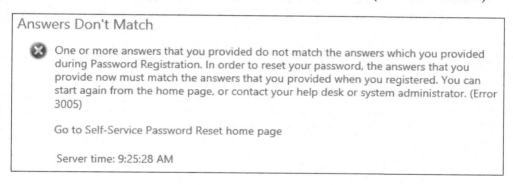

In our settings, if the workflow fails three times for the same account, the user is temporarily locked out of the SSPR for 15 minutes. This is a service lockout, and not an Active Directory lockout:

Access Denied Temporarily

You are temporarily prohibited from resetting your password. Please try again later, or contact your help desk or system administrator for assistance. (Error 3007)

Go to Self-Service Password Reset home page

After 15 minutes, the user can attempt to answer their questions again. Failing the workflow **two** more times would equate to the permanent lockout threshold setting of three, and the user would receive the following error when attempting again:

Access Denied

 Ensure you enter your user name correctly. If you still cannot reset your password, please contact your helpdesk for assistance. (Error 3001)

Go to Self-Service Password Reset home page

At this point, the only way the user would be able to use SSPR again would be to have someone unlock the SSPR account in MIM. To do this, perform the following steps:

1. Go to the MIM portal, and click on **Administration**, then on **Unlock Users**. Search for the user, and click on the name. Click on **Password Reset AuthN Workflow** that indicates SSPR permanent lockout, then click on the **Unlock User** icon:

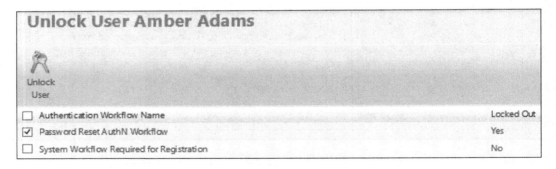

Unlock User Amber Adams	
Unlock User	
☐ Authentication Workflow Name	Locked Out
☑ Password Reset AuthN Workflow	Yes
☐ System Workflow Required for Registration	No

2. Click on the **Unlock Users** button, then on **Submit**. You should receive an **Access denied** response:

Status
Access denied. View Details

3. To grant SSPR unlock permissions, we need to create two sets and three MPRs.

4. The first new set that we will create will be named **TFC SSPR Unlock Admins**. For our example, we will add the administrator in this set, although in your environment, you could make the set criteria-based to refer to your IT helpdesk staff:

5. Next, create a new set named **Lockout gate registration resources** that is criteria-based with gate registration resources that match **Gate Type is D1230EF0-C5FA-4473-BE2A-30918B42EA2B**:

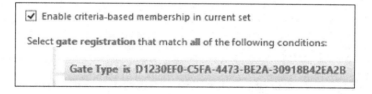

6. We now create a new request MPR named **TFC: SSPR Unlock Admins can modify Lockout gate registration resources** that specifies **Requestors** as **TFC SSPR Unlock Admins**, **Operation** as **Read resource** and **Modify a single-valued attribute**, and **Permissions** as **Grants permission**:

Requestors *
Define who this rule applies to.

◉ Specific Set of Requestors
Requestor is defined as the following user set.

TFC SSPR Unlock Admins

○ Relative to Resource
Select the attribute of resource that defines valid requestors.

Operation *
Define what operation types this rule applies to.

☐ Create resource ☐ Add a value to a multivalued attribute
☐ Delete resource ☐ Remove a value from a multivalued attribute
☑ Read resource   ☑ Modify a single-valued attribute

Permissions
Select if this rule will grant permission to request the operation defined in this rule. Do not select this check box if you want to only define workflows for the operation.

☑ Grants permission

7. In the **Target Resource** tab, the **Target Resource Definition Before Request** and the **Target Resource Definition After Request** settings should be the newly created **Lockout gate registration resources** set. The **Resource Attributes** setting should be **All Attributes**:

Target Resource Definition Before Request *
Define the set the target resource must belong to before the request is processed. This applies only to Read, Modify and Delete operation types.

Lockout gate registration resources

Target Resource Definition After Request *
Define the set the target resource must belong to after the request is processed. This applies only to Modify and Create operation types.

Lockout gate registration resources

Resource Attributes *
Select the target resource attributes for this rule.

◉ All Attributes
Rule applies to all attributes of the resource

8. Click on **Submit** to save the MPR.

9. We will create another new request MPR named **TFC: SSPR Unlock Admins can unlock Password Reset Users Set** that specifies **Requestors** as TFC SSPR Unlock Admins, Operation as Read resource and Remove a value from a multivalued attribute, and Permissions as Grants permission:

Requestors * Define who this rule applies to.	⦿ Specific Set of Requestors Requestor is defined as the following user set. TFC SSPR Unlock Admins ☑ 🗊 ◯ Relative to Resource Select the attribute of resource that defines valid requestors.
Operation * Define what operation types this rule applies to.	☐ Create resource ☐ Add a value to a multivalued attribute ☐ Delete resource ☑ Remove a value from a multivalued attribute ☑ Read resource ☐ Modify a single-valued attribute
Permissions Select if this rule will grant permission to request the operation defined in this rule. Do not select this check box if you want to only define workflows for the operation.	☑ Grants permission

10. The **Target Resource Definition Before Request** and the **Target Resource Definition After Request** settings should be set to **Password Reset Users Set** with the specific attributes **Lockout Gate Registration Data Ids** and **AuthN Workflow Locked Out** selected:

11. The final step is to create a request MPR named **TFC: SSPR Unlock Admins can read Password Reset Users Set** that specifies **Requestors** as TFC SSPR Unlock Admins, **Operation** as **Read resource**, and **Permissions** as **Grants permission**:

12. In **Target Resource Definition Before Request**, set the value to **Password Reset Users Set** with **Display Name** selected as the specific attribute:

Target Resource Definition Before Request *

Define the set the target resource must belong to before the request is processed. This applies only to Read, Modify and Delete operation types.

Password Reset Users Set

Resource Attributes *

Select the target resource attributes for this rule.

○ **All Attributes**

Rule applies to all attributes of the resource

◉ **Select specific attributes**

Rule applies to selected attributes

Display Name:

13. You should now be able to go to **Administration | Unlock Users,** click on a locked out account, and unlock it, assuming that you logged into an account that is in the TFC SSPR Unlock Admins set.

Password synchronization

Another optional MIM feature is password synchronization. Password synchronization allows you to synchronize passwords between connected systems that have appropriately configured Management Agents. Password synchronization does not require run profiles, because the password is intercepted at the configured source system and passed to the configured target system. There are some key takeaways you should know about password synchronization.

First, there are three types of Management Agent:

- Those that support password synchronization by default
- Those that need a custom DLL for password synchronization
- Those that do not support password synchronization

Active Directory, Active Directory Lightweight Directory Services, IBM Directory Server, and Lotus Notes are some of the MAs that support password synchronization without the need to write any special code—there are a few configuration items within the MA that are needed, and you are done. The SQL Management Agent is an example of one that requires custom code to be written, while the MIM MA does not have any password synchronization settings.

To enable password synchronization, an MA is configured to be a source for password synchronization, a target to receive password changes, or nothing at all (default):

1. If you look at the AD MA, in **Configure Directory Partitions**, there is an option named **Enable this partition as a password synchronization source**. Notice the **Targets** button where you can select the targets that this source MA should send its password updates to:

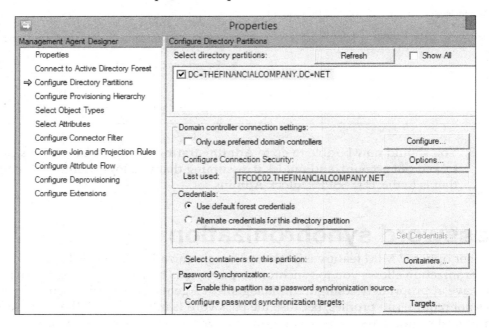

2. If you want to configure an AD MA for a target to receive password updates, go to **Configure Extensions**, and check the **Enable password management** box and click on the **Settings** button, where you can find a few other options such as retry and whether MIM should unlock the account when resetting the password:

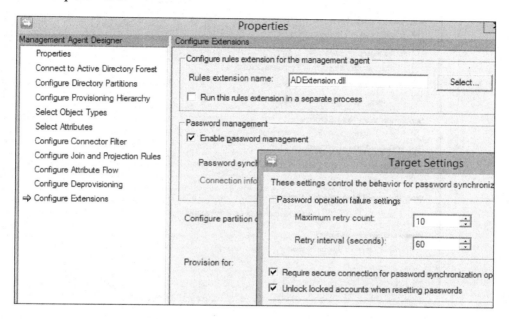

3. Additionally, there is a global password synchronization setting within the Synchronization service itself, available from the **Management Agents** tool by clicking on **Tools | Options**:

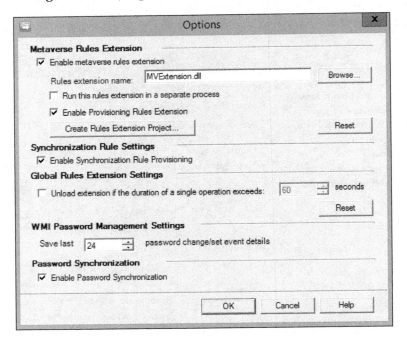

Password Change Notification Service

If you want to use Active Directory as a password reset source, you will need to install Password Change Notification Service. PCNS is a special service you will install on all domain controllers for that source AD domain. PCNS safely intercepts the password change that the domain controller receives, and sends it over securely to the MIM Synchronization service, where MIM will investigate which MAs are configured as targets and send over the password.

Installing PCNS is a six-step process, which is as follows:

1. Extending the AD schema.
2. Installing the PCNS service.
3. Configuring the MIM SPN.

4. Configuring PCNS.

5. Configuring the MAs.

6. Enabling password synchronization.

We have already talked about the last two steps, so we will walk you through extending the AD schema, installing the service on the domain controllers, configuring the MIM SPN, and configuring PCNS. Follow these steps:

1. To extend the AD schema, log in with an account that is a member of schema admins and domain admins. Run an administrative command prompt and go to the `Add-ins and extensions` folder for your installation media. Choose either the `x64` or `x32` folder depending on the system type of your domain controller and enter the following:

```
MSIEXEC.EXE /i "Password Change Notification Service.msi"
SCHEMAONLY=TRUE
```

2. After extending the AD schema, simply run the MSI and walk through the prompts to install PCNS. The domain controller will require a reboot after PCNS is installed.

3. Setting the MIM SPN is a simple command. In our example, we would type the following:

```
setspn -a PCNSCLNT/tfcsync01.thefinancialcompany.net TFC\svc-
mimsync
```

The first entry specifies the user-defined name for the MIM Sync server, and the second specifies the MIM Sync service account in the *domain\ username* format.

4. Next, use the command-line tool `PCNSCFG.EXE` to configure the PCNS settings in Active Directory. PCNSCFG requires membership of the domain admins or enterprise admins, and is located in the `\Program Files\ Microsoft Password Change Notification` folder on each domain controller that has PCNS installed. We use PCNSCFG to set the MIM target server (the synchronization server), maximum password queue length, retries, retry interval, and group inclusion and exclusion among other things. An example command is as follows:

```
Pcnscfg.exe addtarget /N:TFCSYNC01 /A:tfcsync01.
thefinancialcompany.net /S:PCNSCLNT/tfcsync01.thefinancialcompany.
net /FI:"Domain Users" /FE:"Domain Admins" /I:600 /F:1 /WL:30 /
WI:60
```

The parameters used in this example are explained as follows:

- ° /N: This is the user-defined friendly name of the target server.
- ° /A: This is the FQDN or address of the target server.
- ° /S: This is the SPN of the target server running FIM.
- ° /FI: This is the filter inclusion group name to use to permit passwords to be forwarded.
- ° /FE: This is the filter exclusion group name to prevent passwords from being forwarded.
- ° /I: This is the keep alive, or heartbeat, interval specified in seconds.
- ° /F: This is the username format to be delivered to the target. 1 is FQDN and 3 is NT 4.0 format.
- ° /WL: This logs a warning level when the number of objects in the queue reaches or exceeds the number specified. The default value is 30.
- ° /WI: This is the interval (in minutes) that the warning level is logged.

 For more information, check the product help or type PCNSCFG /?.

One common password synchronization scenario is synchronizing passwords across AD forests. If you want to synchronize passwords across AD forests, you should be aware that PCNS installed on each domain controller communicates to the MIM Synchronization server over **Distributed Component Object Model (DCOM)**. That is, if the DCs using PCNS are not in the same forest as the Sync server, you will need a bidirectional trust. You would need to register an SPN in the domain where the MIM Service account resides. The Sync server will need SRV record access to the domain controllers, and have appropriate ports opened: the RPC Endpoint mapper (TCP 135), and the dynamic RPC ports. Some customers find that editing the default dynamic port range of all their DCs and opening up that range in their firewall(s) is a good way to implement PCNS across organizational boundaries.

Summary

In this chapter, we demonstrated two optional MIM components: SSPR and password synchronization. We showed you how to enable and configure the SSPR feature and password synchronization. Before you set up SSPR, make a decision whether you want the same solution for both internal and external access to the SSPR feature. If you would like to separate SSPR access, you need to install a separate set of SSPR registration and reset portals, and modify the MIM Service MPRs and workflows, accordingly.

In the next chapter, we will be looking at certificate management and its installation and configuration.

10
Overview of Certificate Management

Microsoft Identity Management (MIM)—certificate management (CM)—is deemed the outcast in many discussions. We are here to tell you that this is not the case. We see many scenarios where CM makes the management of user-based certificates possible and improved. If you are currently using FIM certificate management or considering a new certificate management deployment with MIM, we think you will find that CM is a component to consider.

CM is not a requirement for using smart cards, but it adds a lot of functionality and security to the process of managing the complete life cycle of your smart cards and software-based certificates in a single forest or multiforest scenario.

In this chapter, we will look at the following topics:

- What is CM?
- Certificate management components
- Certificate management agents
- The certificate management permission model

What is certificate management?

Certificate management extends MIM functionality by adding management policy to a driven workflow that enables the complete life cycle of initial enrollment, duplication, and the revocation of user-based certificates. Some smart card features include offline unblocking, duplicating cards, and recovering a certificate from a lost card.

The concept of this policy is driven by a profile template within the CM application. Profile templates are stored in Active Directory, which means the application already has a built-in redundancy. CM is based on the idea that the product will proxy, or be the middle man, to make a request to and get one from CA. CM performs its functions with user agents that encrypt and decrypt its communications.

When discussing **PKI (Public Key Infrastructure)** and smart cards, you usually need to have some discussion about the level of assurance you would like for the identities secured by your PKI. For basic insight on PKI and assurance, take a look at `http://bit.ly/CorePKI`.

In typical scenarios, many PKI designers argue that you should use **Hardware Security Module (HSM)** to secure your PKI in order to get the assurance level to use smart cards. Our personal opinion is that HSMs are great if you need high assurance on your PKI, but smart cards increase your security even if your PKI has medium or low assurance. Using MIM CM with HSM will not be covered in this book, but if you take a look at `http://bit.ly/CMandLunSA`, you will find some guidelines on how to use MIM CM and HSM Luna SA.

The Financial Company has a low-assurance PKI with only one enterprise root CA issuing the certificates. The Financial Company does not use a HSM with their PKI or their MIM CM. If you are running a medium- or high-assurance PKI within your company, policies on how to issue smart cards may differ from the example. More details on PKI design can be found at `http://bit.ly/PKIDesign`.

Certificate management components

Before we talk about certificate management, we need to understand the underlying components and architecture:

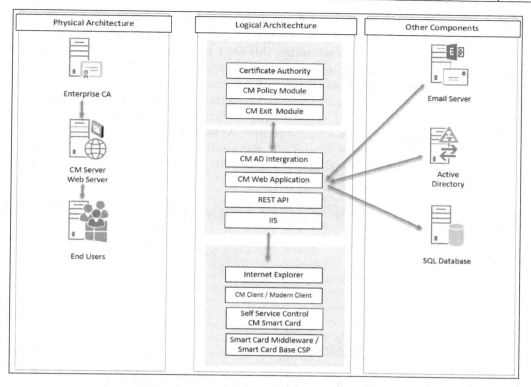

As depicted before, we have several components at play. We will start from the left to the right. From a high level, we have the Enterprise CA. The Enterprise CA can be multiple CAs in the environment. Communication from the CM application server to the CA is over the DCOM/RPC channel. End user communication can be with the CM web page or with a new REST API via a modern client to enable the requesting of smart cards and the management of these cards.

From the CM perspective, the two mandatory components are the CM server and the CA modules. Looking at the logical architecture, we have the CA, and underneath this, we have the modules. The policy and exit module, once installed, control the communication and behavior of the CA based on your CM's needs.

Moving down the stack, we have Active Directory integration. AD integration is the nuts and bolts of the operation. Integration into AD can be very complex in some environments, so understanding this area and how CM interacts with it is very important. We will cover the permission model later in this chapter, but it is worth mentioning that most of the configuration is done and stored in AD along with the database. CM uses its own SQL database, and the default name is `FIMCertificateManagement`. The CM application uses its own dedicated IIS application pool account to gain access to the CM database in order to record transactions on behalf of users. By default, the application pool account is granted the `clmApp` role during the installation of the database, as shown in the following screenshot:

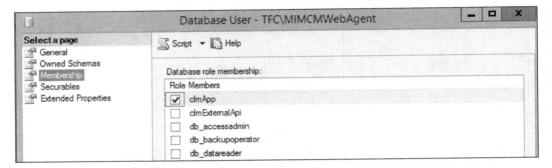

In CM, we have a concept called the profile template. The profile template is stored in the configuration partition of AD, and the security permissions on this container and its contents determine what a user is authorized to see. As depicted in the following screenshot, CM stores the data in the **Public Key Services** (**1**) and the **Profile Templates** container. CM then reads all the stored templates and the permissions to determine what a user has the right to do (**2**):

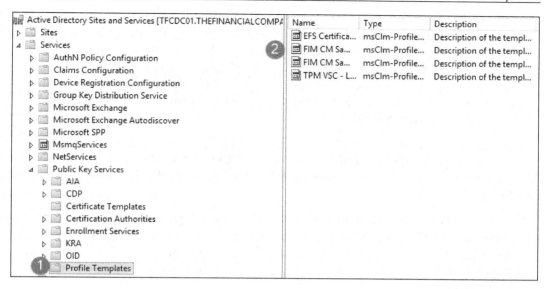

Profile templates are at the core of the CM logic. The three components comprising profile templates are certificate templates, profile details, and management policies. The first area of the profile template is **certificate templates**. Certificate templates define the extensions and data point that can be included in the certificate being requested.

The next item is **profile details**, which determines the type of request (either a smart card or a software user-based certificate), where we will generate the certificates (either on the server or on the client side of the operations), and which certificate templates will be included in the request.

The final area of a profile template is known as **management policies**. Management policies are the workflow engine of the process and contain the manager, the subscriber functions, and any data collection items. The e-mail function is initiated here and commonly referred to as the **One Time Password (OTP)** activity. Note the word "One". A trigger will only happen once here; therefore, multiple alerts using e-mail would have to be engineered through alternate means, such as using the MIM service and expiration activities.

The permission model is a bit complex, but you'll soon see the flexibility it provides. Keep in mind that **Service Connection Point (SCP)** also has permissions applied to it to determine who can log in to the portal and what rights the user has within the portal.

SCP is created upon installation during the wizard configuration. You will want to be aware of the SCP location in case you run into configuration issues with administrators not being able to perform particular functions. The SCP location is in the **System** container, within **Microsoft**, and within **Certificate Lifecycle Manager**, as shown here:

```
Typical location CN=Certificate Lifecycle Manager,CN=Microsoft,CN=Syst
em,DC=THEFINANCIALCOMPANY,DC=NET
```

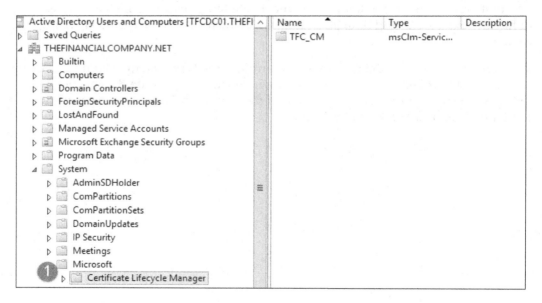

Certificate management agents

We covered several key components of the profile templates and where some of the permission model is stored. We now need to understand how the separation of duties is defined within the agent role. The permission model provides granular control, which promotes the separation of duties. CM uses six agent accounts, and they can be named to fit your organization's requirements. We will walk through the initial setup again later in this chapter so that you can use our setup or alter it based on your need. The Financial Company only requires the typical setup. We precreated the following accounts for TFC, but the wizard will create them for you if you do not use them. During the installation and configuration of CM, we will use the following accounts:

MIMCM - Subscribers	Security Group - Universal	
MIMCMAgent	User	MIM CM Agent
MIMCMAuthAgent	User	CM Authorization Agent
MIMCMEnrollAgent	User	CM Enrollment Agent
MIMCM-HelpDesk	Security Group - Global	
MIMCMKRAgent	User	CM Key Recovery Agent
MIMCMManagerAg...	User	CM CA Manager Agent
MIMCM-Managers	Security Group - Universal	
MIMCMWebAgent	User	CM Web Pool Agent

Besides the separation of duty, CM offers enrollment by proxy. Proxy enrollment of a request refers to providing a middle man to provide the end user with a fluid workflow during enrollment. Most of this proxy is accomplished via the agent accounts in one way or another. The first account is MIM CM Agent (**MIMCMAgent**), which is used by the CM server to encrypt data from the smart card admin PINs to the data collection stored in the database. So, the agent account has an important role to protect data and communication to and from the certificate authorities. The last user agent role CMAgent has is the capability to revoke certificates. The agent certificate thumbprint is very important, and you need to make sure the correct value is updated in the three areas: CM, `web.config`, and the certificate policy module under the **Signing Certificates** tab on the CA. We have identified these areas in the following.

For `web.config`:

```
<add key="Clm.SigningCertificate.Hash" value
<add key="Clm.Encryption.Certificate.Hash" value
<add key="Clm.SmartCard.ExchangeCertificate.Hash" value
```

The **Signing Certificates** tab is as shown in the following screenshot:

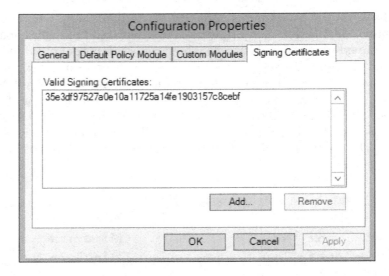

Now, when you run through the configuration wizard, these items are already updated, but it is good to know which locations need to be updated if you need to troubleshoot agent issues or even update/renew this certificate.

The second account we want to look at is Key Recovery Agent (**MIMCMKRAgent**); this agent account is needed for CM to recover any archived private keys certificates.

Now, let's look at Enrollment Agent (**MIMCMEnrollAgent**); the main purpose of this agent account is to provide the enrollment of smart cards. Enrollment Agent, as we call it, is responsible for signing all smart card requests before they are submitted to the CA. Typical permission for this account on the CA is read and request.

Authorization Agent (**MIMCMAuthAgent**) — or as some folks call this, the authentication agent — is responsible for determining access rights for all objects from a DACL perspective. When you log in to the CM site, it is the authorization account's job to determine what you have the right to do based on all the core components that ACL has applied. We will go over all the agents accounts and rights needed later in this chapter during our setup.

CA Manager Agent (**MIMCMManagerAgent**) is used to perform core CA functions. More importantly, its job is to issue **Certificate Revocation Lists (CRLs)**. This happens when a smart card or certificate is retired or revoked. It is up to this account to make sure the CRL is updated with this critical information.

We saved the best for last: Web Pool Agent (**MIMCMWebAgent**). This agent is used to run the CM web application. The agent is the account that contacts the SQL server to record all user and admin transactions.

The following is a good depiction of all the accounts together and the high-level functions:

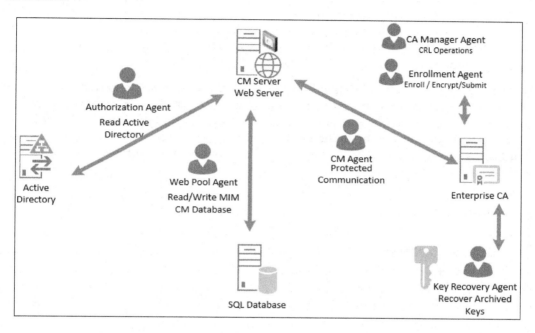

The certificate management permission model

In CM, we think this part is the most complex because with the implementation, you can be as granular as possible. For this reason, this area is the most difficult to understand. We will uncover the permission model so that we can begin to understand how the permission model works within CM.

When looking at CM, you need to formulate the type of management model you will be deploying. What we mean by this is will you have a centralized or delegated model? This plays a key part in deployment planning for CM and the permission you will need to apply.

In the centralized model, a specific set of managers are assigned all the rights for the management policy. This includes permissions on the users. Most environments use this method as it is less complex for environments. Now, within this model, we have manager-initiated permission, and this is where CM permissions are assigned to groups containing the subscribers. Subscribers are the actual users doing the enrollment or participating in the workflow. This is the model that The Financial Company will use in its configuration.

The delegated model is created by updating two flags in `web.config` called `clm.RequestSecurity.Flags` and `clm.RequestSecurity.Groups`.

These two flags work hand in hand as if you have `UseGroups`, then it will evaluate all the groups within the forests to include universal/global security. Now, if you use `UseGroups` and define `clm.RequestSecurity.Groups`, then it will only look for these specific groups and evaluate via the Authorization Agent . The user will tell the Authorization Agent to only read the permission on the user and ignore any group membership permissions:

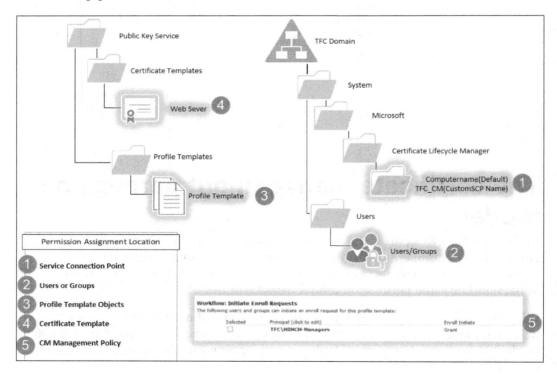

When we continue to look at the permission, there are five locations that permissions can be applied in. In the preceding figure is an outline of these locations, but we will go in more depth in the subsections in a bit. The basis of the figure is to understand the location and what permission can be applied. The following are the areas and the permissions that can be set:

1. **Service Connection Point**: Extended Permissions
2. **Users or Groups**: Extended Permissions
3. **Profile Template Objects**:
   - **Container**: Read or Write
   - **Template Object**: Read/Write or Enroll
4. **Certificate Template**: Read or Enroll
5. **CM Management Policy** within the Web application: We have multiple options based on the need, such as Initiate Request

Now, let's begin to discuss the core areas to understand what they can do. So, The Financial Company can design the enrollment option they want. In the example, we will use the main scenario we encounter, such as the helpdesk, manager, and user-(subscriber) based scenarios. For example, certain functions are delegated to the helpdesk to allow them to assist the user base without giving them full control over the environment (delegated model). Remember this as we look at the five core permission areas.

Creating service accounts

So far, in our MIM deployment, we have created quite a few service accounts. MIM CM, however, requires that we create a few more. During the configuration wizard, we will get the option of having the wizard create them for us, but we always recommend creating them manually in FIM/MIM CM deployments.

One reason is that a few of these need to be assigned some certificates. If we use an HSM, we have to create it manually in order to make sure the certificates are indeed using the HSM.

The wizard will ask for six different service accounts (agents), but we actually need seven.

In The Financial Company, we created the following seven accounts to be used by FIM/MIM CM:

- MIMCMAgent
- MIMCMAuthAgent
- MIMCMCAManagerAgent
- MIMCMEnrollAgent
- MIMCMKRAgent
- MIMCMWebAgent
- MIMCMService

The last one, MIMCMService, will not be used during the configuration wizard, but it will be used to run the MIM CM Update service.

We also created the following security groups to help us out in the scenarios we will go over:

- **MIMCM-Helpdesk**: This is the next step in OTP for subscribers
- **MIMCM-Managers**: These are the managers of the CM environment
- **MIMCM-Subscribers**: This is group of users that will enroll

Service Connection Point

Service Connection Point (SCP) is located under the `Systems` folder within Active Directory. This location, as discussed in the earlier parts of the chapter, defines who functions as the user as it relates to logging in to the web application. As an example, if we just wanted every user to only log in, we would give them read rights. Again, authenticated users, have this by default, but if you only wanted a subset of users to access, you should remove authenticated users and add your group.

When you run the configuration wizard, SCP is decided, but the default is the one shown in the following screenshot:

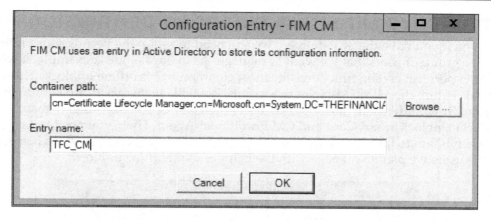

If a user is assigned to any of the MIM CM permissions available on SCP, the administrative view of the MIM CM portal will be shown.

The MIM CM permissions are defined in a Microsoft TechNet article at `http://bit.ly/MIMCMPermission`. For your convenience, we have copied parts of the information here:

- **MIM CM Audit**: This generates and displays MIM CM policy templates, defines management policies within a profile template, and generates MIM CM reports.

- **MIM CM Enrollment Agent**: This performs certificate requests for the user or group on behalf of another user. The issued certificate's subject contains the target user's name and not the requester's name.

- **MIM CM Request Enroll**: This initiates, executes, or completes an enrollment request.

- **MIM CM Request Recover**: This initiates encryption key recovery from the CA database.

- **MIM CM Request Renew**: This initiates, executes, or completes an enrollment request. The renewal request replaces a user's certificate that is near its expiration date with a new certificate that has a new validity period.

- **MIM CM Request Revoke**: This revokes a certificate before the expiration of the certificate's validity period. This may be necessary, for example, if a user's computer or smart card is stolen.

- **MIM CM Request Unblock Smart Card**: This resets a smart card's user **Personal Identification Number (PIN)** so that he/she can access the key material on a smart card.

The Active Directory extended permissions

So, even if you have the SCP defined, we still need to set up the permissions on the user or group of users that we want to manage. As in our helpdesk example, if we want to perform certain functions, the most common one is offline unblock. This would require the MIMCM-HelpDesk group. We will create this group later in this chapter. It would contain all help desk users then on SCP; we would give them CM Request Unblock Smart Card and CM Enrollment Agent. Then, you need to assign the permission to the extended permission on MIMCM-Subscribers, which contains all the users we plan to manage with the helpdesk and offline unblock:

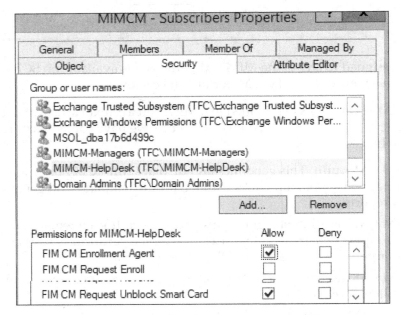

So, as you can see, we are getting into redundant permissions, but depending on the location, it means what the user can do. So, planning of the model is very important. Also, it is important to document what you have as with some slight tweak, things can and will break.

The certificate templates permission

In order for any of this to be possible, we still need to give permission to the manager of the user to enroll or read the certificate template, as this will be added to the profile template. For anyone to manage this certificate, everyone will need read and enroll permissions. This is pretty basic, but that is it, as shown in the following screenshot:

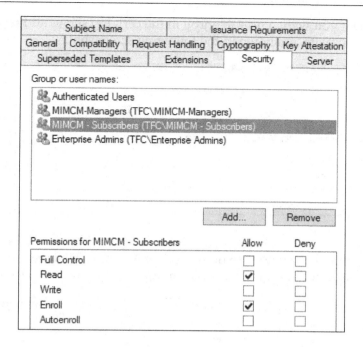

The profile template permission

The profile template determines what a user can read within the template. To get to the profile template, we need to use Active Directory sites and services to manage profile templates. We need to activate the services node as this is not shown by default, and to do this, we will click on **View | Show Services Node**:

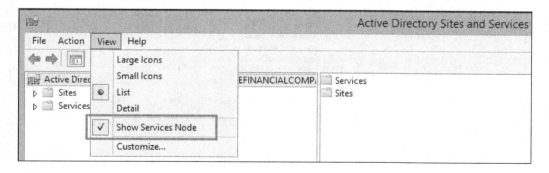

As an example if you want a user to enroll in the cert, he/she would need CM Enroll on the profile template, as shown in the following screenshot:

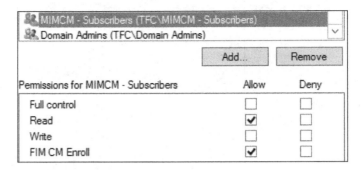

Now, this is for users, but let's say you want to delegate the creation of profile templates. For this, all you need to do is give the MIMCM-Managers delegate the right to create all child items on the profile template container, as follows:

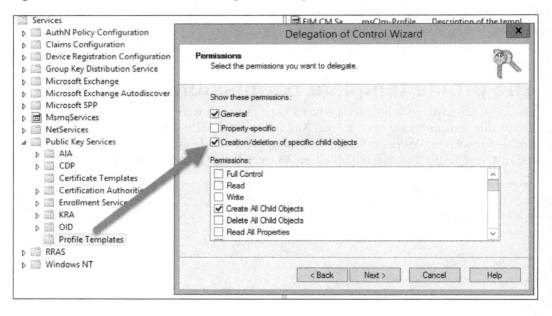

The management policy permission

For the management policy, we will break it down into two sections: a software-based policy and a smart card management policy. As we have different capabilities within CM based on the type, by default, CM comes with two sample policies (take a look at the following screenshot), which we use for duplication to create a new one. When configuring, it is good to know that you cannot combine software and smart card-based certificates in a policy:

☐	FIM CM Sample Profile Template	X	X	0	Description of the template goes here
☐	FIM CM Sample Smart Card Logon Profi...	X	✓	0	Description of the template goes here

The software management policy

The software-based certificate policy has the following policies available through the CM life cycle:

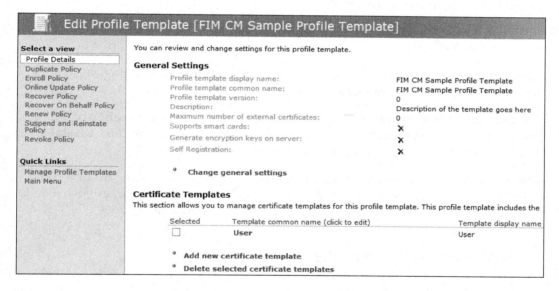

The **Duplicate Policy** panel creates a duplicate of all the certificates in the current profile. Now, if the first profile is created for the user, all the other profiles created afterwards will be considered duplicate, and the first generated policy will be primary.

The **Enroll Policy** panel defines the initial enrollment steps for certificates such as initiate enroll request and data collection during enroll initiation.

The **Online Update Policy** panel is part of the automatic policy function when key items in the policy change. This includes certificates about to expire, when a certificate is added to the existing profile template or even removed.

The **Recover Policy** panel allows for the recovery of the profile in the event that the user was deleted. This includes the cases where certs are deleted by accident. One thing to point out is if the certificate was a signing cert, the recovery policy would issue a new replacement cert. However, if the cert was used for encryption, you can recover the original using this policy.

The **Recover On Behalf Policy** panel allows managers or helpdesk operations to be recovered on behalf the user in the event that they need any of the certificates.

The **Renew Policy** panel is the workflow that defines the renew setting, such as revocation and who can initiate a request.

The **Suspend and Reinstate Policy** panel enables a temporary revocation of the profile and puts a "certificate hold" status. More information about the CRL status can be found at `http://bit.ly/MIMCMCertificateStatus`.

The **Revoke Policy** panel maintains the revocation policy and setting around being able to set the revocation reason and delay. Also, it allows the system to push a delta CRL. You also can define the initiators for this policy workflow.

The smart card management policy

The smart card policy has some similarities to the software-based policy, but it also has a few new workflows to manage the full life cycle of the smart card:

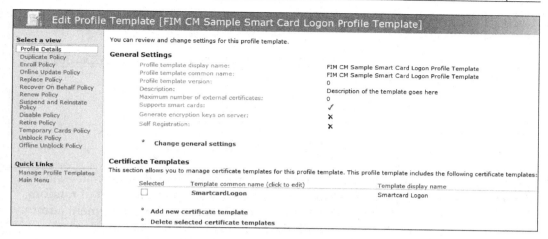

The **Profile Details** panel is by far the most commonly used part in this section of the policy as it defines all the smart card certificates that will be loaded in the policy along with the type of provider. One key item is creating and destroying virtual smart cards. One final key part is diversifying the admin key. This is best practice as this secures the admin PIN using diversification. So, before we continue, we want to go over this setting as we think it is an important topic.

Diversifying the admin key is important because each card or batch of cards comes with a default admin key. Smart cards may have several PINs, an admin PIN, a **PIN unlock key (PUK)**, and a user PIN. This admin key, as CM refers to it, is also known as the administrator PIN. This PIN differs from the user's PIN. When personalizing the smart card, you configure the admin key, the PUK, and the user's PIN. The admin key and the PUK are used to reset the virtual smart card's PIN. However, you cannot configure both. You must use the PUK to unlock the PIN if you assign one during the virtual smart card's creation.

 It is important to note that you must use the PUK to reset the PIN if you provide both a PUK and an admin key.

During the configuration of the profile template, you will be asked to enter this key as follows:

Admin Key initial value:	010203040506070801020304050607080102030405060708
Admin PIN rollover:	✗
Admin PIN length:	Not Applicable
Admin PIN character set:	Not Applicable
Admin PIN initial value:	Not Applicable
User PIN policy:	Server Distributed
User PIN character set:	Ascii
Print card:	✗

The admin key is typically used by smart card management solutions that enable a challenge response approach to PIN unlocking. The card provides a set of random data that the user reads (after the verification of identity) to the deployment admin. The admin then encrypts the data with the admin key (obtained as mentioned before) and gives the encrypted data back to the user. If the encrypted data matches that produced by the card during verification, the card will allow PIN resetting. As the admin key is never in the hands of anyone other than the deployment administrator, it cannot be intercepted or recorded by any other party (including the employee) and thus has significant security benefits beyond those in using a PUK — an important consideration during the personalization process.

When enabled, the admin key is set to a card-unique value when the card is assigned to the user. The option to diversify admin keys with the default initialization provider allows MIM CM to use an algorithm to uniquely generate a new key on the card. The key is encrypted and securely transmitted to the client. It is not stored in the database or anywhere else. MIM CM recalculates the key as needed to manage the card:

Smart Card Configuration

This section displays smart card settings, including information about the card provider and certificate authority (CA) certificates.

Provider name:	Microsoft Smart Card Base CSP
Provider id:	MSBaseCSP
Initialize new card prior to use:	✓
Reuse retired card:	✓
Use secure key injection:	✗
Install CA Certificate(s):	✓
Certificate label text:	{Template!cn}
Maximum number of certificates:	Unlimited
Diversify Admin Key:	✓
Card Initialization Provider Type:	Default
Card Initialization Provider Data:	dd91d2cc31c99804c14ec5ea9fda7731dc925818
Admin Key initial value:	
Admin PIN rollover:	✗
Admin PIN length:	Not Applicable
Admin PIN character set:	Not Applicable
Admin PIN initial value:	Not Applicable
User PIN policy:	Server Distributed
User PIN character set:	Ascii
Print card:	✗

⚙ **Change settings**

The CM profile template contains a thumbprint for the certificate to be used in admin key diversification. CM looks in the personal store of the CM agent service account for the private key of the certificate in the profile template. Once located, the private key is used to calculate the admin key for the smart card. The admin key allows CM to manage the smart card (issuing, revoking, retiring, renewing, and so on). Loss of the private key prevents the management of cards diversified using this certificate.

More detail on the control can be found at `http://bit.ly/ MIMCMDiversifyAdminKey`.

Continuing on, the **Disable Policy** panel defines the termination of the smart card before expiration, you can define the reason if you choose. Once disabled, it cannot be reused in the environment.

The **Duplicate Policy** panel, similarly to the software-based one, produces a duplicate of all the certificates that will be on the smart card.

The **Enroll Policy** panel, similarly to the software policy, defines who can initiate the workflow and printing options.

The **Online Update Policy** panel, similarly to the software-based cert, allows for the updating of certificates if the profile template is updated. The update is triggered when a renewal happens or, similarly to the software policy, a cert is added or removed.

The **Offline Unblock Policy** panel is the configuration of a process to allow offline unblocking. This is used when a user is not connected to the network. This process only supports Microsoft-based smart cards with challenge questions and answers via, in most cases, the user calling the helpdesk.

The **Recovery On Behalf Policy** panel allows the recovery of certificates for the management or the business to recover if the cert is needed to decrypt information from a user whose contract was terminated or who left the company.

The **Replace Policy** panel is utilized by being able to replace a user's certificate in the event of them losing their card. If the card they had had a signing cert, then a new signing cert would be issued on this new card. Like with software certs, if the certificate type is encryption, then it would need to be restored on the replace policy.

The **Renew Policy** panel will be used when the profile/certificate is in the renewal period and defines revocation details and options and initiates permission.

The **Suspend and Reinstate Policy** panel is the same as the software-based policy for putting the certificate on hold.

The **Retire Policy** panel is similar to the disable policy, but a key difference is that this policy allows the card to be reused within the environment.

The **Unblock Policy** panel defines the users that can perform an actual unblocking of a smart card.

More in-depth detail of these policies can be found at `http://bit.ly/ MIMCMProfiletempates`.

Summary

In this chapter, we uncovered the basics of certificate management and the management components that are required to successfully deploy a CM solution. Then, we discussed and outlined, agent accounts and the roles they play. Finally, we looked into the management permission model from the policy template to the permissions and the workflow.

In the next chapter, we will go into the installation in detail and also discuss what is required in the deployment of a modern application.

11
Installation and the Client Side of Certificate Management

Microsoft Identity Management certificate management can be a bit hard to get going, and this is why we have focused on it in multiple chapters. In this chapter, we will discuss the installation of the certificate management solution in full detail.

The topics covered in this chapter are as follows:

- Installation and configuration:
    - Extending the schema
    - Database permission
    - Configuring the CA
    - Configuring the templates and permission
    - CM update service configuration

- The certificate management client
    - Modern App deployment and configuration

Installation and configuration

MIM **certificate management (CM)** can be used in many ways, but to show you a little bit about how we can use its basics, The Financial Company will use it to allow managers (such as Jeff) to issue smart cards to users (such as David) with the help from the Modern App. We will also configure autoenrollment for EFS certificates using the policy module to recap the accounts being used in this setup.

Extending the schema

Before we can do anything, we need to extend the Active Directory schema to support MIM CM. We will go over multiforest configurations later in this chapter under various scenarios.

 All schema changes in Active Directory should be planned carefully.

If we don't, the configuration wizard will stop and tell us to extend the Active Directory schema if we try to run it. As you can see in the following screenshot, the installer is reminiscent of the branding transition:

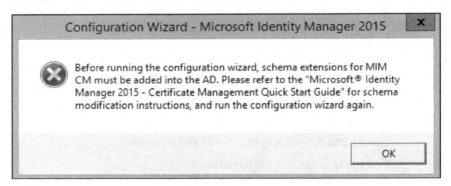

 Remember that all modifications to the schema require the schema admin's permissions.

If you look at the MIM media in the `\Certificate Management\x64` folder, you will find a `Schema` folder from which you can run the `resourceForestModifySchema.vbs` script:

ModifySchemaOnlineUpdate.vbs	6/28/2015 7:24 PM	VBScript Script File	15 KB
onlineupdate.ldif	4/22/2015 5:07 AM	LDIF File	2 KB
resourceForest.ldif	4/22/2015 5:07 AM	LDIF File	9 KB
resourceForestModifySchema.vbs	6/28/2015 7:24 PM	VBScript Script File	15 KB
userForest.ldif	4/22/2015 5:07 AM	LDIF File	6 KB
userForestModifySchema.vbs	6/28/2015 7:24 PM	VBScript Script File	15 KB

If you just run this script, you will get a success message, as follows:

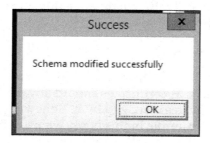

Schema in AD is now upgraded to support MIM CM.

The configuration wizard

If we knew what was coming in the configuration wizard, we might have prepared a bit more before starting it. However, one way of configuring MIM CM is to solve the problems as they arise in the configuration wizard. It is quite common to cancel out from the wizard to fix something and then start it again.

As we know what is coming, we will make some preparations.

Creating certificate templates for MIM CM service accounts

Three of the service accounts will require a certificate, and during the configuration wizard, we will be asked which template to use when requesting the certificate. This can be ignored during the wizard, but then, we need to make sure that the three accounts are configured manually with each certificate. In the case of using an HSM, this is how you need to do it.

We will, however, let the wizard request the certificates we need, but we need to create the templates.

The service accounts using a certificate are as follows:

- `MIMCMAgent`: This account needs a **User** certificate
- `MIMCMEnrollAgent`: This account needs an **Enrollment Agent** certificate
- `MIMCMKRAgent`: This account needs a **Key Recovery Agent** certificate

There are templates already present in AD, but we need to create our own versions to work with MIM CM.

All three of these accounts will be given a lot of power within your organizations and should be handled carefully. If you are not using an HSM, the certificates need to be backed up in a secure way.

So, for each of the three, we need to create a new certificate template.

One common parameter among all three is the validity period. In our opinion, the validity period on the MIM CM certificates should always exceed the maximum validity period of the certificates managed by it. Renewing these certificates might also be challenging. In our example in this book, we use a five-year validity period on these certificates. The idea is that the smart cards will have a maximum two-year validity period.

When you look in our guides, as follows, remember that we only show you the minimum requirements to work with MIM CM. Your PKI might have quite a different set of requirements for the templates.

The MIM CM User Agent certificate template

The MIM CM User Agent needs a User certificate, so let's just use the existing User template as a basis for our template. This certificate is used to secure (encrypt) a lot of data used in CM. In the next few steps, we will need to have the Certificate Authority snap-in open connected to the `TFCMIMCA` server:

> Once you use the certificate in CM, make sure you never lose track of the certificate and the private keys. If you do, you may create a situation in which all data in CM is useless as it is unable to decrypt it.

1. Right-click on the **User** template and select **Duplicate Template**:

🔲 User	3.1
🔲 User Signat Duplicate Template	4.1

2. Select **Windows Server 2003 Enterprise** as the version.

3. Give it a descriptive name. In our example, we used **MIMCM User**.

4. Change **Validity period** to something appropriate; in our example, we use 5 years. Also, extend **Renewal period** to something like 6 weeks:

5. In the **Cryptography** tab, modify the CSPs and select **Microsoft Enhanced RSA and AES Cryptographic Provider**:

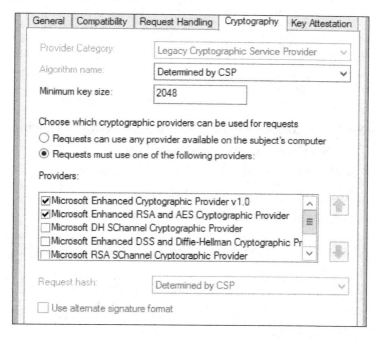

6. In the **Subject Name** tab, clear the **Include e-mail name in subject name** and **E-mail name** checkboxes:

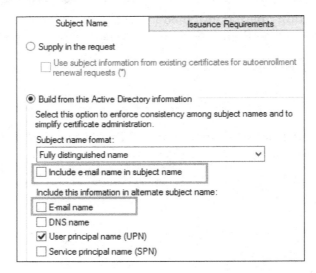

7. In the **Security** tab, remove the domain users. Assign following permissions:

   ○ **Authenticated Users**: **Read** permission

   ○ **MIMCMAgent**: **Read** and **Enroll** permissions

   ○ **Administrator**: **Read** and **Write** permissions

   ○ **Enterprise Admins**: **Read** and **Write** permissions

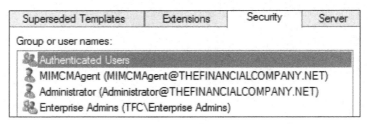

8. Click on **OK** to save the new template.

The MIM CM Enrollment Agent certificate template

The Enrollment Agent certificate is used to sign off all the certificate requests made by MIM CM. An Enrollment Agent basically has the ability to request a certificate to impersonate all users, including the administrator. This is one reason why many people like to use HSMs; they prevent private keys from being stolen. Perform the following steps:

1. Right-click on the **Enrollment Agent** template and select **Duplicate Template**.

2. Select **Windows Server 2003 Enterprise** as the version, as we did in the agent step.

3. Give it a descriptive name. In our example, we called it **MIM CM Enrollment Agent**.

4. Change **Validity period** to something appropriate; in our example, we use 5 years. Also, extend **Renewal period** to something similar to 6 weeks.

5. In the **Request Handling** tab, select **Allow private key to be exported** if you are not using HSMs.

6. In the **Security** tab, remove the domain users. Assign the following permissions:

   ° **Authenticated Users**: **Read** permission

   ° **MIMCMEnrollAgent**: **Read**, **Enroll**, and **Autoenroll** permissions

   ° **Enterprise Admins**: **Read** and **Write** permissions

7. Click on **OK** to save the new template.

The MIM CM Key Recovery Agent certificate template

The Key Recovery Agent is used if MIM CM needs to restore private keys. Perform the following steps:

1. Right-click on the **Key Recovery Agent** template and select **Duplicate Template**.

2. Select **Windows Server 2003 Enterprise** as the version.

3. Give it a descriptive name. In our example, we called it **The Financial Company MIM CM Key Recovery Agent**.

4. Change the **Validity period** to something appropriate; in our example, we use 5 years. Also, extend **Renewal period** to something like 6 weeks.

5. In the **Security** tab, remove the domain users. Assign the following permissions:

   ○ **Authenticated Users**: **Read** permission

   ○ **MIMCMKRAgent**: **Read**, **Enroll**, and **Autoenroll** permissions

   ○ **Enterprise Admins**: **Read** and **Write** permissions

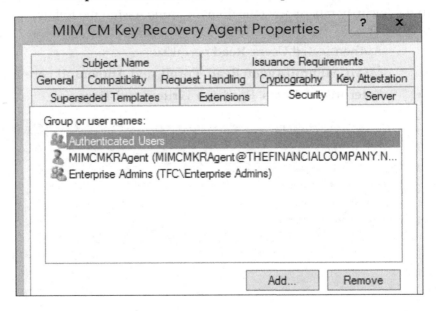

6. Click on **OK** to save the new template.

Enabling the templates

Once the templates are created, you need to remember to enable them on your CA. As you see in the following screenshot, you can simply select **Certificate Templates | New | Certificate Template to Issue**. Select the three templates we just created:

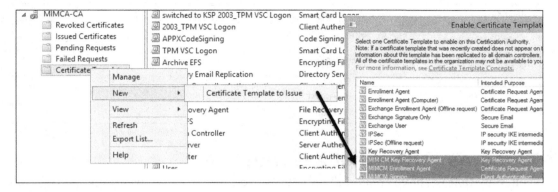

Require SSL on the CM portal

It is highly recommended that you configure your MIM CM portal to require SSL. If not, you will get the following message during the configuration wizard:

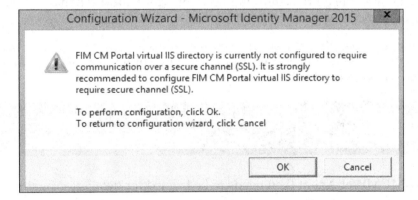

In the IIS manager, you need to configure the `CertificateManagement` virtual directory to require SSL. `CertificateManagement` is the default name, but if you configured the installation to create a site with a different name, you need to change it. We will request a certificate called `cm.thefinacialcompany.net`.

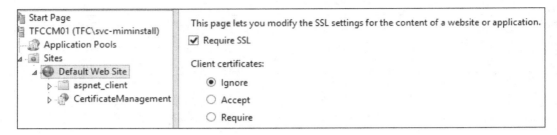

Kerberos… oh, what a world!

Well, now that we have created the accounts used by MIM CM, we might as well verify that all Kerberos Constrained Delegations and SPNs are in place.

Most of the job is done by the `MIMCMWebAgent` account, the one that will be running the MIM CM portal. In The Financial Company, we will be turning off kernel mode authentication so as to set the SPN on the user. In the event of using kernel mode, we would set the SPN on the computer account. More information can be found at `http://bit.ly/CMkernel`:

1. First, we need to make sure the correct SPNs are configured for this account. As this is the web portal application pool account, there will be some HTTP services that need to be registered:

```
C:\Users\Administrator.TFCDC01>setspn -l MIMCMWebAgent
Registered ServicePrincipalNames for CN=MIMCMWebAgent,OU=TFC Service Accounts,DC
=THEFINANCIALCOMPANY,DC=NET:
        http/cm.thefinancialcompany.net
        http/cm
```

2. **MIMCMWebAgent** then needs to be trusted for delegation against the HOST service on the CA server. Information around HOST to build SPNs on computer accounts can be found at `http://bit.ly/mimhost`:

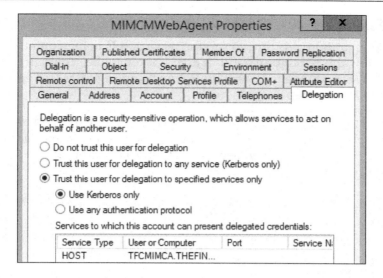

3. The final delegation is **rpcss** from the MIM CM server; in this case, navigate to the computer container and select our CM server. Then, go to **Properties**, and then to the **Delegation** tab. Here, we will enter the certificate authority server name and select **rpcss**; more information can be found at `http://bit.ly/MIMRPC`:

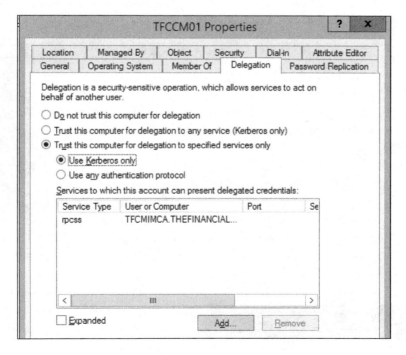

Running the wizard

After some preparation, it is time to run the wizard. It is not uncommon to rerun the wizard a few times, but be careful. It does not remember your current settings, so running it a second time may well break your working MIM CM environment. Perform the following steps:

1. To run the wizard, you need to be a domain admin and also use an account with permission to create the database in SQL. When running the wizard, it will detect the permission needed and return an error when you're not part of this group:

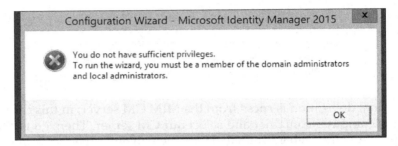

2. If you have multiple Enterprise CAs, select the one that MIM CM should use. We can later configure MIM CM to use multiple CAs if we like. At this point, we will use the **MIMCA-CA** server:

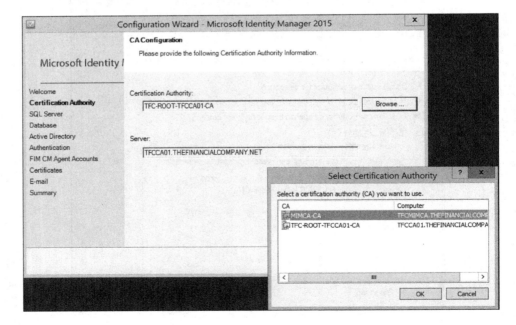

3. Since we will use the SQL alias, we will set **dbMIMCM** as the SQL Server name. If you are not logged on with an account that has permission to create the database, you need to provide credentials for such an account. In an earlier chapter, we used `cliconfg.exe`, as depicted in the following screenshot:

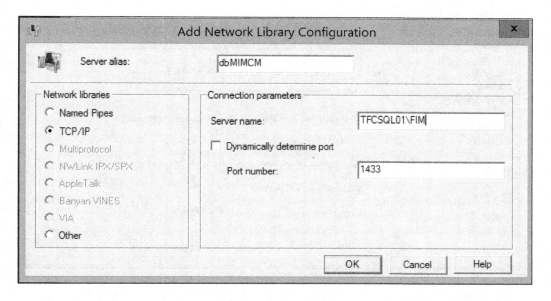

4. Leave the default settings on the **Database** page:

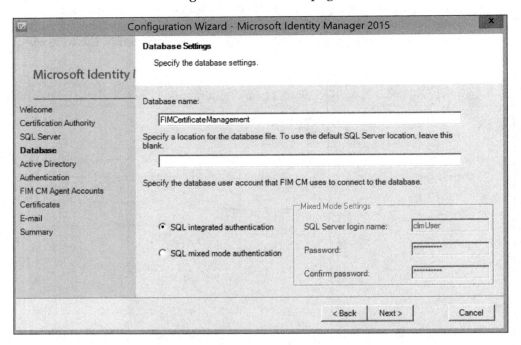

5. In the **Active Directory** page, note the AD path for the so-called Service Connection Point. We will need to configure some permissions on this object later on. We have never dared to change the location, even if it points to an old location, referencing the older version of MIM CM, Certificate Lifecycle Manager.

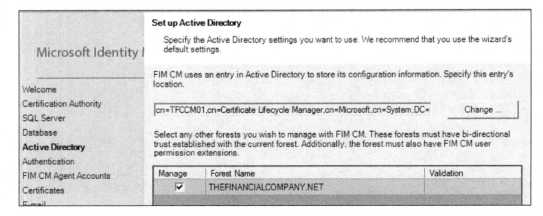

As you see in the preceding screenshot, by default, the wizard uses the default server name. In the enterprise, we recommend you to have a global name so that when we add new servers to the organization, we can use a global name. To do this, we can simply click on the **Change** button you see. Also, you will see a new feature to be able to select the other forest. By default, it will show all the forest that are fully trusted. So, you can enable cross-forest environment. We will cover setting this up in *Chapter 12, Certificate Management Scenarios*:

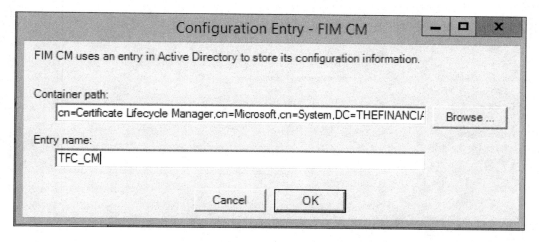

The Financial Company will use the name **TFC_CM** for the company. This will create an SCP with this name.

The next section is new as well, as you see here. This determines whether you will enable ADFS authentication or Active Directory. The current authentication we will use is Active Directory. We will also cover this setup in *Chapter 12, Certificate Management Scenarios*, if you decide to enable this new feature:

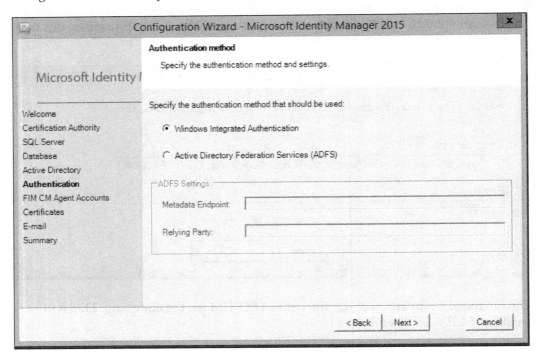

So far, it has been an easy wizard to follow, but now, it is time to really pay attention, especially if this is the first time you are running the wizard. Perform the following steps:

1. On the **MIM CM Agent Accounts** page, you need to configure every one of the agents with the correct information. Clear the **Use the MIM CM default settings** checkbox and click on the **Custom Accounts** button:

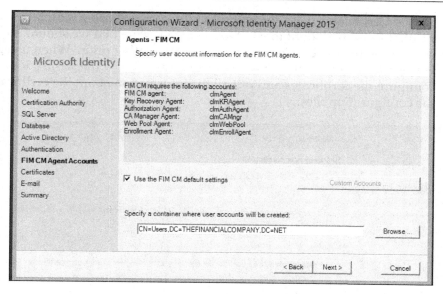

2. On all the six agent accounts, select the **Use an existing user** checkbox and fill in the **User name** and **Password** textboxes for the account. Now you can tell why we named our accounts the way we did; it makes it easy to understand which account to use for which agent.

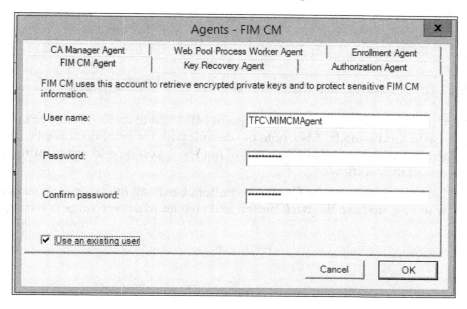

3. On the **Certificates** page, we will select the corresponding template we would like each account to use. Some people argue that we should always use the **Create and configure certificates manually** option. When using HSMs, we always do this. It is, however, nice to allow the wizard to configure the certificates and put all the information about the certificates in the configuration files:

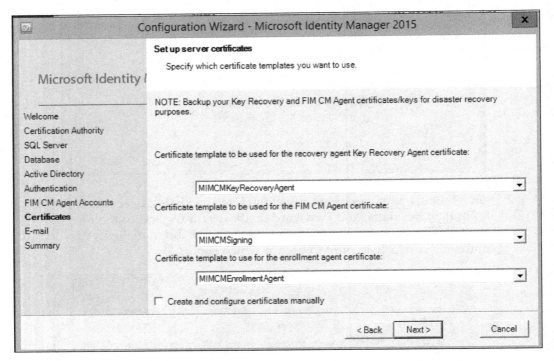

4. On the **E-mail** page, we will just point MIM CM to an SMTP server that it can use to send e-mails. Also, note the default path for print documents. In this short coverage of MIM CM, we will not show you how to use printing and e-mail in workflows.

5. Before you click on the **Configure** button, verify all the settings. If something is wrong, just use the **Back** button and change whatever value is wrong:

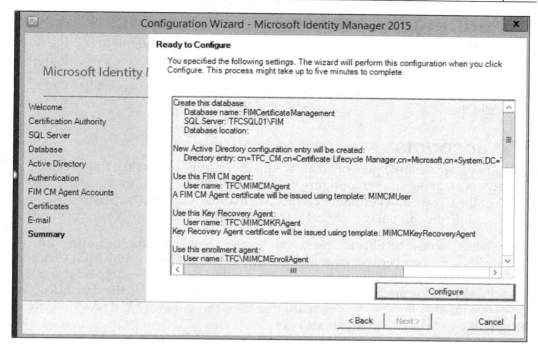

6. The wizard will take a few minutes to complete the execution. It is not uncommon for it to fail as there may be many parameters that might not have been correctly set.

Backup certificates

As soon as the configuration wizard is finished, you need to log in to the MIM CM server as the three users—MIMCMAgent, MIMCMEnrollAgent, and MIMCMKRAgent—and make sure you get a backup of the certificates. Do not forget the private keys they received.

 Do not ever lose track of the agent certificates! This is key to recovery.

Rerunning the wizard

If something goes wrong or you need to change something, you might need to rerun the wizard. This is fine as long as you keep a close eye on what you are changing.

There are two critical parts where you might end up destroying your MIM CM deployment.

The accounts

If you have successfully generated and requested certificates for the three MIM CM accounts, make sure to configure the wizard with the same accounts and also to select the **Create and configure certificates manually** checkbox. Otherwise, you might end up creating new certificates without this actually being your intention.

If you generate new certificates, make sure to also create backups, including the private keys. Remember that once an FIM agent certificate is used by MIM CM, you have to keep track of it until you are certain that no data is encrypted using its keys. If MIM CM is unable to use the private key to decrypt data, the data is lost. We have seen cases where every smart card had to be thrown away and new ones were bought due to the loss of the private keys.

The database

If there is already an MIM CM database, we will receive an option to either use the existing one or create a new one. Make sure you select the correct option. Answering **No** will delete all the data that MIM CM has so far stored in the database, and a new database will be created.

Configuring the MIM CM Update service

By default, the Forefront Identity Manager CM Update service runs under the local system account. It is considered best practice to change it and use a service account instead.

We have already created the MIMCMService user that we intend to use for this purpose. Before we can configure it for the service, we need to assign a few user rights to it.

The account needs the following User Rights Assignment:

- To act as part of the operating system
- To generate security audits
- To replace a process-level token
- To log in as a service

It then needs to be added to the following local groups on the MIM CM server:

- Administrators
- IIS_IUSRS

After this, we will reconfigure the service to use the account and start automatically.

Database permissions

Once the database is created by the configuration wizard, we need to assign permissions to it. If you are not comfortable managing your SQL database, your DBA can help you with this.

On the `FIMCertificateManagement` database, we need to allow the CA server and the MIM CM Update service with the `clmApp` role.

Usually, this also means that we need to create the logins since these accounts never had any.

So, what we need is to create logins for `TFC\TFCMIMCA$` and `TFC\MIMCMService` and then assign them the `clmApp` role in the MIM CM database, as depicted in the following screenshot:

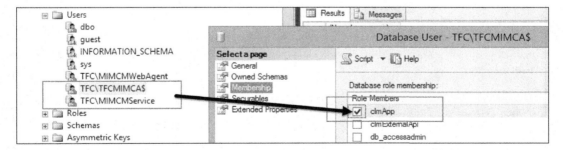

Configuring the CA

The CA used by MIM CM needs to be configured before we can use it.

First, we need to install the MIM CM CA files, and then we need to configure the modules we just installed.

Installing the MIM CM CA files

You install the CA files by running the same setup as when installing the MIM CM server.

The only trick is to remember to unselect the **MIM CM Portal** and **MIM CM Update Service** options in the feature selection during setup. We only want to install **MIM CM CA Files**:

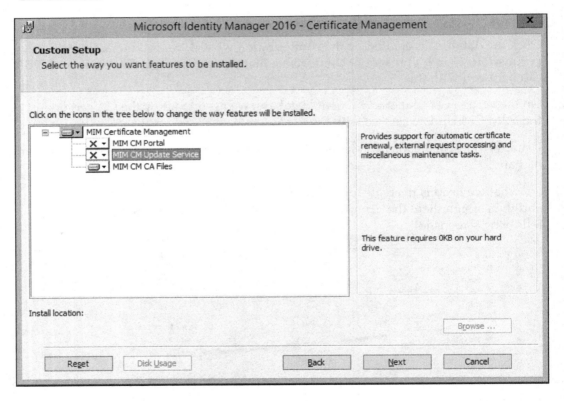

Configuring the Policy Module

Once we install the modules, we need to configure them with some information regarding MIM CM.

In the properties of **Exit Module**, we need to tell the CA how to connect to the MIM CM database by supplying it with a connection string:

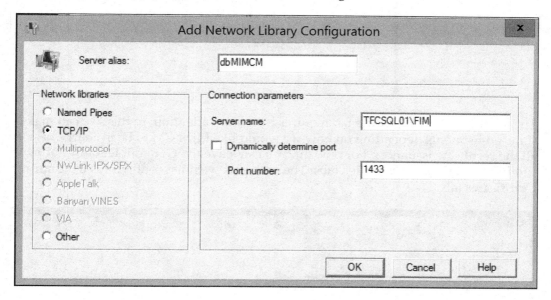

A typical connection string looks as follows:

```
connect Timeout=15;Integrated Security=SSPI;Persist Security
Info=True;Initial Catalog=FIMCertificateManagement;Data Source=dbMIMCM
```

In this example, we used a SQL alias on the CA server as well, similar to what we did with the other server installs.

Check for errors in the event log when restarting the CA service to verify that the connection to the MIM CM database is successful. You can also take a look at the CertificateAuthority table and see the registered CA, as follows:

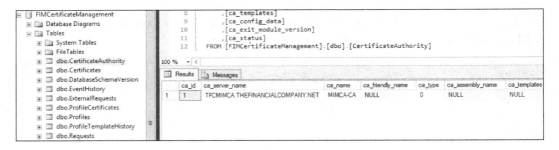

The MIM CM **Policy Module** tab requires a bit more attention. In this, we can make some adjustments depending on how we would like MIM CM to be in charge of all the certificate issuances. For now on, you can leave the **General**, **Default Policy Module**, and **Custom Modules** tabs. The only part we must configure is the **Signing Certificates** tab:

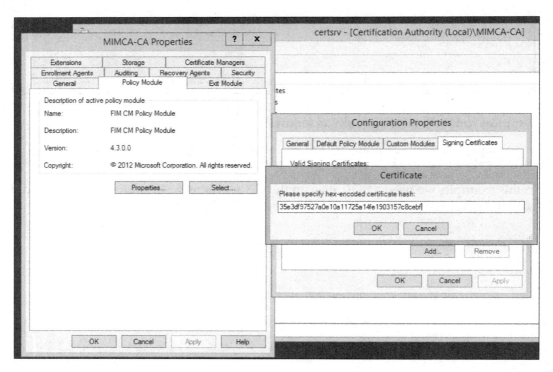

In this tab, we need to add the hex-encoded hash value of the certificate that the MIM CM agent will use to sign requests.

You can get this value by either taking a look at the certificate or by looking into the configuration file of MIM CM. We almost always get this from the configuration file as reading the information from the certificate requires you to reformat them.

The configuration file we are talking about is the `web.config` file used by the MIM CM portal. If you open up IIS Manager and right-click on the **CertificateManagement** site and choose **Explore**, you will end up in the right spot.

The default path is `C:\Program Files\Microsoft Forefront Identity Manager\2010\Certificate Management\web`.

As a MIM CM administrator, you will find yourself looking at this `web.config` file quite often. Within this configuration file, you will find the hash of the currently used certificate as well as hashes of previous certificates, if any. Locate the following section in the `web.config` file:

```
<add key="Clm.SigningCertificate.StoreLocation" value="CurrentUser" />
<!-- hex-encoded certificate hash. -->
<add key="Clm.SigningCertificate.Hash" value="35E3DF97527A0E10A11725A14FE1903157C8CEBF" />
<!-- URI of the signing certificate. If this value is not empty then
     Digital signature will only contain a reference to the certificate, not the
     encoded certificate itself.
     -->
<add key="Clm.SigningCertificate.URI" value="" />
<!-- Additional Valid Certificates~~~~~~~~~~~~~~~~~~~
     Define the list of additional certificates that are considered valid
     signing certificates. Current signing certificate is valid by definition.
     -->
<!-- comma-separated list of hex-encoded certificate hashes. -->
<add key="Clm.ValidSigningCertificates.Hashes" value="35E3DF97527A0E10A11725A14FE1903157C8CEBF" />
<!-- controls how signing certificate is validated. -->
<add key="Clm.ValidSigningCertificates.ValidationFlag" value="-1" />
<!-- CLM Decryption Certificates~~~~~~~~~~~~~~~~~~~
```

In our example environment, the hash was on line 126.

Now, you can copy the hash value and place it into the **Policy Module Signing Certificates** setting.

If you have renewed your user agent certificate, you might also have additional valid signing certificates that you need to add. These should be listed a few lines below, in your configuration file:

```
<add key="Clm.ValidSigningCertificates.Hashes" value="35E3DF97527A0E10A11725A14FE1903157C8CEBF" />
<!-- controls how signing certificate is validated. -->
<add key="Clm.ValidSigningCertificates.ValidationFlag" value="-1" />
```

As in our case, this is a new installation, we only have one certificate and thus, the same value for SigningCertificate and ValidSigningCertificate.

The Policy Module will only accept an input in uppercase without spaces when entering the value. Be sure to stop and restart the certificate service on the CA after configuring the Policy Module.

Certificate management clients

MIM comes with two options for enterprises to allow users to enroll or manage certificates. We have the classic ActiveX plugin that has been with us since the **CLM (Certificate Lifecycle Manager)** days of the CM smart card enrollment. Now, we also have a new option using the Modern App with the new REST API. In this chapter, we will go over the installation of these components and also the configuration of the MIM CM Modern App depending on your environment.

Installing the MIM CM client

On the client computers where users manage smart cards (in some cases, all workstations), you will need to install some client components.

 You should install the x86 client software, even if the operating system is a 64-bit one. You have to match your MIM CM client with the type of Internet Explorer that the users are using. (Even on 64-bit Windows, we almost always use the 32-bit version of IE.)

The installation can be automated and settings controlled using GPOs, but showing a few manual steps gives you an idea of what might need to be changed:

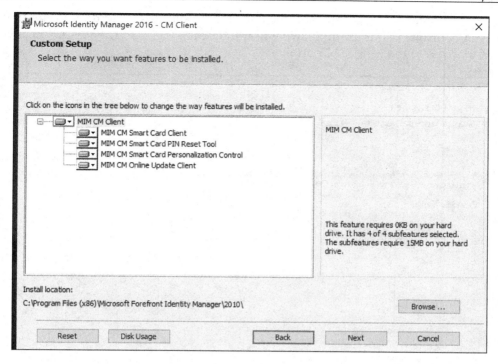

Usually, we select all the components of the client software because we would like to support all the features. If you are using a separate tool for the PIN reset, for example, you might exclude this component.

We then need to tell the component the name of the sites it should trust to run the ActiveX controls. In our example, we will use the alias `cm.thefinancialcompany.net` for access to the MIM CM portal:

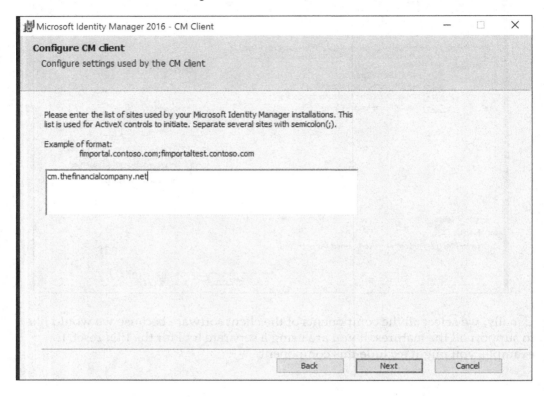

If you are not using the self-service option while using the MIM CM portal, we still suggest you install the client components in case you decide to start using some workflows within CM, which require the users to interact with MIM CM.

Modern App deployment and configuration

The Modern App brings new freshness to how we can manage certificates within the enterprise for users. The Modern App has a few configuration options from enterprise deployment using Windows Authentication or even Active Directory Federation Services. The Modern App has the concepts of admin and non-admin modes.

Within the Modern App, the default configuration is that it assumes the user is a local administrator. Of course, in many cases as we know, this is definitely not standard practice, so the Modern App allows us to customize this default setting and other settings, such as whether we want to use ADFS.

In the next section, will go through these configurations as for The Financial Company, we want to use the non-admin mode as this is the typical configuration that most companies are comfortable using.

Configuration and deployment

In the configuration of the Modern App, we first need to copy the Modern App from the MIM media disk, as we can see in the following screenshot:

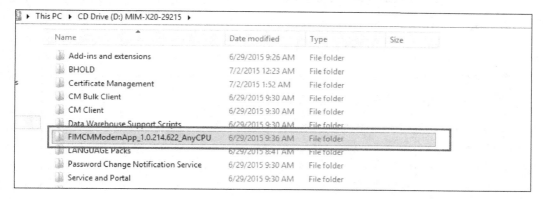

Once we have copied the folder to our Windows 8, 8.1, or 10 machine. We will then need to make sure we installed the **MakeAppx** utility. This utility allows for the creation or extraction of the Modern App to disk. More details can be found at `http://bit.ly/MIMMakeapp`.

Now we have that in place, we need to sign the application with a trusted certificate. Now, the Modern App does come with a self-signed certificate, but in most cases, you would want to sign it with a trusted source because most self-signed certificates are not welcome within the enterprise, as is the case for The Financial Company. You can skip this if you want to just go through the steps in a test environment by updating the local machine group policy (`http://bit.ly/MIMModernaaptest`). But you must still update the `Custom.data` file accordingly and repackage the app as described further ahead.

To do this, we need to make a software-signing certificate on our CA, or if you already have a service that does software signing, then you can skip the step you are about to perform.

So, let's open up the certificate templates and duplicate the code signing template with the following details:

- **Compatibility**
  - ○ **Certificate Authority**: Windows Server 2008 R2
  - ○ **Certificate Recipient**: Windows 8.1/Windows 2012 R2

- **Request Handling**
  - ○ Allow private key to be exported

- **Subject Name**
  - ○ Supplied in the request

- **Extensions**
  - ○ **Application Policies**: Code Signing

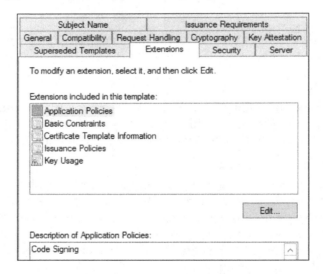

After you complete the code signing template, go ahead and publish it as we did with the CM certificates.

Right-click on **Certificate Template** | **New** | **Certificate Template to Issue**. Select the signing template and click on **OK**.

After this, we will go to our Windows desktop and open up MMC. Once MMC is open, we will go ahead and navigate to **Personal | Certificates** in **Certificate - Current User**. Right-click on the right-hand side, then, on **All Tasks | Request New Certificate**, as you see in the following screenshot:

Now, in the wizard, once the enrollment screen appears, you need to select the default Active Directory enrollment policy. In this screen, you should see our new code signing certificate template. In our case, we will see **APPXCodeSigning** as being available for enrollment, as follows:

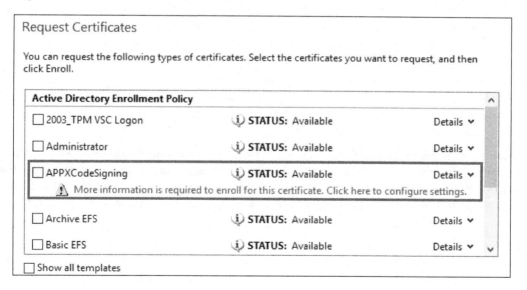

Now, we can see that it does require more information, and this information will be required for the Modern App to be signed using the common name. In our case, we will use CN=MIMCMAPP as a common name, and we will use this later on when we compact the customized Modern App. In the following screenshot, you will see the CN name, then we simply click **Add**, then **OK**, and then on **Enroll**.

The following screenshot is the CN screen of the enrollment:

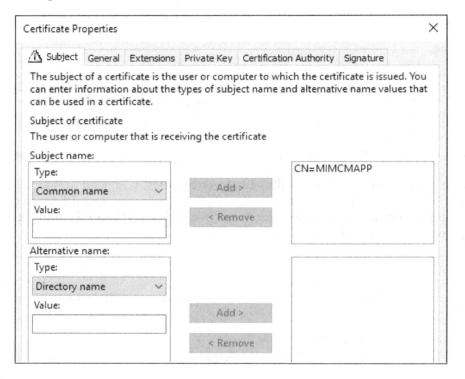

Once we complete the enrollment, we need to export the certificate to a PFX file for later use. During the export of the certificate, we need to make sure that we select the **Export private key** option, and then on the next screen, we will confirm that we are exporting all the extended properties, as you can see in the following screenshot:

Certificate Export Wizard

Export File Format
Certificates can be exported in a variety of file formats.

Select the format you want to use:

○ DER encoded binary X.509 (.CER)

○ Base-64 encoded X.509 (.CER)

○ Cryptographic Message Syntax Standard - PKCS #7 Certificates (.P7B)

☐ Include all certificates in the certification path if possible

◉ Personal Information Exchange - PKCS #12 (.PFX)

☑ Include all certificates in the certification path if possible

☐ Delete the private key if the export is successful

☑ Export all extended properties

☐ Enable certificate privacy

○ Microsoft Serialized Certificate Store (.SST)

So now, we've got all the prerequisites ready for us to customize the configuration. In our case, the first thing we need to do is unpack the Modern App application. To do this, we simply need to run the following command:

```
makeappx unpack /l /p FIMCMModernApp_1.0.219.1111_AnyCPU.appx /d ./.\appx
```

Once this is complete, we want to make sure that we don't overwrite the default Modern App. Again, it can be easy to recover the Modern App by simply going to buy the license. The next command that we will run, the `ren` command, will rename the Modern App for safekeeping:

```
C:\Users\dsteadman\Desktop\FIMCMModernApp_1.0.219.1111_AnyCPU_Test>
C:\Users\dsteadman\Desktop\FIMCMModernApp_1.0.219.1111_AnyCPU_Test>
C:\Users\dsteadman\Desktop\FIMCMModernApp_1.0.219.1111_AnyCPU_Test>ren FIMCMModernApp_1.0.219.1111_AnyCPU.appx FIMCMModernApp_1.0.219.1111_AnyCPU.appx.original
```

Next, we will change (using the `cd` command) into the `appx` directory.

Open up the `AppxManifest.xml` file and look for the `Publisher` attribute in the `Identity` element. Then, replace it with `MIMCMAPP`, the value you used as the subject name of the code signing certificate exported before. The publisher name must match the certificate subject name when you sign the Modern App.

Next, open Explorer, and in the `appx` directory, we will see a file called `CustomDataExample.xml`. We will rename this file `Custom.data`, and it will serve as the Modern App customization file.

Now, let's open up the `Custom.data` file in Notepad, and you'll notice six key areas. The first area is FQDN of your claims base provider. If you're not using a claims base provider, leave this value blank. The second configuration item is FQDN of the certificate management server. The third item is the privacy URL that companies can use to educate what is being collected from the certificate management service. The fourth item is essentially the support e-mail address if the customer runs into an issue. The fifth item is `LobComplianceEnable`; this line item is enabled by default. It is unclear what this compliance setting is for or maybe it was added but never used during the spec. The sixth item is around minimum PIN length; by default, this is set to six. The last setting that we were interested in is the non-admin value; by default, this value set to `False`. In our case, we want to set it to `True` so that the Modern App knows that it can't create virtual smart cards dynamically on the TPM chip. These settings that The Financial Company will use can be found in the following screenshot:

```xml
<?xml version="1.0" encoding="utf-8" ?>
<!-- This is an example of CustomData -->
<!-- To install the package, the command in PowerShell should be: -->
<!-- Add-AppxProvisionedPackage -PackagePath .\<PackageName>.appx -CustomDataPath .\<CustomDataFileName>.xml -SkipLicense -Online -->
<CustomData>
  <!-- insert MIM CM and ADFS absolute server address as demonstrated in template-->
  <ServersAddresses>
  ① <ADFS Url=""/>
  ② <MIMCM Url="https://cm.thefinancialcompany.net/certificatemanagement"/>
  </ServersAddresses>
  <!-- Insert privacy policy absolute URI address as demonstrated in template. -->
  <!-- see link for more examples: http://msdn.microsoft.com/en-us/library/system.uri.iswellformeduristring%28v=vs.110%29.aspx -->
  ③<PrivacyUrl Url="https://Your privacy URL"/>
  <!-- Insert email address for support issues. To predefine a subject, add the following to the "Mail" string: "?subject="+subject. -->
  <!-- example: "support@supportMail.com?subject=VSC support issue" -->
  <!-- If support is provided through a web page, a URI can be inserted instead. -->
  ④ <SupportMail Mail="support@supportmail.com"/>
  ⑤ <LobComplianceEnable Value="True"/>
  ⑥ <MinimumPinLength Length="6"/>
  ⑦ <NonAdmin Value="True"/>
</CustomData>
```

Once we've entered all the information, we will go ahead and save and close the file. We will then compact the application back on for deployment. To do this, we will use the MakeAppx utility again and run the following command against our `appx` directory, followed by the name of the application:

```
makeappx pack /l /d .\appx /p FIMCMModernApp.appx
```

Now, we are ready to sign the application with the PFX certificate that we exported earlier. With this, we will use a utility called **Sign Tool** and run the following command (Sign Tool is found within Visual Studio; more detailed information can be found at `http://bit.ly/MIMSigntool`):

```
signtool sign /f ModernAppTestOnlyTFC.pfx /p <your password> /fd "sha256" FIMCMModernApp.appx
```

Now, if you've done everything correctly, you should see our `appx` directory and our new customized Modern App that is signed in the original Modern App. The next thing we need to do is actually run or add the application so that we can test it. So, to deploy the app, we will use the `Add-AppDevPackage` PowerShell script that is provided with the Modern App package and run it:

Add-AppDevPackage.resources	2/10/2016 3:28 PM	File folder	
appx	2/10/2016 8:05 PM	File folder	
Add-AppDevPackage.ps1	7/24/2014 1:22 PM	Windows PowerS...	61 KB
CustomDataExample.xml	1/20/2015 8:55 AM	XML Document	2 KB
FIMCMModernApp.appx	2/10/2016 8:13 PM	APPX File	491 KB
FIMCMModernApp_1.0.219.1111_AnyCPU.appx.original	11/11/2015 10:04 ...	ORIGINAL File	486 KB
ModernAppTestOnlyTFC.pfx	2/10/2016 8:13 PM	Personal Informati...	7 KB

Once installed, you will see it in the Start menu, so let's go ahead and test the launching of the application:

Now, once the application launches, if you already have certificates from the certificate management server, you can see that the app has already detected that you have active certificates you can manage. If you do not have any certificates here, then this is a new deployment of the complete certificate management server, and there would be a prompt to enroll software certificates that you have configured or even virtual smart cards.

One last bit of information regarding the Modern App is that it has a log enabled by default. To understand what is happing under the hood, you can navigate to `%localappdata%\Packages\CmModernAppv.01_gpzb379ef946y\LocalState` to troubleshoot the Modern App.

In the next chapter, we will go over common scenarios with and without the Modern App now that we have configured and installed the certificate management core. This includes extending the schema, configuring the service accounts, and deploying any plugins that may be required.

The following are some more useful links to use around deploying certificate management:

- Non-admins (`http://bit.ly/MIMNonadmins`)
- Working with the certificate manager (`http://bit.ly/MIMCMManager`)

Summary

In this chapter, we covered a lot of ground on the installation of the certificate management solution. We are well on our way to have a great certificate solution for The Financial Company. We also looked in grave detail the Modern App from deployment to the signing and customizing of the Modern App.

The next chapter will be the final documentation of the scenarios and configuration to include the ADFS setup and typical models.

12
Certificate Management Scenarios

The Financial Company is interested in the management of its certificates and has decided to deploy MIM **Certificate Management** (**CM**). This chapter will discuss step-by-step instructions to implement and test various CM scenarios and models. We will cover configuration files, permissions, and error files and provide some of our personal feedback on what to avoid. Furthermore, we will discuss new features not found in earlier versions of the product, such as enabling one forest to provide certificates to another forest.

In this chapter, we will cover the following topics:

- Virtual smart card with TPM (Modern App)
- Using support for non-MIM CM
- Multi-forest configuration
- **Active Directory Federation Services** (**ADFS**) configuration
- Models at a glance

Modern app and TPM virtual smart card

In the previous chapter, we configured the Modern App for The Financial Company. Our next step is to allow the enrollment of the virtual smart card deployment by deploying the certificate template and updating the policy template.

First, enable the MIM CM REST API by setting `CLM.WebApi.Enabled` to `true` inside the `web.config` file and make sure `CLM.WebApi.Enabled` is set to `true`, as follows:

```
<!--
The FIM CM Web API provides a RESTful interface against which clients can perform
management and enrollment.
-->
  <add key="Clm.WebApi.Enabled" value="true" />
  <!--
```

Another useful setting is adding error logging for the REST API controllers under `<system.diagnostics>` of `web.config`, as follows:

```
<add name="Microsoft.Clm.Web.API" value="4" />
```

This setting allows errors from the REST interface to be written to the event log along with a correlation ID. The correlation ID is sent to the client, and you can trace the error all the way back to its origin. More information on the REST API for CM can be found at `http://bit.ly/MIMCMRestAPI`.

Creating a certificate template

We will now create a certificate template in the CA. Open CA MMC and manage the certificates, as you can see in the following screenshot:

We will duplicate the smart card login template. In the **Compatibility** screen, select **Certification Authority** as **Windows Server 2008** or later and **Windows 8 / Windows Server 2012** or later as **Certificate recipient**. This step is important because the Modern App does not support the management of Windows XP or Windows Server 2003 smart card certificates. The option selection is shown as follows:

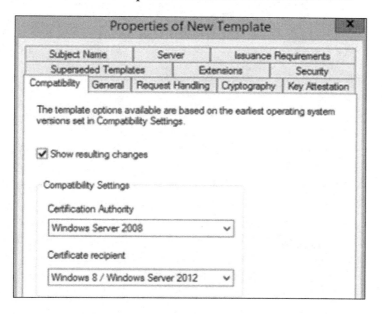

In the **General** Tab, in the **Display name** field, type TPM VSC Logon. In the **Request Handling** tab, we want to set the **Purpose** option to **Signature and encryption**:

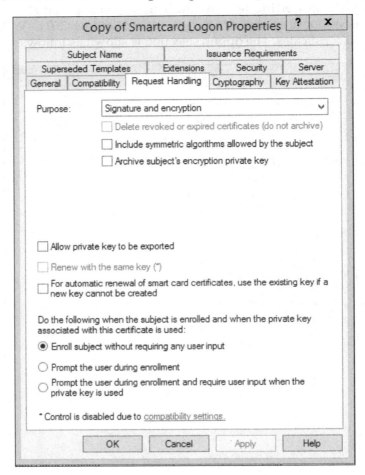

Click on the **Cryptography** tab, and under **Provider Category**, select **Key Storage Provider** and then select **Requests can use any provider available on the subject's computer**. You must select KSP as the provider, as the Modern App will not recognize this certificate template type for TPM:

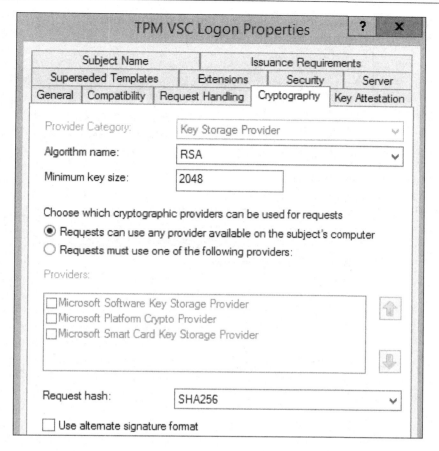

Next, we will set up the permissions on the certificate template. Navigate to the **Security** tab and add the security group that you want to give **Enroll** access to. For example, if you want to give access to all users, select the **Authenticated Users** group and then select the **Enroll** permission. In our situation, we want the following permissions for The Financial Company:

- **Authenticated Users**: **Read** permission
- **MIMCM-Managers**: **Read** and **Write** permissions

- **MIMCM – Subscribers**: **Read** and **Enroll** permissions
- **Enterprise Admins**: **Read** and **Write** permissions

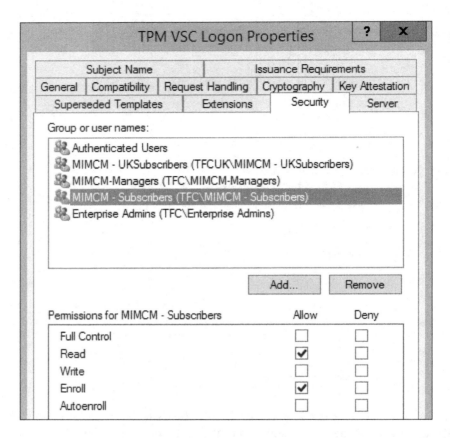

Finally, we need to set the subject name from Active Directory. Click on the **Subject Name** tab and unselect **Include e-mail name in subject name**. Then, under **Include this information in alternate subject name**, unselect **E-mail name**:

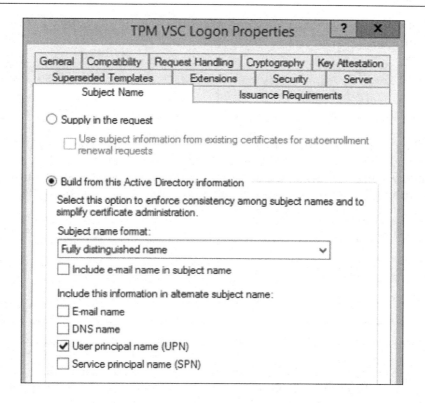

Click on **OK** to complete the certificate template. When you see your template in the MMC console, you can publish the certificate as we did with the agent certificates in the previous chapter.

Creating the profile

We now need to tell CM what we want to do with the virtual smart card. We will create our profile template and the driver for the workflow and enrollment. The first step is to log on to the CM website as profile template admin, which can be a full admin or a delegated admin of the template.

Navigate to **Manage profile templates** and click on the link:

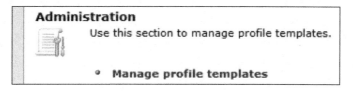

Select **FIM CM Sample Smart Card Login Profile** and click on **Copy a selected profile template**:

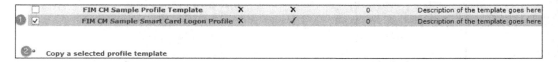

You will be prompted for the name of the certificate. In this version of MIM CM, the name you provide will be the CN name of the certificate and will be the current name listed when enrolling in the Modern App. We hope that in the future, the Modern App will be updated to use the profile display name, as described in the profile template under general settings:

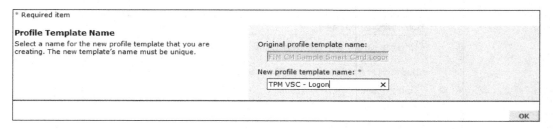

Now that we have our template created, we need to add the certificate template we created. To add the certificate template, select **Add new certificate template**:

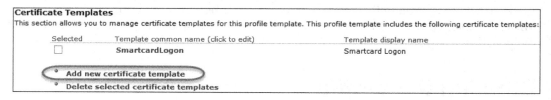

Select the CA, and the templates will be available:

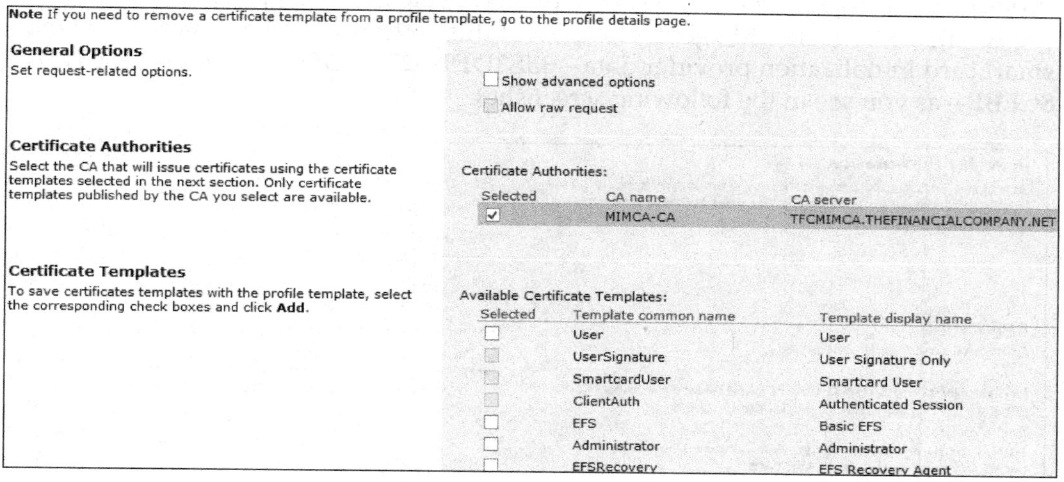

Select the CA, then select the **TPMVSCLogon** template, and finally, click on **Add**:

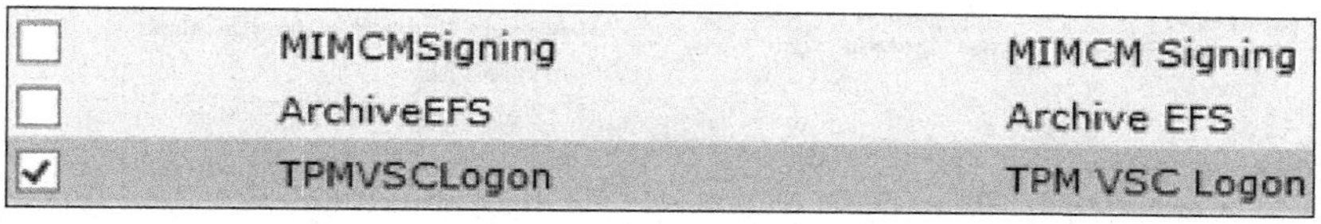

You should now be back at the main screen with two templates defined. We will select the default template and then click on **Delete selected certificate templates**:

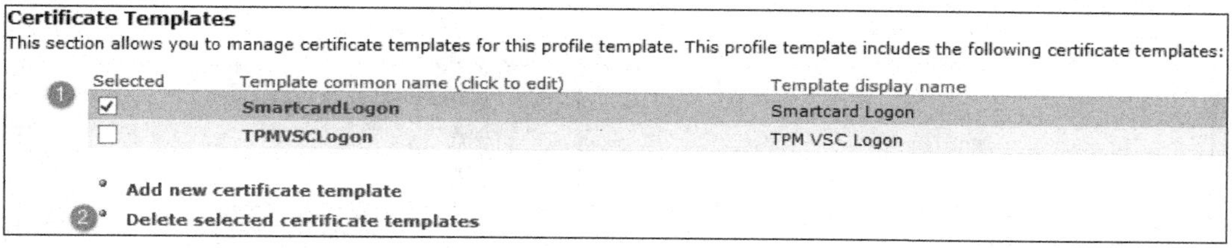

Next, we will update the smart card configuration:

1. Select **Create/Destroy virtual smart card**.

2. Select **Diversify Admin Key**.

3. You need to set the initial admin key to the default virtual smart card, which is as follows: **010203040506070801020304050607080102030405060708**

We will use the agent certificate to diversify the admin key. It is good practice to protect the admin key of a smart card. This certificate must be present in the "my" (personal) store of the CM agent. The hash of this certificate will be entered into the smart card initialization provider data—**35E3DF97527A0E10A11725A14FE1903157C 8CEBF**—as you see in the following screenshot:

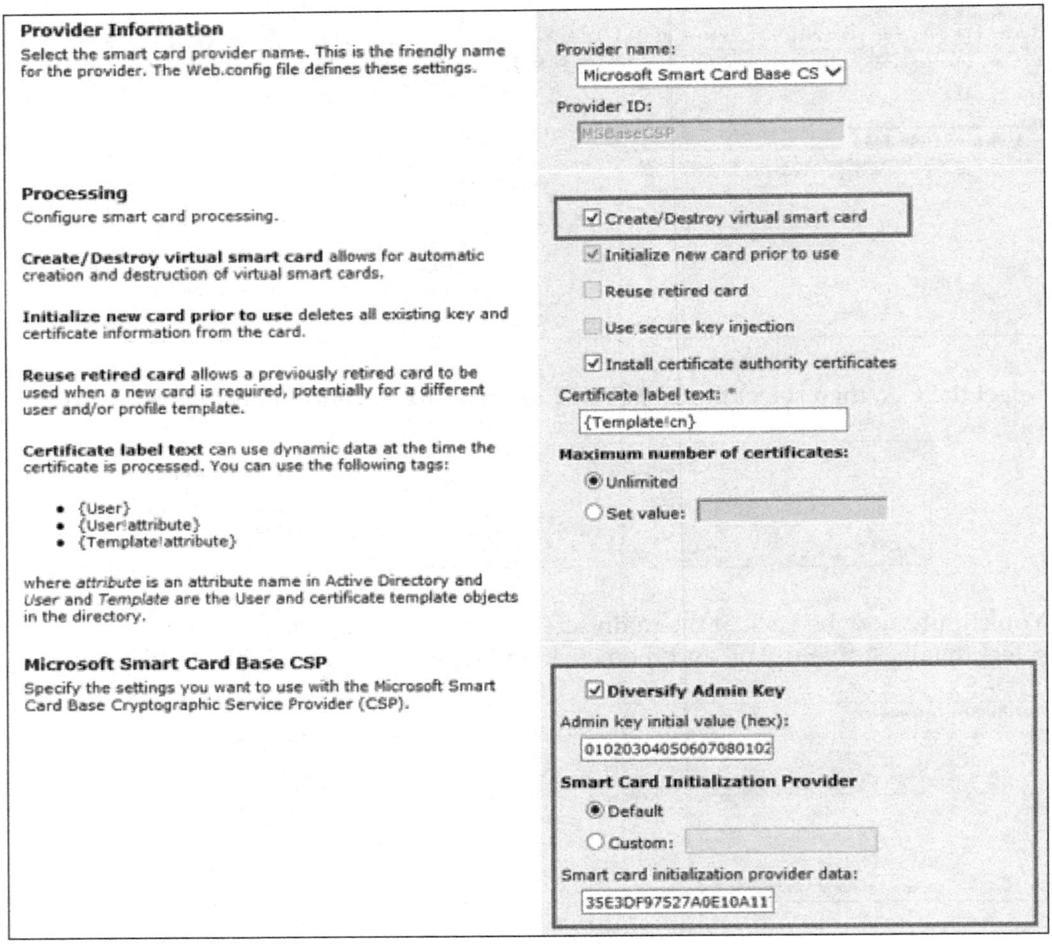

We now we need to update the PIN policy. In our Modern App, we will set the minimum pin to **6**; then, in the profile template, we want to have the user enter the pin. Select **User Provided**, as in the following screenshot:

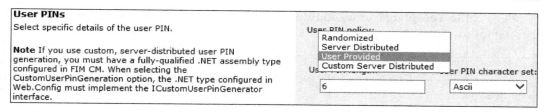

The last step is that we need to clear the data collection on the Renew and Enroll policy, as the Modern App doesn't support this collection currently:

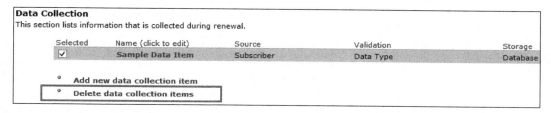

Now, we will configure the permissions on the policy template. Policy template permissions can be done in two areas, as previously discussed. In this case, we do not want to have permissions set at the policy level, so we will go to the policy permissions within the Active Directory Sites and Services profile template container.

As we did earlier, to get to the profile template, we need to use Active Directory Sites and Services to manage profile templates. Click on **View | Show Services Node**:

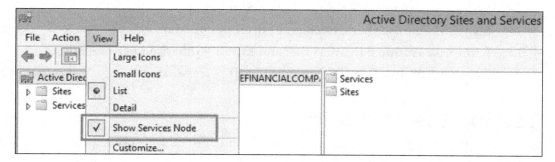

Under **Profile Templates**, you should see **TPM VSC – Logon**. In the **Security** tab, set the following permissions:

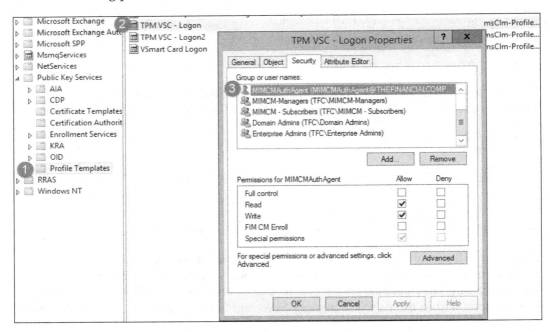

- **MIMCMAuthAgent**: **Read** and **Write** permissions
- **MIMCM-Managers**: **Read** and **Write** permissions
- **MIMCM – Subscribers**: **Read** and **Enroll** permissions
- **Enterprise Admins**: **Read**, **Write**, and **Enroll – Inherited** permissions
- **Domain Admins**: **Read**, **Write**, and **Enroll** permissions

Testing the scenario

Log in to our desktop as `dsteadman`, who is a member of the subscriber group that is allowed to enroll on the virtual smart card. Our test account, `dsteadman`, is not a local admin, so we need to create the virtual smart card before he can enroll. To create the virtual smart card, open the command prompt window using `runas`, as follows:

```
runas /user:TFC\administrator "cmd"
```

We will use the `TpmVscMgr` command to create a virtual smart card called `MyVSC`, which has the default admin PIN and default key. More information about the `TpmVscMgr` command can be found at `http://bit.ly/MIMTpmVscMgr`.

In the administrator command prompt window, type the following command:

```
TpmVscMgr create /name MyVSC /pin default /adminkey default /generate
```

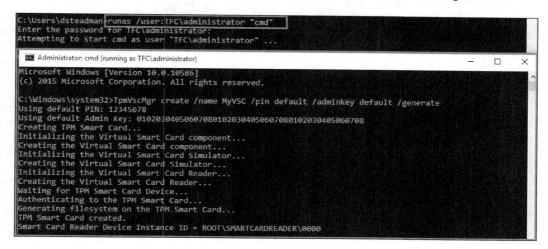

We can now launch the Modern App. The Modern App will inform us that we do not have any certificates to manage, as in the following screenshot:

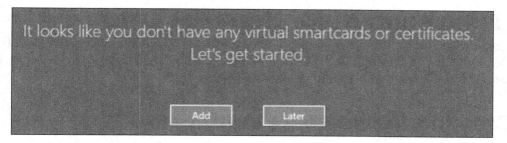

At this point, we can click on the **Add** button and select **TPM VSC – Logon**:

During enrollment, we will see a PIN prompt and the installation of a virtual smart card:

We have now enrolled a virtual smart card using the REST API.

Using support for Non-MIM CM

Most organizations want auto-enrolment of certain certificate templates, while still having MIM CM capabilities. In the following example, The Financial Company will use the EFS certificate for enrolment and recovery.

Creating the software certificate

The first step in this process is to set up the certificate template. We will navigate to the CA to duplicate the Basic EFS template, as depicted in the following screenshot:

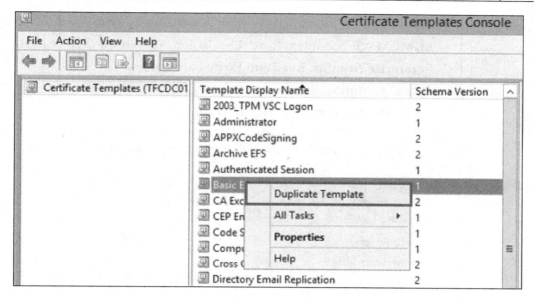

In the template screen, enter the following information:

- The **General** tab:
    - **Template Display Name**: Archive EFS
    - **Validity Period**: 2 years
    - **Renewal Period**: 6 weeks
    - **Publish certificate in Active Directory**: Enabled
    - **Do not automatically re-enrol if a duplicate certificate exists in Active Directory**: Enabled
    - Leave all the other settings at default values

- The **Request Handling** tab:
    - **Archive subject's encryption private key**: Enabled
    - Leave all the other settings at default values

- The **Subject Name**, **Server**, **Issuance Requirements**, and **Extensions** tabs:
    - Leave all the settings at their default values

- The **Superseded Templates** tab:
    - **Add**: Basic EFS (this is the template we duplicated)

- The **Security** tab:
  - ○ **MIMCM - Subscribers**: **Read, Enroll,** and **Autoenroll** permissions
  - ○ **Enterprise Admins**: **Read** and **Write** permissions
  - ○ **Domain Admins**: **Remove** permission
  - ○ **Authenticated Users**: **Read** permission

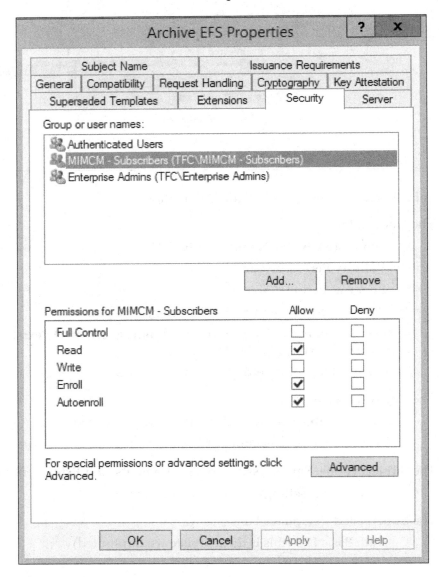

After creating the template, we need to publish the certificate in order to use it. Certificate publishing is done similarly to the other templates we created earlier — by navigating to **Certificate Template | New | Certificate Template to Issue**.

Next, we need to add or confirm that the MIMCM managers have the **FIM CM Request Recover** permissions on the Service Connection Point:

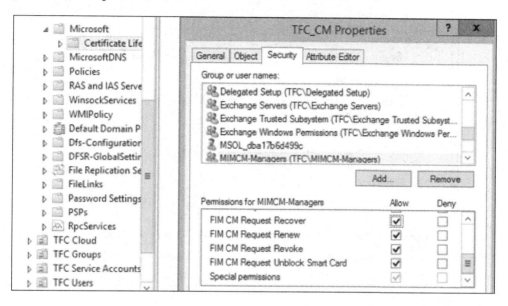

Based on our earlier reading, we know that the manager needs permission on the SCP as well as the target users. We, therefore, created a security group called **MIMCM – Subscribers** and assigned the FIM CM permission to include **FIM CM Request Recover**:

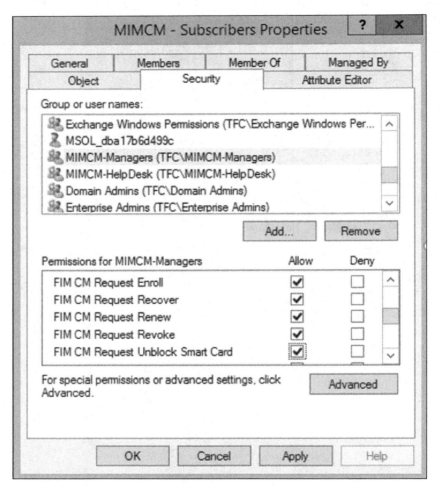

Creating the profile

We now need to create an EFS profile template. As in the smart card scenario, we will duplicate the **FIM CM Sample Profile** template under **Manage profile templates** in the web interface. We will name this template **EFS Certificates**, add **ArchiveEFS** to the certificate template list, and remove the default template (**User**).

Let's now navigate to the Enroll policy and click on **Change General Settings**. Unselect the **Enable policy** checkbox:

General Workflow Options

Notes

Use self serve specifies whether users can initiate enroll requests.

Number of approvals specifies the number of certificate managers who must approve an enroll request before the request can be completed.

The number of active or suspended profiles/smart cards allowed is the number of profiles that a user is allowed to have of this profile template.

☐ Enable policy

☑ Use self serve

☐ Require enrollment agent

☐ Allow request priority to be collected

Default request priority:

[0   ×]

Number of approvals:

[0]

Number of active or suspended profiles/smart cards allowed:

◉ Unlimited

○ Set value: [   ]

In order to support recovery options, we need to click on the Recover policy and make sure **Use self serve** is disabled:

You can review and change workflow settings for this recover policy.

General Workflow Options For Recover

Use self serve controls whether users can initiate recover requests.

Number of approvals determines the number of certificate managers who must approve a recover request before the request can be completed.

☑ Enable policy

☐ Use self serve

☐ Require enrollment agent

☐ Reissue archived certificates

☐ Allow request priority to be collected

Default request priority:

[0]

Number of approvals:

[0]

The next few configuration options are needed for recovery, and we need to make sure the revocation settings are properly set to the requirements of The Financial Company. For **Workflow: Revocation Settings** and **Workflow: Duplicate Revocation Settings**, we need to set to the following for both:

- **Set old card or profile status to disabled**: Enable
- **Revoke old certificates**: Disabled

Workflow: Revocation Settings
This section displays the revocation configuration for the existing certificates being replaced.

Set old card or profile status to disabled:	✓
Revoke old certificates:	✗

○ **Change revocation settings**

Workflow: Duplicate Revocation Settings
This section displays the revocation configuration for duplicate profiles or smart cards.

Set old card or profile status to disabled:	✓
Revoke old certificates:	✗

○ **Change duplicate revocation settings**

In the profile, we need to set who can initiate a recovery option. We will use **MIMCM –Managers**, so we will need to add them to the following section and remove the default value of **NT AUTHORITY\SYSTEM**, as shown here:

Workflow: Initiate Recover Requests
Specify which users and groups can initiate a recover request for this profile template:

Selected	Principal (click to edit)	Recover initiate
	NT AUTHORITY\SYSTEM	Grant
☐	TFC\MIMCM-Managers	Grant

The Financial Company requires a reason for the recovery operation. We will update the **Data Collection** item. Currently, it shows as **Sample Data Item**. We will update the item to a recovery reason, as shown in the following screenshot:

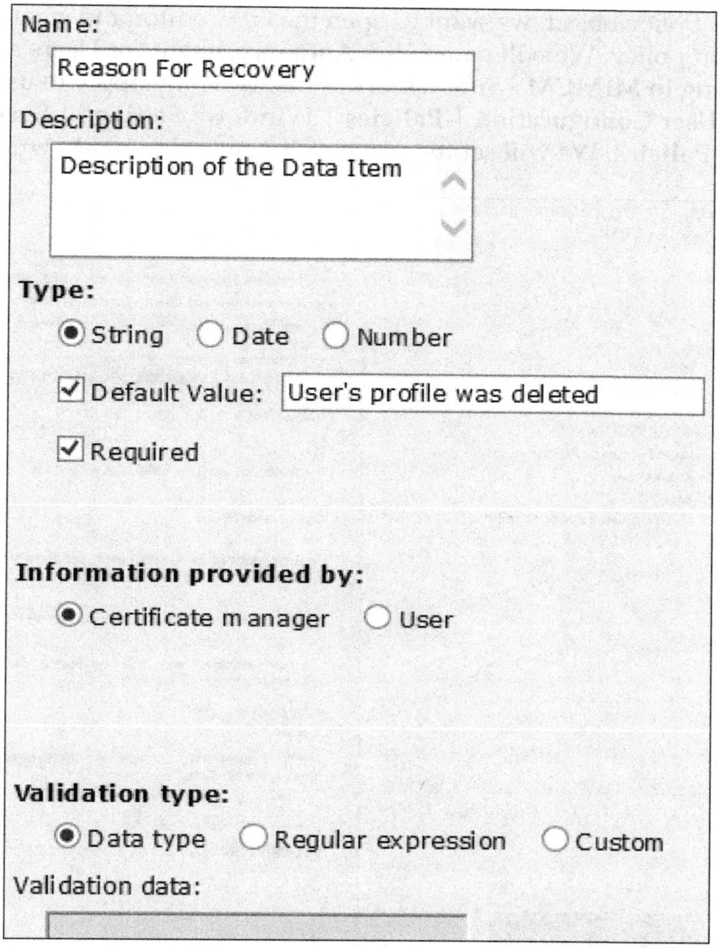

Name:

Reason For Recovery

Description:

Description of the Data Item

Type:

◉ String ○ Date ○ Number

☑ Default Value: User's profile was deleted

☑ Required

Information provided by:

◉ Certificate manager ○ User

Validation type:

◉ Data type ○ Regular expression ○ Custom

Validation data:

When selecting encryption, the agent certificate is used to encrypt the data in the database. We will leave the one-time password setting to be displayed onscreen, but as an option, it can be e-mailed to the subscriber or target user. More information on the notification mechanism can be found at http://bit.ly/MIMCMNotification.

The last step of this process is to set up the Group Policy object and update the policy module in the CA. Let's finalize this setting now and test the scenario.

For the Group Policy object, we want to open the GPO editor and create an autoenrollment policy. We will name ours **Autoenrollment for Users** and then add security filtering to **MIMCM - Subscribers** as this will only apply to users in this group. Go to **User Configuration | Policies | Windows Settings | Security Settings | Public Key Policies**. We will set the autoenrollment policy as shown here:

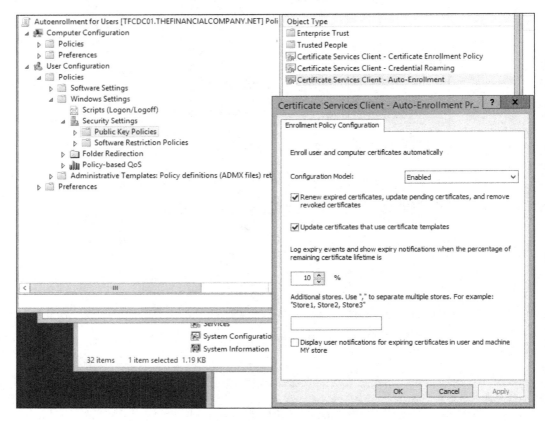

Next, we need to map the autoenrollment to the profile template upon user autoenrollment. Let's go back to the CA. On the CA, click on **Properties** and then on the **Policy** module. Finally, on the **Custom Module** tab, click on **Add**, as you can see in the following screenshot:

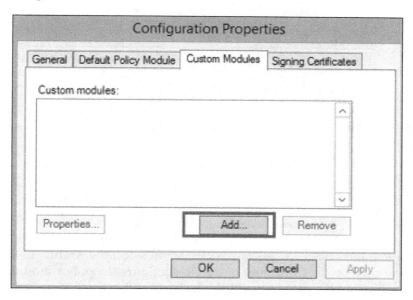

You should now see a prompt for custom modules. The module we want comes with CM and is located in the `Microsoft.Clm.PolicyModulePlugins.dll` DLL. The DLL comes with four plugins, as follows:

- Certificate SMimeCapabilities Module 1.0
- Certificate Subject Module 1.0
- SubjectAltName Module 1.1
- Support for non-FIM CM certificate requests

More information on these plugins can be found at `http://bit.ly/MIMCMModules`.

The template we are interested in is **Support for non-FIM CM certificate requests**:

We will name this CLIENT EFS - AUTOENROLL and select the **ArchiveEFS** certificate. Next, we will click on the **Configure** button to configure the policy module connection, allowing the processing of the certificate. One key setting is the mapping to the profile template. We need to select the EFS certificate we created earlier and the maximum number of active certificates that we are allowed to create per user. We will set the maximum number of active certificates to **5**:

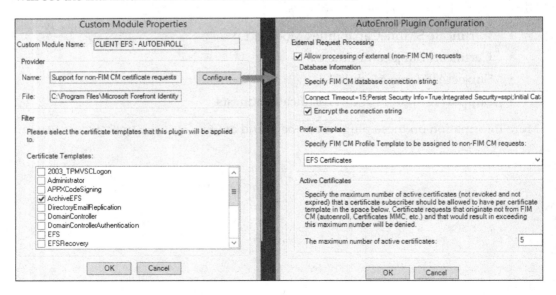

We have now completed all the backend work to hook this all together. The work we performed configured the certificate and permission for the user and the manager. We created the template, the workflow needed to recover a certificate, and the GPO to initiate the enrollment on login. Lastly, we told the CA to record the enrolments in CM up to five times.

Testing the scenario

Log in as a user that is part of the issuers group, and the autoenrollment should initiate and install our certificate. We can now encrypt items using the certificate:

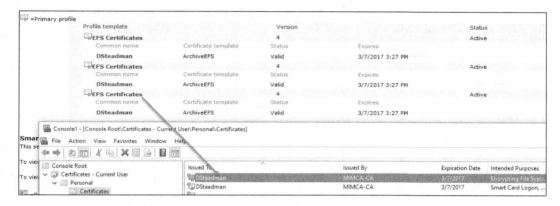

As shown before, a new certificate was issued. Note that we see two other profiles that are EFS certificates. Recall that in our configuration, we set a maximum of five certificates, which means we would issue a certificate on any new machines `dsteadman` logs in to, up to five machines.

Testing certificate recovery requires a CM manager that has appropriate permissions. The manager would log in to the web interface and search for the user to recover. In our example, Jeff is a CM manager and will log on to the portal and click on **Find a user to view or manage their information**, as in the following screenshot:

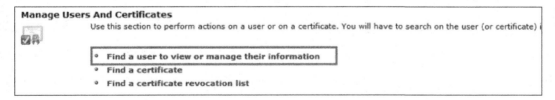

Enter the e-mail or username of the user we want to initiate the recovery of. We have an option to search all of the forest or perform a selected scoped search. Once found, we will see the three profiles the user sees. We will select the first EFS certificate because David has indicated that he secured a document using this certificate:

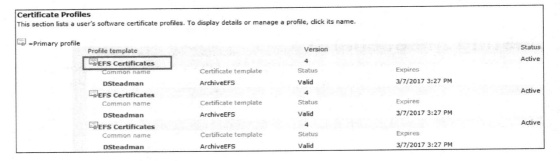

Clicking on this profile provides the following option:

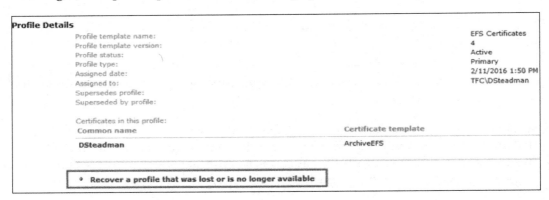

The manager will be prompted for a recovery reason, which is prefilled with the default value we entered on the profile. We will leave the default value and click on **OK**:

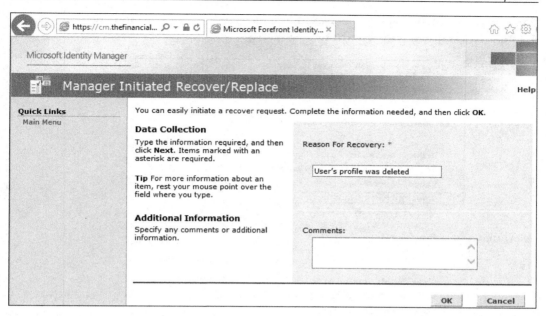

We also have an option to recover the certificate. In this case, we will give David the one-time password option to complete the recovery:

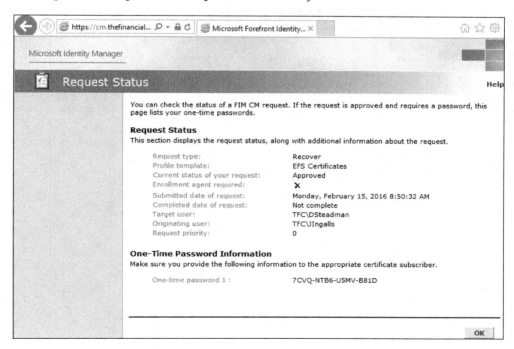

Let's log on to the web portal as David to complete the recovery and click on **Complete a request with one-time passwords**:

Enter the one-time password and click on **Next** twice:

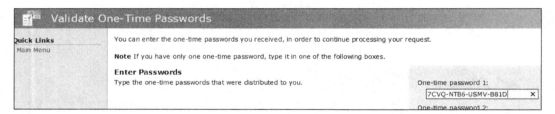

David will now be prompted, typically twice, that a certificate operation is being performed on his behalf. Click on **Yes**:

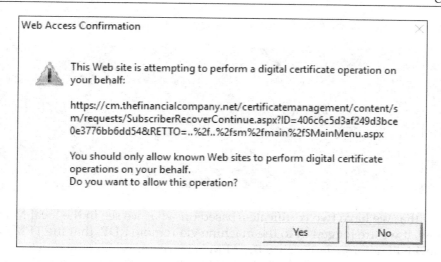

David is redirected to a screen informing him that the recovered EFS certificate is installed, as seen in the following screenshot:

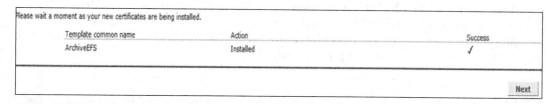

To confirm that the EFS is truly recovered and installed, we will open the MMC console and find two EFS certificates:

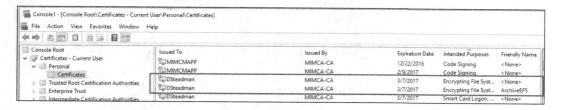

If we launch the Modern App remotely, we will not see any certificates:

We know that we have two certificates, based on what we see in the local MMC. We also know, if we are logged in to the machine via remote RDP, that the TPM/virtual smart card will not appear because the TPM is inaccessible. So why don't we see the certificates from the Modern App? The Modern App looks at the profile template if, and only if, you have Enroll rights to the profile. In our example, we will use the policy module and autoenrollment to do the work. So, to see these certificates, we need to add the **FIM CM Enroll** permission to the profile template. We do not know whether this behavior will change in the future. It does seem as though we should see all our profiles even if we don't have the Enroll permission on the CM profile, but as of writing this, you need the permission:

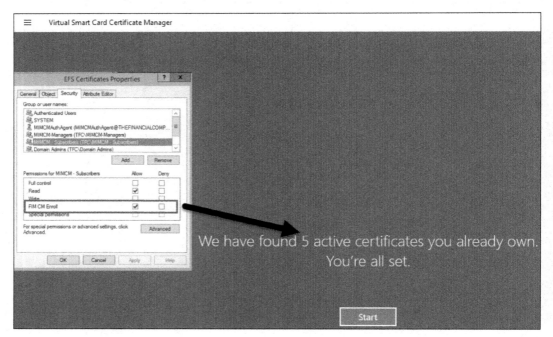

Multiforest configuration

We will now discuss the new multiforest CM capabilities. Multiforest CM enables an enterprise to issue certs to users from another forest that is trusted by TFC. The Financial Company is bringing on a new UK domain called TFCUK.LOCAL, which only hosts users. The UK group plans to use CM in the future, but it needs to issue certs immediately.

First, we will verify that our requirements are working properly, such as DNS and the trust; then, we will extend the schema.

Step 1 – CM DNS setup

Perform the following steps:

1. Go to the domain controller hosting DNS, open the DNS manager, and add conditional forwarders to The Financial Company.

2. Expand the server name in the left-hand side pane and right-click on **Conditional Forwarders**.

3. Select **New Conditional Forwarder** and click on **Next** on the first wizard page:

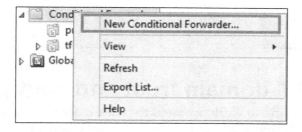

4. Then, in the DNS domain, type `tfcuk.local`.

5. In the next section, select **DNS Domain**.

6. On the next page, select **To all DNS ... on this forest** and click on **Next**.

7. In **IP Address**, enter the target domain controller IP, `192.168.5.240`, and then click on **Next**.

8. Finally, click on **Next** and then on **Finish**.

9. We will need to do this on the `tfcuk.local` domain as well, pointing back to `thefinacialcompany.net`.

10. The following screenshot shows what this would look like once completed:

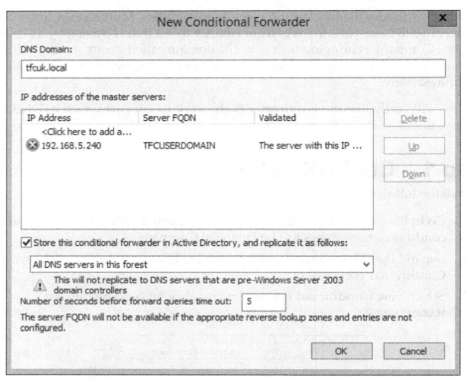

Step 2 – CM domain trust and configuration

In order for the scenario to work, we need to create a domain trust and extend the schema for the new forest as we did in The Financial Company's domain.

Now that we have our DNS routing in place, we can create the two-way trust. For more information on two-way trusts, refer to `http://bit.ly/MIMCMTrust`. We will create the trust from The Financial Company's side, but in some cases, you might not have this luxury as the organization may not allow domain admin access to the trusted forest. Open up the Active Directory Domains and Trusts console, click on the domain, and then go to **Properties**. Click on **New Trust**, and once the trust wizard opens, click on **Next**.

On the next screen, we need to enter `tfcuk.local`, as you can see in the following screenshot. Then, click on **Next**:

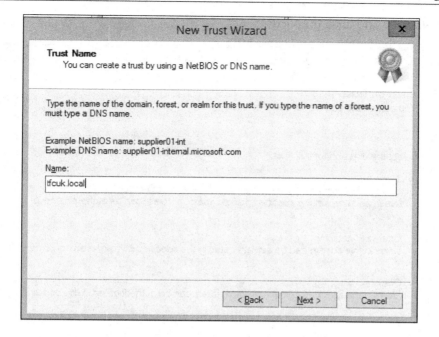

Select **Forest trust** and then click on **Next**:

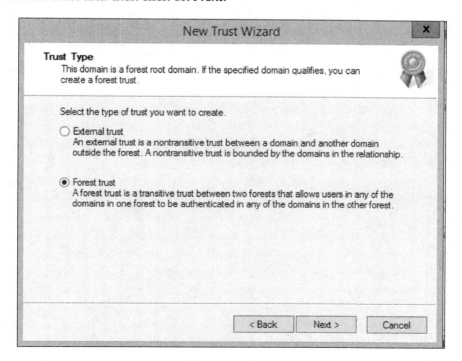

Select **Two-way** and click on **Next**:

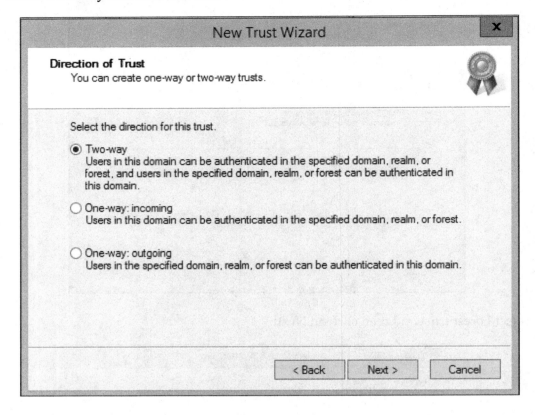

We are now at the point where you might have to select this domain only if you do not have permissions on the other side. In our case, the tfcuk.local domain allows us to create the trust on their side, as well; therefore, we will select **Both this domain and the specified domain** and click on **Next**:

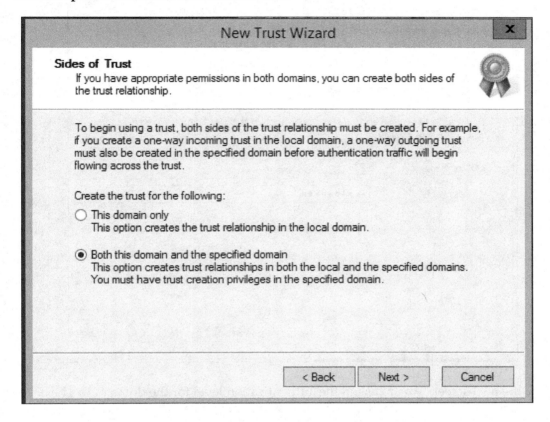

Then, the next screen will prompt us for an account that has administrative privileges in the target forest. Enter the credentials and click on **Next**:

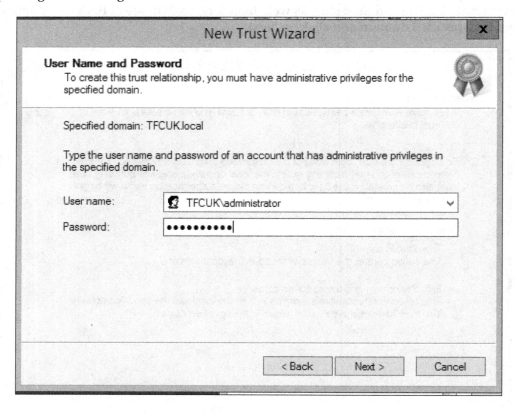

In the next screen, we are asked the authentication level for the domain. In The Financial Company, we will allow forest-wide authentication. In some scenarios, you will want to use selective authentication. From the CM perspective, you may have to work around a few configuration items when using selective authentication, but don't let this stop you from choosing this level. More information on authentication levels can be found at `http://bit.ly/MIMCMselectiveAuth`.

For our situation, select **Forest-wide authentication** for both forests and then click on **Next**:

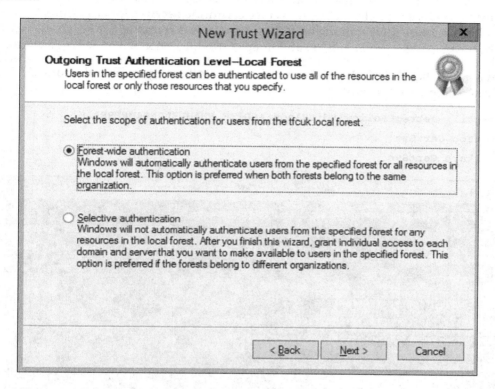

Click on **Next** until we are prompted to test the trust. We recommend that you test the trust at least once during the setup. The wizard should now report that the trust is successfully created.

We are now ready to update the schema for the TFCUK user forest. There are two options to run: the userForestModifySchema.vbs or the resourceForestModifySchema.vbs script. Which one should we run? In our situation, the target forest plans to raise their own CM environment to support other activities. The userForestModifySchema.vbs script is specifically written for the user forest only, which is not where this forest plans to be in the future. Therefore, we will run resourceForestModifySchema.vbs in the TFCUK domain.

After the `resourceForestModifySchema.vbs` script is complete, we will be ready for our final step. This last step is critical to the success of the cross-forest scenario; set up the Active Directory certificate services for cross-forest enrollment. More information about these scenarios is found at http://bit.ly/MIMCMCAEnrollmentprocessing and http://bit.ly/MIMCMCrossForestCAlab.

Navigate to the TFC MIMCA server and run the following commands from an elevated command prompt:

```
certutil -setreg Policy\EditFlags +EDITF_ENABLELDAPREFERRALS
net stop CertSvc
net start CertSvc
```

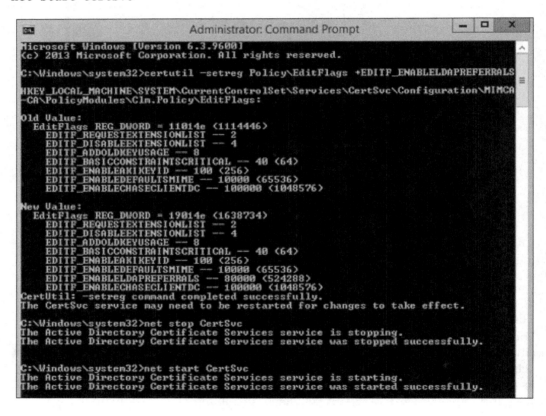

Step 3 – CM forest configuration

We need to tell Microsoft Identity Certificate Manager about our new forest. One way to accomplish our goal is to run the configuration wizard we ran earlier in this chapter to set up the environment, as shown by the following screenshot:

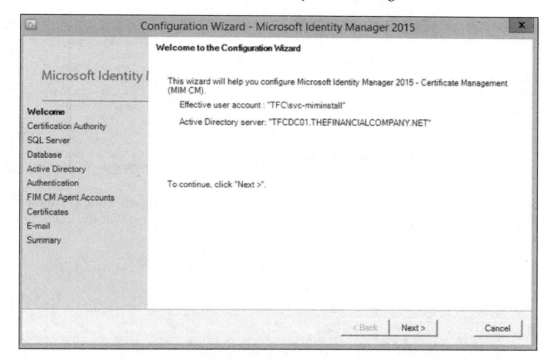

 As a precautionary step, make a backup of the web.config file before proceeding.

In the wizard, you would use all the same accounts used earlier. Click on **Next** through the SQL connection using dbMIMCM as the SQL server name. Then, on the database screen, click on **Next**. At the Active Directory screen dialog, select the Service Connection Point we used during setup earlier in the chapter, as the configuration wizard always defaults to the server name.

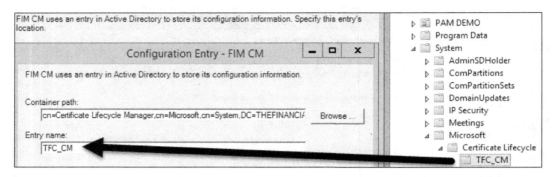

Select the forest checkbox of TFCUK. Once selected, the wizard will work to validate that all the settings are correct. If successful, the wizard will report that the validation is passed:

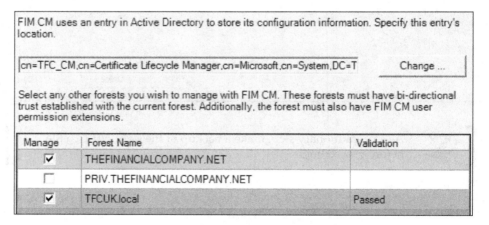

Under authentication, we will keep the default and click on **Next**. We are now at the part of the configuration where the CM agent accounts are specified. Enter the same accounts for the configuration:

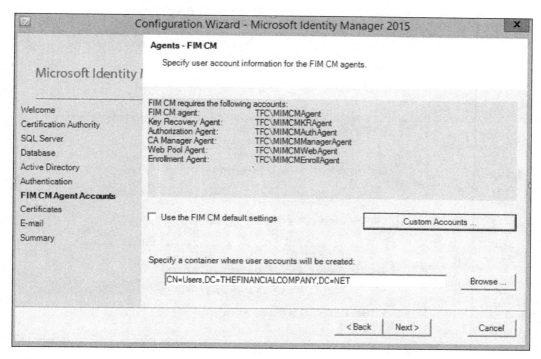

We are now at the certificate generation part of the setup. There is no need to generate certificates again because this is an existing setup, so we will select **Create and configure certificates manually** and then select the same templates as in *Chapter 11, Installation and the Client Side of Certificate Management*:

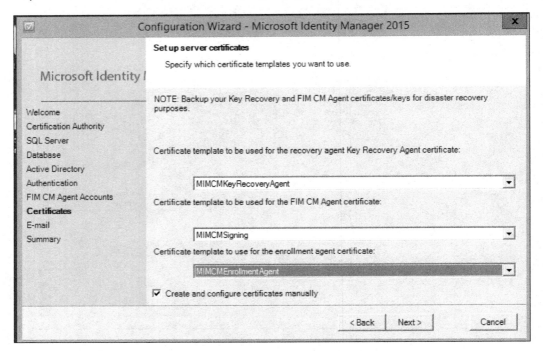

Click on **Next** twice. We will click on **Configure**, wait for the completion of the setup, and then test. If you encounter any errors during this step, refer to the wizard log located at C:\Program Files\Microsoft Forefront Identity Manager\2010\ Certificate Management\Config.txt.

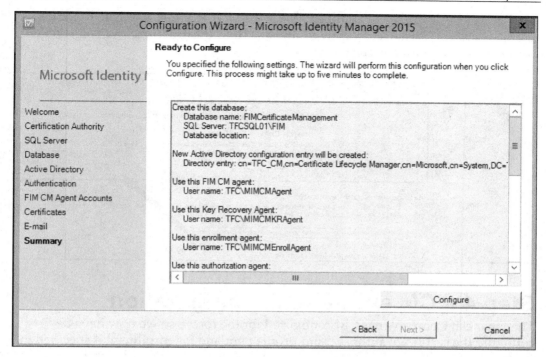

All this wizard is doing is adding the forest to `web.config` without adding anything to The Financial Company's baseline configuration. Why use the wizard at all? If you have already met all the prerequisites, you can avoid the wizard and modify `web.config`, which is typically located at `C:\Program Files\Microsoft Forefront Identity Manager\2010\Certificate Management\web`.

Open the file with Notepad and look for the entry named `Clm.ActiveDirectory.ManagedForests`.

Enter the FQDN of the trusted forest, as follows:

```
<add key="Clm.ActiveDirectory.ManagedForests" value="TFCUK.LOCAL" />
```

Save and close `web.config` and then restart the web services. Navigate to the CM portal, click on **Find a user to view or manage their information**, and you should see the forest we added in the `web.config` file:

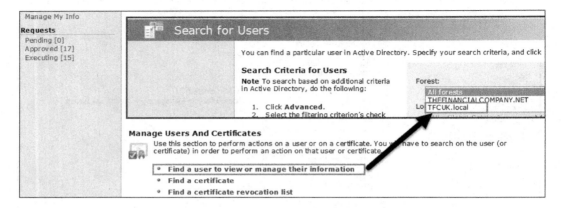

Step 4 – CM enrollment configuration

The Financial Company has CM configured for the forest, so we now have to configure the certificate authority and profile template for enrollment if specified in the profile template. We want to be able to issue virtual smart cards for this forest, so we will use our existing template for enrollment.

Create a security group called **MIMCM – UKSubscribers** and add our user Justin to the group:

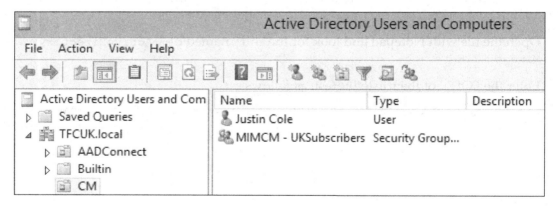

Navigate to the certificate template and open the certificate authority. Manage the template and select **TPM VSC Logon** on the properties. Add the UK subscriber group as you see here and add the **Read** and **Enroll** permissions. Click on **OK** and close the certificate management screen:

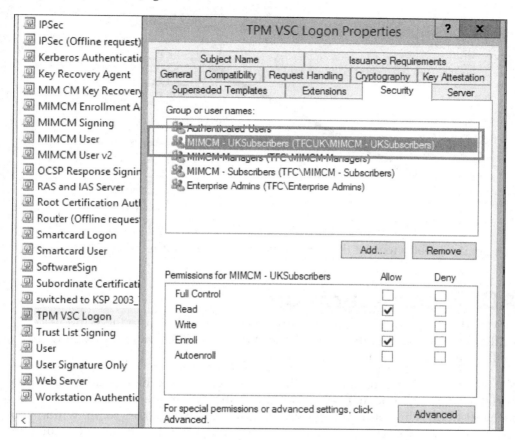

We will set the permissions on the profile template directly and not within the profile template itself. We now need to add the permission for enrollment in the template within the AD Sites and Services node, just as we did earlier in this chapter:

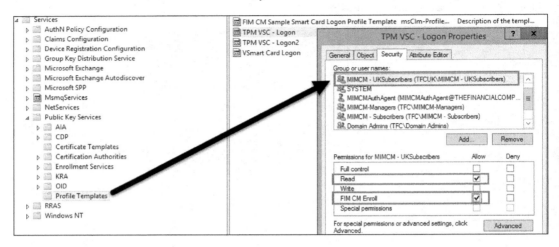

You are now ready to start the enrollment of the users in the TFCUK user forest!

ADFS configuration

MIM CM configuration for ADFS installation is quite similar to the Windows Authentication configuration. We will outline the installation to the existing CM configuration of The Financial Company.

The ADFS installation requires a dedicated server because the web administration portal is not compatible with the ADFS authentication model's claims-based authentication. This setup assumes that you already have ADFS set up within your environment, so we will not go through this configuration. The Financial Company has already set up ADFS, but if you need help with setting it up, visit `http://bit.ly/MIMCMADFSGuides`.

Step 1 – the CM installation and prerequisites

The first step is to install CM software on the CM2 (TFCCM02) server. Request a domain certificate for the IIS website and call it `cm2.thefinacialcompany.net`:

Once we have the certificate, we will make sure it is tied to the default site by navigating to **IIS <Server name> | Sites | Default Web Sites**. Open the **Bindings** setting in the **Action** menu on the right-hand side of the page and create an HTTP binding:

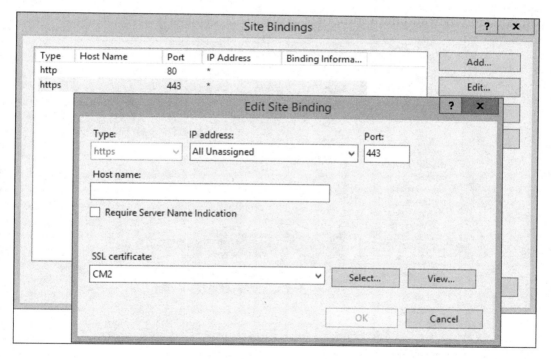

Confirm that the DNS and SPN are set for our app pool account. Open the DNS management MMC for The Financial Company and create an **A** record, as we did for the current CM server. We have captured the configuration in the following screenshot for clarification:

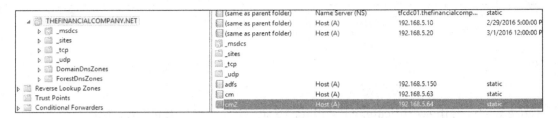

For the SPNs, we will add two records for our CM2 server. Open the Active Directory object and view the **Service Principal Names (SPN)** via the editor. Click on **Edit** and add the new SPN. As you can see here, we will select the attribute, click on **Edit**, and then add the appropriate SPN:

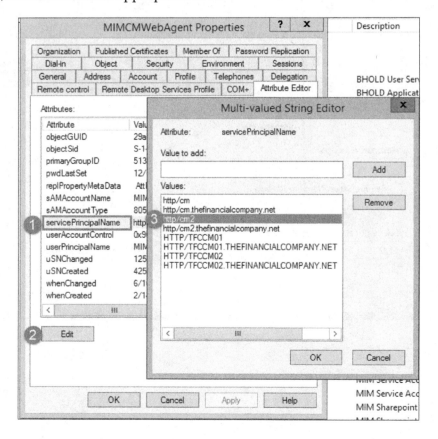

Step 2 – the configuration wizard

We are ready to run the wizard as we did earlier on CM1. It is not uncommon to rerun the wizard a few times, but be careful. The wizard does not remember your current settings, so running it a second time could break your working MIM CM environment if you are not careful.

To run the wizard, you need to be a domain admin and use an account that has the SQL database creation permission. The wizard will detect the permission needed and return an error if you're not part of this group:

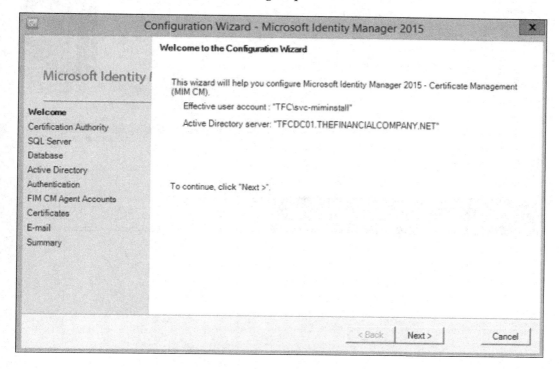

If you have multiple Enterprise CAs, select the one that MIM CM should use. We can later configure MIM CM to use multiple CAs if we like. At this point, we will use the **MIMCA-CA** server:

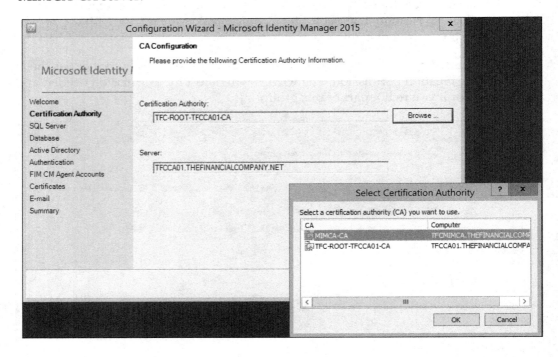

Leave the default settings on the **Database Settings** page:

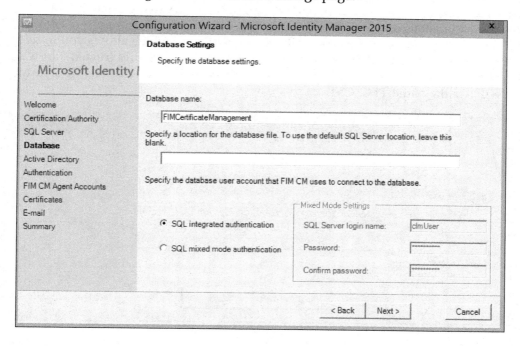

On the **Active Directory** page, note the AD path for the Service Connection Point. We will need to configure some permission on this object later. We have never dared to change the location, even if it points to an old location referencing the older version of MIM CM, Certificate Lifecycle Manager:

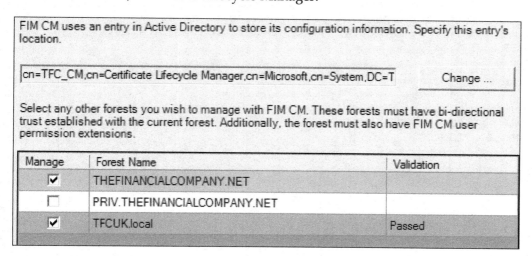

The wizard will use the default server name. In an enterprise, we recommend that you have a global name so that when we add new servers to the organization, we can use a global name as we did on CM2. To set up a global name, simply click on the **Change** button. Note that you will see a new feature, which allows you to select another forest. By default, it will show all the forests that are fully trusted, but we can select any forest we configured in the earlier chapters. At The Financial Company, we will use the name **TFC_CM**:

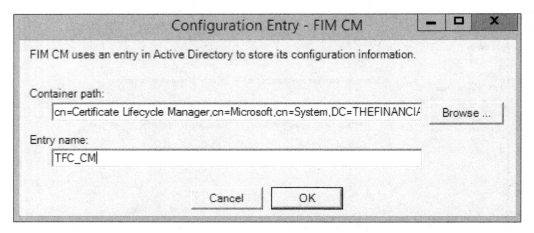

The next section of the wizard is new and determines whether you will enable ADFS authentication or Active Directory. We will select Active Directory Federation Services because it will be the endpoint for all ADFS CM requests via the REST API. We will apply the following settings:

- **Metadata Endpoint**: `https://adfs.thefinancialcompany.net/`
  `federationmetadata/2007-06/federationmetadata.xml`

- **Relying Party**: `https://cm2.thefinancialcompany.net/certificatemanagement`

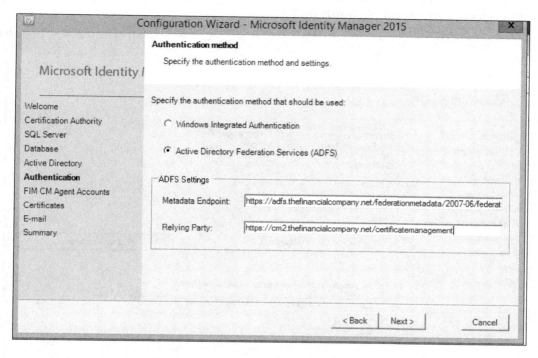

Thus far, the wizard has been easy to follow, but it is time to really pay attention, especially now that we have another server in the mix.

On the **FIM CM Agent Accounts** page, you need to configure every one of the agents with the correct information. Clear the **Use the FIM CM default settings** checkbox and click on the **Custom Accounts** button:

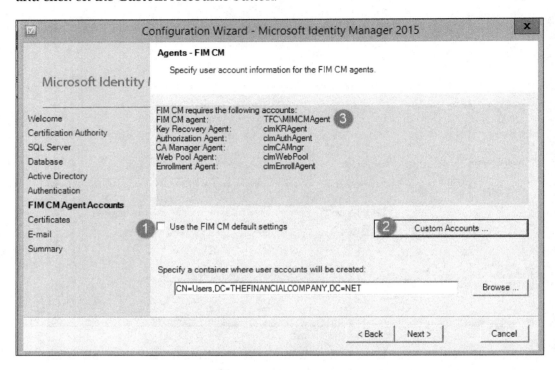

On all the six agent accounts, select the **Use an existing user** checkbox and fill in the **User name** and **Password** textboxes for the account. You can see why we named our accounts the way we did, because we can easily determine which account to use for each agent:

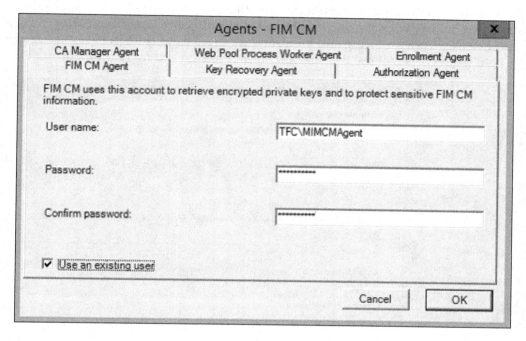

On the **Certificates** page, we will select the corresponding template that we would like each account to use. Some people argue that we should always use the **Create and configure certificates manually** option. When using HSMs, we always do this. It is, however, nice to allow the wizard to configure the certificates and put all the information about the certificates into the configuration files. For the ADFS configuration, we will select the **Create and configure certificates manually** checkbox as we are exporting and importing the certificates from the TFCCM01 server. So, both the servers will use the same certificates to sign and for enrollment:

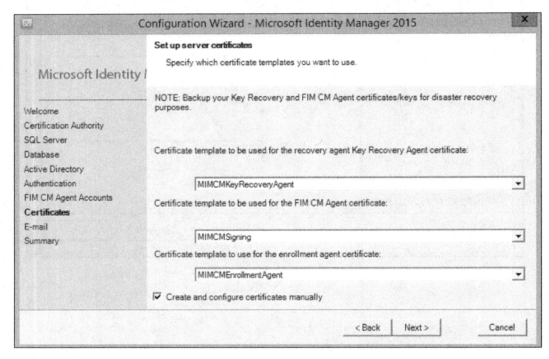

On the **E-mail** page, we will point MIM CM to an SMTP server that it can use to send e-mails. Also, note the default path for print documents. In this short coverage of MIM CM, we will not show you how to use printing and e-mail in workflows.

Before you click on the **Configure** button, verify the settings. If something is wrong, just use the **Back** button and change whichever value is wrong:

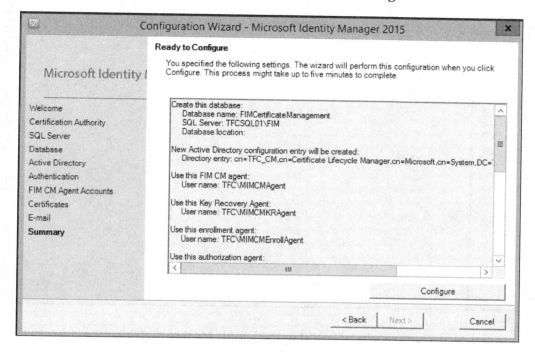

The wizard will take a few minutes to complete the execution. It is not uncommon for it to fail because there may be many parameters that might not have been correctly set:

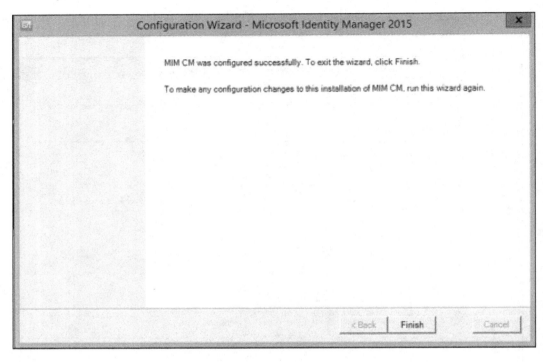

As stated earlier, errors can be found in the log file located at `C:\Program Files\Microsoft Forefront Identity Manager\2010\Certificate Management`.

Step 3 – continued configuration

We now need to export all the certificates from the `TFCCM01` server that are used within the CM configuration. For this activity, we will log in as our install account and perform three `runas` commands using the three accounts, as follows:

- `MIMCMAgent`: Agent account
- `MIMCMEnrollment`: Enrollment account
- `MIMCMKRAAgent`: Key Recovery Agent account

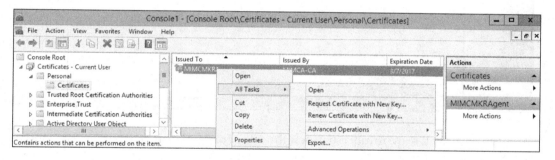

Open the MMC on each `runas` command prompt. Add **Certificates - Current User** for each of the three accounts and then export each certificate as you see in the following screenshot:

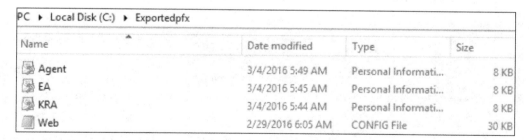

We now need to consolidate the certificates and copy the web configuration file, which will be needed to update some entry values on CM2:

Name	Date modified	Type	Size
Agent	3/4/2016 5:49 AM	Personal Informati...	8 KB
EA	3/4/2016 5:45 AM	Personal Informati...	8 KB
KRA	3/4/2016 5:44 AM	Personal Informati...	8 KB
Web	2/29/2016 6:05 AM	CONFIG File	30 KB

On CM2, copy the certificates from CM1 and the `web.config` file. Next, proceed with the same steps performed on the CM1 server: first, run the `runas /user:TFC\MIMCMAgent cmd` command (**1**); second, run the MMC (**2**); and finally, import the certificate that corresponds to the agent account (**3**):

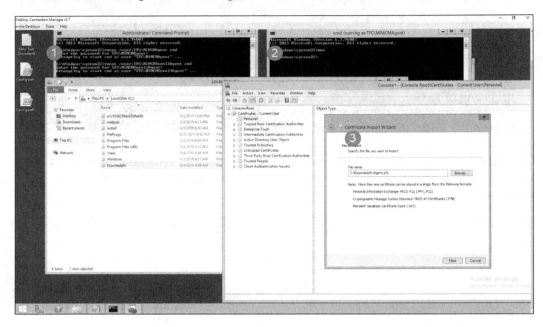

Once the certificates are imported, open the `web.config` file from the `TFCCM01` and `TFCCM02` servers. Look at all the hash entries from CM1 and add them to CM2. As you see in the following screenshot, the CM1 file is on the left-hand side, and the CM2 file is on the right-hand side; the CM2 file is missing the CM1 hash entries. Add all the hash settings in the `web.config` file on the CM2 server:

Once we have updated `web.config`, we will make two configuration changes in the `CertificateManagement` virtual IIS directory, disabling **Windows Authentication** and enabling **Anonymous Authentication**:

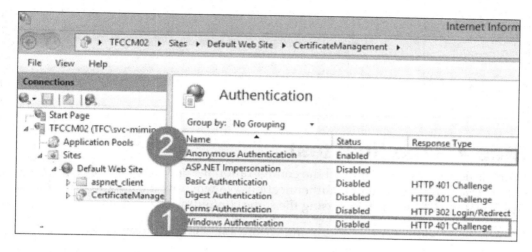

Next, perform `IISreset`. We will now move on to configuring the ADFS sever. To configure the relying trust, use the `ConfigureFIMCMClientAndRelyingParty.ps1` script found at `http://bit.ly/ConfigureMIMCMClient`. Run the script on the ADFS server(s). You will need to update the URL in the script to point to your environment:

```
Configuring ADFS Objects for OAuth E2E tests..
Creating Client Objects...
Found existing instance of the FIM CM Modern App, removing
Client object removed
Adding Client Object for FIM CM Modern App client
Client Object for FIM CM Modern App client Created
Creating Relying Party Objects
Found existing instance of the FIM CM Service RP, removing
RP object Removed
Creating RP Trust for FIM CM Service
RP Trust for FIM CM Service has been created

PS C:\Users\administrator.TFC\Desktop>
```

You should see the relying party trusts and authentication policies as follows:

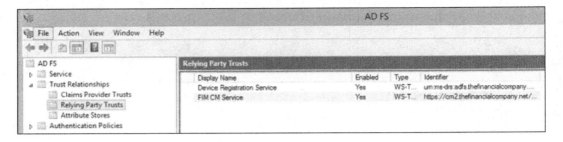

Step 4 – the final test

In an earlier section, we outlined the configuration needed for the Modern App to talk to CM using claims-based authentication. We will now reconfigure the Modern App to talk to CM with claims using the same configuration.

Launch the Modern App. At this point, we are still using Windows Authentication:

We have three active certificates. Click on the upper-left screen for the context menu and then click on **Settings**:

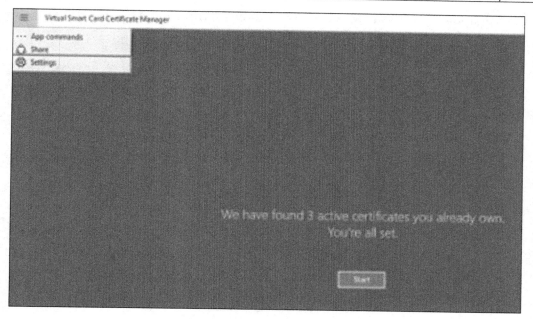

Click on **Settings** on the right-hand side task bar:

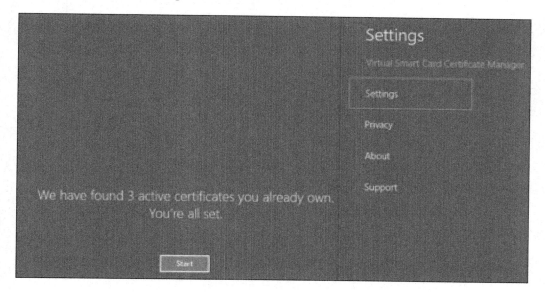

We will update **Certificate Management Server Address** and **Active Directory Server Address** to the following:

- **CM Server**: `https://cm2.thefinancialcompany.net/certificatemanagement`

- **ADFS**: `https://adfs.thefinancialcompany.net/adfs`

Close and reopen the Modern App, and you should see the application quickly connect to the ADFS server and display your current certificate, as before:

You have now successfully integrated the Modern App with ADFS authentication, utilizing your existing configuration!

Models at a glance

There are some high-level models that most environments use to manage certificates. In the next few sections, we will uncover these models and the requirements and permissions needed to succeed with them. The Financial Company has already applied the self-service registration model as part of the manager-initiated model. The models are not explicit, but they are flexible, and TFC could use a mixture of both. Let's now look at the centralized management model.

The centralized management model

The centralized management model works well when there is a tightly controlled HR process or a security officer enrolls a smart card for the user, and in general cases where a random PIN is assigned to the card. When the card is received by the subscriber (that is, the user), then they would perform the initial online unblock. The helpdesk would be able to assist if an offline unblock operation is needed. In the centralized model, the following permissions would be needed:

Service Connection Point (Active Directory) and MIMCM-Subscriber

MIMCM – Managers (HR/Security)	Read
	All FIM/MIM Extended Permission
MIMCM - Helpdesk	Read
	FIM CM Request Unblock Smart Card
	FIM CM Enrollment Agent
MIMCM – Admins	Full permission

Profile Template (Site and Service)

MIMCM – Subscribers (Users)	Read
	FIM CM Enroll
MIMCM – Managers (HR/Security)	Read
	FIM CM Enroll
MIMCM - Helpdesk	Read
	FIM CM Enroll

Certificate Template (CA)

MIMCM – Managers (HR/Security)	Read Enroll
MIMCM – Admins	Read Enroll

Management Policy (Workflow)

General Settings	Self Service Disabled	
Enroll Policy	Initiate Enroll Requests	MIMCM – Admins
	Enroll Agent for Enroll Requests	MIMCM – Managers (HR/Security)
Offline Unblock Policy	Initiate Offline Unblock Requests	MIMCM – Admins
	Unblock Agent for Offline Unblock Requests	MIMCM – Managers (HR/Security)
		MIMCM - Helpdesk

The preceding permissions provide a centralized management workflow for enrollment and recovery.

The self-service model

The self-service model is most common when we want a person to initiate the requesting of a smart card or software certificates. In some cases, the request the subscriber initiated could be left in a pending state until a certificate manager approves the request. The permissions required for the self-service model are straightforward, as shown by the following tables:

Service Connection Point (Active Directory) and MIMCM-Subscriber

MIMCM – Managers (HR/Security)	Read CM Audit

Profile Template (Site and Service)

MIMCM – Subscribers (Users)	Read FIM CM Enroll

Certificate Template (CA)

| MIMCM – Subscribers (Users) | Read |
| | Enroll |

Management Policy (Workflow)

General Settings	Self Service Enabled	
Enroll Policy	Number of approvals 1	MIMCM – Managers (HR/Security)
	Approve Enroll Requests	

The manager-initiated model

The manager-initiated model is not as commonly implemented as the centralized or self-service models. In the manager-initiated model, we have a select group of certificate managers, with the manager initiating the request. There could be other approvals that then need to happen or requests that need to be sent to another group or approving authority. Once approved, the subscriber will receive a one-time password and would then go to the portal and complete the request, similarly to the EFS certificate recovery scenario earlier. Here, we have provided the required permissions for the manager-initiated model:

Service Connection Point (Active Directory) & MIMCM-Subscriber

| MIMCM – Managers (HR/Security) | Read |
| | CM Request Enroll |

Profile Template (Site and Service)

MIMCM – Subscribers (Users)	Read
	FIM CM Enroll
MIMCM – Managers (HR/Security)	Read

Certificate Template (CA)

| MIMCM – Subscribers (Users) | Read |
| | Enroll |

Management Policy (Workflow)

Enroll Policy	Number of approvals 1	MIMCM – Managers (HR/Security)
	Approve Enroll Requests	
	Initiate Enroll Requests	

Summary

As you can see, certificate management provides a company with many options and features. In this chapter, we discussed implementing the enrollment of virtual smart cards, support for non-MIM CM scenarios, and the configuration and requirements necessary for multi-forest CM capabilities. We also walked you through the installation of CM with ADFS and its prerequisites. We ended the chapter by looking at three CM models and their required permissions.

In the next chapter, we will explore one of the new features in Identity Manager 2016, the built-in reporting support.

13
Reporting

One of the new features in Identity Manager 2016 is built-in reporting support. During installation, we discussed the need for System Center Service Manager 2010/2012 R2 in order for the Reporting feature to work.

Once you have managed to install and configure the SCSM environment, using the built-in Reporting feature is quite easy, similar to how we installed SCSM back in *Chapter 2, Installation*.

In this chapter, we will discuss the following topics:

- Verifying the SCSM setup
- Default reports
- The SCSM ETL process
- Looking at reports
- Modifying the reports
- Hybrid reporting

Verifying the SCSM setup

We usually start by looking at the SCSM Management console to verify that the MIM settings are there. In *Chapter 2, Installation*, we showed you how to install the SCSM infrastructure.

Follow these steps to verify your SCSM setup:

1. On the MIM Service server, where we will add the MIM Reporting feature, start the System Center Service Manager console. It will ask you to connect to your SCSM Management server:

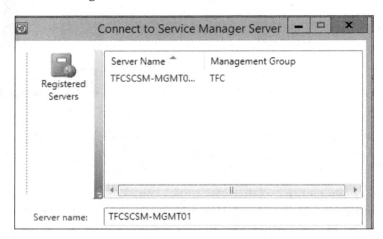

2. What happens usually (but not all the time) is that you will find that the Reporting node is missing in the navigation pane, as shown in the following screenshot:

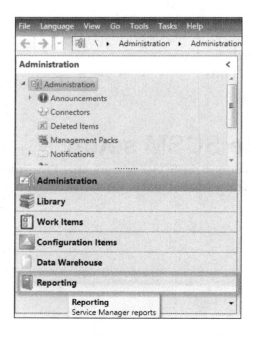

Don't worry! It just takes some time. On some occasions, you may also need to restart the SCSM Management console for it to appear. We have not yet figured out what causes this issue. This issue may occur due to network timeouts or overall system health.

However, we are now ready to set up MIM Reporting. Some of these steps may take time to run through the cycles, but the steps are similar to the ones at `https://technet.microsoft.com/en-us/library/jj133845(v=ws.10).aspx`:

1. Verify that the initial data warehouse schema is created and SCSM is set up correctly.

2. Perform the environmental prerequisites.

3. Install MIM Reporting.

4. Ensure that `MPSynch` has finished and the MIM Management packs are now visible in SCSM.

5. Install data warehouse support scripts.

6. Run the `Start-FIMReportingInitialSync` PowerShell cmdlet.

7. Run the `Start-FIMReportingIncrementalSync` PowerShell cmdlet.

8. Run the `ETLScript` PowerShell script.

Steps 1 and 2 were completed earlier, in *Chapter 2, Installation*. We just need to verify from the that chapter and based on the screenshots, we are all set.

The next thing we want to do is enable Reporting by going to the MIM instance that will be processing it. Again, this doesn't have to be the same node processing user requests or sync requests; a dedicated MIM service is preferred to do this as it will be under a heavy load. In earlier chapters, we discussed how to set up partitioning and how to update the service configuration to isolate nodes from the workload. In our case, we are fine with the same node as this is a proof-of-concept. However, in a production environment, we might need to put the MIM and SCSM services on the same node to eliminate network timeouts as the MIM service user:

3. Run the MIM 2016 service and portal `Service and Portal.msi` as an elevated user. Click on **Change**, as shown in the following screenshot:

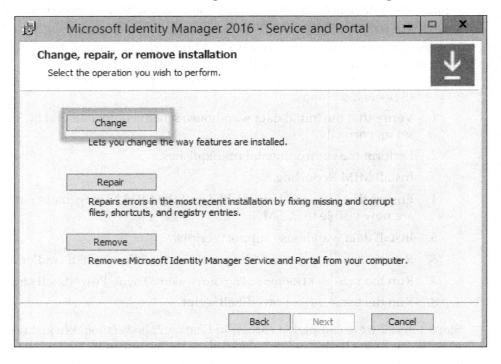

4. Then, we will select the **MIM Reporting** option to be installed on the local drive:

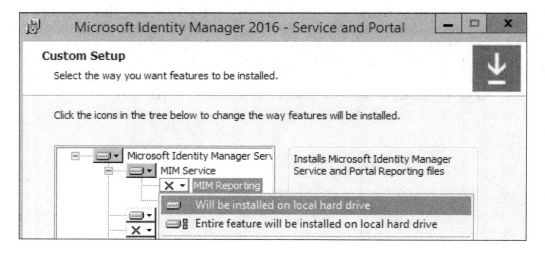

5. During the change mode, it will ask you for the SCSM management machine; in our environment, this is **TFCSCSM-MGMT01**:

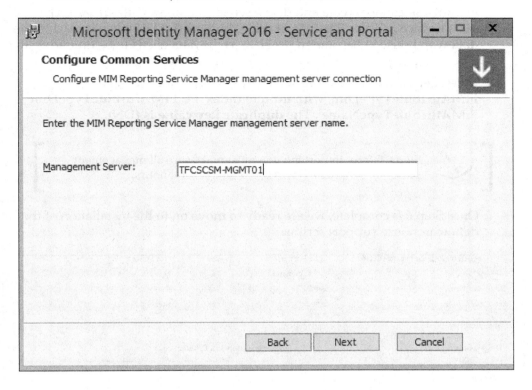

6. Next, you will go through the setup steps and see that Reporting is installing and using the SCSM client to install the management packs. This process may take a while to run, but these steps are needed to import the schema and management packs:

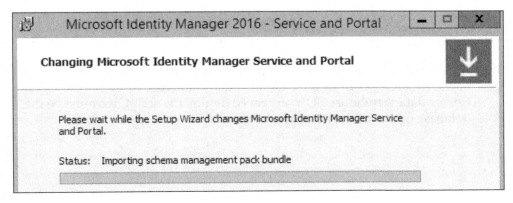

All requests and management of the MIM service are logged and transferred to the SCSM, including new attributes and schema changes. So, from here on out, you cannot create and delete schema changes without care. The MIM service handles this type of thing quite nicely, but when it reaches the data warehouse, it becomes a problem as the data needs to be unique on the index. Again, just as a word of caution, here is a sample error:

Message: Cannot insert duplicate key row in object 'dbo. FIMAttributeTypeDim' with unique index 'IX_FIMAttributeTypeDim_ FIMAttributeTypeName'. The duplicate key value is (DN).

 Step 6 is very important; you must make sure all management packs are synced, and this could take several hours.

Once Step 6 is complete, we are ready to move on to the installation of the data warehouse support scripts:

Process.SystemCenterConfigItemCube	Cube Processing	Yes	Not Started
MPSyncJob	Synchronization	Yes	Not Started
Load.Common	Load	Yes	Running
Extract_TFC	Extract	Yes	Running

MPSyncJob

Description:		**Synchronization Job Details:**		
MPSyncJob		Id	Data source	Management Pack ▲	Status
Category:	**Status:**		TFC	Microsoft.FIMGroupMembershipCha	Associated
Synchronization	Not Started		TFC	Microsoft.FIMMPRHistory.Report.Lib	Associated
Last run:	**Next run:**		TFC	Microsoft.FIMRequestHistory.Report	Associated
12/26/2015 1:50:00 PM	12/26/2015 2:50:00 PM		TFC	Microsoft.FIMSetHistory.Report.Libra	Associated
Schedule:			TFC	Microsoft.FIMSetMembershipChang	Associated
Every 1 hour(s) 0 minute(s)			TFC	Microsoft.FIMUserHistory.Report.Lib	Associated
			TFC	Microsoft.Forefront.IdentityManager	Associated
Job Progress: (183/183)					

7. To deploy the data warehouse support script, you can copy `Data Warehouse Support Scripts` from the RTM installer to the root drive of your System Center data warehouse SQL server. To deploy the script, we must be the database owner of the data warehouse.

8. Open PowerShell as an elevated user:

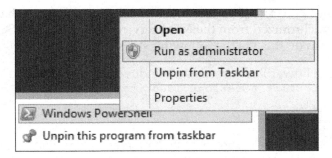

9. Then, navigate to the directory and run
FIMPostInstallScriptsForDataWarehouse.ps1. You will be asked for
the SQL server and instance. In this case, the data warehouse server is local
on the default instance, so we will use localhost. Then, we will specify the
MIM service account. We will see the complete message as follows:

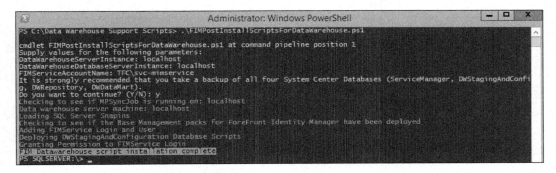

Finally, you will see the Reporting tool and the default Forefront Identity Manager
Reporting reports. This at least shows us that MIM reports are imported into SCSM;
however, don't try them just yet! We have a few more things to do before we have
useful data in the reports.

Synchronizing data from MIM to SCSM

Before we can start generating any reports, we need to make sure that the information is synchronized from the MIM service database to the SCSM data warehouse. We can do this via the following steps:

1. Open up a PowerShell command window and navigate to `C:\Program Files\Microsoft Forefront Identity Manager\2010\Reporting\ PowerShell`.

 This is the location of some PowerShell scripts that you use to manage the Reporting feature.

2. On the SQL server used by the MIM service, you will find a SQL Server agent job that is scheduled to run every 8 hours:

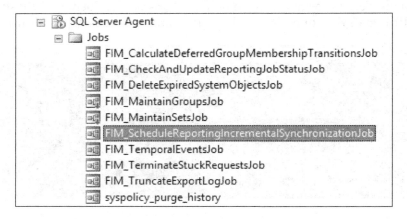

This, however, is running an incremental synchronization between the MIM and SCSM data warehouses.

3. Once we have decided that it is time to start using the Reporting feature, we need to run an initial synchronization. We can do this by running the `Start-FIMReportingInitialSync.ps1` PowerShell script from the `Reporting` folder of our MIM service machine:

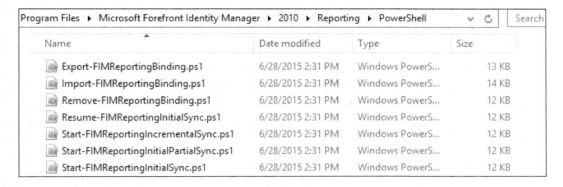

The feedback from this PowerShell script is nothing; it just kicks off a job, and you will have to check the status of this job manually:

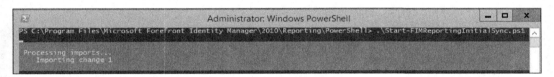

4. In the MIM portal, navigate to the **All Resources** section in the **Administration** panel and search for the **Reporting** resources:

Here are some points to keep in mind:

- ° The **Reporting Job** resource will contain information about the manual and scheduled jobs transferring information from MIM to SCSM.

- ° If you click on **Reporting Job**, you will see all the reporting jobs in the order of oldest to newest, so the newest one will be on the last page.

- ○ If you click on the **Created Time** column, you can reorder them so that the last one comes first. You can then open up the newest reporting job to verify the status.

- ○ If you look at the initial job you just started, you will see whether it is completed without errors. If **Reporting Job Status** still shows **Running**, just wait a few minutes and check the status again:

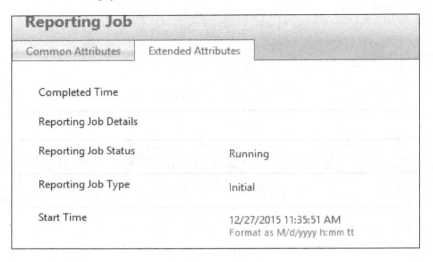

5. Once you have completed this, as depicted in the following screenshot of the initial sync job, you should also run an incremental job by firing the `Start-FIMReportingIncrementalSync.ps1` script. Once this is completed successfully, you will soon have some reports to look at:

Completed Time	12/27/2015 11:38:26 AM
	Format as M/d/yyyy h:mm tt
Reporting Job Details	
Reporting Job Status	Completed
Reporting Job Type	Initial
Start Time	12/27/2015 11:35:51 AM
	Format as M/d/yyyy h:mm tt

Default reports

The MIM Reporting service automatically installs management packs to create a number of reports. At http://bit.ly/MIMMOOBReports, the default reports are described, but we have the information copied here for your convenience:

- **The Group Membership Change report**: This report provides key information about group membership modifications in MIM, including the user account that approved the group change, the type of change, and any related requests or policy rules related to this change.

- **The Set Membership Change report**: This report provides key information about set membership modifications in MIM, including account information about the user who joined or left a set, approvers (if any), and any related requests or policy rules related to this change.

- **The Group History report**: This report provides information about changes to key attributes on group resources in MIM, including the group filter, owner, type, domain, and membership.

- **The Management Policy Rule History report**: This report provides information about changes to key attributes on the management policy rule resources in MIM, including the MPR type, principal set, and change type.

- **The Request History report**: This report provides information about requests that have been committed to the database in MIM, including the request originator, the request target, the approver account name, and any modified attributes.

- **The Set History report**: This report provides information about the changes to key attributes on set resources in MIM, including the set filter, change type, membership, and creator.

- **The User History report**: This report provides information about changes to key attributes on user resources in MIM, including the account name, e-mail, job title, and employee start/end date.

The SCSM ETL process

The SCSM ETL process is broken into several steps, which we will outline here. To understand this, we will first start with the MIM service. As we have discussed previously in this chapter, we executed the initial job and watched this job get created in the portal. Now, we will explain what is happening under the hood so that it can help you troubleshoot and manage the reporting system.

The steps to move the data are defined as follows:

- **Initial**: This process reads data directly from the Service Objects database.
- **Initial-Partial**: This process allows for the movement and configuration of the schema attribute.
- **Incremental**: This process runs every 8 hours, or as set by the SQL agent job. This ETL job reads the export log table only.

When you first kick off reporting the Initial job, this job extracts data from the [fim].[Objects] table. So, if you're just turning on Reporting but you have had MIM up for a while and have a large set of data, your initial sync could take a bit of time to complete. So, most people ask, how long will it take? To answer this, the first thing we would do is query the FIM service database to understand the amount of data we have, by running the following script:

```
USE FIMService
GO
SELECT MAX(ObjectKey)
FROM [FIMService].[fim].[Objects]
```

In our case, we are looking at 85716. This also includes and objects during your retention period. Now we need to run the initial sync, and then we can run the following script to see FIMWatermark:

```
USE [ServiceManager]
GO
SELECT *
FROM [ServiceManager].[dbo].[MT_FIMDW$FIMWatermark]
```

We would typically run a collection on the Service Manager DB to see how many records we are processing and to know how long the initial would take. In the case of TFC, we are looking at an initial sync of 4 hours, based on a 30-minute run:

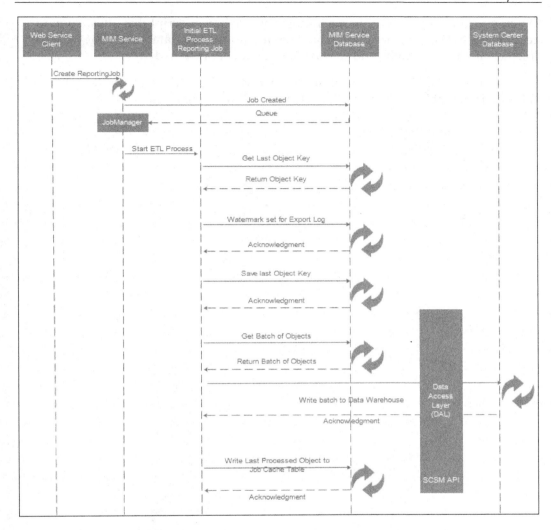

The preceding diagram explains the initial process once the job is created by the client, and the job manager within the service receives the execution command and the type of job. This job then executes the preceding process to move data from the objects table directly. The initial process only needs to be run once, unless the watermarks get messed up due to performance or other errors within the system. However, you must have a successful initial run as it populates the dimension properties within the data warehouse.

If you encounter errors within the initial sync, we have a script that allows you to resume the initial sync based on what is sent to the SCSM database, what we have logged into the jobs table, and the last object key that is recorded.

The incremental process is a bit similar in nature to the initial one, but we will use the export log table for this process, as in the following diagram:

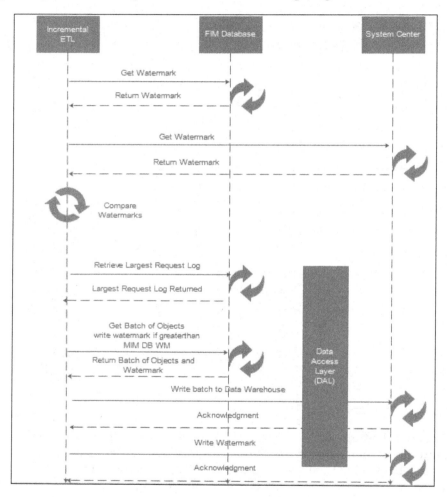

The job manager within the service monitors the creation and execution of the `fim.reportingjobs` table. If there is a row created because of the SQL agent job or because someone ran a PowerShell script to create the job, only one job can be defined and running at one time. The job table holds the key that generates the service identifier, and this identifier tells you which server service is holding or running the reporting job. Take a look at the following example of running a reporting job. The job manager's sole responsibility is to manage the `ReportingManager` process. Once this is complete, the job manager will then complete the request and clear and complete the reporting job:

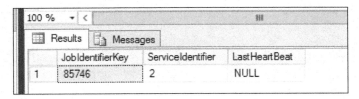

The **Extract, Transform, and Load** (ETL) process within SCSM refreshes the data in the warehouse. This is logically a sequential flow of data, as follows:

1. The Extract job acquires data from registered management servers.
2. The Transform job optimizes the data needed for reporting and shapes the data according to the defined business rules.
3. The Load job populates the data mart for long-term retention and access.

[For further reading, a great explanation can be found at `http://bit.ly/MIMReportingETL`.]

Looking at reports

There are several ways of looking at MIM reports. You can use the SCSM Management console, but you can also use the web interface of SQL Reporting services.

Using the SCSM Management console (from the MIM Service server, for example) is a way for you, as an administrator, to verify that everything looks alright.

It is not uncommon for the reports to be empty, with the message **There is no data available for this report**. This is due to the fact that the reports show the data for the last three days by default:

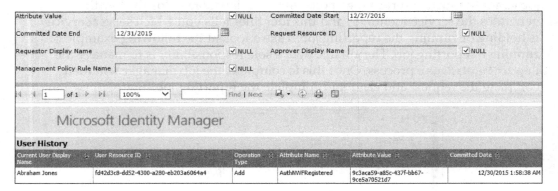

What you need to do is expand the **Parameter** section at the top of the SSRS site and modify it to match your needs. Once you have done this, you can click on **View Report** in the **Tasks** pane to regenerate the report.

The following example shows a report filtered to show all the events regarding the **Hunters** group, with the display name **Hunters**:

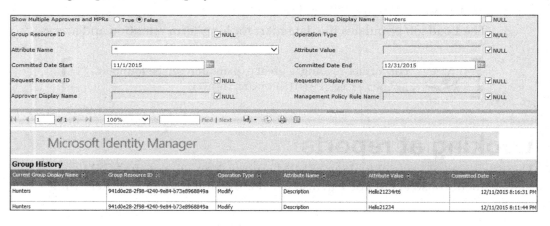

The web interface is typically the way normal users would access the reports. However, if David (our manager) would like to look at the reports and does not have sufficient permissions to do so, he will receive the error page shown in the following screenshot:

Allowing users to read reports

In order for selected users to read reports, we need to give them some permission on the Reporting server side.

Service Manager supports a delegation model for different user roles. However, if you want non-administrators to see and use specific reports, this is not possible using one of the default roles. To make this happen, we need to use the permission model of SQL Reporting services.

Let's take a look at how we can give John (our manager) exclusive permission to only look at the FIMUserHistory report and nothing else:

1. As an administrator, access the web interface of the Reporting services server. In our example, this is http://tfcscsm-dw01/Reports.

2. Navigate down the tree to **Forefront.IdentityManager.Reporting**.

3. Drop down the little menu to the right of the `FIMUserHistory` report and select **Security**:

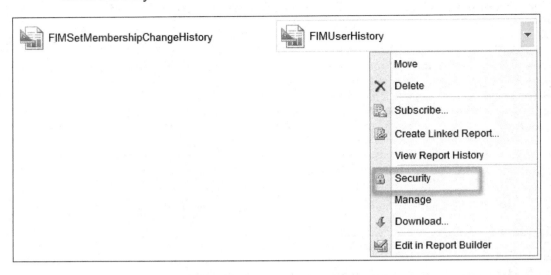

4. Click on the **Edit Item Security** option to change the security setting for this particular report.

5. A warning appears asking whether you really want to have special permissions and stop using the inherited security settings:

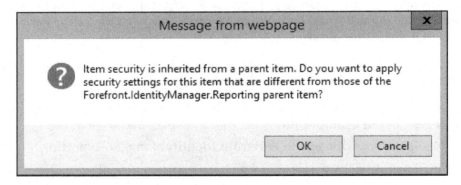

If we had wanted David to run all the MIM reports, we could have done this at the folder level instead.

6. After clicking on **OK**, the user interface changes and allows you to assign new roles:

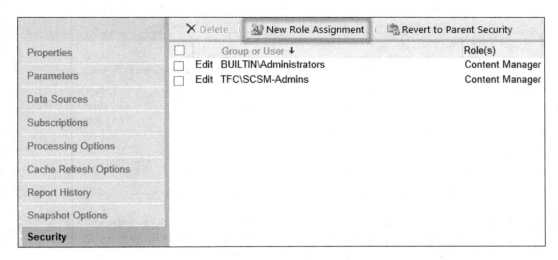

7. We can now click on the **New Role Assignment** option and give David the **Browser** role, which will give him permission to run this report:

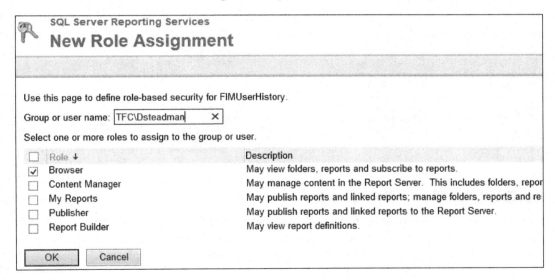

As you can see, we have the opportunity to allow David to get additional roles as well. In most real cases, we would be using the Active Directory groups managed by MIM to assign these permissions, rather than assigning them to individuals:

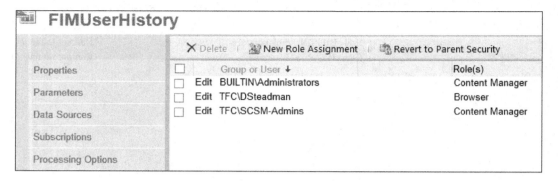

One problem remains, though. This does not allow David to access the default Report site and navigate down to the `FIMUserHistory` report. One way of solving this problem is to give him a direct URL to this report. Once he has this, he can access the `FIMUserHistory` report using his browser:

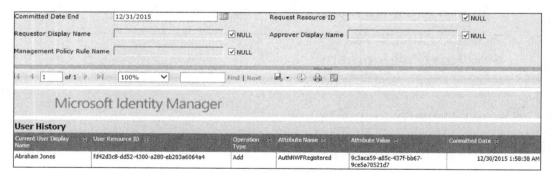

Modifying reports

While MIM provides reports based on the default MIM schema, you can also extend MIM Reporting to accommodate custom resources and attributes that you have created in the MIM schema, or customize the way reports are displayed.

 For detailed guidance on extending MIM Reporting, take a look at http://aka.ms/FIMReporting.

As mentioned earlier, the MIM Reporting service automatically installs several SCSM management packs to define the default MIM schema and reports. Once you have modified the MIM schema with new resources or attributes, you will need to create another management pack so that SCSM is aware of the new resources.

The following is a summary of this process from the TechNet article at http://technet.microsoft.com/en-us/library/jj133861. It outlines the general process of extending MIM Reporting:

1. Create a new schema management pack for SCSM that contains definitions for the new schema elements.

2. Create a new MIM Reporting binding file. An MIM Reporting binding file is an XML file that is used to define the resource mapping between the data warehouse and MIM. A default binding file, DefaultBinding.xml, is installed with MIM and can be used as a template for your customized reports.

3. Using a PowerShell script, import the schema management pack to the SCSM server.

4. Using a PowerShell script, import the MIM Reporting binding file to the MIM server.

5. Using SQL Server Management Studio, create a new, stored procedure to return the data that you require for your report.

6. Create a new **Report Definition Language** (**RDL**) file using the stored procedure from the previous step. The RDL file defines how the report is structured and displayed to the end user.

7. Create a new report management pack that uses the stored procedure and RDL file from the previous steps. This management pack will define a new report in the SCSM Service Manager console.

At this point, all the required customization work is done. Next, you will run a PowerShell process that will:

- Verify that the MIM and data warehouse schemas referenced in the MIM Reporting binding file are valid and free of collisions

- Create management pack files (.MP) from the schema and reporting management packs that you created

- Bundle the .MP files and RDL files into a new management pack bundle

- Import the bundle into SCSM

- Import the MIM binding into MIM

The last step is to synchronize the new management packs on the data warehouse.

This process instructs the data warehouse to look for any new management packs that have been added, create any new schema elements that have been defined, and deploy any new reports that have been defined.

Once the management packs have been synchronized, you must take the following steps to check whether the new data appears in the data warehouse:

1. Run the MIM Reporting Initial-Partial ETL process. This will move the new schema elements, which you have just defined, over to the data warehouse.

2. Once this is complete, you may optionally start a MIM Reporting Incremental ETL process to pick up any changes that have occurred since Incremental ETL was last run.

3. Either start the SCSM ETL processes manually or wait for a scheduled run to occur. Once a full cycle is complete (Extract, Transform, and Load), you will see the data appear in the SCSM console or the SSRS web view.

We typically get questions on sizing Reporting and SCSM. General guidance is given around this at the following sites:

- Considerations for deploying Reporting (`http://bit.ly/MIMReportingConsiderations`)

- System requirements for System Center 2012 R2 (`http://bit.ly/MIMSCSMrequirements`)

Hybrid reporting in Azure

While Microsoft Identity Manager provides reports based on the default MIM schema, you can also take advantage of a new feature that provides another reporting option. Reporting in Azure is another simple solution.

The service currently requires the tenant to be a premium feature. This could change in the future, but as of right now it is the requirement:

1. To enable the service first, we need to log in to Azure and download the client:

identity manager reporting

Download and install the Microsoft Identity Manager reporting agent on your Identity Manager servers. Download now

2. Once we have the client, we need to install this on the MIM server that is hosting the MIM Server service. To install it, simply click on `MIMHybridReportingAgent.msi` and go through the prompts.

3. The agent uses a certificate-based authentication for the transfer of data. This is generated when clicking on the download of the agent, as you can see in the following screenshot:

MIMHybridReportingAgent.msi	Windows Installer Package	625 KB	No
tenant.cert	CERT File	4 KB	No

4. While going through the install, you will get the license agreement dialog box. Click on **Install**.

   The install only takes a moment to complete:

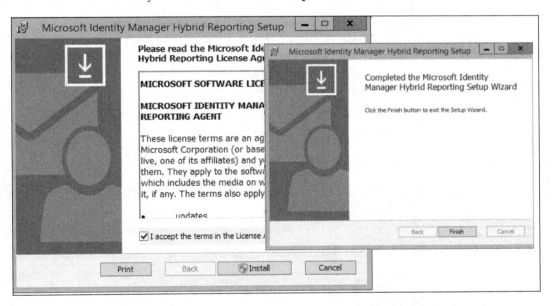

5. Once installed, we need to check a few things to confirm that we are working as we should. The first item to look at is the MIM Service config, and we should see a new configuration entry called `hybridReportingRequestLoggingEnabled`, as depicted here:

```
ddress="mimservice.THEFINANCIALCOMPANY.NET"/>
THEFINANCIALCOMPANY.NET" hybridReportingRequestLoggingEnabled="true"/>
```

6. The next item we want to confirm is that we have a new event log in **Applications and Services Logs**:

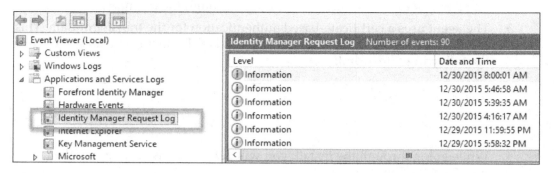

So at this point, with all the little checks, we can assume that data is flowing as we see no errors related to the client in the log that it is unable to communicate. As you guessed, there are only a few pieces to the solution: two stored procedures that handle the data collection `[fim].[GetResourceProperties]` and transformation `[fim].[GetMultipleResourceProperties]` via the MIM service, and then the registering of that data in the event log in JSON format.

7. The final step is the agent that is running and monitoring the event and passing the information to the Azure service.

Here is an example of an entry in the event log:

```
{"HybridObjectID":"80e6e017-41f7-4b65-be39-58c45530cb89","ObjectType":"Request","Creator":{"HybridObjectID":"7fb2b853-24f0-4498-9534-
4e10589723c4","CreatedTime":"Mar 30 2015 5:13AM","ObjectID":"2340","Creator":"2340","DomainConfiguration":"2730","AccountName":"svc-
miminstall","DisplayName":"svc-miminstall","Domain":"TFC","Email":"","FirstName":"svc-miminstall","MailNickname":"svc-
miminstall","ObjectType":"Person"},"Operation":"Create","Target":{"HybridObjectID":"0068ba38-9a40-48b0-a623-4b075637cd06","CreatedTime":"Dec 30 2015
1:46PM","Creator":"2340","ObjectID":"85746","DisplayName":"Reporting
Job","ObjectType":"msidmReportingJob","msidmReportingJobStatus":"NotRunning","msidmReportingJobType":"Incremental"},"RequestStatus":"Completed","Management
Policy":[{"HybridObjectID":"86f43496-931f-4d30-967b-2c64d6333bad","Disabled":"0","GrantRight":"1","CreatedTime":"Mar 30 2015
12:16PM","PrincipalSet":"2732","Creator":"2931","ResourceCurrentSet":"3150","ResourceFinalSet":"3150","ObjectID":"3152","ActionParameter":"*","ActionType":
["Create","Delete"],"Description":"Reporting Administration: Administrators can control reporting job resources. ","DisplayName":"Reporting Administration: Administrators
can control reporting job resources.","ObjectType":"ManagementPolicyRule","ManagementPolicyRuleType":"Request"}],"DisplayName":"Create msidmReportingJob:
'Reporting Job' Request","CreatedTime":"12/30/2015 1:46:57 PM","TargetObjectType":"msidmReportingJob","CommittedTime":"12/30/2015 1:46:58 PM","RequestParameter"
[{"Calculated":"false","PropertyName":"ObjectType","Value":"msidmReportingJob","Operation":"Create"},
{"Calculated":"false","PropertyName":"msidmReportingJobType","Value":"Incremental","Operation":"Create"},{"Calculated":"true","PropertyName":"ObjectID","Value":
{"HybridObjectID":"0068ba38-9a40-48b0-a623-4b075637cd06","CreatedTime":"Dec 30 2015 1:46PM","Creator":"2340","ObjectID":"85746","DisplayName":"Reporting
Job","ObjectType":"msidmReportingJob","msidmReportingJobStatus":"NotRunning","msidmReportingJobType":"Incremental","Operation":"Create"},
{"Calculated":"true","PropertyName":"Creator","Value":{"HybridObjectID":"7fb2b853-24f0-4498-9534-4e10589723c4","CreatedTime":"Mar 30 2015
5:13AM","ObjectID":"2340","Creator":"2340","DomainConfiguration":"2730","AccountName":"svc-miminstall","DisplayName":"svc-
miminstall","Domain":"TFC","Email":"","FirstName":"svc-miminstall","MailNickname":"svc-miminstall","ObjectType":"Person"},"Operation":"Create"},
{"Calculated":"true","PropertyName":"DisplayName","Value":"Reporting Job","Operation":"Create"}
```

As you can see, it holds a lot of information, so this type of logging could have far more reach than just Azure for consuming.

When looking at the spooling of the service, we can see the trigger and the upload of the event and its success:

```
10.00:00:00., TID:14 Time:10:25:46 AM
UpdateChecker.CheckForAndApplyUpdates;No new updates available., TID:15 Time:10:
25:46 AM
UpdateChecker.MonitorThreadProc;Next update check is in 06:00:00., TID:15 Time:1
0:25:46 AM
BufferManager.QueueUploadIfNoActivity;Upload due to inactivity:MIMEventLogPlugin
Monitor, TID:12 Time:10:26:45 AM
UploadManager.UploadStream;Heartbeat:True,Pos:0,Len:5096000,Name::MIMEventLogPlu
ginMonitor, TID:11 Time:10:26:45 AM
AzureUploader.UploadBuffer.EventHub;MIMEventLogPluginMonitor:Success:Heartbeat,
TID:11 Time:10:26:46 AM
AzureUploader.BuildAndWriteQueueMessage;MIMEventLogPluginMonitor:Success:Heartbe
at, TID:11 Time:10:26:47 AM
BufferManager.RecycleBuffer;Position:0, Capacity:5096000, TID:11 Time:10:26:47 A
M
MIMHReportingEventLogProcessor::EventLogEventWrittenCallback;MIMEventLogPluginMo
nitor,Microsoft.IdentityManagement.Service.1, TID:8 Time:10:27:07 AM
BufferManager.QueueUploadIfNoActivity;Upload due to inactivity:MIMEventLogPlugin
Monitor, TID:12 Time:10:27:45 AM
UploadManager.UploadStream;Heartbeat:False,Pos:2548,Len:5096001,Name:20151209T18
2707Z-20151209T182745Z-TFCMIM01-688a18956871454492a259db9ef8fa09.log:MIMEventLog
PluginMonitor, TID:11 Time:10:27:45 AM
AzureUploader.UploadBuffer.EventHub;MIMEventLogPluginMonitor:Success:https://pks
proddatastorewestus08.blob.core.windows.net/4681113a-2874-4744-8467-8d11d3858c66
-mimdev-20151207/20151209T182707Z-20151209T182745Z-TFCMIM01-688a18956871454492a2
59db9ef8fa09.log, TID:11 Time:10:27:46 AM
AzureUploader.BuildAndWriteQueueMessage;MIMEventLogPluginMonitor:Success:https:/
/pksproddatastorewestus08.blob.core.windows.net/4681113a-2874-4744-8467-8d11d385
8c66-mimdev-20151207/20151209T182707Z-20151209T182745Z-TFCMIM01-688a189568714544
92a259db9ef8fa09.log, TID:11 Time:10:27:47 AM
BufferManager.RecycleBuffer;Position:2548, Capacity:5096001, TID:11 Time:10:27:4
7 AM
BufferManager.QueueUploadIfNoActivity;Upload due to inactivity:MIMEventLogPlugin
Monitor, TID:12 Time:10:28:45 AM
UploadManager.UploadStream;Heartbeat:True,Pos:0,Len:5096000,Name::MIMEventLogPlu
ginMonitor, TID:11 Time:10:28:45 AM
AzureUploader.UploadBuffer.EventHub;MIMEventLogPluginMonitor:Success:Heartbeat,
TID:11 Time:10:28:46 AM
AzureUploader.BuildAndWriteQueueMessage;MIMEventLogPluginMonitor:Success:Heartbe
at, TID:11 Time:10:28:46 AM
BufferManager.RecycleBuffer;Position:0, Capacity:5096000, TID:11 Time:10:28:46 A
M
```

On a new service, it could take up to 24 hours to have everything flowing. Typically, it is faster than this, but this is just a warning for you.

Currently, there are only a few select reports for hybrid, as the service is in its early stages:

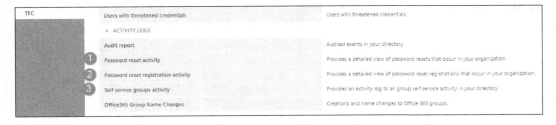

Now, when you select a report, you need to be aware that you need to select the source as **Identity Manager**. By default, it will show only **Azure AD**:

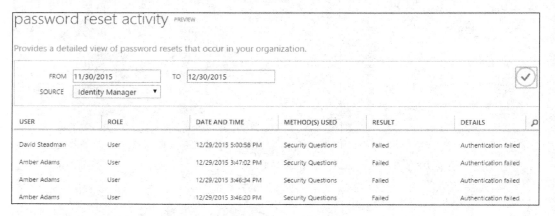

The development team is working hard on the service and looking at new ways to bring new and exciting reports to its customer base.

Summary

The MIM Reporting and hybrid reporting features are a great way of tracking historical events related to your MIM objects. However, setting up dependency using the SCSM functionality for data warehousing and Reporting makes it hard to troubleshoot and get set up correctly the first time. The use of standard SQL Server Reporting services does, however, make it very easy to make your own custom reports and also to granularly define permissions around your reports. Hybrid reporting opens up the door for customers such as TFC to decide why this type of reporting would work for them.

In the next chapter, we will go into some of the basics of troubleshooting and common errors.

14
Troubleshooting

The last two chapters of the book are to help you operate and support Microsoft Identity Manager. We will approach MIM troubleshooting in terms of its components and show you how and where to find data that will lead you to the root cause. We will also discuss some of the common errors for each component and how to solve them.

In this chapter, we will cover:

- The basics
- The sync engine
- The FIM service
- The FIM portal
- The password change notification service

The basics

Sometimes, the hardest part of troubleshooting is figuring out where to start, especially when MIM involves so many technologies. A single problem could be caused by one or more MIM server(s), an MIM component, the MIM configuration, a rules extension logic problem, the network, invalid or incorrect data entered at the source system(s), or other things such as the underlying infrastructure of domain controller(s), DNS, SQL Server, SharePoint, or IIS.

One way to start troubleshooting is to think of how the components are installed in your specific environment—that is, determining the systems or components involved in a particular problem.

Let's take the basic data problem in which an account has missing or wrong data and list a few possible causes. The source system could be down, source data could have been accidentally deleted or entered incorrectly, or the service account being used by MIM could have issues such as incorrect permissions, password reset, or the account being disabled. You could be missing MIM attribute flows; there could be an error in a rule extension (missing or bad logic); the source object could be out of scope; the object could be disconnected; the object could be in error in MIM; or the data synchronization itself could have stopped, have an error, or just not been run yet. The target system may reject the requested change due to permissions or invalid data or, in the case of Active Directory and other distributed systems, there may be a replication wait period or problem.

Let's organize these possibilities into categories, as follows:

Category	Possible causes
Source system problem or business communication gap	Source system could be down.
	Source data could have been accidentally deleted or entered incorrectly.
	System account problems.
MIM configuration problem or business communication gap	There could be missing MIM attribute flows.
	There could be an error in a rule extension (missing or bad logic).
	The source object could be out of scope.
	The object could be disconnected.
	The object could be in error in MIM.
	The synchronization could have stopped, have an error, or not been run yet.
Target system problem or business communication gap	The target system could be down.
	The system requirements could be not fulfilled.
	There could be service account problems.
	There could be a replication/distributed system problem.

You will notice a common category theme: a business process gap. Does the organization understand which attributes are flowing between systems and when? The most successful identity management implementations are those that have great communication between teams.

Outside communication problems and misunderstandings between people, you will notice that this problem can be broken down into a source system problem, an MIM problem, or a target system problem. As we are identity professionals, we will start at MIM and depending on what we see, determine the problem within MIM itself or look at the source or target system.

Operation statistics

A quick and simple way to determine whether an MIM solution is working as you expect is by looking at the MIM synchronization statistics and the FIM service statistics. MIM provides the synchronization engine with operational statistics through Synchronization Service Manager by clicking on **Tools | Statistics**:

Statistics

Management agent statistics:

Name	Objects	Total Connectors	Connectors	Explicit Connectors	Total Disconnectors	Disconnectors	Expli
Exam...	155	0	0	0	151	151	0
Phone	1024	1024	1024	0	0	0	0
MIM	1071	1056	1056	0	2	0	0
AD	1048	1038	1038	0	7	7	0
AD_...	4	1	1	0	2	2	0
BHO...	10	8	8	0	0	0	0
BHO...	94	18	18	0	76	76	0
HR	1022	1022	1022	0	0	0	0

Metaverse object count: 1064

Metadirectory object count: 5492

How can looking at numbers help you troubleshoot a problem? Let's say your environment has a source system responsible for projecting to the Metaverse, yet when you look at the statistics, you notice that less than half of the objects are connectors. There could be a data issue or a misconfiguration (or misunderstanding) with the connector filter or rules extension. That is, the synchronization statistics provide a sense of a potential problem. A large number of explicit disconnectors or explicit connectors is another sign that there are (or used to be) data issues or that the Management Agent configuration may need adjustment.

The FIM service provides operational statistics that can help diagnose problems too. Using SQL Server Management Studio, connect to the server hosting the MIM Service database and run the following:

```
USE [FIMService]
GO
EXEC  [debug].[CalculateOperationalStatistics]
    @startTimeUTC = N'1/13/2016',
    @endTimeUTC = N'1/14/2016',
    @includeDataStoreStatistics = 1
GO
```

The `startTimeUTC` and `endTimeUTC` arguments specify the timespan to use for analysis. Choosing yesterday's date and today's date should be sufficient. A value of 1 with the `includeDataStoreStatistics` argument provides statistics for the entire data store and includes data such as the number of tables, objects, attributes, bindings, sets, large sets, and groups, whereas a value of 0 (default) would not display the data store statistics. It is recommended to retrieve the data store statistics once per session and turn it off (a value of 0) for a faster execution of subsequent runs. Here is a sample snippet of running the MIM Service operational statistics:

	Name	Value	Comment
17	RequestStatusFinalSummary	100.00	% of Requests; Count 489
18	RequestStatusPostProcessingError-ErrorTotal	0	0.00% of total Requests
19	RequestStatusFailed-ErrorTotal	8	1.64% of total Requests
20	RequestStatusFailed-ErrorCount	8	Sample RequestKey 137320 RequestIdentifier F72CE3D5-2E19-4C1E-8F!
21	RequestStatusDenied-ErrorTotal	0	0.00% of total Requests
22	RequestStatus-ShortLived-LikelyStuck	0.00	% of total Requests; Count 0
23	RequestStatus-LongLived-LikelyStuck	0.00	% of total Requests; Count 0
24	SetCorrections	2	Number of sets corrected
25	DataStore-ExpiredRequests	2	if > 0, run FIM_DeleteExpiredSystemObjectsJob SQL Agent Job to Delete
26	TotalLoad-RequestAndQuery	489	Number of 1 Minute Intervals with Load 260

Note that `DataStore-ExpiredRequests` is greater than 0, and we should run the SQL agent job `FIM_DeleteExpiredSystemObjectsJob`. Note that there's also two `SetCorrections`, and we can click on the `DetailsXML` hyperlink to find the GUID of the corrected sets:

	Name	Value	Comment	DetailsXml
24	SetCorrections	2	Number of sets corrected	<data><row requestKey="137348" requestIdentifier="0A5

A simple data problem

The sync engine server is a great place to start because we can easily see data sync errors, the state of the Metaverse object(s), and that of the connector space object(s). The quickest way to know whether the sync engine is experiencing errors is to look at **Operations Tool**. If a run profile returns a status of anything other than **success**, then there is an error, such as shown here:

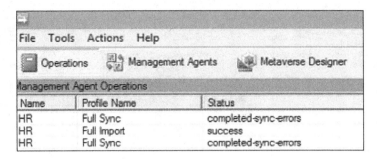

If you click on the row containing the error, the lower pane is split into a statistics window and an error window. With a few exceptions, the error window will contain a hyperlink to the object reporting an error, which you can click on and receive more information:

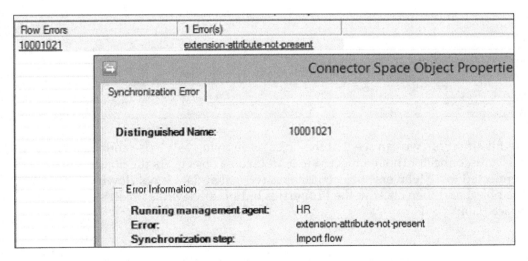

Another method to identify and work through problems is to search the Metaverse or the connector space directly. We have already discussed how searching using the **Metaverse Search** tool should be intuitive. Let's look at troubleshooting as its typically done: from the point of the object having issues or at the connector-space level.

To search the connector space, go to the **Management Agents** tool of the appropriate Management Agent. In our example scenario, the object having an error is an AD object not being updated, so we will click on the AD Management Agent, click on the Search Connector Space icon (or right-click and select **Search Connector Space**), then enter the object's DN, and finally click on the **Search** button:

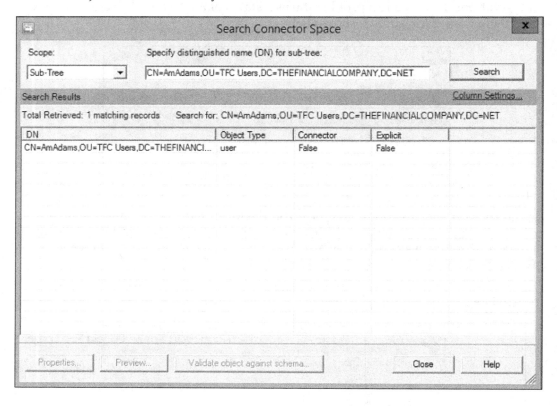

In this situation, we can see that the object is showing as a **False** connector, meaning it is a disconnector (not connected to a Metaverse object). As the object is not connected to a Metaverse object, it makes sense that data is not flowing to it. Select the object and then click on the **Properties** button to view the object's connector space data:

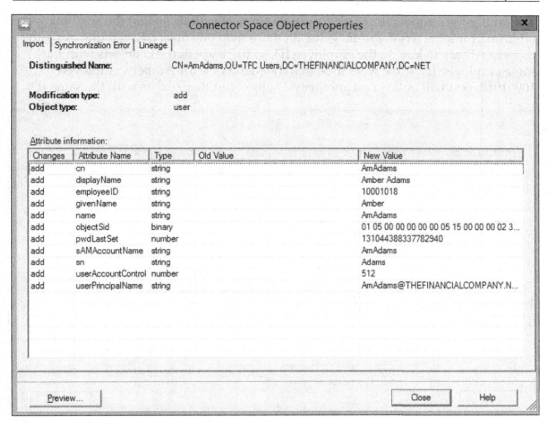

There's nothing out of the ordinary in this first view; the object has a display name, employee ID, and other bits of data. Let's look at the **Synchronization Error** tab in the following screenshot:

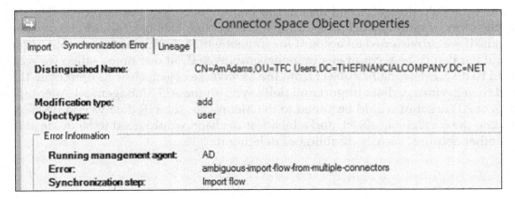

The ambiguous import flow from multiple connectors tells us that the attribute we are using for joins has the same value on more than one object. Recall that our join rules in AD are to join on the employee ID, so there are two AD objects with the same employee ID. If we were to search the Metaverse for Amber's employee ID, 10001018, you will notice that another AD object out there exists with the same ID:

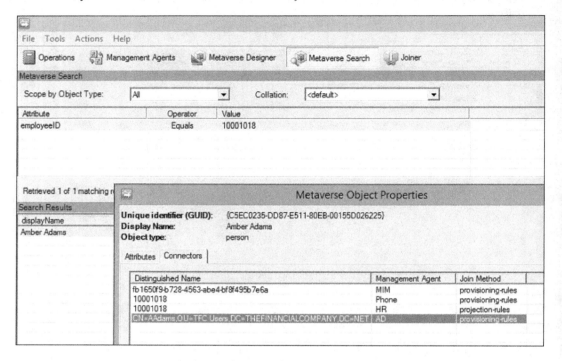

The solution is determined on which AD account should be used. If the end user should use the provisioned AD account that is currently joined to the Metaverse, then you would direct the end user to this account and clear the employee ID value on the other account (or delete it). If the disconnected AD object should be used — that is, if we provisioned an account for someone that already had an account (this could happen if the account is missing its employee ID at one time) — then we would need to disconnect the AD object from the Metaverse object, clear its employee ID, and then perform a delta import and delta sync on the AD Management Agent. The correct AD account would be joined to the Metaverse, the HR data would need to update the correct AD object, and a business decision would need to be made about the other account, such as disabling or deleting it.

Rule extension debugging and logging

Let's take another example in which data is not flowing from the source system to the target system. We will use a simple error for our example; however, the steps we will now show can be applied to any scenario. When debugging rules, the extension code is needed. In this scenario, you have come back from vacation after some changes have been made and are told that several objects are not updating their displayName attribute in AD. One such object is Ed Bush, TFC\EBush, who should have the displayName attribute of Edward Bush. Here, we will look at the connector space object and find a **Synchronization Error** tab that tells us that HRExtension.dll has a problem, specifically a problem with the import flow on displayName. If we click on the **Stack Trace** button, we can see more information about the error:

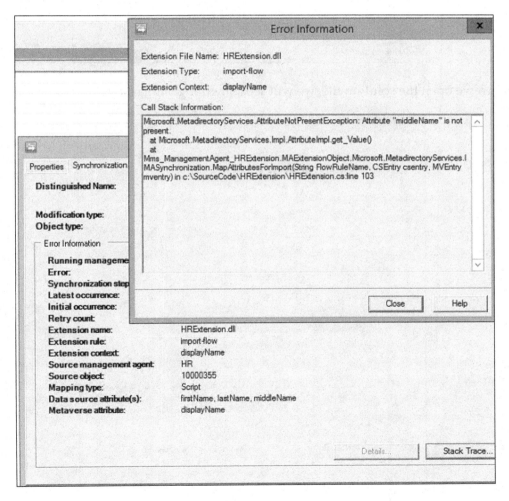

The error informs us that we are attempting to use `middleName` in `HRExtension.dll`, but Edward Bush's HR record does not have a `middleName` value. Sometimes, these kinds of error aren't so straightforward, so let's walk through how you would go about stepping through `HRExtension.dll` (or any other rules extension code).

Open up the rules extension in Visual Studio by clicking on the `HRExtension.sln` file:

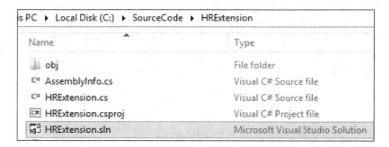

When we open the solution file, we will see something similar to this:

```csharp
HRExtension.cs*  + X
Mms_ManagementAgent_HRExtension.MAExtensionObject

using System;
using Microsoft.MetadirectoryServices;

namespace Mms_ManagementAgent_HRExtension
{
    /// <summary>
    /// Summary description for MAExtensionObject.
    /// </summary>
    public class MAExtensionObject : IMASynchronization
    {
        public MAExtensionObject()
        {
            //
            // TODO: Add constructor logic here
            //
        }
        void IMASynchronization.Initialize ()
        {
            //
            // TODO: write initialization code
            //
        }

        void IMASynchronization.Terminate ()
        {
            //
            // TODO: write termination code
            //
        }

        bool IMASynchronization.ShouldProjectToMV (CSEntry csentry, out string MVObjectType)
        {
            //
            // TODO: Remove this throw statement if you implement this method
            //
            throw new EntryPointNotImplementedException();
        }

        DeprovisionAction IMASynchronization.Deprovision (CSEntry csentry)
        {
            //
            // TODO: Remove this throw statement if you implement this method
            //
            throw new EntryPointNotImplementedException();
        }
```

As the stack trace said that the problem is within the `MapAttributesForImport` method, let's scroll to this section, click on the line where the `displayName` case exists, and then right-click and select **Breakpoint | Insert Breakpoint**:

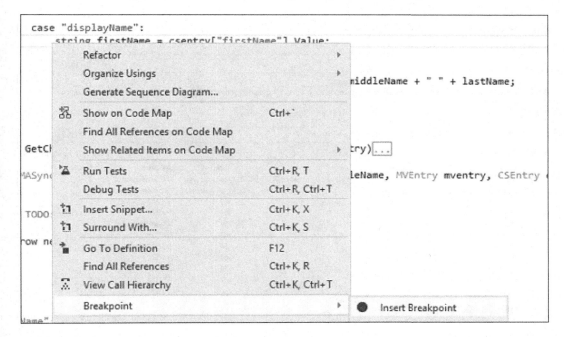

You will then notice that the first line in the `case` statement has a solid dot indicating that you've set a breakpoint:

```
case "displayName":
    string firstName = csentry["firstName"].Value;
    string lastName = csentry["lastName"].Value;
    string middleName = csentry["middleName"].Value;
    mventry["displayName"].Value = firstName + " " + middleName + " " + lastName;
    break;
}
}
```

On the Visual Studio toolbar, click on **Debug | Attach to Process**, and a window will appear, showing you all the processes running on the system. Click on the **Show processes from all users** checkbox if not already checked:

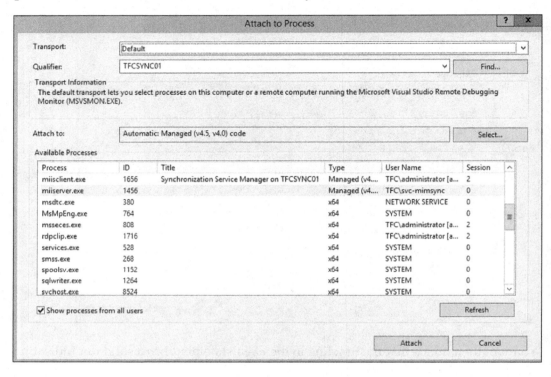

Find the `miiserver.exe` process (this is the MIM server service process), and then click on the **Attach** button. You will be presented with another window. Click on the **Attach** button:

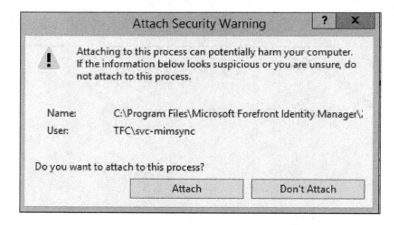

Now that we have attached to the MIM Synchronization server service process, go back to MIM Synchronization Service Manager and open up the connector space object in error (the HR connector object):

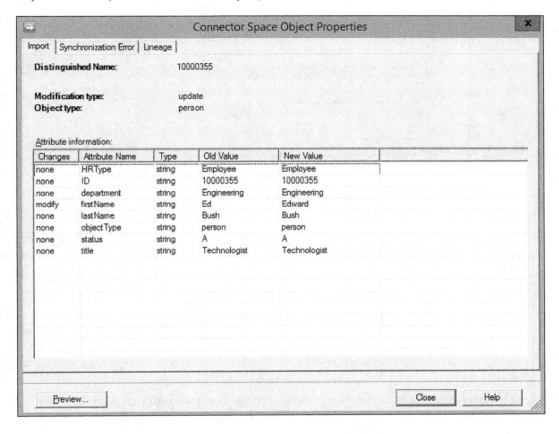

Click on the **Preview** button. In the **Preview** window, click on **Delta Synchronization** and then on the **Generate Preview** button to simulate what happens during a delta synchronization:

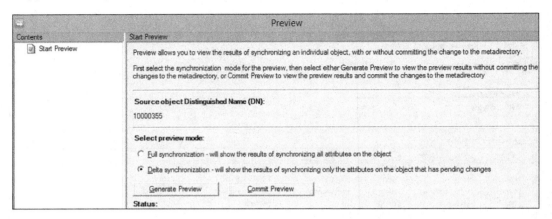

As soon as you click on the **Generate Preview** button, Visual Studio should appear stopped on the breakpoint you have set:

```
        case "displayName":
            string firstName = csentry["firstName"].Value;
            string lastName = csentry["lastName"].Value;
            string middleName = csentry["middleName"].Value;
            mventry["displayName"].Value = firstName + " " + middleName + " " + lastName;
            break;
    }
}
```

Note the arrow to the left showing us where in the code we will run next. In other words, we have not yet run the line where we stopped. Press the *F11* key to process the line and move to the next line:

```
        case "displayName":
            string firstName = csentry["firstName"].Value;
            string lastName = csentry["lastName"].Value;
            string middleName = csentry["middleName"].Value;
            mventry["displayName"].Value = firstName + " " + middleName + " " + lastName;
            break;
    }
}
```

In the Visual Studio toolbar, click on **Debug | Windows | Immediate** to change
your focus to **Immediate Window**:

We can use **Immediate Window** to look at the value of our variables by typing a
question mark (?) and then the variable. Here, we could type ?firstName and press
Enter, and Visual Studio would return the value of the firstName variable:

Which value is stored in the `lastName` variable? Let's type `?lastName` and press *Enter*:

Why is the `lastName` variable showing null? This is because we have not processed that line of code yet. If we press the *F11* key to step to the next line and then look at the value of `lastName`, we will see something similar to the following screenshot:

Let's continue stepping through the code until we get to assigning a value to
`middleName`:

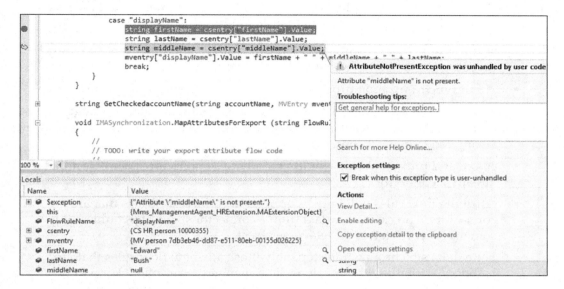

This connector space object does not have a value set for `middleName`, so the
`AttributeNotPresentException` error will occur. The solution, of course, is to
verify that a value exists before setting the variable. Here's one way to approach
the issue:

```
case "displayName":
    string firstName = string.Empty;
    string middleName = string.Empty;
    string lastName = string.Empty;

    // If firstName, lastName, and middleName exists
    if (csentry["firstName"].IsPresent && csentry["middleName"].IsPresent && csentry["lastName"].IsPresent)
    {
        mventry["displayName"].Value = csentry["firstName"].Value + " " + csentry["middleName"].Value + " " + csentry["lastName"].Value;
    }

    // If firstName and lastName exists
    if (csentry["firstName"].IsPresent && csentry["lastName"].IsPresent && !csentry["middleName"].IsPresent)
    {
        mventry["displayName"].Value = csentry["firstName"].Value + " " + csentry["lastName"].Value;
    }

    // If only firstName exists
    if (csentry["firstName"].IsPresent && !csentry["lastName"].IsPresent && !csentry["middleName"].IsPresent)
    {
        mventry["displayName"].Value = csentry["firstName"].Value;
    }

    // If only lastName exists
    if (csentry["lastName"].IsPresent && !csentry["firstName"].IsPresent && !csentry["middleName"].IsPresent)
    {
        mventry["displayName"].Value = csentry["lastName"].Value;
    }
    break;
```

What happens if you don't know where to set a breakpoint? Remember that inbound synchronization must process before outbound synchronization can begin and that not all rules are necessarily applied due to the state of the connector and the run step you performed. Here are a few rules to keep in mind:

- A run profile that is combined with delta import and delta sync will only process objects that have changed in this step.

- A full synchronization processes all the objects except explicit connectors.

- A filter rule does not apply to an explicit connector. We strongly suggest that you don't make explicit connectors as the future filter rules you make will not be applied to explicit connectors.

- A join and projection rule wouldn't apply to a connector space object that is already a connector.

- Attribute flow rules will only be applied to connector objects that are connectors. You can't flow data from a connector space object unless it is somehow connected to a Metaverse object.

- For a delta synchronization step, only those attribute flow rules that are based on attributes whose values have changed are applied. For a full synchronization, all attribute flow rules are applied. In other words, within a Management Agent, if you add an attribute or change the import or export attribute flow, join rule, projection rule, provision rule, deprovision or object deletion rule, you need to run a full synchronization.

If you have no idea where to set the breakpoint, look at the error message and refer to this table:

Order of processing	Rule	Method	Rules extension
1	Connector Filter	`FilterForDisconnection`	Management Agent
2	Join	`MapAttributesForJoin` and `ResolveJoinSearch`	Management Agent
3	Projection	`ShouldProjectToMV`	Management Agent
4	Import Attribute Flow	`MapAttributesForImport`	Management Agent
5	Provision	`Provision`	Metaverse
6	Export Attribute Flow	`MapAttributesForExport`	Management Agent
7	Deprovision	`Deprovision`	Management Agent
8	Object Deletion	`ShouldDeleteFromMV`	Metaverse

Rule extension logging

If you have a rules extension, it may be useful to utilize logging. You can create a log file for a rules extension by adding the `\Program Files\Microsoft Forefront Identity Manager\2010\Synchronization Service\Extensions\Logging.dll` reference to your Management Agent project:

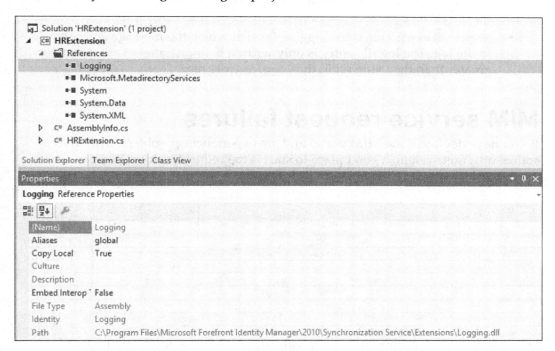

Then, within your rules extension code, add a logging event similar to this:

```
Logging.Log("Error in account: " + csentry.DN.ToString(), True, 2)
```

The three parameters are as follows:

```
Logging.Log(logMessage, addTimeStamp, loggingLevel)
```

Here is what they mean:

- `logMessage`: This is a string message to write to the log. In the preceding example, we concatenate a custom string with a string value of the connector space's DN.

- `addTimeStamp`: This is a Boolean value that determines whether a time stamp should be included.

- `loggingLevel`: This is the logging level at which the message is written to the log. The log file entry is only written if `loggingLevel` is equal to or greater than the value set in the `logging.xml` file.

MIM service request failures

If you have deployed the MIM portal and are experiencing problems with it as a source or target system, a good place to start is the request history. You can search the request history by clicking on **Search Requests**:

Let's take a look at a common support call where a MIM request is failing and figure out the problem simply by looking at the request history. In this situation, an update to the **Jeff Ingalls Direct Reports** group is failing, as shown in the following screenshot:

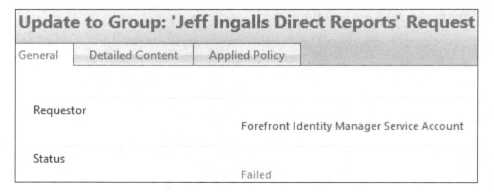

If we click on the **Detailed Content** tab, we can see that we are trying to update description on the group:

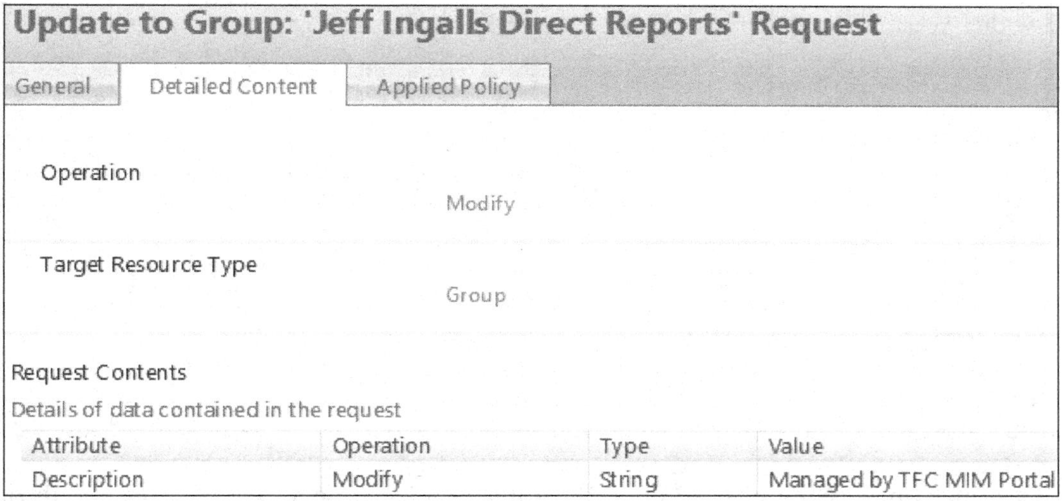

Update to Group: 'Jeff Ingalls Direct Reports' Request

General	Detailed Content	Applied Policy

Operation

Modify

Target Resource Type

Group

Request Contents

Details of data contained in the request

Attribute	Operation	Type	Value
Description	Modify	String	Managed by TFC MIM Portal

Click on the **Advanced View** button and the **Extended Attributes** tab and look for **Parent Request**:

Parent Request	
The Request that created this Request. If this Request was not created by a workflow, this attribute will not have a value.	Create Group: 'Jeff Ingalls Direct Reports' Request

Next, click on the **Applied Policy** tab, and we can see numerous Management Policy Rules that were applied, as seen here:

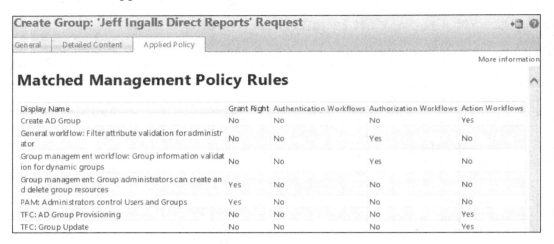

If we click on the MPR object **TFC: AD Group Provisioning** and look at the details of its workflows, we will see a **Set Description** function that sets the value **Managed by MIM Portal** successfully, as follows:

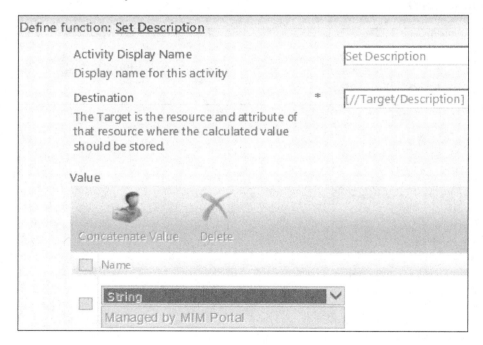

We have found that we have two workflows connected to two different MPR objects that are attempting to write different values on the same attribute, which is a clear problem!

Debugging a custom activity

You can debug the execution of a custom activity the same way as a rules extension. Open the project in Visual Studio, and in the **Debug** menu, select **Attach to Process**. In the **Attach to:** field, select **Managed Code**, and in **Available Processes**, select `Microsoft.ResourceManagement.Service.exe`. Set breakpoints as already described. Debug a custom activity UI by attaching to the `w3wp.exe` process, creating a workflow, and selecting the custom activity.

Increasing application logging

You can increase the events sent to the Forefront Identity Manager Application log by editing `\Program Files\Microsoft Forefront Identity Manager\2010\ Service\Microsoft.ResourceManagement.Service.exe.config`, changing `switchValue` from `Error` to `Verbose`, and then restarting the MIM service (the Forefront Identity Manager service).

Password change notification service

One of the most common problems for PCNS is the service not installed or running on a domain controller that handled a user's password reset. Recall that PCNS must be installed on all source domain controllers. Another common problem is that password synchronization is not enabled within the synchronization engine. There are three places to verify within the synchronization engine: the source MA's **Configure Directory Partitions** section should have **Enable this partition as a password synchronization source** checked and targets specified, the target MA should have **Enable password management** enabled in the **Configure Extensions** tab, and the global setting should be **Enable Password Synchronization** in **Tools | Options**. MIM logging is enabled by adding a `REG_DWORD` entry `FeaturePwdSyncLogLevel` to the registry subkey `HKEY_LOCAL_MACHINE\System\ CurrentControlSet\Services\FIMSynchronizationService\Logging`. A value of 0 indicates minimal logging, 1 is normal (default) logging, 2 is high logging, and 3 is verbose logging.

Summary

In this chapter, we discussed using statistics to find potential problems, how to use the Synchronization Service Manager tool to find a data problem, and how to debug a rules extension and custom activity. We showed you how to increase application logging and investigate MIM service requests to find the cause of a failing request.

In the next chapter, we will look at some operational best practices that can be used to help you with your implementation and keep your Microsoft identity solution operationally sound and healthy.

15
Operations and Best Practices

Our last chapter will focus on helping you keep your MIM system operationally healthy. We will attempt to consolidate known best practices that carry over from previous versions and add some new items that have come from support cases along with the common issues we've seen out in the field.

In this chapter, we will cover the following topics:

- Expectations versus reality
- Automating run profiles
- Backup and restore
- SQL health
- Sync engine
- Rules extensions
- The MIM portal

Expectations versus reality

Consider the following real-world scenario: HR IT does not want to provide read-only production access to their system. Instead, they will provide access to their development environment that has production data without private details such as salary and home address. A Management Agent is configured to connect to the development system, and all is working well until it is discovered that a high-ranking executive had access to the business' confidential files for a week. HR confirm that the employee was properly terminated, so the identity management system is blamed for the security breakdown. Analysis discovers that the HR development system is only updated once a week. Different departments voice how they thought the system worked. The building facilities and IT security thought that termination updates disabled accounts immediately even though HR performs terminations at the end of the day. Organizational expectations need to be addressed, which will impact the identity's design.

Consider another real-world scenario in which the identity system is working perfectly for a period of time, and then the source system, such as HR, changes the format or meaning of attributes. Accounts are removed from criteria-based groups, sets, and distribution lists. All critical attributes needed for provisioning, deprovisioning, filters, and criteria-based sets and groups have to be well understood by everyone, and there are change control processes involving, well, everyone.

We bring these two situations up in *Chapter 14*, *Troubleshooting*, because the identity operations team has to be involved in changes to the connected systems as well as those to associated business processes.

Automating run profiles

Let's first talk about automating your run profiles. Organizations typically run their Management Agents using Task Scheduler or some other task scheduler. To set this up, click on a Management Agent and then click on **Configure Run Profiles**. Click on the **Script** button and save the file:

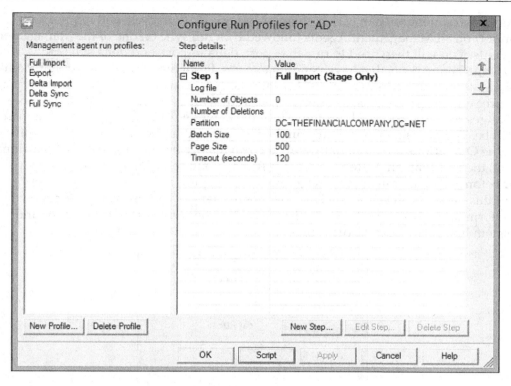

If you save it as a VB Script file, you can run the particular run profile by running `cscript filename.vbs`. As VB Script is making a simple call to WMI, you could use PowerShell too. Whether you want to run your imports, synchronizations, and exports using Task Scheduler or some other product is up to you; just know that you will need to start the run profiles with a WMI call.

If you save the run profile as a C# file, you can compile the file into an executable (`.exe`) with `csc.exe` from a Visual Studio command prompt. Here is an example of compiling `C:\SourceCode\HRFullImport.cs` into `C:\Scripts\HR-FI.exe`:

```
csc C:\SourceCode\HRFullImport.cs /out:C:\Scripts\HR-FI.exe
```

As we have mentioned in earlier chapters, your initial run cycle will require a full import on all Management Agents followed by a full sync on one of the Management Agents. You will then need to run an export, delta import, and delta sync on Management Agents that have pending exports. From the normal, day-to-day point of view, you can perform a run cycle (imports, synchronizations, and exports of your source and target systems) as often as you want with a few caveats. First, the more changes that are processed through MIM, the bigger your synchronization database will be. The Management Agent's run history is saved in the database as you will see in the **Operations** tool. Manually clear the run history by clicking on the **Operations** tool, then clicking on **Actions** and **Clear Runs...**, and selecting to clear all history or before a certain date. A general guideline is keeping 15-30 days of run history, but this depends on factors such as how many changes you process; how often you perform imports, exports, and synchronizations your business requirements; and system limitations such as disk space.

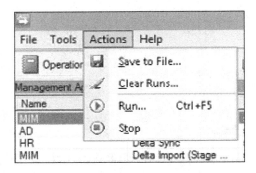

Similar to starting a run profile, you can clear the run history with a WMI call. Markus Vilcinskas has published a PowerShell script to clear run history on TechNet at http://bit.ly/MIMClearRunHistory.

There are a few scripts floating around that start run profiles at the same time, which leads us to the next caveat. You can run an import of multiple Management Agents asynchronously, but running a synchronization of two different Management Agents at the same time can result in a SQL deadlock and is therefore not supported. Further, you cannot run an export and import on the same Management Agent at the same time. Additional run profile guidance is given by the MIM product support team at http://bit.ly/MIMRunProfileGuidance.

Best practices concepts

Any best practice worth repeating should apply to any MIM solution no matter how complex. Some MIM best practices are industry-standard concepts, such as performing a backup and verifying system backups, while others refer to specific technology, such as the operating system or SQL. We will now point you to the resources for the backup and restoring of the main components and discuss specific SQL and MIM best practices.

Backup and restore

Rather than rewriting Microsoft's backup and restore guidelines, we have chosen to direct you to the official documents and then to summarize some key points. Note that some of the documents were written for MIM's predecessor, FIM, but still hold true:

- *Backup and Restore Guide for FIM 2010* (`http://bit.ly/MIMBackupRestoreGuide`)
- *FIM CM Backup and Restore* (`http://bit.ly/MIMCMBackupAndRestore`)
- *FIM Reporting Disaster Recovery* (`http://bit.ly/MIMReportingRecovery`)
- *SCSM Disaster Recovery Guide* (`http://bit.ly/SCSMDisasterRecoveryGuide`)
- *High availability and PAM disaster recovery* (`http://bit.ly/MIMPAMDisasterRecovery`)

Backing up the synchronization encryption key

Back up the synchronization encryption key by running the Synchronization Service Key Management tool, select **Export key set**, and enter the Synchronization Service account credentials. Keep this file in a secured location as the key is used to securely store the password for accounts not yet provisioned.

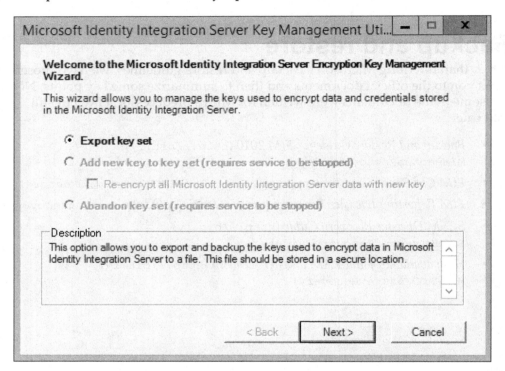

Restoring the MIM synchronization DB

A backup of the SQL database will include the schema, Management Agents, and even the rules extensions (they are stored as binary blobs in the database), but it can be handy to have just the Management Agents and Metaverse configuration saved and backed up separately. You do not need to stop the MIM Synchronization service before performing the backup, but you should verify no Management Agents are running because a running Management Agent means data is being processed.

The most common restore problem with the MIM Synchronization service database is a lost encryption key. If you need to restore the database without providing the encryption key, you will lose all MA connection settings and will have to reconfigure them. Re-entering service account passwords and clicking on **Next** a few times may seem a minor thing, but keep in mind that you will lose any initial passwords of users that are in the process of being provisioned. If you look at the pending exports in your MAs, you can track whether any users are in the process of being provisioned, and if the initial password is used. If so, you can disconnect the user and reprovision them or export them and then manually set the passwords for these users.

Restoring the MIM service DB and portal

The MIM service database is probably the most important database for you to back up because you probably have authoritative data in it. The MIM portal database will hold resources, attributes, workflows, MPR objects, and resource relations, among others. If you are using the MIM portal to create or update resources or you've deployed self-service password reset, backup is critical.

According to the *Backup and Restore* guide for FIM 2010, the recommendation is to perform at least a full daily backup of the FIM service database. If you are not performing incremental backups, then set the database in simple recovery mode. You do not have to stop the FIM service when you create the backup.

Other files that should be backed up when modified are as follows:

- The .NET application configuration file in `%programfiles%\Forefront Identity Manager\2010\Service\Microsoft.ResourceManagement. Service.exe.config`

- The registry keys under `HKEY_LOCAL_MACHINE\SYSTEM\ CurrentControlSet\Services\FIMService`

- The SQL Server Agent jobs `FIM_DeleteExpiredSystemObjectsJob`, `FIM_ MaintainGroupsjob`, `FIM_MaintainSetsJob`, and `FIM_TemporalEventsJob`

Assuming you have made changes to the SharePoint installation, you should back up the SharePoint configuration and database in addition to the portal database:

- SharePoint Foundation 2010 Backup and Recovery (`http://bit.ly/ SharePoint2010BackupAndRecovery`)

- SharePoint Foundation 2013 Backup and Recovery (`http://bit.ly/ SharePoint2013BackupAndRecovery`)

Additional backup considerations

Custom source code of rules extensions and workflows should be backed up as well as any scripts used in conjunction with the identity system or overall system functionality. We suggest using a source management package to maintain configuration settings and custom code.

Operational health

There are a lot of moving parts to the system depending on the components you have installed. How do you know if your system is healthy? Here are a few items to watch:

- The Synchronization Service Operation tool should have no errors
- MIM portal requests should show successful completion (Completed)
- MIM SQL jobs should be successful
- The Windows Application and Forefront Identity Manager event logs should be shown
- SQL and/or clustering logs should be shown
- The duration of synchronizations and imports and exports over time for each Management Agent should be monitored

Database maintenance

If a Management Agent is taking longer to complete its run operation, there are few things to consider. If you have a delay in an export or import operation, there could be a problem with the source system or network. Initial investigations for longer-than-expected synchronizations should determine whether a large number of groups is being synchronized, whether non-indexed attributes are being used as joins, or whether there are SQL Server performance problems.

If the MIM portal takes a long time to respond or times out while performing a "contains" search, it could be because the full-text search catalog needs to be rebuilt. Start SQL Management Studio and click on **Databases | FIMService | Storage | Full Text Catalogs**. Right-click on **ftCatalog** and select **Rebuild**:

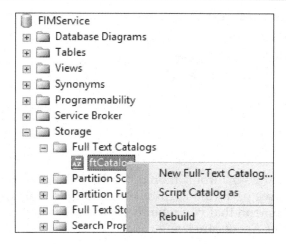

If your portal's search performance is slow for "non-contain" searches, then you may need to rebuild the indexes and update the statistics of the service database. The following query can be used to determine the average fragmentation as a percentage:

```
SELECT a.index_id, name, avg_fragmentation_in_percent

FROM sys.dm_db_index_physical_stats (DB_ID(), OBJECT_ID(N'fim.
ObjectValueString'),

    NULL, NULL, NULL) AS a

    JOIN sys.indexes AS b ON a.object_id = b.object_id AND a.index_id =
b.index_id;
```

The official SQL documentation on reorganizing and rebuilding indexes at http://bit.ly/SQLReorgAndRebuildIndexes says to rebuild the index if fragmentation is greater than 30%.

You should also periodically reindex all of the tables in the Synchronization service database. Tim Macaulay, senior support escalation engineer for Microsoft, posted the following SQL script for table reindexing:

```
USE FIMSynchronizationService

DECLARE @table_name varchar(1000)

declare c1 cursor for SELECT name

FROM   sysobjects

WHERE xtype = 'U'

open c1
```

```
fetch next from c1 into @table_name
while @@Fetch_Status = 0
begin DBCC DBREINDEX (@table_name,  '')
fetch next from c1 into @table_name
end
close c1
deallocate c1
GO
```

Note that reindexing the synchronization database while performing synchronization will see performance problems and potential SQL locking problems, so we strongly recommend that you rebuild the index during a maintenance window when no Management Agents are being run.

SQL best practices

Microsoft's official best practices for FIM holds true for MIM too. These items should be implemented before releasing the system to a production environment. We have highlighted several SQL practices that we've found to solve customer problems:

- Never modify any of the MIM database tables directly in SQL because you can corrupt the database.
- Do not query the Metaverse table within a rules extension, workflow, or external process. Doing so creates SQL deadlock conditions that MIM would not expect.
- Do not change SQL permissions set by the MIM installer.
- The Synchronization service database and MIM Service database should be in their own SQL instances and on different disks, if possible.
- Isolate the SQL data and log files on different disks.
- Presize the SQL databases and avoid relying on SQL autogrow to improve performance.
- Monitor SQL databases to ensure that there is enough disk space.
- Limit the amount of memory that SQL will use if SQL is running on the same server as the sync engine or MIM Service.
- Before placing your MIM databases on a shared corporate cluster server, investigate its response time and performance first. Some performance issues (slow synchronizations) can be tracked back to an already taxed SQL server.
- Configure the synchronization database to use a full recovery model if you need to recover from the time of failure.

MIM synchronization best practices

Here are some of MIM synchronization's best practices to follow:

- Index any Metaverse object you are using for a join.

- The account used for the MIM Synchronization service should be different from the account used for the MIM Service MA.

- The source code for all rules extensions should be backed up and maintained in a source control program. You will need the source code if you ever need to debug a rules extension.

- When writing a rule extension, check whether the attribute is present before looking for a value. An example is as follows:

```
if (csentry["department"].IsPresent) {...}
```

- We suggest performing a full import run profile and a full synchronization on each MA at least every 30 days.

- Clear the synchronization operational run history regularly as the data will make the database grow over time and have an impact on its performance.

- Avoid using the Joiner tool as much as possible because any explicitly joined or projected object will not honor existing or future connector filter rules.

- Try to keep domains of the same forest in the same MA because it allows MIM to automatically manage references between domains.

- When you install MIM, you have the choice to make the MIM security groups (MIMAdmins, MIMSyncBrowse, MIMSyncJoiners, MIMSyncOperators, and MIMSyncPasswordReset) local to the synchronization server or Active Directory groups. We recommend making the MIM security groups similar to Active Directory groups as it allows you to have a standby synchronization server.

- Closely monitor the membership of the MIM security groups that have access to the MIM databases and physical access to the MIM servers involved in the solution.

- Restrict access to the Program Files\Microsoft Forefront Identity Manager\2010\Synchronization Service\Extensions and ..\ ExtensionsCache folder because an attacker could compile malicious code and have it be run by the Synchronization service.

- If you have deployed the MIM portal, the MIM MA should have two connector filter rules: one that blocks the synchronization account and another that blocks the administrator account. The best way is to use GUIDs, as follows:

```
<dn> Equals fb89aefa-5ea1-47f1-8890-abe7797d6497
<dn< Equals 7fb2b853-24f0-4498-9534-4e10589723c4
```

MIM portal best practices

The following are some best practices of the MIM portal:

- Minimize the use of dynamic nesting and the use of negative (NOT) conditions in sets and groups. A good rule of thumb is to stay under five NOTs.

- Disable the verbose tracing of MIM Service when not needed.

- Be aware that exposing self-service reset internal and external could be a Denial of Service endpoint if you have Active Directory configured to lock out.

- Back up custom workflow code and pages and manage them as you would any production source code.

- Do not delete the default workflows that come with the product.

- Keep an eye on expired portal requests. If you see requests building up beyond the retention time (default 30 days), then you may need to run the SQL job `FIM_DeleteExpiredSystemObjectsJob`.

Other best practices

- Hear us now and thank us later; back up the databases and configurations prior to making a configuration change or applying an update.

- Do not run your MIM service accounts in the enterprise admin, domain admin, schema admin, or account operator Active Directory groups.

- Disable SharePoint indexing if you have deployed the MIM portal.

- Try to keep the product up to date with the latest update as much as possible as the latest update fixes bugs and sometimes add new features and performance enhancements. Updates are found at `http://bit.ly/MSFTIDMUpdates`.

Also refer to the MIM 2016 `Help` file for Best Practices and Microsoft's own best practices page at `http://bit.ly/MIMMSFTBestPractices`.

Summary

We discussed some best practices, informed you how to perform maintenance on your MIM databases, referenced backup and restore procedures, showed how to automate run profiles, and discussed how business assumptions can turn into operational issues. Did we cover everything about MIM? Absolutely not. We did cover the core functionality of the product from installation to troubleshooting, the primary concepts and terminology, and potential pitfalls and best practices. We hope you find the book informative and helpful in your identity management adventures.

Index

CPSIA information can be obtained
at www.ICGtesting.com
Printed in the USA
FSOW03n0007030816
23366FS